Genealogies of Citizenship

As market fundamentalism has moved from the margins of debate to global doctrine, three decades of market-driven governance is transforming growing numbers of rights-bearing citizens into socially excluded internally stateless persons. Against this perilous movement to organize society exclusively by market principles, Margaret Somers argues that the fragile project of sustaining socially inclusive democratic rights requires the countervailing powers of a social state, a robust public sphere to hold it accountable, and a relationally sturdy civil society. In this original and path-breaking work, from historical epistemologies of social capital and naturalism, to contested narratives of civil society and the public sphere, to Hurricane Katrina's racial apartheid, Somers alerts us that the growing moral authority of the market is distorting the meaning of citizenship from noncontractual shared fate to conditional privilege, making rights, inclusion, and moral worth dependent on contractual market value. *Genealogies of Citizenship* advances an innovative view of rights as necessary public goods rooted in an alliance of public power, political membership, and social practices of equal moral recognition – in short, the right to have rights. A remarkable rethinking of freedom, human rights, and social justice, this is political, economic, and cultural sociology and social theory at its best.

MARGARET R. SOMERS is Professor of Sociology and History at the University of Michigan. A leading figure in historical, political, economic, and cultural sociology and social theory, she recently received the Inaugural Lewis A. Coser Award for Innovation and Theoretical Agenda-Setting in Sociology.

D1593523

Cambridge Cultural Social Studies

"The contributions Margaret Somers has made to our understanding of citizenship and rights are legion. Written with a sense of urgency, and directed to publics beyond her discipline, *Genealogies of Citizenship* continues her quest to build knowledge that is historical and analytical, empirical and ethical. Concerned with current threats to the standing of citizens, the book offers a timely plea to appreciate and defend the public sphere against depoliticization.' and market pressures, lest democratic institutions and human dignity erode."

Ira Katznelson
Ruggles Professor of Political Science and History, Columbia University

"Somers has provided us with a broad, multi-faceted and immensely inspiring provocative account of modern 'western' societies' problems in combining citizenship rights and market principles which should be required reading not just for those of us interested in such questions, but for anyone who intends to use the words 'social capital' or 'civil society' in future."

Andreas Fahrmeir, *Sehepunkte*

"In eloquent essays Margaret Somers sheds new light on citizenship as a central concern of modern political life. She shows the tensions, aporias, repressed possibilities, and potential vitality in everyday usage and scholarly conceptualization alike. This is a book scholars have been waiting for and one that should be widely read."

Craig Calhoun
University Professor of Social Science, NYU

"Margaret Somers' *Genealogies of Citizenship* is a profound and original defense of the moral ideal of socially inclusive democratic citizenship. It combines a sophisticated theoretical and philosophical defense of the normative foundations of this ideal with a range of compelling sociological explorations of the conditions for its robust sustainability. The book's central provocative thesis – that under-regulated, expansionary markets constitute a deep threat to this form of citizenship – is powerfully and convincingly argued. It deserves to be widely read and debated by anyone worried about the future of democratic society."

Professor Erik Olin Wright
Department of Sociology, University of Wisconsin-Madison

"This book is required reading for anyone interested in the consequences of neo-liberalism for the redefinition of social boundaries. With characteristic elegance, breadth, and theoretical mastery, Somers develops a detailed and complex analysis of processes of social exclusion and inclusion. Knowledge cultures, narratives and the law figure prominently in this new account of the redefinition of social citizenship. A *tour de force* that will be long remembered . . ."

Michele Lamont, Robert I. Goldman Professor of European Studies, Professor of Sociology and African and African-American Studies, Author of *The Dignity of Working Men: Morality and the Boundaries of Race, Class, and Immigration*

"Disinterring histories of the market-fundamentalist present, this is a devastatingly trenchant, yet profoundly creative, critique of privatized citizenship. Reclaiming the right to have rights, Somers puts critical social theory to work in what amounts to a radical new vision for social justice and progressive politics."

Jamie Peck
Canada Research Chair in Urban Regional Political Economy, University of British Columbia

"Margaret Somers is a renowned polymath, and in *Genealogies of Citizenship* she obliterates common divisions among sociology, history, moral philosophy, and politics to fashion an exhilarating new form of social inquiry that simultaneously advances core debates long-standing in social theory and offers a searching mediation on contemporary citizenship *in extremis*."

Charles Camic
Professor of Sociology, Northwestern University

"*Genealogies of Citizenship* might well provide the definitive sociological and political critique of the era of market fundamentalism. Building on the insights of Karl Polanyi, T. H. Marshall, and Hannah Arendt, Margaret Somers demonstrates that civil society rests on the 'right to have rights'. But this right has been swept away by three decades of market-dominated discourse and policies. Somers brilliantly shows how Hurricane Katrina's devastating impact on New Orleans' African American community was the culmination of this dynamic.

Fred Block
Professor of Sociology, University of California at Davis

"With extraordinary erudition and theoretical acuity, Margaret Somers examines the dominant ideas that link many of us together as a community, and marginalize others of us. She argues that the rise of the ideology of market fundamentalism is an assault on democratic rights. Nor is the assault a mere abstraction. Political ideas are embedded in legal practices and economic and social relations. Market fundamentalism is thus a profound threat to democratic possibilities."

Frances Fox Piven
Distinguished Professor of Political Science and Sociology, Graduate Center of the City University of New York

"*Geneologies of Citizenship* offers many intellectual rewards. Somers provides, at once, an incisive analytic for approaching the internal exclusions of liberal democratic societies, a sophisticated meditation on the career and meanings of the citizenship concept in social theory, and an eloquent indictment of a 'market fundamentalism' which, she shows, ultimately subverts citizenship's highest aspirations."

Professor Linda Bosniak
Rutgers University School of Law

"Margaret Somers breaks the traditional link between constitutionalist discourse and the formalities of citizenship, and demonstrates the diversity of circumstances in which citizenship fails. This book is an exhaustive history of Anglo-American citizenship theory . . . interweaving the work of Karl Polanyi, Hannah Arendt, and T. H. Marshall to provide an genealogical history of the diverse forms of citizenship theory."

Alan Hunt
Canadian Journal of Sociology

Genealogies of Citizenship

Markets, Statelessness, and the Right to Have Rights

Margaret R. Somers

CAMBRIDGE UNIVERSITY PRESS
Cambridge, New York, Melbourne, Madrid, Cape Town, Singapore, São Paulo,
Delhi, Dubai, Tokyo

Cambridge University Press
The Edinburgh Building, Cambridge CB2 8RU, UK

Published in the United States of America by Cambridge University Press, New York

www.cambridge.org
Information on this title: www.cambridge.org/9780521793940

First published 2008
Reprinted with corrections 2010

Printed in the United Kingdom at the University Press, Cambridge

A catalogue record for this publication is available from the British Library

Library of Congress Cataloguing in Publication data
Somers, Margaret R.
Genealogies of citizenship: knowledge, markets, and the right to have rights / by Margaret R.
Somers.
p. cm. – (Cambridge cultural social studies)
Includes bibliographical references and index.
ISBN 978-0-521-79061-1
1. Citizenship. 2. Civil rights. I. Title. II. Series.
JF801.S65 2008
323.6–dc22

2008005101

ISBN 978-0-521-79061-1 hardback
ISBN 978-0-521-79394-0 paperback

Resignation was ever the fount of man's strength and new hope. Man accepted the reality of death and built the meaning of his bodily life upon it. He resigned himself to the truth that he had a soul to lose and that there was worse than death, and founded his freedom upon it. He resigns himself, in our time, to the reality of society which means the end of that freedom. But, again, life springs from ultimate resignation ... Uncomplaining acceptance of the reality of society gives man indomitable courage and strength to remove all removable injustice and unfreedom.   (Karl Polanyi)

We became aware of the existence of a right to have rights ... and a right to belong to some kind of organized community, only when millions of people emerged who had lost and could not regain these rights. [S]tateless people could see ... that the abstract nakedness of being nothing but human was their greatest danger ... It seems that a man who is nothing but a man has lost the very qualities which make it possible for other people to treat him as a fellow-man. The loss of home and political status became identical with expulsion from humanity altogether.
(Hannah Arendt)

By social citizenship, I mean the whole range from the right to a modicum of economic welfare and security to the right to share to the full in the social heritage and to live the life of a civilized being according to the standards prevailing in the society ... which in turn means a claim to be accepted as full members of the society, that is, as citizens.
(T. H. Marshall)

Contents

Figures

Preface

In *After Virtue* the moral philosopher Alasdair Macintyre suggests that all moral and political philosophy presupposes a sociology. To argue for how the world *ought* to be, one must have a set of assumptions about how the world already *is*. Unfortunately, sociologists have all too rarely returned the compliment to philosophers. To this day there exists no such thing as a real sociology of rights. Since its nineteenth-century origins, sociology has self-consciously and militantly carved out for itself a separate professional identity as an empirical science in contrast to the "normative speculations" of philosophy. Because questions of what counts as right or just are seen as normative, not empirical, worries, a division of labor and turf divides sociologists who write about people who fight *for* rights from philosophers who worry about the *meaning* of those rights. The philosophical and sociological traditions have rarely been joined. Although sociologists too cautiously respect this distribution of intellectual turf, one of the most popular subjects of our discipline – social movements and their participants – have displayed no such cautious professionalism. Social movement actors have almost always articulated their motivations and goals in (often competing) languages of justice, entitlement, and above all rights. Disciplined by the discipline, however, students of social movements have by and large not focused on the meanings and normative impulses behind these rights-based desiderata; instead they have concentrated on the structures, resources, mechanisms, and "frames" of mobilization, organization, and contentious politics. To be sure, organizational mechanisms and the dynamics of power are of critical import to the work of making sense of the social world. But they should not crowd out attention to the more normatively driven powers of justice and rights. In a pluralist knowledge culture, the empirical and the normative are mutually interdependent.

This volume is intended to contribute to a new sociology of rights. Its goal is to identify the processes and relationships that support or disable democratic citizenship regimes, which requires historicizing rights. Throughout the chapters, I aim to identify the conditions – institutional, associational, cultural, normative, economic, etc. – that can account for varying genealogies of citizenship and rights over time and space. By putting together a picture of the different frameworks that have embedded the claims, violations, and support for citizenship rights, we can gain critical glimpses into a sociology of human rights more broadly.

My passion for citizenship theory did not begin as such. Rather it began with an abiding ache and an unrelenting itch – an ache for social justice and human rights, and an itch to understand why they always seemed to be increasingly distant possibilities. First as an undergraduate and then in graduate school I, like so many others of my generation, turned to sociology to salve that ache and scratch that itch. I turned to a sociology of citizenship only when I recognized its signature role as a proxy and sublimation for a sociology of rights. In so doing, however, I discovered that the two are really one, for citizenship rights and rights as such are inescapably mutually implicated and constituted. Citizenship is the *right to have rights.*

Without an existing sociology of rights from which to draw, mine is also by necessity a project in the invention of knowledge. While I am by training a historical sociologist, the scholarly work in this volume is wide-ranging and eclectic, and the research does not fit neatly under any single area in sociology. I consider myself in equal parts a practitioner of sociolegal studies and citizenship formation, a sociological theorist, an economic sociologist, a sociologist of knowledge and ideas, a political sociologist, and a critical theorist. Beyond sociology, my work draws from the fields of legal theory and history, political and social theory, British, American, and French economic and cultural history, anthropology, historical demography, and politics. My methodology is eclectic and includes comparative historical, theoretical, epistemological, philosophical, and cultural approaches.

Still, there is a unifying impulse to this multiplicity. It is that same preoccupation with social justice and human rights with which I began, a belief in the necessity and power of history to provide alternative futures, and a deep conviction that the work of building a sociology of rights is through the genealogies of citizenship. In this respect, my work is clearly more than academically detached. I am motivated by the urgency of holding back the corrosive impact on democratic citizenship and human rights of both market fundamentalism and the overreaching of state power today. Rather than passively accepting the current erosion of citizenship and rights, we need to reclaim their original promise, and to address the racial, ethnic, and gender injustices submerged beneath their beneficent sheen. And as rights are inexorably matters of the public sphere, it is also a project in public sociology. I aspire to work as a public sociologist to bring to the surface for inspection and demystification all the complexities of citizenship and human rights. I thus take on board the mandate of Michael Burawoy, recent president of the American Sociological Association, in his exhortation to include that of public sociologist among legitimate sociological practices. This book was written with this vision of the public sociologist clearly in mind.

Acknowledgments

My list of acknowledgments is especially long and deep as I have accumulated a true embarrassment of riches and debts in the course of writing the chapters that comprise this volume. For a glorious year and a half between 1995 and 1997 I was in residence at the European University Institute (EUI), Florence, Italy – first, as a Jean Monnet Fellow in the European Forum, and then as a visiting professor in the Department of History. I am enormously grateful to Steven Lukes and Klaus Eder, co-directors of the Forum's theme year on "Citizenship," for inducting me into the rich intellectual life of the EUI, introducing me to the addictive wonders of Florence and, above all, for their enduring friendships and abiding confidence in my work. I am also grateful especially to John Brewer who made possible my subsequent appointment in the History Department. While it is John who deserves credit for my good fortune in being able to extend my stay in Florence, it was only possible thanks to generous support from the German Marshall Fund of the United States, which awarded me a research fellowship for 1996–7. While in residence at the EUI, in addition to the aforenamed, I was surrounded by a wonderful group of colleagues and friends, each of whom contributed in critical ways to my thinking and writing on citizenship, political culture, and historical epistemology: Carlos Closa, Laurence Fontaine, Jack Goody, Patricia Grimaldi, Agnes Horvath, Christian Joppke, John McCormick, Alessandro Pizzorno, Gianfranco Poggi, Giovanna Procacci, Yasemin Soysal, Arpad Szakolczai, and John Torpey.

In 1998–9 I was honored to be appointed to be the A. Bartlett Giamatti Faculty Fellow at the University of Michigan's Institute for the Humanities. So many people contributed to that rewarding year, starting with Tom Trautman, then the Director, as well as Mary Price and Eliza Woodford – the Institute's two spectacular administrators and friends, who made my year not only productive but also fun and funky. Over the course of the same period, some critical research needs were met by a small grant I am grateful to have been awarded by the Fund for the Advancement of the Discipline, under the auspices of the American Sociological Association and the National Science Foundation. In 2000–1, I was awarded a residential Research Fellowship at Yale University's Program in Agrarian Studies. James Scott (one of my long-time intellectual heroes) directed the program and led the legendary Friday seminar with a flair, generosity, and attention that made the year so intellectually gratifying. Several colleagues and lasting friends made my stay in New Haven even richer, especially Arun Agrawal, Debbie Dacunto, Rebecca Hardin, Donald Moore, Sylvia Tesh, and Carol Rose. During this time I was surprised and delighted to incur yet another debt from the George and Eliza Howard Foundation (located at Brown University), which awarded me their generous "Outstanding Mid-Career Fellowship." It is an award that I especially cherish as I shared the honor with only one other sociologist, Roger Gould, a friend and great social scientist who died so tragically young in 2001.

In 2003–4 I spent a wonderful year as an External Fellow at the Center for Critical Analysis of Contemporary Culture (CCACC), Rutgers University. It was an exciting year, both intellectually and collegially, thanks largely to Linda Bosniak's skillful and creative directorship. Thanks to her own scholarly accomplishments, I benefited not only from Linda's critical contributions to the theme year on "Citizenship," but also from the other seminar members and the extended presence of several extraordinary visitors, among whom I must single out Étienne Balibar, someone whose work has for years inspired me and who has since become a friend and generous reader of my work. In addition to Linda and Étienne, I want to note how much my visit that year was enhanced in every way by David Abraham, Sandy Abraham, Susan Anable, Martin Bunzl, Deborah Hertz, and Yoav Peled.

For making it possible for me to finish this book, my heartfelt gratitude goes to the National Endowment for the Humanities for a 2006–7 Faculty Fellowship for university teachers, and to New York University's International Center for Advanced Studies (ICAS), where I spent the academic year 2006–7 as a Center Fellow on the theme of "Rethinking the Social," the last of ICAS's stimulating three-year project on "Globalization and the Authority of Knowledge." My thanks go especially to the program directors Tim Mitchell and Tom Bender. In addition, I want to thank Amy Koteles and Greg Morton for making ICAS such a comfortable place to work, as well as the many colleagues and friends whose warmth and generosity so greatly enhanced my New York sojourn, especially Monique Girard, Kathleen Gerson, Linda

Gordon, Atina Grossman, Allen Hunter, Hadassah Kosak, Molly Nolan, Uri Ram, Nava Schreiber, David Stark, Ann Stoler, and Miriam Ticktin.

The challenge of trying to identify by name all of the intellectual communities, colleagues, and friends who have sustained me over the years is daunting, and I can only apologize in advance to those I will have inevitably neglected to list. Among the many students who have performed critically important tasks with brains, brawn, and good-naturedness, I would like to thank especially Weining Gao, Camilo Leslie, Jane Rafferty, and Chris Roberts. Our "Goils Group" was a wonderful setting for intellectual discourse, and served as a fun and stimulating site for a critical reading of a very early version of the introduction. At that time, the group included Julia Adams, Julie Skurski, Ann Stoler, and Katherine Verdery, and I owe them all thanks for their careful suggestions and insights. My intellectual debts to those who read and commented on one or more chapters are ample, and include Julia Adams, Jeff Alexander, Elizabeth Anderson, Renee Anspach, Dan Bell, Mabel Berezin, Fred Block, Rogers Brubaker, Craig Calhoun, Frank Dobbin, Geoff Eley, Gloria Gibson, Wally Goldfrank, Tom Green, Ira Katznelson, Michael Kennedy, Howard Kimeldorf, Hadassah Kosak, Marion Kozak, Michele Lamont, C. K. Lee, Rick Lempert, Terry McDonald, Mark Mizruchi, Gina Morantz-Sanchez, Frances Piven, Art Stinchcombe, Ann Stoler, George Steinmetz, Marc Steinberg, Ron Suny, Charles Tilly, and Mayer Zald. Tom Bender, Tim Mitchell, Steven Lukes and the members of the ICAS Friday seminar provided energetic feedback and excellent comments on the introduction and chapter 1, as did Elizabeth Anderson, Deb Cowen, Julia Elyachar, Wolf Heydebrand, Alondra Nelson, Chris Otter, Marc Steinberg, Diana Yoons, and, above all, Allen Hunter, who gave so generously of his time and searing intellect. Finally, I owe special heartfelt thanks to Jeff Alexander, Renee Anspach, Fred Block, Chas Camic, Leslie DePietro, Geoff Eley, Wally Goldfrank, Tim Mitchell, and Tobin Siebers who not only read and commented on the introduction and chapter 2 but kept faith with me when all else had failed to get me to let go of this volume.

Several heroic figures are owed special thanks for their remarkable abilities to meet the unusual and truly daunting challenges that have been involved in this book's production. Thanks go to Claire Whitlinger for her generosity of spirit and computer, organizational, and time-management skills; to Liz Warburton who gave of her scarce time when I most needed it; to Patricia Preston, who never blanched at the extended trials of contributing to a legible manuscript; to Megan Remaly, who seemed to appear almost magically exactly when I needed her to solve emergency technical crises, to apply her boundless computer skills to tame recalcitrant diagrams and figures, and to patiently work through iteration after iteration of my illegible hand-written editing – all during the crucial last six or seven months of this book's preparation; and to Carrie Cheek of Cambridge University Press who worked with me with unfailing patience throughout the process of preparation and production.

My final appreciations go to Fred Block, Wally Goldfrank, and Leslie DePietro, for whom words escape me that are adequate to express just how blessed I feel for their presence in my life and for all they have given me in the way of support, inspiration, and exemplary generosity. My mother, Anne R. Somers, continues to amaze and inspire me. Indeed, the more I try to honor her long, brave, and accomplished life, the more grateful I am for her continuous support over the years. I dedicate this book to my mother and to my father, Herman "Red" Somers, as well as to Enid and Stan Adelson, Lynne Klein, Anna Keifer, Ralph Miliband, and Marion Kozak. As corny as it may sound, I also dedicate it to the remarkable people of New Orleans who were betrayed not by Hurricane Katrina but by an indifferent market-driven government.

I am grateful to the following for giving me permission to republish essays that first appeared in their pages. All of these have been revised substantially for this book.

"Citizenship, Statelessness and Market Fundamentalism: Arendtian Lessons on Losing the Right to Have Rights." In *Migration, Citizenship, Ethnos: Incorporation Regimes in Germany, Western Europe and North America*, ed. Y. M. Bodemann and G. Yurdakul: 35–62. London: Palgrave Macmillan, 2006.

"Beware Trojan Horses Bearing Social Capital: How Privatization turned *Solidarity* into a Bowling Team." In *The Politics of Method in the Human Sciences*, ed. George Steinmetz: 346–411. Durham, NC: Duke University Press, 2005.

"Citizenship Troubles: Genealogies of Struggle for the Soul of the Social." In *Remaking Modernity*, ed. Julia Adams, Lis Clemens, and Ann Orloff: 438–69. Durham, NC: Duke University Press, 2005.

"Narrating and Naturalizing Civil Society and Citizenship Theory: The Place of Political Culture and the Public Sphere." *Sociological Theory* 13 (3), 1995: 229–74.

"What's Political or Cultural about the Political Culture Concept? Toward an Historical Sociology of Concept Formation." *Sociological Theory* 13 (2), 1995: 113–44.

Margaret R. Somers
New York City
January 2007

1

Theorizing citizenship rights and statelessness

> Citizenship is man's basic right for it is nothing less than the right to have rights. Remove this priceless possession and there remains a stateless person, disgraced and degraded in the eyes of his countrymen. His very existence is at the sufferance of the state within whose borders he happens to be ... [H]e will presumably enjoy, at most, only the limited rights and privileges of aliens, and like the alien he might even be ... deprived of the right to assert any rights.
>
> (Earl Warren, Chief Justice, US Supreme Court, 1958)[1]

This book is about citizenship rights – what they are, how we think about them, why they are currently in peril. Through a mix of historical, conceptual, and epistemological lenses, I engage these questions by creating multiple genealogies of citizenship and statelessness – genealogies that range from the story of Hurricane Katrina's racial apartheid to contested narratives of civil society and the public sphere, from the Trojan horse of social capital to historical epistemologies of concept formation and the metanarrative of Anglo-American citizenship theory. Common to all these are conflicts over the balance of power among the institutions, practices and discourses of states, markets, and civil societies. Whether these conflicts result in regimes of relatively democratic socially inclusive citizenship rights or regimes of social exclusion and statelessness largely depends on the ability of civil society, the public sphere, and the social state to exert countervailing force against the corrosive effects of market-driven governance. My central

---

[1] This version of "the right to have rights" is taken from a Supreme Court opinion written by Chief Justice Earl Warren in 1958. In a case called *Perez* v. *Brownell*, the Court narrowly upheld an order stripping a man of United States citizenship. Warren wrote an impassioned dissent, however, which over the next thirty years provided a basis for the Supreme Court to shield native-born citizens from the government's efforts to "denationalize" them, and also to protect naturalized citizens against efforts to denaturalize them.

claim is that ideal-typical democratic and socially inclusive citizenship regimes rest on a delicate balance of power among state, market, and citizens in civil society, which is mediated through collective adjudications in the public sphere. Disproportionate market power disrupts this carefully constructed balance, as the risks and costs of managing human frailties under capitalism once shouldered by government and corporations get displaced onto individual workers and vulnerable families.

Rights imperiled

Today, global society is drastically out of balance. With the United States in the vanguard, we are in an era in which market fundamentalism – the drive to subject all of social life and the public sphere to market mechanisms – has become the prevailing ideational regime. An ideational regime is comprised of those public narratives and assumptions that have become widely taken for granted in the political culture; it sets the parameters for what counts as worthwhile argument in social and political debates. Through the alarm of "citizenship imperiled," I caution that the rise of market fundamentalism to the position of dominant ideational regime has created a radically unbalanced power dynamic between the market and state on the one side, and civil society on the other. Inequality in America has reached a level not seen since the Gilded Age, as a once thriving middle class feels itself on the brink of collapse into the ranks of the invisible working poor.[2] Indeed, three decades of what has become market-driven governance are transforming growing numbers of once rights-bearing citizens into socially excluded internally rightless and stateless persons.[3] A political culture that tolerates, even legitimates, these brute disparities in life chances has a corrosive effect not only on citizenship and human rights, but equally on perceptions of what we owe each other as fellow humans.

  The most prominent force in this eroding of rights is what I call the *contractualization of citizenship* – an effort to reorganize the relationship between the state and the citizenry, from noncontractual rights and obligations to the principles and practices of quid pro quo market exchange. The contractualization of citizenship effectively collapses the boundaries that protect the public sphere and civil society from market

[2] On the current state of economic inequality in America, see *American Prospect* (2007), *The Economist* (2007), Frank (2007a), Gross (2007), Kuttner (2007), Mishel *et al.* (2006), *New York Times Magazine* (2007), and Uchitelle (2007).
[3] The post-9/11 surveillance society and the G. W. Bush administration have intensified this trend dramatically. They did not, however, create it.

penetration. Contractualizing citizenship distorts the meaning of citizenship from that of shared fate among equals to that of conditional privilege. The growing moral authority of both market and contract makes social inclusion and moral worth no longer inherent rights but rather earned privileges that are wholly conditional upon the ability to exchange something of equal value. This is the model by which the structurally unemployed become *contractual malfeasants* (see chapter 2).

Much of market fundamentalism's great success has been facilitated by what Fred Block and I have dubbed *conversion narratives*. These are fear-inducing predictions intended to convert a culture's dominant narratives from social to market precepts by foretelling the dire moral and economic implications of continuing on the present social policy course. Among the most effective of these conversion narratives have been the "Personal Responsibility Crusade" (Hacker 2006) and "the Perversity Thesis" (Hirschman 1991; Somers and Block 2005). These are both public discourses that reassign responsibility and blame for social problems from structural conditions to alleged defects of individual moral character, such as dependency, indolence, irresponsibility, lack of initiative, promiscuity, and parasitism on the body politic. At the same time, market fundamentalist conversion narratives have worked to substitute alternative understandings of reality, which aim to normalize and justify the market's ever-increasing expansion into political, cultural, social, and civil sites once insulated from market penetration. The successful deployment of such conversion narratives has enabled market fundamentalist advocates over the last thirty-five years to delegitimate once popular legislative agendas that embodied a modest acceptance of the social ethos of shared fate, equal risk, and social justice, as well as a commitment to redressing centuries of gender and racial exclusions.

Throughout this volume I engage the epistemological aspects of both citizenship rights and statelessness by deconstructing numerous public discourses, disciplinary claims, and political conversion narratives. To explore the epistemological consequences of market fundamentalism and the contractualization of citizenship, I probe the shift from a primarily sociologically driven knowledge culture built on relational social assumptions to an economics-driven one based on market models of society.[4] It is important to keep in mind that the different types of regimes

---

[4] In discussing epistemological issues throughout this volume, and in other work, I use the term *knowledge culture* to characterize the same notion of an orthodox spectrum of what are considered competing truth claims, rather than a single hegemonic Truth. See especially chapter 7, as well as Somers 1996a, 1998.

and spheres I discuss throughout the book are ideal types, not empirical claims about precise social entities. Empirically, in fact, civil societies, states, and public spheres are never autonomous or unpenetrated by markets, any more than any actual citizenship regime has or will ever achieve absolute solidarity, equality or full social inclusion (Zelizer 1997, 2005; Fraser 1989). Least of all are markets autonomous self-regulating entities; rather they are at root a set of social institutions comprising legal rules and relations (e.g. contractual obligations, legal exchanges, property rights), which structure, organize, and legitimate commodity exchanges. As such, markets are not merely embedded in but actually constituted by political institutions, social practices, and cultural constructs (Hodgson 1988; Krippner 2001; Sen 1981). For analytic and heuristic purposes, however, as well as to measure changes and variations in the degree of their interpenetration, it helps to conceive of the political, economic, and social domains as analytically separate spheres.

Following in this vein, market fundamentalism is itself an ideational movement, not an empirically viable reality. I accentuate its *ideational* quality to underscore a paradox: on the one hand, its ideology of absolute market freedom is almost totally at odds with actually existing successful market societies, which rely heavily on social institutions (e.g. laws and tax codes) to protect the rich from full market exposure while forcing market "freedoms" on the rest of us.[5] On the other hand, this distance from reality seems to matter not at all, but even to contribute to the beguiling notion that prosperity is associated with complete market freedom. The visibility of so much wealth, coupled with the invisibility of poverty and the poor, seems only to lend credibility to the market as the arbiter of moral authority – one that is recalibrating our notions of citizenship rights and the citizen from that of social inclusion, shared fate, and membership to only conditional inclusion, quid pro quo exchange, and social exclusion for those whose worth falls short when measured by market metrics. Market-driven freedom may only be an illusion, but no matter. As a capacious vision, it has conquered the current social imaginary.

Nowhere has this conquest been more complete than in the United States. Thus my arguments about marketization's worrisome effects on citizenship rights tend to focus on contemporary America. Yet from its

---

[5] See especially Sunstein (2004); Block (1990); Polanyi (1957a, 1957b). This of course is the foundational precept of Polanyi-influenced institutional analysis with its critique of the "scarcity postulate" and the "self-regulating" market, as well as of the field of economic sociology. See e.g. Dobbin (2004); Granovetter and Swedberg (2001); Smelser and Swedberg (2005).

inception, American society has been a culture divided by internal boundaries; the land of self-evident equal human rights has thrived uneasily on the backs of people considered neither fully human nor even partial rights-bearers (Smith 1993, 1999; Shklar 1991). And just as the parameters of the socially included are revealed only by demarcating the boundaries of the socially excluded, so too does the ideal of inclusive citizenship depend on recognizing citizenship's stateless Others. A benign view of citizenship has purchase only from the perspective of the insiders. It is the cold instrument of exclusion to those outside its borders, both internal borders based on race and gender exclusion, as well as nation-state ones based on xenophobia and nationalism. Market fundamentalism has by no means been the sole cause of today's social exclusions. Yet since the 1970s it has served to radically exacerbate the exclusions of race and class by first delegitimating affirmative action and then grafting the impersonal cruelties of a "color-blind" market onto these preexisting "primordially" defined differences. The outcome has been an ever-growing superfluous population, no longer accommodated by a regime in which market value is the chief criterion for membership. This population makes up America's socially excluded and internally stateless who have lost the right to have rights, and they figure greatly in my opening chapters.

The right to have rights

Against the perilous movement to organize society exclusively by market principles, I argue that the fragile project of sustaining socially inclusive democratic rights requires the counteracting powers of a social state, a robust public sphere to hold it accountable, and a relationally sturdy civil society. Reconstructing the social, historical, and epistemological conditions that support or disable this project makes it possible to theorize more generally about the cluster of rights at the heart of democratic and socially inclusive citizenship regimes. Included among these are legal and civil freedoms, and equal access to justice; participatory rights in democratic governance; and the social inclusionary rights that allow for the meaningful exercise of all the others. Conceived as individual possessions, however, these rights are ethereal. Like all rights, rather, they are *public* goods, and thus can only be sustained by an alliance of public power, political membership, and social practices of equal moral recognition. Following Earl Warren (1958) and Hannah Arendt ([1951] 1979), this makes citizenship the *right to have rights*. The right to have rights is both normative and empirical. The term parses two distinct kinds of rights. The first is an existentially foundational right, without which the second set of rights has no meaning. It entails both *de jure* and *de facto* rights to membership in a political community – the scale of which can vary from local to national to global (Arendt herself was at once deeply skeptical and melancholic about the nation-state, even while she was reluctantly resigned to it). In line with Karl Polanyi ([1944] 2001) and T. H. Marshall ([1950] 1992), however, I stipulate that the first right to political membership must equally include the *de facto* right to *social* inclusion in civil society. By social inclusion I mean the right to *recognition* by others as a moral equal treated by the same standards and values and due the same level of respect and dignity as all other members.[6] The second bundle of rights contains the civil–juridical ones, often summed up in Marshallian terms as civil, political, and social rights, and recently expanded to include such rights as cultural, economic, indigenous, and same-sex rights. In addition, I insist that both kinds of rights must include human rights, since they too require the recognition that only membership and social inclusion can ensure.

My conception of citizenship as the right to have rights is at once both "thinner" and "thicker" than many more familiar definitions. It is thinner because, unlike other approaches, for something to count as citizenship I do not require a foundation of any particular civil–juridical rights, such as those of participation or individual property rights. Membership alone is the minimalist definition of citizenship. This allows me to think comparatively about citizenship regimes as variable, along a continuum from lesser to greater degrees of democratic and rights-based social inclusiveness. At the same time my conception is thicker because it *does* require in the first instance the foundational right to political and social membership as well as both *de jure* and *de facto* inclusion and recognition. So unconditional is this primary requirement of social and political membership that I ascribe to it an ontological status. It is only this primary right of inclusion and membership that makes possible the mutual acknowledgement of the other as a *moral equal*, and thus worthy of equal social and political recognition. As philosopher Charles Taylor puts it: "Due recognition is not just a courtesy but a vital human need" (Taylor and Gutmann 1992).

The conflict between citizenship rights and human rights can to some extent now be challenged. To be sure, citizenship is a relational and inclusionary right whose claim to universality is only partial and internal

---

[6] The origins of "recognition ethics" are in Hegel's famous discourse on the master–slave relationship in his *Philosophy of Right* (Hegel 1955).

as it has purchase only in the context of membership in a particular political and/or social body – usually, although not necessarily, conceived as a nation-state. Human rights, by contrast, are believed to be possessed by all humans for the simple reason of their being human. Thus human rights are called *natural* (presocial and prepolitical), as they are justified by the existence of humanity as such and not by any particular membership attachments. Human/natural rights theory stipulates that to discover the ontological truth of humanity, a person must be stripped metaphorically of all political and social attachments, and considered in her natural state in the perfect freedom of the "state of nature." According to natural/human rights theory, even when totally unencumbered by all things social, this stateless person is by nature still a *rights-bearer*. Such is the optimism of the thought-experiment on which natural rights theory rests its claims.

My approach to citizenship theory, by contrast, draws from history, which is considerably more revealing, though much less consoling. Indeed, as Arendt demonstrates, the Holocaust provided us with a natural experiment of what happens to people when they *actually* are stateless, rather than simply metaphorically so. Arendt explains how the Nazis created the conditions that facilitated genocide. First, they revoked the citizenship of the German Jews; then they expelled them into the condition of statelessness. Now divested of all political attachments and social identity, Jews became unrecognizable as fellow humans. They became, in the words of Goebbels, the "scum of the earth," wanted nowhere, and easily rounded up and shipped to extermination camps with virtually no objection from the Western nations. The lesson Arendt draws is that it is *not* freedom and autonomy *from* all social and political entities that liberate us to be rights-bearers. Bare life (Agamben 1998) in fact makes humans who are "nothing but human" as rightless as they are stateless (Arendt 1979). Instead, it is embeddedness, political membership, and social inclusion that are necessary to have any rights at all, especially the human right to life itself. My focus on inclusion and membership as the ontological preconditions for recognition blurs the radical dichotomy between human and citizenship rights. If recognition is the precondition not only to citizenship but also to human rights, and membership is the prerequisite to recognition, then human rights and citizenship rights are *both* rooted in that which endows us with our humanity – the recognition that comes only from attachments and inclusion. If we want to advance the cause of actual (rather than metaphysical) human rights, we must embrace them as being anything *but* natural. As Étienne Balibar has recently written "Man [sic] does not make citizenship; citizenship makes the man" (2004a: 35).

Throughout the book I often use the term the citizenship *ethic* or *ethos* to denote not the actuality but the normative ideal embodied in the right to have rights – the foundational right to inclusion, membership, and recognition to which the term refers. But precisely because it is but an ideal and an aspiration, the right to have rights is sociologically incomplete unless complemented by institutional foundations, both historical and structural, that can explain the social requirements for its realization – or not. Thus my analysis of citizenship also contains a methodology for comparative empirical analysis. Specifically I deploy a structural model of a continuous triadic assemblage among the institutions of state, market, and civil society, with an internally free-floating public sphere. The model is situated on a continuum that makes it possible to measure how the relative levels of institutional power among competing institutions vary over time and space. I treat this model as the *architectonics* of different citizenship regimes, or the infrastructural design of how the parts fit together into a complex whole. Exploring the conditions and consequences of these spatial and temporal shifts of power makes it possible to theorize the genealogies of different citizenship regimes.[7]

The thesis I develop throughout this book is that rights must be recognized to be public goods. As such, socially inclusive democratic citizenship regimes (including human rights) can thrive only to the extent that egalitarian and solidaristic principles, practices, and institutions of civil society and the public commons are able to act with equal force against the exclusionary threats of market-driven politics. To accomplish this, the expansionary drives of both state and market must be impeded. Only in this way can market-driven governance be prevented from converting civil society and the public sphere into pathological reflections of undue market wealth and political power.

Multiple angles of vision: genealogy and history of the present

Throughout this book, I approach citizenship from diverse perspectives and multiple angles of vision. In this introduction, my aim is to signal the overall intellectual project and to present the unifying assumptions that guide my work as a whole and form the basis for a coherent intellectual agenda. This agenda is to craft a social theory of citizenship and sociology of rights. It is a project of compelling urgency in this age of increasing human rights abuses, global poverty, inequality, and social exclusion.[8]

---

[7] See Somers (1993, 1994a) for examples of this methodology in practice.
[8] See Somers and Roberts (forthcoming 2009).

In each of the chapters I grapple with a set of questions that increasingly haunt me: Why are democratic citizenship regimes currently in peril? Why are rights and entitlements, long held to be self-evident characteristics of liberal democracies, under attack? What does citizenship imperiled look like? Why are the risks of market society (jobs, health, retirement, education, etc.) shifting away from government and corporate responsibility onto the increasingly vulnerable shoulders of individual workers and families? What are the consequences of citizenship in peril? What causes the differences in types of citizenship regimes? How and why are people included or excluded from different citizenship regimes? What sustains and legitimates practices of citizenship?

I explore these questions by constructing new stories and genealogies. Genealogy aims to take up "minor" or repressed knowledge – not to reproduce dominant mythologies. Foucault describes it as the "insurrection of subjugated knowledges" (Foucault 1997b: 7). By subjugated knowledges, he means those ways of seeing and understanding the world which have been disqualified for their supposed lack of rigor or "scientificity," those knowledges that have been present but which are often made invisible.[9] Following this reasoning, genealogies of citizenship should look very different when they focus on these "outsider" perspectives.[10]

Doing history as genealogy entails active practices of selection; like all practices these are driven by one's place and concerns in the world. Thus while my analyses are infused by historical epistemologies, it is contemporary problems of late twentieth- and early twenty-first-century America and Europe that serve as points of departure in most of the chapters. My approach is that of a problem-driven "history of the present." It draws its inspiration from many sources, including James Baldwin. "History," Baldwin writes, "does not refer merely, or even principally, to the past. On the contrary, the great force of history comes from the fact that we carry it within us and are unconsciously controlled by it in many ways, and history is literally present in all we do."[11] Also prominent in my thinking is the Faulknerian assumption that "the past is never dead; it's not even past." A history of the present rejects the conceit that it is possible to tell the past "as it was," independent of

---

[9] On genealogy see Dean (1994), Foucault (1979b).
[10] I believe this is what Engin Isin tries to do in his *Being Political: Genealogies of Citizenship* (2002). Thanks to Deb Cohen for reminding me of this point.
[11] Baldwin, cited in Foner 2002, p. ix.

contemporary concerns.[12] No story can be told nor any theory proposed that is not responding to prior (implicit or explicit) questions, and our questions are always the products of our situated selves. To be sure, historical writing must refer to "events, irruptions, discourses, and social practices" that occur within "a particular time-space." But this in no way negates that it is "in fact an activity that is irrevocably linked to its current uses" (Dean 1994: 14).

From this point of view, it is folly to try to make sense of the present without recognizing the historical stories that live within it. Looking at the present social world through time and space changes not only what we actually can see, but also the meaning of that world. We cannot look forward until we look back to learn how we came to be who we are, and until we know what we have lost, or gained.[13] This is the meaning of what I call causal narrativity: the present is always an episode in a much longer story; it is unintelligible without exploring the temporal and spatial narratives that come before and might come after, thereby constituting its inner life (Somers 1996a, 1998).

Some critics worry that a history of the present is the same thing as teleology, in which the present is viewed as the inexorable purposeful end-point of history, and the past is the necessary prologue to the present. But problem-driven histories of the present such as mine are just the opposite. Like path-dependence, they ask how – given multiple possible routes, times, places, and branches – our present social world was created. Indeed, in a fundamentally antiteleological move, my strategy is to denaturalize the present – to show that things we take as self-evident and necessary are in fact but contingent historical outcomes; they simply take on the appearance of being the only possible reality. These are the perspectives that I have used to fashion the book's genealogies and narratives of citizenship – genealogies and narratives with causalities and meanings that only emerge by looking at the present through some very long and very wide lenses.

Indeed, underlying all of my work has been the central interplay between history, ideas, and theory. Although I have tried to make them stand on their own, many of the theoretical concepts and epistemological arguments I have developed have been driven by empirical historical puzzles. My exploration, for example, of a "historical epistemology of

---

[12] There is an enormous literature on Foucault's uses of "genealogy" and "history of the present." For especially enlightening discussions see Dean (1994); Davidson (2001); Gutting (1989); Hacking (1979, 1990b); Stoler (1995, 2002).

[13] Daniel Mendelsohn (2006).

concept formation" is informed by many of the same historical methods that I use in my more recognizably empirical research, thus making the theoretical project at once a historical sociology. And because I believe that underlying most macro-level social theory is a particularistic view of historical events and causal processes in the making of the modern world, I have consistently argued that theoretical renewal in social theory requires a simultaneous historical retelling of that embedded metanarrative of "Anglo-American citizenship theory" (see chapters 5 and 7). For a sociology of rights, it is not possible to privilege either theory or history; both must proceed at once.

My discussion of Hurricane Katrina in chapter 2 reveals important lessons about problem-driven narrative, genealogy, and the history of the present. At the time of the tragedy, the hurricane was generally perceived as a shocking and unexpected event characterized by almost incomprehensible ineptitude of FEMA in particular, and, more generally, of all levels of government – local, state, and federal. But deconstructing the tragedy reveals it to have been neither unexpected nor anomalous – however shocking. Hurricane Katrina was (and is) part of an ongoing story, not a single event. It was an episode, as much as a long chapter, in an almost four-decades long genealogy entailing the steady disarticulation of citizenship rights and civil society from their noncontractual foundations and reattaching them to the contractual requisites of a market-driven politics. All of the critical ingredients that went into making the tragedy had been nurtured over a period of decades by the powers and effects of market fundamentalism. The sight of so many forgotten New Orleanians without the resources to evacuate the city was but a momentary snapshot in a steady process of increasing social exclusion and an eviscerating of the public sphere. On the surface it began with the government's failure to adequately construct and maintain the city's levees. At the core, however, it was driven by an ideational assault on the idea of poverty as a social problem, and poisoned with the stigmatizing venom of personal blame and cries of dependent immorality. A milestone was reached in the 1996 welfare bill that removed much of the remaining barrier between unprotected citizens and full exposure to an unforgiving and often unattainable labor market. Only by reconstructing this much longer story of the displacement of the noncontractual principles of solidaristic social provisioning by those of market and contract, can we understand how and why those left behind in New Orleans to face the storm alone were *already* a rightless, stateless, and expendable population deemed unworthy of the mutual recognition due moral equals. That's why they had been left behind in the first place.

Citizenship has today become a topic of overwhelming urgency. Throughout this volume I engage that urgency by moving from Locke's revolutionary narrative social imaginary to the recent tragedy of Hurricane Katrina. The range of perspectives I take should not be surprising in light of the breadth of citizenship's recent impact on the world scene in the post-Cold War period. These decades have been caught in the crossfire of globalization, immigration, multiculturalism, nationalist resurgences, and market-driven pressures to increasingly privatize the public world of citizenship. The position I take in this book is that questions such as whether immigration and globalization will decouple the nation-state from citizenship, or human rights from citizenship rights, or how such a catastrophic and preventable tragedy as that of Katrina could have happened, can best be answered historically. It is a mandate for critically rethinking the genealogies of citizenship's ascendancy in tandem with the currently imperiled condition of citizenship and human rights.

The rediscovery of citizenship

Since being awakened from a long dormancy at the end of the twentieth century, studies of citizenship have been making up for lost time at a breathtaking pace. Over the course of a few years, the field has produced a staggering amount of research and theoretical innovation. The rediscovery has been a product of history and scholarship. Although history played the greater part, the contribution of scholarship has not been negligible. While no single intellectual process or any particular event can be singled out as *the* catalyzing "citizenship moment," shortly after its initial burst onto the scene it was clear we were witnessing the birth of a new field of *citizenship studies*.[14]

From one disciplinary point of view in the social sciences, the process began when historical sociologists began to be frustrated by the lack of fit between their theories and the seemingly unprecedented world events of the 1980s and 1990s. Their dominant state centrism had already been propelling them toward new questions about the relationship of political institutions to the economy and civil society. It was a short step from there to hypothesizing the state as causally implicated in market relations, or as Karl Polanyi (2001) conceptualized it, to recognizing the necessary centrality of institutional embeddedness. There were deep affinities between Polanyi's explanation for the American New Deal

---

[14] In 1997 the new flagship journal *Citizenship Studies* began publication. See also Isin and Turner (2002).

and Marshall's analysis of citizenship – specifically, their mutual focus on the necessary countervailing powers of politics and civil society to reconfigure the market-driven inequalities of social class. This approach also nudged welfare state studies toward a broader causal conception of political/legal dynamics as mechanisms of equality, as well as toward a more sociologically inflected conception of citizenship.

Comparative-historical sociology's rediscovery of citizenship was signaled by the work of the leading state-formation theorists of the 1970s and 1980s – Michael Mann (1986, 1987) and Charles Tilly (1995a), in particular. Mann focused especially on the mechanisms and comparative processes by which citizenship was extended in the nineteenth century by state and dominant class elites, while Tilly developed an empirical and sociological definition of citizenship as the "rights and mutual obligations binding state agents and a category of persons defined exclusively by their legal attachment to the same state" (Tilly 1995: 369). Substantial contributions were also made by historians and social scientists who combined their focus on state formation with research on class formation. Instant classics, such as Gareth Stedman Jones's (1983) essay on nineteenth-century English Chartism, demonstrated that even the most iconic of working-class movements at the height of the Industrial Revolution was motivated by demands for participatory *political* inclusion and the legal rights of citizens, neither of which were reducible to class interests alone. These were historical actors driven by collective expectations of political and legal entitlements born of workers' self-identities as "Freeborn Englishmen."[15] Inherited formulations were inadequate to capture this kind of political agency, yet state-centric comparative-historical sociology could not provide the necessary degree of fundamental reformulation. Finding a vocabulary for these politically driven movements led to an engagement with the language of *rights* – something long outside the intellectual vocabulary of the empirical social sciences. This triggered a recognition that it was primarily through the prism of their rights as *citizens* that workers came to discover and articulate their interests in the first place. For comparative-historical sociologists (along with other historically minded social scientists and theoretically oriented historians) in the late 1980s and early 1990s, recognizing working-class social movements as expressions in part of

---

[15] See Thompson (1963) for the definitive analysis of pre-Chartist English working-class consciousness. Polanyi also focuses on Chartism as a classic example of a non-interest-based social movement that sought to reclaim the institutional relationships that the Industrial Revolution was wrenching away.

citizenship identities brought together the now well-accepted focus on state formation with the study of class formation (Barbalet 1988; Giddens 1982; Somers 1992, 1993, 1996b; B. S. Turner 1986).[16]

In a kind of parallel universe to that of historical sociology, the field of political theory began forging its own path toward the rediscovery of citizenship in the 1960s and 1970s with a series of remarkable changes oriented toward a rediscovery of politics, civil society, and republicanism. Its impetus was a powerful critique of the hegemony of both utilitarianism and classical political liberalism for their common erasure of politics and community through the postulate of the deontological prepolitical and presocial individual (Wolin 1960; Rawls 1971; Sandel 1982, 1984). By resurrecting the long-buried tenets of republicanism, political theorists shifted their focus to political identities and practices based not on the isolated self but in the context of relationships, civil society, and, inevitably, citizenship and membership (Cohen 1982; Cohen and Arato 1992; MacIntyre 1981, 1989; Oldfield 1990; Taylor 1989; Walzer 1983, 1988, 2005; Wolin 1960). Several ancillary new trends developed that dovetailed with citizenship's focus on membership, such as the new "communitarianism," also based on a critique of liberalism's excessive fixation on the individual (Bellah *et al.* 1985; Etzioni 1997; MacIntyre 1981; Sandel 1982, 1984).

Historical eruptions

Developments in political theory and the logical maturation of comparative-historical sociology were only part of the story of the rediscovery of citizenship. The other necessary component was – with poetic justice – history itself. With numerous interpretations available, it is not necessary to rehearse all the possible configurations of social, political, and economic conditions that combined to trigger a new attention to the issue of citizenship. I will simply touch on some of those issues that most dramatically illustrate how broad was the spectrum of concerns that catalyzed the new citizenship studies.

Some credit the decline of the welfare state in the 1980s for reviving attention to the significance of social citizenship rights that had long been

---

[16] That it was as early as 1982 that Giddens published his important article on the centrality of popular movements in the development of citizenship rights points to just how ahead of the curve he was with respect to an intellectual movement that only became fashionable a decade later. In retrospect and with just a hint of what was to follow, Giddens, along with Mann (1986, 1987) and B. S. Turner (1986), were clearly harbingers of a scholarly reconsideration of citizenship in general and Marshall in particular.

taken for granted (Leibfried and Pierson 1995; Pierson 1994; Crouch 2001; Eder *et al.* 2001; Esping-Andersen *et al.* 2002; Freedland 2001; Huber and Stephens 2001; Pierson 2001; Procacci 2001; Somers and Block 2005). Others point to the radical transformation of the federal judiciary over the last quarter-century in the US, in which a successful assault has been launched against virtually all the civil rights that Marshall made foundational to the very possibility of democratic citizenship rights. According to one of today's most acclaimed legal scholars "[t]o a degree that has been insufficiently appreciated, and is in some ways barely believable, the contemporary federal courts are fundamentally different from the federal courts of just two decades ago" (Sunstein 2003: A2). And because they have a causally reciprocal relationship to each other, these challenges to civil and legal rights can in no way be separated from those of political and social rights. Long-term attacks on welfare and other forms of entitlement (Mead 1997; Murray 1984; Olasky 1992) also placed the blame on an "excess" of democracy for the reckless spread of a system of "handouts" (Crozier *et al.* 1975).[17]

Among the most important international factors were the striking new patterns of immigration and movements of guest workers and migrant labor throughout the global labor market. Large numbers of immigrants and their descendants have become permanent denizens of advanced industrial societies, yet the status of full citizenship remains either beyond reach or available in a less than complete form (Bauböck 1991, 1994; Bauböck *et al.* 1998; Joppke 1998; Soysal 1994). The permutations of this peculiar diaspora continue to be wide-reaching and include the effects of ethnic differences on full political inclusion (Benhabib 2001, 2004; Oommen 1997a, 1997b). Often characterized as a conflict of particularistic identity movements asking for inclusion in (or in some cases withdrawal from) a polity defined by universalistic politico-juridical criteria, this has been theorized – and criticized – as a conflict between states that practice *ethnic* citizenship versus those that are built upon *civic* citizenship (Benhabib 2007a; Brubaker 1992; Rex 1996; Rex and Drury 1994; Schnapper 1998).

Regardless of a nation-state's juridical practices with respect to citizenship, porous national boundaries and global labor movements of immigrants from poor to rich countries, from postcolonial societies to the metropolis, have made most advanced Western societies irreversibly

---

[17] This reference to the Tri-Lateral Commission underscores the fact that the emergence of market fundamentalism as a social and political movement began long before Reagan's presidential tenure. For its even earlier European roots in the 1950s, see Mirowski 2005; Mitchell 2005; Peck 2008).

multicultural (Benhabib 2002; Hollinger 1995; Lukes and Joppke 1999; R. Smith 2003). Attention to multiculturalism has been triggered not only by new immigrant arrivals, but also by recognition of indigenous peoples and national minority groups who, despite having the formal status of citizenship, have nonetheless long been excluded from most of its rights and privileges (Benhabib 2004; Joppke 1998; Kymlicka 1995, 1997; Walzer 2005). The claims for full inclusion that many of these groups have expressed through social movements and other political activities often have been made in terms of the rights and unfulfilled ideals and obligations on the part of the governing polity – a language immediately recognizable as that of the inclusionary claims of citizenship (Alexander 2006; Cohen and Arato 1992). When specifically focused on rights to an increasing share of the economic and social pie, these claims to redistribution have brought attention to Marshall's famous *social* citizenship (Fraser and Gordon 1998; Handler 2004, 2006; Kessler-Harris 2001; Twine 1994) in relationship to the identity politics of recognition (Fraser 1997; Fraser and Honneth 2003; Isin and Wood 1999).

One of the most interesting challenges for citizenship has been that of "post-nationalism" (Bosniak 2006; Cohen 1999; Sassen 1996, 1998, 2001, 2006a; Soysal 1994). Several iterations of the idea have been generated by transformational dilemmas of the last decades. Should there be a new kind of citizenship that attaches to the formation of the European Union? Is there now such a thing as a "European citizenship" (Balibar 2002, 2004a, 2004b; Bellamy and Warleigh 2001)? If so, should it endow dual citizenship to the holder who maintains her original national status? As a "supranational" legal entity, should the European Union be able to trump the citizenship laws, rights, and obligations of individual nation-states?[18] If so, what is left of the European system (the 1648 Treaty of Westphalia) that defined nation-states by their sovereign territorial boundaries and laws?

A second reason for the interest in post-nationalist citizenship is the far-reaching implications of globalization, most important of which has been what some believe to be the shift of power away from nation-states toward the abstract, decentered global marketplace, where business and finance capital operate in a zone outside the reach of any global polity or international political/legal entity (Brysk 2004; Brysk and Shafir 2004; Habermas 2001; Ong 2003, 2006; Sassen 2001, 2006a, 2006b). Some scholars argue that the global market is functionally efficient not only for economic transactions, but also for the well-being of citizens more generally. Turner (1990: 195), for example, writes that "the problem

---

[18] This is the worry many have about the European Court of Justice in particular.

with Marshall's theory is that it is no longer relevant to a period of disorganized capitalism since it assumed nation-state autonomy in which governments were relatively immune from pressures within the world-system of capitalist nations." In response to this, there have developed theories of "cosmopolitan citizenship," what Habermas (2001) calls a "post-national constellation," and Bosniak (2006) a "denationalized" citizenship (e.g. Archibugi and Held 1995; Benhabib 2007b; Cohen 1999; Habermas 2001; Heater 1996; Held 1995, 1999; Held and McGrew 2002; Hutchings and Dannreuther 1999; Kymlicka 1997; Linklater 1990, 2000; Nussbaum and Cohen 1996; Sassen 1996, 1998; Walzer 1997).

The explosive recognition that we are living in a new world of multiculturalism has posed a strong challenge to traditional understandings of the rights and obligations of citizenship (Joppke and Lukes 1999; Kymlicka 1995).[19] While demands for social inclusion have traditionally been made in the name of the principle of redistribution, many new social movements have mobilized under the right to recognition – the right to be acknowledged by others as a moral equal – despite group differences (Benhabib 2002; Fraser 1997; Fraser and Honneth 2003; Taylor and Gutmann 1992). Supporters of these identity movements argue that they are piercing the illusory veils of (false) universality and equal rights to reveal not Marx's conflictual economic foundations but the deep fissures of race, gender, sexuality, and ethnicity that comprise the fault lines of contemporary advanced political cultures. Identity politics, from this perspective, are rightly pushing the limits of political/juridical citizenship and forcing it to accommodate such novelties as *group* rights based on group difference, the rights of institutions to practice diversity, and the rights to recognition and protection for different expressions of sexuality (Benhabib 1996, 2002; Fraser and Honneth 2003; Fraser 1997; Kymlicka 1995, 1997; Nussbaum 2000; Okin *et al.* 1999; Young 1990, 2000). The new attention to issues of inclusion, participation, and identity has thus vastly expanded the legitimate scope of citizenship studies to include gender, sexuality, race, and even environmentalism – to name just a few (e.g. Siim 2000; Isin and Wood 1999; Lister 1997; Voet 1998).

The intense attention in the United States to recent Supreme Court decisions concerning sexuality and racial diversity prove just how deep a

---

[19] Marshall himself was *not* innocent of these issues, despite claims to the contrary, and his essays in Marshall (1981) reveal that he had for years been cognizant of how attention to race and ethnicity would impose significant adjustments on his earlier work. Indeed he makes such an adjustment in some of these later essays on race and power.

challenge these claims for recognition pose for existing definitions of citizenship. Critics of identity politics (from both the left and the right) are alarmed by the specter of group rights; the focus on difference and identity, they worry, threatens to tear asunder the principle of universality and egalitarianism that forms the very foundation of modern democratic citizenship (Shachar 2001; Walzer 2005). The idea that primordial attachments and loyalties to particular groups could trump the attachment to national membership in a polity held *in common* is felt by many liberals to threaten a "neonationalism" in which "questions of identity eclipse those of citizenship and democracy" (Morley and Robins 1995: 186). Others famously have worried that support for multiculturalism entails the "twilight of common dreams" (Gitlin 1995) and the "disuniting of America" (Schlesinger 1992, 1998). Even feminists with otherwise shared commitments have debated this issue of "recognition versus redistribution" (Benhabib 1995; Fraser 1997; Young 2000). However one views the phenomenon, a central issue has emerged in the field of citizenship studies. A complex relationship, if not an irresolvable conflict, exists between citizenship and identity and demands deep intellectual engagement (Isin 1992, 2002; Isin and Wood 1999; Mouffe 1995; Preuss 1995; Procacci and Salamone 2000; Rajchman 1995; Trend 1996).

One of the most significant catalysts to citizenship's rediscovery was the recuperation in the 1980s and early 1990s of the idea of *civil society*. The vehicles for this were both practice-based and theory-driven (e.g. Alexander 1993, 2006; Calhoun 1993; Cohen and Arato 1992; Janoski 1998; Kennedy 1990, 1991, 2002; Kymlicka and Norman 1995; Seligman 1992; Somers 1995b, 1999, 2001; Taylor 1990; Wolfe 1989). Revisionist approaches to West European democratization focused new attention on the importance of the three citizenship concepts – civil society, the public sphere, and civil political participation (Beiner 1995; Habermas [1962] 1989; Putnam 1993; Somers 1993, 1994a; Walzer 1995). The processes that captured the world's attention included the political and human rights achievements of the civil society movements in Latin America, the trade unionist Solidarity movement in Poland, Charter 77 in Czechoslovakia, and the widespread anti-authoritarian revolutions across Eastern Europe, more broadly – especially the 1989 fall of the Berlin Wall, and the collapse of the Soviet state.

In all of these, civil society played a role as both a normative ideal and a practical site for democratic social action. It was exciting to discover a political vocabulary free of the manichaean and stifling Cold War dichotomies between state and market. Civil society came to be seen as a "third sphere," not reducible to either the ruthless individualism of unregulated capitalism or the bureaucratic apparatus of the communist state. This contributed mightily to a new appreciation of citizenship as a social phenomenon, which broke apart seemingly immutable, age-old obstacles to a sociology of citizenship and made available for future democratizers an empirical explanation for the success of the revolutions that over-turned communism. In this effort, civil society theorists pointed to the significance of *social organization* and *associational life* – both formal (e.g. civic clubs) and informal (underground communities of shared resistance) (see Putnam 2000; and chapter 6, this volume). There were social networks, labor associations, and community solidarities that provided both the actual and the normative foundations for the third sphere of civil society. It was part of a reinvigorated citizenship ideal associated with the "dynamics of contention" (McAdam *et al.* 2001). It was a novel political and social terrain, one that provided the spring-board for those popular movements and multiple forms of mobilization that overturned oppressive regimes in the name of a participatory citizen-ship and democratic public life.

Above all, then, it was the rediscovery of civil society both intellec-tually and as a practical site for democratic social action that broke apart seemingly immutable, age-old obstacles to a sociology of citizenship. The hegemony of the great dichotomy between public and private gave way to a long suppressed third sphere, and there emerged for social theory this new social site of citizenship practices. Even more significant is that these practices were expressed in the voice of both individual rights and civic participation. They were taken from both the liberal and republican traditions and reflected the voices of people not as isolated individuals, but as citizens whose identities were shaped by their relationships to others. Only from the site of the social could these voices be heard with-out being absorbed back into either the competitive chaos of market governance or the domination of the administrative state. Alas, this was not to last; the lifespan of civil society as a quasi-autonomous third sphere was brief indeed. In short order, as I argue in chapters 6 and 7, civil society as a theoretical rallying cry returned to its original roots as a site of civic opposition to the tyranny of the communist state (in Eastern Europe) and the welfare state (in the West), and fully in alliance with the market.

Theorizing citizenship

In chapter 2, I begin by suggesting that the story of Hurricane Katrina is a parable of citizenship in America today. Deconstructing Katrina – excavating the hidden stories of what came before it, exposing the well-guarded assumptions and submerged practices that belied the public alibis for so many lost and abandoned lives – reveals much about the fragility of citizenship rights today and the costs of their erosion. But, as I hope will become evident, Katrina also serves as a parable for this book's central theoretical precepts and for those concerns that drive my current explorations and theorizations. Rather than try to spell these out in a single grand "theory of citizenship," here I simply highlight several aspects of my approach, elaborate on some of my theoretical precepts, and place them on the wider canvas of citizenship studies. Although it is entirely arbitrary, I have decided to focus on five areas.

1. *The question of borders.* Whereas citizenship research is usually divided between those who look at the rights of citizens in the "soft inside," and those who focus on national borders and the "excluded hard outside" faced by noncitizens, I emphasize internal borders of exclusion within the nation state.[20]

2. *Normativity and empirical social science.* Whereas citizenship studies often reflect a division of labor between normative philosophical scholarship and empirical social science, my approach to citizenship and rights underlines their indivisibility; citizenship and citizenship rights are at once normative and empirical.

3. *What is citizenship?* Whereas many theories of citizenship are organized around a single normative political theory (for example, liberalism or republicanism), my approach eschews a single theory in favor of the capacious hybrid of the right to have rights.

4. *What is civil society?* As an "essentially contested concept," multiple definitions of civil society have vied to make critical contributions to the new citizenship studies. I define civil society as "the site of citizenship," and discuss it in terms of "the fragile centrality of the social."

5. *An architectonics of citizenship: a triadic variable for comparative empirical analysis.* Whereas many empirical studies of citizenship portray it as a status constructed out of a two-party relationship between the individual and the state, I argue, by contrast, that citizenship is essentially the name we use for a triadic assemblage of shifting institutional and discursive relationships and struggles for power among state, market and civil society.

---

[20] Balibar (2004b) and Bosniak (2006).

Global, national, or internal borders?

Citizenship at its most basic is a mechanism for inclusion and exclusion, and thus a means for establishing or prohibiting membership in political entities that vary in scale from supranational to local. This makes citizenship studies a "two-sited" research field, with most scholarship inhabiting primarily one or the other site. The first straddles and stretches across the geopolitical and conceptual borders of citizenship's exclusionary lines of demarcation. This site is populated inter alia by scholars of immigration, international labor migration, guest worker policies, post-colonial ethnic migration, globalization, post-nationalism, and transnational citizenship. Call this the "inside/outside" site of citizenship studies, for it focuses on how citizenship serves as a mechanism to distribute people among political entities, as well as on how the criteria are established for these rules and practices of distribution and exclusion. Citizenship's second research site can loosely be called the "inside/interior" one, for it asks the essential question of what is citizenship's meaning and what are the substantive benefits and costs, the rights (if any) and obligations, that accrue to those who already possess its status – that is, those who are its legal citizen-members. With the exception of my attention to the epistemology of human rights, I focus on the site of citizenship's interior meaning.

Let me say immediately that this division of labor between citizenship sites is demonstrably porous. It would be difficult, for example, for studies of "illegal" immigrants qua would-be citizens to focus exclusively on membership criteria and exclusionary policies without attention to the benefits and resources that hold out such promise to the excluded. In my own work, the division of labor has become even more blurred, its porousness more pronounced, as the exclusions of exteriority at the borders are increasingly being grafted onto interior membership sites. As I suggest in my argument about how the citizens of New Orleans were made stateless by the man-made tragedy of Katrina, the borders and boundaries once used solely as external demarcations designed to exclude people from nation-state entry are increasingly expanding to the center of our polities, creating sharp interior borders of internal social and political exclusion (see especially Bosniak 2006; and Balibar 2004b, for the European dimensions of this phenomenon, as well as the many sociological analyses of the new phenomena of gated communities in America). Resembling a fractal devolution of national borders, this type of internal apartheid is increasing in this age of globalization, when "winners" and "losers" are distributed not exclusively between

nation-states, but equally within single nation-states. There is an important interaction between internal and external borders, however, which
cannot be ignored since it further contributes to internal social exclusion.
While empirical economic studies differ in how much immigration
contributes to wage depression, there is no question but that it is used
as a check on the powers of citizen-workers to organize into unions, to
demand liveable wages, and to secure a minimally nondegrading quality
of life. While they have no real right to have rights, illegal immigrants are
still "welcomed" into our economy where their presence has the effect of
suppressing the rights of citizen-workers. They are in effect indentured
servants – at once rightless and exploited. Chapter 2 engages these
internal borders of social exclusion that are being increasingly produced
by the expanding marketization and contractualization of citizenship.

Normative, empirical, or both?

Citizenship studies today are notable for just how much they are divided
between those who primarily write normative political theory, philosophy, and legal theory, and those whose work is explicitly empirical. In
general, normative work tends to be driven by recurring concerns in
moral and political philosophy, while empirical research is more problem-
driven (which explains why it is less likely to have crisp philosophical
moorings and more likely to resemble a bricolage of history, political
science, economics and sociology). In the social sciences, where there is a
constitutive mandate to avoid normativity, and by implication theories of
rights, it is hardly surprising that sociologists tend to confine themselves
to generating causal explanations and/or cultural interpretations of specific empirical problems in citizenship formation and rights more generally. This split between the normative and the empirical should not be
overstated; the borders between them are also porous and there are of
course those whose work encompasses both sites, especially Étienne
Balibar (1994, 2004a, b), Seyla Benhabib (2001, 2004, 2007a, b), Linda
Bosniak (2006), Engin Isin (2002), Will Kymlicka (2001, 1995), Banting
and Kymlicka (2006), Jeff Alexander (2006), and Bryan Turner (1993,
2006).[21] I call attention to this division of labor because it precludes much

---

[21] Other leading voices in this group include Cohen and Arato (1992), Fraser and Gordon
(1997, 1998), Lukes (2004, 2006), and Habermas (1996, 2001). Among the most prominent
empirical voices in citizenship studies are Mann (1986, 1987), Brubaker (1992), Soysal
(1994), Sassen (2006), and Tilly (1995, 1998).

conversation between the two kinds of citizenship work, which has left a marked imprint on the theoretical output. There are exceptions, of course. Tilly recounts an incident in which he commented on Robert Dahl's (2000) definition of democratic citizenship by pondering whether Dahl's philosophically normative definition should be rejected because it was "empirically empty," in that no state or political community had ever fully met its requirements. Or do we justify it because it sets a standard against which we can array real political arrangements or even ask, "What political arrangements are worth sacrificing for?" (Tilly 1995: 370).[22] This model of cross-conversational query could be more frequently emulated by social scientists.

My own thinking and writing has been equally shaped by normative philosophy and by empirical analysis, which is evident in my efforts to speak in both voices. But it is not only an abstract commitment to bring them together that drives my approach. It is also because citizenship *is*, willy-nilly, both a normative and an empirical concept.[23] Even those empirically driven scholars who question the advantages of introducing normativity into citizenship studies usually concede that it is already there and cannot be expunged. Social action is shaped as much by narratives, myths, ideational regimes, and cultural codes as it is by sociology's more traditional causal suspects, such as the economy, the state, the class structure, and so on (Somers and Gibson 1994). The case for normativity is even stronger when we recognize the causal force of normative commitments. Citizenship, however much an empirical institution of governance, is perceived as a *desideratum* and a good, and these normative qualities have causal powers.

"Ideational embeddedness" is the term Fred Block and I use to capture the causal powers of ideas and ideational regimes in embedding, constructing, deconstructing, and transforming markets, and market relationships (e.g. with the state), over the last four decades (Somers and Block 2005). Recognizing the degree to which ideas, beliefs, meaning structures, and public narratives actually inform the very "material" dynamics that we have tended to privilege in causal arguments allows me to dispose of the very distinction between "ideal" and "material"

---

[22] For Tilly, "rights exist when one party can effectively insist that another deliver goods, services or protections and third parties will act to reinforce (or at least not to hinder) their delivery" (1998: 56).

[23] On the normativity of the market, see especially Zelizer (1997, 2005).

interests, assuming the concept of interest to denote a motivational force inherent in a person's structural location and practices of intentionality. The working-class social movements for citizenship rights at the heart of my historical research on English citizenship formation, for example, were motivated by normative ideas of equality, freedom, justice, fairness, solidarity, and the equal rule of law. To be sure, the actual developmental processes of these movements depended on many opportunity structures, such as the porous "multiple-use" structure of English law, civil society's autonomy from the market and state, and partible family inheritance patterns. But it is ideas and ideals that move people, and fighting to achieve the rights of citizenship is one way to at least partially realize those ideas/ideals. Without such motivating ideas and expectations, these structural features would be causally inert. Attempting to purge these powers from theories of citizenship would not only be futile; it would also make them less than fully intelligible and incompletely theorized.

This normative aspect of citizenship is most apparent in the dimension of identity formation. As a mechanism of membership distribution, citizenship has cultural, identitarian, and practical implications. Culturally, membership and social inclusion give identity a distinct form and meaning. Hence Marshall (1992: 6, 8) characterizes social citizenship not as income transfers or quantifiable economic benefits but as a matter of social recognition and full inclusion in the body politic. Ditto Judith Shklar (1991): in her discussion of the relative importance of the practical exercise of citizenship rights versus their cultural and symbolic implications for identity, she demonstrates how the cultural meaning of citizenship and the identity of inclusion they endow appear to significantly outweigh its practical implementation. People appear to be motivated to avoid the stigma of social exclusion associated with being "second-class citizens" without the right to vote, more than they are committed to actually exercising those rights that citizenship confers.[24]

The voices of the left-behind of New Orleans tell us a lot about the strength of this normative bond between identity and citizenship. For the Katrina survivors interviewed by the media after their prolonged ordeals and days of abandonment, rather than what so understandably might have been anger expressed as African-Americans betrayed by racism, the shock and despair they expressed at being abandoned were those of citizenship betrayed. It appears that at this moment of existential

---

[24] In addition to Shklar, Smith (1993, 1999) argues that slavery served this cultural purpose of creating identitarian feelings of inclusion over and against these excluded others.

crisis, their attachment to citizenship-based identities trumped those of difference-based identities of race and class. Through the concept of narrative identity, I argue that citizenship identities are shaped through narratives of membership rights obtained through (or lost despite) struggle and hardship (Somers 1992, 1994a). The Katrina story gives heft to the power of narratives to shape our sense of who we are – especially the narrative of belonging through membership. Identity is both constitutive and a product of citizenship institutions, practices, and expectations, even when – or perhaps especially when – the rights of citizenship are not delivered, as in New Orleans, late August 2005. Historically, nation and citizenship have worked together, or co-produced, the kind of meaningful identification tied up with political membership. In medieval cities and in the period of European nation-state formation, citizenship dominated nation as the dominant affective source of meaning (Somers 1994a, 1995c). Among America's white population today, and in contrast to the majority of African-Americans, patriotic attachment to nation is increasingly displacing commitment to constitutional rights as the primary source of meaning and identity formation, as I discuss in chapter 3. Embracing both normative and empirical approaches allows me, for purposes of analysis and clarity, to disarticulate into distinct concepts the two dimensions of my definition of citizenship and citizenship rights.

What is citizenship? The right to have rights

In line with Arendt's most Delphic of phrases, citizenship is about having the right to have rights – not any single civil, juridical, or even social right, but the primary right of recognition, inclusion, and membership in both political and civil society. I read this as a radical distinction between the formal rights (e.g. civil rights, political rights) attached to the legal status of citizen, versus the right to human personhood – recognition as a moral equal, that is – endowed by full inclusion in a social and political body. Implicit in this conception of citizenship is a critique of classical liberalism's conception of rights as possessions owned by already fully constituted human beings – persons whose originating and sustaining ontology remains mysteriously ambiguous, whether simply a given part of the "state of nature," or a being whose rights-bearing status is adduced by the Lockean capacity to "mix one's labor with the soil" (Shapiro 1995). One thing we do know is that the rights-bearer is ontologically presocial and prelegal and the rights remain "natural," without institutional foundations, without relationships, without membership.

For Arendt the tragedy of this eighteenth-century liberalism is that the statelessness that paved the way to the actual historical Nazi genocide also represents liberalism's highest ideals of absolute freedom from political belonging. As she so poignantly explains, to effectively make the world safe for genocide, the Germans created a population of stateless people by depriving Jews of nationality and citizenship. Hence, they made the Nuremberg Laws one of their earliest orders of business. The Nazis understood all too well that statelessness would deprive the Jews of membership in a political community. Statelessness also deprived them of the very qualities that made them recognizably human. It would transform them from fellow humans into the "scum of the earth" – Goebbels' term evoking nonhuman slime, which Arendt uses purposively to provoke repulsion and misrecognition in her readers, and so to prick the bubble of denial that safely insulated the self-satisfied West from the consequences of their own indifference. As "scum," Jews would be unworthy of rescue by every Western country to which they pleaded for asylum. This is exactly what happened. With no disturbance whatsoever to the sacred Rights of Man and with their "natural rights" fully in hand, the stateless were annihilated with virtually no objection from the rest of the world (Arendt 1979).

This story informs the conception of citizenship that I embrace in this book. I take the right to have rights to involve two analytic levels of rights. The first right is to membership in a political body, and thus the right to be recognized by others as a moral equal and full part of the human community. For Arendt this existential right to recognition and inclusion can only be conferred by a political body, but she is deeply agnostic about the necessity of that body being a nation-state. Indeed as we will see clearly in my discussion of Hurricane Katrina in chapter 2, *de jure* legal citizenship and formal nation-state citizenship may have been necessary, but they certainly were not sufficient to secure the rights of the abandoned of New Orleans. The treatment inflicted on those left behind teaches us that without *de facto* citizenship, possessing formal nation-state citizenship alone is an inadequate foundation for being recognized as a fully rights-bearing person. Social inclusion in a robust civil society is also a precondition of the first right to membership and belonging. Absent that civil membership, so too will be recognition by others as a fellow human of equal worth and value.

Unlike belonging to a nation-state, however, where the question of national citizenship is settled by documents, there are no passports or papers that testify to membership in civil society. Nor are there customs officials, 700-foot walls, or "Welcome to . . ." signs to signify the boundaries demarcating where civil society ends and social exclusion begins. How then do we determine inclusion or exclusion from civil society? The drama of Hurricane Katrina reveals that we do not need to see any papers to identify the socially excluded. They were demonstrably treated as the "scum of the earth," and were evidentially pushed outside the circle of human recognition. Their formal nation-state membership notwithstanding, the left-behind of New Orleans had become *de facto* internally stateless superfluous people. Rightlessness and exclusion from civil society go hand in hand.

By defining the right to have rights as the heart of my citizenship theory I am bypassing the usual approach in which citizenship is defined by a dominant organizing theory. Dominant organizing theories are like metatheories, in that they specify less a single causal explanation than a whole set of interrelated assumptions, such as the meaning of agency, the relationship of state and market, and so on. The approach is both reasonable and useful, as these metatheories are capacious enough to be able to differentiate classes of citizenship regimes using only their own bundle of assumptions and concepts to address citizenship's main concerns – the meaning of citizenship, its criteria for inclusion, and in what practical goods it actually consists and delivers – to name a few. If I were to do justice to even a fraction of the theories that have been deployed to address these I would have to include not only the standard ones of republicanism, liberalism, communitarianism, and post-nationalism, but also neoutilitarianism, law and economics, rational-choice theory, critical legal studies/Marxist critiques of rights, neorepublicanism, civic humanism, recognition politics/multicultural-ism/identity politics, discourse ethics/procedural theory of democracy, and post-liberal rights theories. I will avoid torturing my readers with a thorough survey, especially since several of them are the subjects of my chapters.

Despite this abundance, several dominate the field – liberalism, repub-licanism, communitarianism and/or ethnonationalism – and hence merit comment. Each has a central organizing principle and concomitant foundational assumptions. For liberalism, it is liberty, autonomy, and natural rights; for republicanism, it is equality and political participa-tion; for communitarianism, it is moral self-regulation and duty; and for ethnonationalism, it is ethnic belonging to the nation. Not surpris-ingly, many split the difference, mix and match, and reconfigure. Habermas (1996), most famously, invented "constitutional patriotism" to mix three of them, as well as "procedural democracy" to join liberal-ism and republicanism. Étienne Balibar (1994, 2004a) does likewise with his neologism "equaliberty," while Van Gunsteren (1998) imaginatively theorizes "neorepublicanism."

I, too, plead guilty to this desire to combine the best of all theories, and were I to use the dominant theory approach to define citizenship I would take my inspiration from Balibar's (1994, 2004a) mixing of liberalism, communitarianism, and republicanism through the hybridity of equaliberty. Indeed, I believe that the right to have rights takes the best of each theory and combines them into one, using the principle that each is "necessary but not sufficient." Thus although liberalism's dedication to liberty and individual rights is absolutely necessary for any adequate conception of democratic citizenship rights, it is not sufficient. And republicanism's focus on equality, membership, and the principle of participation (if not the unrealistic Aristotelian "to rule and be ruled") is also necessary but not sufficient. Finally, communitarianism's insistence on the sphere of the social as a critical site of solidarity is also necessary, but insufficient.

My revised version of the right to have rights, in effect, combines the necessary elements from each theory while abandoning their less appealing auxiliary assumptions, such as liberalism's insistence on grounding liberty in the market and rights in the state of nature. The resulting configuration should be familiar: the right of membership and inclusion inherent in the right to have rights combines aspects of republicanism and communitarianism, while at the same time it regrounds the principle of individual liberty not in nature but in the solidarism and membership of civil society. And parts of liberalism, republicanism, and communitarianism all find their way into the second group of substantive rights. In principle, the second group of rights could include as many theoretical principles as there are social concerns and their associated claims to equality, recognition, and inclusion.

Nonetheless, this understandable impulse to have it all ways pays too little attention to some of the theories' fundamental and perhaps even mutually exclusive assumptions. Unlike the enormous attention paid to the stark tensions between the two different political theories of republicanism and liberalism, less has been directed to how those tensions have been incorporated into the seemingly unproblematic concept of "citizenship rights." In chapter 4, I identify the consequent internal tensions, destabilizing aporias, and outright negations as some of the many "citizenship troubles" to which I attribute the precarious condition of citizenship rights. The problem is that in classical liberalism, however generous an interpretation we now read into it, there are no citizens to be found; instead, there are only discrete rights-bearing individuals who come together as parties to a contract. To attach citizenship to these autonomous rights-bearers is to graft a political membership-centered identity onto a view of the person who originates in the prepolitical state of nature – surely the recipe for a confused agent of political and moral action. In the right to have rights, I have posed an alternative conceptualization of both citizenship and (human) rights that overcomes this inherent instability by grounding both in an ontology of social inclusion. In doing so, however, I have violated some of the fundamental precepts of both liberalism and republicanism. When Arendt argues that the Holocaust can in part be attributed to what she defines as the zero-sum relationship between citizenship and the Rights of Man, she is pointing to the antipolitics that the abstract universalism of natural rights theory requires, as I discuss in chapter 3. Theories of citizenship may not have to solve this internal conflict in citizenship rights' hybrid mix of republicanism and liberalism, but at the very least, they should engage it.

Civil society – the site of citizenship and the fragile centrality of the social

Throughout this book I stress the centrality of civil society and social inclusion as a foundational right and necessity for democratic socially inclusive citizenship. Civil society has several conceptual histories, which explains why there are so many competing points of origin in the effort to recoup the power of its narrative path. The Lockean version of civil society is what Charles Taylor (1990) calls the "L" stream – which conveniently for him covers both its namesake and the classical liberalism that Locke arguably did more than anyone to invent. As I chart in chapter 7, in the classical liberal metanarrative, civil society exists in a zero-sum dyadic relationship with the state. It is the familiar story of civil society emerging from the state of nature to create a prepolitical, self-sufficient autonomous site entirely independent of any authority deriving from state institutions, as the political state is the force which civil society has been invented to resist. Other than begrudgingly accepting the necessity of the state carrying out minimal functions of security and property protection, civil society qua market society focuses on the singular threat of coercive state intervention, where it is poised to repel the inexorable threat of state colonization. As for the actual space of civil society, for the liberal narrative it is the site of both property exchange and individual freedom – which are causally interrelated. When civil society and the site of the market are conceived as one and the same, then free and self-regulating markets are considered the only requisites for individual rights and social justice. This is the dominant metanarrative of market fundamentalism and neoliberalism. Today it is most commonly expressed in the political discourse of spreading democracy around the world (Hertzberg 2002).

The second variant of civil society is that which Taylor dubs the "M" stream in recognition of Montesquieu's earliest articulation. It is most celebrated of course in the writings of Tocqueville, and today is associated with communitarian theory. Again civil society is in a zero-sum dichotomy with the state, only this time the market is ambiguously hidden in the shadows. This time civil society is defined internally and exclusively by its associational social practices, externally by its fiercely constituted opposition to state regulation. It is the associational strength of its practices and institutions that empowers civil society to continually resist and patrol against the invasive designs of the state into the site of the social. This is associated with struggles against communism and dictatorship, which explains why, in normative terms, the focus is placed entirely on civil society's ability to repel the state, usually without equal concern expressed about the effects of extreme marketization (Putnam 2000).

By contrast, a "triadic" approach to civil society is best characterized by those who include the market in this heuristic model, while preserving civil society as the space of social solidarity and ongoing noncontractual relationships. Here civil society represents a "third sphere" in between both state and market, constantly engaged in resisting the imperial designs of the market no less than those of the state.[25] Another variant of this triadic approach can be traced back to Durkheim and is today most dynamically articulated by Jeffrey Alexander (2006). Alexander identifies civil society as a site in perpetual struggle – a "people of individuals" striving for social solidarity while by necessity engaged in an inexhaustible effort to sustain their autonomy from both the utilitarianism of the market and the coercive bureaucratization of state power. Because it is comprised of inclusive democratic structures *and* repressive vilifications, of practices of solidarity as well as those of exclusion, the civil sphere is where citizenship, solidarity, and justice are possible, but by no means inevitable. According to Alexander, civil society is a social world that is at once a product and productive of cultural codes and normative binaries – both the "dark" and the "light" sides of democracy and politics, the

---

[25] Today's most celebrated advocates of this approach are Cohen and Arato (1992) and Jürgen Habermas (1996).

solidaristic and the repressive/exclusionary – that enmesh us no less than the rational discourses to which we more willfully aspire. Civil society's normative ideal combines solidarity and rights, freedom and equality. All too easily, however, these can invert into exclusion and inequality.

In chapter 2, I demonstrate through the story of the abandoned Hurricane Katrina victims the degree to which much of human freedom is contingent upon the existence of a thriving civil society – one fully capable of resisting the expansionist drives of both state coercion and market fundamentalism. At the same time, a healthy civil society is not autonomous of markets and states. Indeed the contrary is true; civil society's very capacity for resistance against external market incursions requires support from the state in the form of market regulations, social insurance policies, public services, redistributive tax schemes, and legal mechanisms to institutionalize and enforce the rights to livelihood. Recalling that a foundational element of democratic citizenship is the right to freedom from the tyranny of want, so too must civil society be supported by access to living-wage employment, especially to those labor markets which are willing and/or able to buck the pressures of the global economy (Sunstein 2004). In alliance with these institutionalized relationships of both support and resistance, and in tandem with the equitable rule of law, it is on a balance of power among civil society, market, and state – mediated through the site of the public sphere, in which pressure on the state from democratic participation is nurtured – that citizenship depends. Only through social inclusions in civil society can the right to have rights be sustained.

However, there is also a duality to civil society's centrality, as well as to its concomitant fragility. In the first instance, its centrality is metaphorically spatial and refers to its place in relationship to other spheres of society. Civil society, in my view of democratic citizenship, must thrive as the social site situated between the market and the state, albeit fully independent of neither. By disrupting what would otherwise be only a dyad of state and market, civil society is thus central to the balance of power in the triadic configuration of state, civil society, and market. But it is also central in a second sense of ethical significance. Civil society is critically important to the making and the survival of egalitarian citizenship regimes. In the interest of democracy, it is critical in an empirical and sociological sense that civil society and its independent egalitarian and solidaristic ethos survive at the center of state and market, where it must prevent the spilling over or boundary transgressions into civil society of either market or state powers. Only then can it thrive as a site that supports practices and precepts that are neither market- nor power-driven. As the only site in which people constitute themselves as citizens and as "a people," an independent civil society is thus necessary for situating the social movements that are called upon to defend society as a whole.

By now it should be evident that the centrality of civil society, in all of these senses, is deeply fragile. Historically, it has been the first sphere to be conquered and corroded by both or either market or state. And the duality of its fragility parallels the duality of its centrality. In the first case, as I show in chapter 6, its place in the center in between market and state can be too easily displaced by the powers of market fundamentalism to domesticate it into social capital, and thus to conquer its autonomy. If this happens, the triadic configuration will collapse into an unequal dyad in which power is concentrated in a market-driven state and a governance-driven market. Having lost its autonomy, civil society can no longer do the boundary work of protecting the nonmarket sites of society from illegitimate market invasion, nor facilitate those social movements so necessary for society to defend itself.

Parallel developments in social theory reflect equally this fragility, as talk of the social and recognition of the constitutive relationality of society, indeed of the very idea of "society," is too often dissolved into contractual models of utility-maximizing individuals responding to market-driven (or perverse) incentives, a view most famously associated with Margaret Thatcher in the 1970s and 1980s. Theories of our social universe have morphed into perspectives informed by social naturalism, the scarcity fiction, and the discipline of economics. Poverty, for example, once the province of sociological analysis has over the last decades been almost entirely appropriated by economists and economic precepts based on stern incentive management of what are now considered individual behavioral "choices." Economics, however, is not the only threat to the social. As we saw under communism, civil society and social theory are equally at risk of being squashed by state tyranny. Whether the threat is economic or political, the social perspective on the world is critical to advance the rights and norms of civil society as a whole, rather than the interests of either market or state, which are served by the disciplines of economics and political science respectively.

But perhaps the greatest threat to the ideational centrality of civil society and social analysis is that of the intractable staying power of what Bobbio (1992) calls the "great dichotomy" of social and political theory, namely the dichotomy between the mutually exclusive spheres of public versus private. This enduring conceptual divide has proved to be intransigent in the ability of its binary representation of state versus market to dominate the entire conceptual landscape of social and political life, thus crowding out all competing representations. As I discuss in chapter 7, the problem for civil society as the "third" sphere in between state and market is that of placing three pegs into two holes. In this struggle for dominance, the dyad of public versus private has consistently been the winner. In the process of driving out the triadic perspective it has too often eliminated civil society entirely by returning it to its Lockean roots as part of private market society.

These are some of the reasons for the fragile centrality of civil society and the idea of the social. Identifying fragility as an essential characteristic of civil society might once have primarily served as a normative cry of alarm – a description that is also a prescriptive warning. No more. Its fragility is a post-hoc tragic observation – made real, increasingly, by history itself.

. . . and the inclusion/exclusion of the citizenship ethic

At the core of civil society are competing political and knowledge cultures, as well as ideational regimes. As I discuss in chapter 7, these are made up of a mix of binary and narrative logics. While Alexander (2006) points to the cultural opposition of the sacred versus the polluted, I focus on the binary logic of *social naturalism*, an epistemological construct of the seventeenth- and eighteenth-century scientific revolution and nineteenth-century positivism. Social naturalism divides the social world into those practices and entities that conform to the self-regulating laws of nature, and those that fall under the rubric of nonnatural phenomena. It then assigns epistemological privilege and ontological superiority to those entities deemed natural, such as the market, and demeans all that is deemed unnatural, such as the state. The critically important struggle for the soul of civil society as a site of the social, especially its autonomy from the market, is at stake in the distribution of entities across the binary divide between the natural and the nonnatural. Market fundamentalism strains to subject civil society exclusively to the side of the natural, hence as its own auxiliary. Civil society, to maintain its noncontractual core, strains against this naturalistic subjection – but in a zero-sum binary, the only alternative is the nonnatural side of the state. Civil society struggles to establish itself as the third site of the social in a binary universe that is limited to the mutually exclusive dichotomous sites of market and state.

The noncontractual relations of civil society are not natural, of course, but institutional. Access to public services and social insurance are institutionalized expressions of rights internal to the inclusionary ethic of citizenship and the common good. The noncontractual citizenship ethos differs from contractual logic in that there is no assumption that one has to exchange commensurable quid pro quos to be treated as a valued member of civil society who is entitled to protection as a right of membership. In some theories of citizenship, members have rights because of their obligation to participate in the common project of "ruling and being ruled" or to contribute in ways that are neither commensurable nor contractual (paying taxes, for example, or serving in the military, raising children, and so on). But as I define it, citizenship is a distinct ethos precisely because the right to have rights does not depend on individual capabilities or on the capacity for participation; nor does it require passing any other kind of litmus test of moral worthiness.[26] This citizenship ethic is manifested in the idea of *social insurance* – social, because as Hacker (2006) reminds us, the "social" in social insurance derives from the principle of "shared fate." It is a principle that leads to the conviction that inevitable threats to well-being, which include "sickness, injury, disability, unemployment, penurious old age – [are] not the responsibility of individuals alone. They [are] a widespread and often unavoidable feature of an interdependent industrial society. And because they [are], the costs of these risks should be distributed widely across the citizenry, not concentrated on those unlucky enough to experience them." Whereas the wealthy can always take for granted basic economic security (in large part because of corporate and business tax breaks and safety nets), the citizenship ethic of social insurance "extend[s] economic security to those least capable of obtaining it on their own – namely those with modest means or a high probability of needing assistance" (Hacker 2006: 41–3). The ethic of citizenship requires a conceptual site of civil society where principles of social insurance are protected from market mechanisms.[27]

Citizenship's conceptual architecture: a triadic variable for comparative empirical analysis

The right to have rights is an ideal and an aspiration. Therefore, it needs to be complemented by empirical foundations that specify the social

---

[26] Contrast this normative view that prohibits bargaining over rights to Tilly's (1998) empirical argument that it is precisely bargaining that answers the question of "where do rights come from?"

[27] See also Alexander (2006).

requirements for its realization. To translate the right to have rights into a conceptual tool for sociological and historical analysis, and to explore the structural conditions that enable or disable varying types of citizenship regimes, I have developed an *architectonics* of citizenship – an infrastructural design that models how the parts fit together. Metaphorically, it is a continuous relational triadic assemblage among the state, market, and civil society, in which the site and direction of power is the object of constant struggle – a struggle mediated through the public sphere. This shifting model represents the analytic infrastructure at the heart of my citizenship theory. It represents the morphology of citizenship – the metaphorical shape that citizenship takes when the relationships among the institutions and practices of each of these three sites are configured diagrammatically. Exploring the conditions and the consequences of these shifts of power and place constitutes the historical work – the genealogizing – of theorizing citizenship.

Drawing from Polanyi's (1957b) famous formulation of the "economy as an instituted process," I define citizenship as an "instituted process" to capture its inherent temporality, as well as the constantly changing balance of power among its institutional sites.[28] Citizenship is at heart a matrix of institutional relationships, technologies, political idioms, and rights-claiming practices that are always dynamic and contingent.[29] As an instituted process, it is comprised of membership rules and political cultures shaped by competing narratives of egalitarianism and social inclusionary rights in opposition to both unfettered marketization and to hyper-securitization by the government. Deploying this analytic heuristic of citizenship as a three-sided instituted process allows me to examine over time the continuous struggles for dominance among these institutional sites. Citizenship can at times blunt the market's inherent drive to convert noncontractual relationships to contractual ones, but this depends on the shifting balance of power among the three sites. Struggles for power among these sites are channeled through the public sphere, the outcomes of which set the parameters of any given citizenship regime and alert us as to whether we are moving toward or away from periods of more or less market fundamentalism. This approach supports my view that citizenship is very much a *practice*. These practices are also a source of identity, or what Shklar (1991) calls one's "standing" relative to

---

[28] This conceptualization and its empirical application is most explicitly demonstrated in Somers (1993, 1994a).
[29] This reconceptualization dovetails with social science's move away from categories and attributes, towards relationality, networks, and narratives (see Somers 1994b).

other citizens and noncitizens. How and whether they will translate into rights depends on their contexts of activation.

My triadic scaffolding of state, market, and civil society contrasts with the prevailing view of citizenship as a two-party relationship between the individual and the polity.[30] To be sure, in the narrowest sense of formal legality, an individual's citizenship status is strictly granted by the state. But this can mislead us into thinking that citizenship can be understood, even in preliminary terms, without recognizing the economic and market dimension already embedded within the public sphere and the state. Moreover, it tells us little to nothing about how citizenship actually works, not *de jure* "on the books" but *de facto* "on the ground," where market relationships and civil societies are always present and entangled with questions of equality and inclusion – or exclusion. Since contractual and property rights are included among the essential guarantees of civil citizenship, markets are constitutive to its workings. As long as humanity's survival includes the need to secure livelihoods and to allocate goods, as long as membership and inclusion are in part tied not just to the fruits of paid labor but to the inclusion attached to actual employment, and as long as we accept that politics and civil society are in part constituted by markets, a focus on the individual and state alone will be wrongheaded. To be sure, for purely analytic reasons we must conceptualize the spheres of the economic, the civil/social, and the polity as separate sites; without that heuristic step, variations in how they actually interact under different conditions are impossible to establish. It is the varying balance of power among all three sites, and how the public sphere negotiates and mediates that struggle, that set the parameters for what kind of citizenship regime will prevail, including the question of the dominant ideational regime, and whether we are moving in the direction of a robust social inclusionary or an attenuated market-driven citizenship.[31]

Constructing the architectonics of citizenship in a triadic configuration is especially valuable methodologically for the task of identifying why and how we have different citizenship regimes. A three-sided institutional

---

[30] The exception to this is when social or what is sometimes called economic citizenship alone is the subject of analysis.
[31] Here I agree with Allen Hunter, who suggests that the spatial metaphor of spheres should be complemented by either a temporal metaphor or by types or modes of practices that are differentially distributed spatially and over time.

configuration in continual struggle for dominance helps to explain variations in citizenship regimes – from those with the most expansive rights, participation, and capacities for solidarity, to those where membership exists in name only, having been overwhelmed by market principles or authoritarian government. By developing different models of citizenship regimes in terms of changing balances of power, we avoid the danger of confusing ideal types with empirical variations. Indeed, here it is worth remembering that the models I devise of both socially inclusive citizenship regimes and those of dystopian social exclusion are empirical fictions. The US version of inclusive citizenship is especially at variance with my ideal-typical characterization, even in its most inclusive years. To theorize the conditions that enable and disable more or less inclusive citizenship regimes, it is still useful to identify the ideal-typical architectonics underlying the two distinct poles of a continuum that stretches between market fundamentalism and a socially inclusive citizenship. In reality, of course, citizenship regimes do not transform from one to the other, like black to white, without stopping at many shades of gray along the way. Transformations in the balance of power occur along the continuum, creating gradations of practices, rather than changing from one distinct and discrete type into another. To understand and explain why and how the meaning and extent of citizenship and rights vary over time, we must reckon with the multiple forces at work in this process, identify where any particular citizenship regime is situated on that continuum, and determine in what direction it is moving. Here I sketch out two contrasting models: first, that of dystopian citizenship imperiled; and second, that of citizenship expanding toward greater social inclusion.

A dystopian model of citizenship imperiled: conditions, consequences and conversions

To marketize and contractualize citizenship, practical and ideational changes must convert the ethos of a socially inclusionary citizenship to one of contractual morality. These conversions amount to a complete inversion: from a triadic balance of power, in which the social state protects citizens in civil society against full exposure to the market, to one in which citizenship collapses into a dyadic instrument of unbalanced power pitting an alliance of state and market against individuals – now bereft of both state protection and membership in civil society. What occurs in the domains of the market, the state, and civil society that causes citizenship to morph into such a dystopian regime?

The market   An inclusive citizenship regime requires that the market be socially embedded in two different ways – it must be regulated by laws, rules, and ethics that constrain its practices, and it must be restricted from over-expanding its scope. Market fundamentalism violates both forms of constraint. First, through market-driven governance and the conquest of regulative agencies, business is able to "undo" those existing regulative practices instantiated by the social state, and rewrite them to support market principles – e.g. using incentives to reduce carbon dioxide voluntarily, rather than regulating it directly. At the same time, market fundamentalism's Congressional branch of lobbyists writes the very statutes signed off by politicians – e.g. the energy policy written by Vice-President Cheney and the oil industry. Finally, the business world ignores its own ethics and fair business practices, and invents more convenient ones of its own, such as stock option salary compensation and backdating account books.

Second, the market's principles and mechanisms expand beyond their place in the economic sphere to convert other nonmarket spheres of life to their organizing logic. The sites of market "invasion" are primarily the state and civil society and their ideational and discursive regimes. This drive to invade and convert noncontractual sites entails marketization, contractualization, and privatization. Since market fundamentalism is a regime on the move, it is always involved in an effort to gain the balance of power by subjecting both polity and civil society to contractual powers and principles. The content of these invasive market principles and discourses, for the sake of simplicity, can be grouped into three categories:[32]

1. The market is the most *efficient*, *just*, and *natural* form of social interaction, which is organized by multiple natural acts of buying and selling, and in which prices are set not by external factors (e.g. need) but according to what the market will bear and the constraints of generating profits.
2. Contractual quid pro quo exchange, in which there can be no expectation of commensuration or balancing of accounts, displaces other kinds of reciprocity (Lukes 2004: 305).
3. Incentives, as market-model tools, increasingly become the dominant instrument for organizing social programs (Frank 2007b). Politicians develop a *deus ex machina* approach to tax credits and

---

[32] That there are many other market principles, such as the place of property, of efficiency, wealth, etc. should go without saying.

incentive management as "the cornerstone of modern life" (Levitt and Dubner 2005), based on the assumption that "instead of taking charge of problems and putting real money and programs behind them, government should deploy incentives to gently prod the natural forces of the world in the direction we want them to go" (Schmitt 2007a: 9). This fixation is based not only on market fundamentalism's social naturalism. It also takes on board the conservative public-choice approach to politics, which stipulates that "people are *homo economicus*, always calculating their decisions based on rational and fully informed analyses of their economic utility" (Schmitt 2007a: 9). Inversely, the concomitant claim is that liberal social insurance programs for protection and inclusion policies will always instantiate perverse incentives and moral hazards (e.g. social welfare, FEMA), and so must be eliminated or contractualized. The incentives and sanctions of compulsory workfare, for example, are central to the landmark 1996 welfare reform bill (the Personal Responsibility and Work Opportunity Act [PRWOA]) (Handler 2004).

When these market-organizing logics are able to capture nonmarket sites, there are at least four results:

1. Because in the market the highest recognition, rewards, power, and influence go to those who accumulate great wealth, financial assets and property, this same market metric of power and influence displaces and replaces civil society's nonmarket criteria for recognition.
2. The newly dominant market ethos captures the rhetoric of efficiency, moral goodness, justice, freedom, and prosperity. Inclusion, moral worth, and recognition in civil society now become conditional on successful contractual behavior, such as employment or workfare for the poor.
3. To force the unemployed to work, incentives are reorganized and restructured to reimpose scarcity and hunger as natural conditions that can only be eliminated by work – work that often is not available or that pays too little for a living wage.
4. Market fundamentalists claim that power is always coercive, resides exclusively in the state, and is a force that must be resisted and minimized. Market fundamentalism justifies its invasion of the political sphere on the grounds that governmental power is dangerous for liberty, causes market inefficiencies, and supports a system of morally corrupting social giveaways. By contrast, the market is defined as a self-regulating natural system entirely devoid of power.

The state: market-driven big government   Under market fundamentalism the institutions of the state are conquered by powers constituted in the economic sphere that have crossed the boundary into the polity, where market power is illegitimately exercised. The extension of market principles into the polity transforms it into a market-driven state. The market ethic of contract displaces that of the social state, and translates the relationship between citizen and state into one of contractual quid pro quo conditionality. In that conversion the state's mediating position between citizens and market is dissolved. As a result:

- political power becomes a reflection of economic wealth and market power;
- the rule of law is penetrated by the rules of the market;
- the state's role in social citizenship is restructured from that of providing protection and social insurance to its citizens into that of demanding quid pro quo obligations in exchange;
- at the level of the polity the result is a two-track displacement of democratic citizenship, led by a two-track public narrative:
  1. *"Big-government" is dangerous, so we must "starve the beast."* The social state, locus of social insurance and other regulative agencies that protect people against full exposure to the market and the risks of modern capitalism, is conquered by contractual principles of quid pro quo exchange. This amounts not to a smaller state (as promised) but to "market-driven big government" which in actuality simply shifts its provision of protection, monopolies, and welfare to corporate and global capital, leaving full exposure to harsh market competition for everyone else (Schmitt 2007b).[33] It is, in effect, socialism for the rich, and capitalism for everyone else. Under the narrative of the necessity of liberating society from "failed social programs" and into the "ownership society," the state shifts tax burdens from wealth to wages. These government policy changes in turn contribute to an entrenchment of internal borders based on social exclusion.
  2. *The rise of the security state.* War is the essential stance of the military and security state. The rise of the security state supports unchecked and unaccountable executive power, and legitimates the suspension of civil and legal rights. It also divides a population between those included by virtue of patriotic acceptance of

---

[33] See Dean Baker, "The Conservative Nanny State," available at: conservativenannystate.org (accessed December 2006) and *American Prospect* 2005.

unchecked executive powers versus those "America-haters" who do not accept the tradeoff. These internal cultural borders do not map neatly onto the internal borders based on market-driven inclusion and exclusion. As I argue in chapter 3, cultural inclusion through the mantle of loyal Americanism often compensates the white middle classes for their increasingly precarious economic condition, thus mitigating the possibility of popular unrest.

The dark side of civil society: competing narratives   The effect of market fundamentalism on civil society is disabling in several ways. The conversion of civil society's citizenship ethic into that of contractualization is facilitated by the shift in the dominant knowledge culture from a social problems approach that valorizes the common good, to economics and a market model of human organization. The consequences for civil society are several.

First, power accrued in the market is converted illegitimately into power and hierarchical influence in civil society. Market success spills over to civil society where it is able to buy outright or to influence the media, universities, democratic institutions, political parties, and the judiciary. Market logic displaces civil society's ethic of inclusion, membership, solidarity, and egalitarianism. Civil society's distribution of rights, inclusion, moral worth, and recognition, are restructured and recalibrated to coordinate with market value. Absent a robust civil society, social movements to resist market penetration cannot be organized.

Second, with the casualties of market fundamentalism increasing – surging inequality, decreases in absolute wages of all but the rich, and a disappearing job market – civil society becomes more exclusionary on traditional ascriptive grounds (Frank 2007a). It no longer holds out the normative promise of universal and equal citizenship. Xenophobia and anti-immigrant talk balloons; affirmative action for women and African-Americans is blamed for white middle-class troubles. The exclusionary anti-universalistic dark side of civil society becomes increasingly prominent, and increasingly naturalized (Alexander 2006; Kuttner 2007).

Third, as the relationship between the citizen and the state turns into a contractual one, citizens are converted into quantities and qualities of human capital, while families and communities are increasingly viewed as sources of social capital. Their worth, value, and inclusion are accordingly determined by contractual successes or failures in relationship to utility. Those without marketable skills or those for whom jobs are no longer available become incapable of engaging in contractual relations, which in turn marks them as morally unworthy.

With increasing corporate layoffs, even education and skills cannot save middle-class professionals from becoming disposable factors of production (Bernstein 2007; Uchitelle 2006). Both kinds of "failure" lead to social exclusion.

Fourth, in the absence of access to labor market opportunities, and when the market-driven state no longer assumes its obligation to protect civil society from full exposure to the market, the result is a destabilized civil society that becomes isolated from the market, the body politic, and the public sphere.

Fifth, unlike the state, which is conquered but left structurally intact to benefit the market regime, civil society and its institutions cannot survive except as market and state auxiliaries. Instead of relying on the state, individuals are directed to exploit their own social capital – i.e. their network of advantageous relationships. ("Public schools are inadequate? Get home-schooled.") Poor communities fail on that count, as they do not harbor advantageous connections, networks, or relationships. Because civil society is the site of primary membership, poor communities are perceived as without worth. In communities of distress, civil society disintegrates, leaving few opportunities for meaningful democratic participation, popular resistance, associational oppositional networks, or even incipient social movements. Neither citizens nor their civil societies can survive or thrive in a setting that is viewed by the larger political culture as without moral worthiness. Social exclusion from the mainstream is the handmaiden of a civil society reduced to social capital.

Genealogizing a democratic socially inclusive citizenship: conditions and consequences of its making

Just as identifying the conditions of citizenship's erosion gives us the materials for constructing an abstract model of what a dystopian citizenship regime looks like, by inverting the balance of power among the three sites we can also deduce the conditions for sustaining and enhancing healthy pluralist democratic citizenship regimes. In direct contrast to a market fundamentalist one, a democratic citizenship regime requires a recalibrated balance of power in which the state, market, and civil society all coexist in a pluralist universe, each able to sustain its own discursive logic. The one twist is that the discourses and practices of civil society must be a little "more equal" than those of market and state. In order to restrain the inherently expansionary tendencies of class and political power, the citizenship ethic must have normative influence over both market contractualism and state bureaucratization and militarization.

The state: The power of the public sphere Under pluralist socially inclusive citizenship the state has to obstruct the market's potential for undue influence in governance and its illegitimate incursions into civil society. To do so, it must exercise power as a countervailing force to the market. To make this kind of power productive, not merely coercive, it must be subject to the democratic pressures of civil society and the public sphere.[34] Political power can be mobilized in the service of justice and citizenship, rather than ceding it to the unforgiving power of market forces. The state bureaucracy would still function, just as would the other institutional dimensions of government, but they would not function as autonomous instruments of rationalizing control, nor as shelters for a market-driven politics. Democratic pressures on the state must be guided by what Alexander (2006) calls the "civil power" of solidarity, equality, and rights, and what I called earlier the citizenship ethic. Civil society's resuscitation would be especially critical for the institutions and agencies of social citizenship, where social insurance and other nonmarket means to protect citizens are situated. Where the market has taken over the state's organizations and agencies, it would be displaced by institutions of social insurance, protection, and provisioning. In the normative ethos of social inclusion, it is the state's responsibility to protect individuals and families without the resources needed to protect themselves.

In contrast to the doddering and decrepit market-driven social state (the victim of decades of starvation, privatization, market invasion, degradation, and vilification) that I depict in chapter 2's discussion of Hurricane Katrina, a strong democratic citizenship requires a regulative state institutionally robust enough to impose rules and restraints on the expansive governing aspirations of global markets, and strong enough to provide protective security to civil society. At the same time, it must be sufficiently rule-bound to be subordinate to constitutional rule, to civil society's regulative interventions, and to muscular democratic participation from civil society. Only by being bound to such rules of law and democratic empowerment will the state be forced to support (rather than attempt to appropriate) an autonomous public

---

[34] Following Polanyi (2001), Parsons (1969), and Foucault (1977b, 1990). See also Kuttner (2007) and Starr (2007).

sphere – without which the delicate balance of power favoring social inclusion would collapse.

Democratizing the market   Democratic citizenship requires the active presence of markets that are rule-bound internally, restricted in scope, and mediated by the state and civil society. The capacity to contain marketizing impulses depends on a pluralist regulated state held legally and democratically accountable by the public sphere and a robust non-subjugated civil society. Under market fundamentalism, pluralism and institutional balances of power are eroded by the contractualization of citizenship – citizenship reverses from status to contract, its rights become conditional on quid pro quo obligatory exchange (usually of labor), and its modalities of policy implementation convert to market-driven technologies (and sanctions) of incentive management. Under an ideal-typical democratic socially inclusive citizenship regime, civil society practices and political institutions must maintain and deflect market intrusions while supporting its basic allocative functions.

Building a citizenship-guided market entails more than simply apply-ing the concept of democracy to economics, democratizing the work-place, or including the right to a decent living among citizenship's bundle of rights – although it certainly is all of these. Rather, it is the commit-ment to what BIEN (Basic Income Earth [formerly European] Network), a growing international movement, calls a *basic income right*, or a *citizen income*, and which I dub as the right to a *citizenship livelihood*.[35] Both words are critical: *livelihood* – because the rights of social provision-ing entail not only the rights due to those who participate in income-generating activity, but also the rights due to children, the elderly, the disabled, the chronically unemployed; rights, in other words, that cannot be stigmatized by means-testing, or the epithets of "dependency," "charity-case" and other words of social exclusion (Fraser and Gordon 1997, 1998). One of the goals of a socially inclusionary citizenship, moreover, would be to transform the livelihood paradigm in such a way as to normalize and valorize monetary reward for much of what is currently unpaid and devalued labor (e.g. raising children, doing household work, unpaid childcare). In the meantime, the currently non-income-generating status of unpaid but essential household labor cannot be used to justify continuing the hierarchy of moral worth between "gainful" employment and unpaid labor.

---

[35] See for example, *Citizen's Income Newsletter 2001–2007*, and *BIEN Newsletter*.

The first word of the right to a *citizenship* livelihood is equally critical. The precepts of citizenship emphasize what is true of all social concerns related to livelihood – namely, that protections against the risks of life in market society represent moral obligations we have to each other. These are, as I argued above, less about income levels or economic measures per se than they are about social inclusion and recognition of all people as moral equals. This is where citizenship's normative ideal of solidarity meets its challenge in the tough realities of our political culture, which has, since the eighteenth-century specter of pauperism and Malthusian warnings of the link between poor relief and socially perilous population growth, divided the "deserving" from the "undeserving" beneficiaries of social relief – a distinction based on an illegitimate conversion of market value (work effort) into civil society's moral metrics (Malthus [1798] 1992). Moreover, the characterization of "undeserving" is consistently used to describe and denigrate those groups of people who have long suffered exclusion based on the nonmarket discourses of race, gender, and ethnic primordialism, exclusions justified by the same distortions to the vocabulary of morality as the market-driven ones. In her cultural approach to citizenship, Judith Shklar (1991) lays bare how the deep exclusionary roots of chattel slavery, which denied to African-Americans the "right to earn," continues to fuel today's moral condemnation of those unable to earn. She attributes to the specter of slavery the moral judgments people attach to employment status – judgments most commonly invoked by those anxious to distance themselves from slaves who were denied just that right. During the Great Depression, despite widespread structural unemployment, Americans without work "still regarded both their lack of income and their need to rely on some form of assistance as a shameful loss of independence and beneath the dignity of a citizen" (Shklar 1991: 22). Even today, despite efforts oriented to treating unemployment as a social problem, Louis Uchitelle has discovered through in-depth interviews that when one is laid off one loses one's moral stature in America (Uchitelle 2006). Worse off are the long-term unemployed who are "treated as less than full members of society. In effect, the people who belong to the under-class are not quite citizens" (Shklar 1991: 22). As Handler (2004), who argues along the same lines, writes: "although ostensibly about work effort, these moral judgments [about unemployment] involve race, ethnicity, gender, family responsibilities, sexuality, and various forms of deviant behavior. Thus, citizenship is also used in an ideological symbolic sense – to distinguish people from either within the borders or from those who are outside ... it is [therefore] often used as a term of exclusion, of moral superiority, a construction of the 'Other'" (2004: 10; see also Fraser and Gordon 1997, 1998; Gordon 1990).

Echoing Shklar's causal linkage between fair employment and the "standing" of inclusive citizenship, Alice Kessler-Harris (2001) has recently argued that for women "access to economic equality" through decent and dignified work is "a necessary condition of citizenship." She stipulates that it begins "with self-support, generally through the ability to work at the occupation of one's choice, [but] it does not end there. Rather, it requires customary and legal *acknowledgment of personhood*, with all that implies of expectations, training, access to and distribution of resources, and opportunity in the marketplace" (Kessler-Harris 2001: 283, 12–13, my italics). Similarly, Carole Pateman writes that "paid employment has become the key to citizenship, and the recognition of an individual as a citizen of equal worth to other citizens is lacking when a worker is unemployed" (Pateman 1989: 10).[36] Nothing guarantees social exclusion more than the inability to participate in the right to livelihood or being forced to live, as Richard Sennett (2006) so aptly puts it, under the "specter of uselessness."[37]

Under socially inclusive citizenship, then, the labor market plays a critical part in supporting the right to a *citizenship livelihood*. The social inclusion and moral worth on which citizenship depends requires access to and participation in the institutions of earning and providing by which livelihood is procured. Yet several caveats are necessary lest this discussion of the link between full citizenship recognition and the right to earn too easily be misread as condoning the *obligation* to work as a condition of full citizenship, especially through such punitive measures as workfare; or being forced to accept any available job regardless of conditions or circumstances. Let me address briefly these caveats.

The long shadow of racism in America supports a political culture that continues to make employment a condition subject to moral judgment by others. "When they cease to earn whatever the character of their work, Americans lose their standing in their communities" (Shklar 1991: 98). But it would not make sense to imply, conversely, that employment leads to social approbation and political inclusion regardless of the kind of work. For there is work, and then there is work that veers too closely to that specter of slavery. From the founding of the country, Americans both endorsed the institution of slavery as well as held contempt for those

---

[36] Cited in Bosniak (2006: 105–6).

[37] This is not to minimize the importance of the right to livelihood more generally, especially through such strategies as developed by BIEN.

unable to achieve the independence that only paid labor could provide. Since republican ideology valorized only the independent producing citizen, the unpaid work of slavery further justified excluding all African-Americans from recognition as citizens. Even freedmen had no standing within the polity, both before and after emancipation. This was a political culture in which the conditions of work mapped onto the exclusions of race and gender to define personhood, which in turn delimited political rights. Among white women and the newly industrialized working classes, this conjuncture of slavery, lack of independence, and political exclusion inexorably linked the fact of slave labor to their status as both earners and political beings. Women more often than not rejected the association of their unpaid household work with slavery, as they felt degraded and shamed by being likened to slaves. By contrast, in deploying the rhetoric of "wage slavery," the industrial working classes used the discourse of shame attached to unpaid work to organize against the pittance of a wage they were earning at the hands of factory owners. Throughout the history of the labor movement, in fact, the cry of "wage slavery" became a constant rhetorical refrain in the association the term conjured between exploitative wage levels and exclusion from full citizenship. Today the degradation imposed on the working poor by an indecently low minimum wage makes it clear that it is not earning per se that supports the rights of citizenship, but only being able to earn a living wage under conditions of dignity.[38]

This makes the heavily sanctioned workfare requirements of the PRWOA seem all the more mean-spirited in its straightforward prioritization of "personal responsibility" through work at even the most degrading of low-wage jobs, over any commitment to reducing poverty or inequality. Dubbed welfare reform, the PRWOA had only one overriding goal: to reduce and eventually eliminate altogether the welfare rolls. Absent from the Act's presuppositions was acknowledgment that it is poverty that leads people to request public assistance. Rather, the bipartisan market fundamentalist stipulation that propelled the PRWOA to victory under the Democratic Clinton administration was that it is the lack of personal responsibility and the refusal to work that underlies the turn to welfare. The requirement to take any job, regardless of its conditions, along with disallowing the job training or education that might prepare for better jobs – in short, the reality of being coerced to participate in workfare – invokes the specter of slavery and indentured servitude among welfare recipients. For the welfare reformers, however, the beneficiaries' alleged "culture of dependence" more than

---

[38] See Tony Atkinson (2002) on participation in the labor market as right of citizenship.

justifies revoking their rights to civic equality and the independence of citizenship. After all, as Shklar reminds us, workfare has nothing to do with economics or monetary self-sufficiency. It is about moral judgment – a paean to the long-standing principle that able-bodied adults who do not earn are undeserving of full citizenship. Workfare is a punitive measure intended to instill "acceptable standards of civic conduct" (1991: 97–8). That more than a decade after its passage, the PRWOA has increased rather than decreased the level of poverty among ex-recipients is rarely acknowledged; what matters is that the welfare rolls have been drastically reduced (Handler 2006). Clearly, workfare cannot be part of any program for a socially inclusive citizenship regime.

Civil society   Democratic citizenship regimes require robust civil societies, which are deeply entangled with both the state and the market, while still doing the boundary work necessary to protect their own integrity. It is in civil society that citizens constitute themselves as such, and it is in civil society that Polanyi's "counter [market]-movements" of social protection are nurtured, just as are social and labor movements more generally (trade unions, environmentalism, civil rights movements, feminism, gay rights, etc.). And it is in civil society that social movements develop the capacities to pressure the state to build adequate social insurance programs and non-contractual policies to protect against market-generated risks to health, retirement, education, and social life. At the same time, a strong civil society also depends on access to the labor market, especially to a full range of employment opportunities for all levels of skill and education.

Civil society is always threatened by radical imbalances of market and/ or state power, to the point where society as a whole is at risk (Polanyi 2001). Since market fundamentalism does not recognize this threat, seven decades ago the New Deal took on the role of housebreaking laissez-faire capitalism – and saved capitalism from itself. To put a canonical twist on it, one could say that social democratic state policies added an unexpected coda to the famous nineteenth-century teleology of modernization – a reinvasion of an (inegalitarian) modern contract by the egalitarianism of status.[39] It is in civil society that social movements and other democratic forces cultivate the public narratives that pressure the "housebreaking" toward solidarism and inclusion. The Durkheimian (1984) noncontractualism of contract is an essential element of this work, not only for the sake of social solidarity but also for the survival of the market itself, which cannot run recklessly along its own instrumental

---

[39] On civil society invading the market sphere, see Estlund (2003).

tracks without risking the survival of the social *tout court*. As Alexander (2006: 173) elaborates, the courts recognized this as early as 1889 when a New York court ruled that even contract law must submit to egalitarian moral maxims when civil solidarity is at stake. Justice Felix Frankfurter in the case of *United States* v. *Bethlehem Steel* most eloquently stated the ethos of civil society in relationship to the market and the state:

> Is there any principle which is more familiar or more firmly embedded in the history of Anglo-American law than the basic doctrine that the courts will not permit themselves to be used as instruments of inequity and injustice? More specifically the courts generally refuse to lend themselves to the enforcement of a "bargain" in which one party has unjustly taken advantage of the economic necessities of [the] other. (Frankfurter, cited in Alexander 2006: 175)

By preventing those who exercise market power from using the law as an "instrument of inequity and injustice," Frankfurter is flexing the muscle necessary to fortify the boundary that protects civil society against political or market invasion. Civil society depends on this kind of boundary patrol to sustain its ballast in the always-unsettled contest of power among state, market, and civil society.

Much of civil society's boundary work thus entails democratizing the law to prevent those who wield outsized instruments of market power (corporate assets, property, and wealth) from converting these into mechanisms of civil domination. Conversely, law can be mobilized to prevent market "failures" such as poverty, propertylessness, and lack of marketable skills from spilling over into civil society to become added instruments of powerlessness and social exclusion, thereby further denying access to the only institutions that support inclusion, social dignity, and moral worth – e.g. education, health care, and decent employment. As if this were not enough, civil society must also be constantly alert to the propensity of the market to use civil society as a dumpsite for its own externalities and privatizing fiascos (as I discuss in chapter 6). And, finally, civil society must patrol against the state's security-driven imperial aims, which threaten the constitutional protections on which civil society depends. These are civil society's normative ideals in a democratic and pluralist citizenship regime. They represent a picture of civil power that is an increasing distance from our current condition.

Three muses and three principles

The arguments and theoretical perspectives in this book clearly wear more than one disciplinary hat, just as the substantive reach of my

material crosses disciplinary boundaries. Both attest to the pluralist cast
of mind this project demands. Still, there is a unifying meaning to my
multiplicity. I have been inspired and motivated by years of engagement
with three towering intellects of the twentieth century, each of whose
life's work was dedicated to human emancipation and to the responsibility of disseminating a public sociology: Karl Polanyi, the great founder
of modern economic sociology and anthropology; Hannah Arendt, post-
Holocaust republican political theorist, historian, and moral philosopher
of the polity; and T. H. Marshall, whose small book established the very
possibility of a sociology of citizenship and rights.

Stimulated by these muses I have been working my way through a
research program in which I attempt to theorize the conditions that
constrain and/or enable greater degrees of social justice and a democratic
culture of human rights. As with Polanyi, Arendt, and Marshall, this
effort entails continuously interrogating the deep conundrums and liabil-
ities, the cultural and political meanings and consequences, of classical
political and economic liberalism – in particular, its tendencies to enable
market fundamentalism, to conflate markets and civil society, and to
systematically degrade the political. At the same time, like my muses,
I have recognized, admired, and explored the indeterminate potential-
ities and promises inherent in liberalism's rule and institutions of law,
as well as its normative commitment to human rights (Starr 2007;
E. P. Thompson 1975b).

Thus inspired by an admixture of Polanyite, Arendtian, and
Marshallian assumptions, I have brought to bear on all my work some
variant of three principles: (1) the authority and powers of knowledge,
culture, and ideational regimes; (2) a critique of social naturalism; (3) a
commitment to institutionalism in the constitution and preservation of
human rights.[40] From these principles I have assembled and woven
through my work the following hypothesis: that people's life-chances,
their access to equality, to social inclusion, to the dignity of recognition,
indeed their very right to have rights, are all dependent on using the
powers of institutionalism to demystify social naturalism – the idea that
certain social entities are in fact part of nature and subject to its laws such
as the "self-regulating" market, free voluntary contractual exchange,
natural rights, and the self-motivating agency of human nature. My
belief is that these naturalized objects must be denaturalized by those

---

[40] There are actually four foundational principles. But since I deal so extensively in the
chapters with the *necessity of power and the public sphere*, I have decided not to include
the fourth in this introductory discussion.

social institutions which are in fact the *least* natural and require the greatest degree of human and social intervention: specifically, the institutions and practices of human rights and citizenship, the rule and rules of law, the solidarism of civil societies and of constitutional power under democratic control. I will say a bit about the origins of this hypothesis in thinking through the three foundational precepts I have associated with Arendt, Polanyi, and Marshall.

The authority and powers of knowledge and ideational regimes

To avoid the idealism that the social sciences were born to refute, sociologists have a long history of dismissing or explaining ideas as reflections of deeper economic and/or political forces. Over the last several decades I have been part of an ever-enlarging group of cultural sociologists that has been mounting a determined – and I believe a remarkably successful – effort to undo this sociological mistake. Like all such cohorts, that of cultural sociology has its founding mothers and fathers – Durkheim, Weber, Foucault and Bourdieu being the most prominent of what can already be called a canon. Virtually unrecognized by this new cultural sociology, however, is the work of Polanyi, Arendt, and Marshall, for whom the causal powers of liberalism's epistemologies and ideational practices were at the very core of their theorizing.

Like all ideas, those at work in the genealogies of citizenship are not isolated signifiers of material objects; rather, they are part of much larger conceptual networks. That which is considered *true* knowledge is contained within the parameters of what in chapter 7 I call a knowledge culture. Since knowledge is that which claims scientific grounds for its truths, attaching culture to knowledge transforms the norms of standard epistemology as well as the means by which knowledge qua truth is represented, expressed, and conveyed.[41] Knowledge can be represented in numerous cultural forms, including public, symbolic, meaning-driven conceptual stories, binary codes, cultural myths, and unconscious discursive associations. The cultural expressions that

---

[41] In addition to Polanyi and Arendt, my use of the knowledge culture concept is loosely associated with the Bourdieuian/Foucauldian "new cultural history" as reflected in the work of Hunt (1989a); Durkheimian/Saussurian cultural sociology, e.g. Alexander (1988); Alexander and Smith (1993); Hacking (1990b). See also Bourdieu (1984), Bourdieu and Wacquant (1992), Saussure ([1916] 1959), Durkheim ([1912] 1995), and Durkheim and Mauss ([1903] 1963).

dominate the knowledge cultures in my research are those of public narratives, binary codes, and the metanarratives and master narratives whose social naturalism gives them enormous epistemic privilege.

Social naturalism

There is one idea that I give pride of place for its pernicious effects on rights and citizenship. This is social naturalism – a way of organizing societal knowledge and perceptions around the schematic worldview that human society is subject to the same laws of nature as the natural world. Social naturalism is not just an epistemological stance; it is also an ontology – a theory of being – in which the characteristics of the natural order are mapped onto and conflated with those of the social order. As an ontology it should not be confused with the more familiar methodology of naturalism – the methodological postulate that because nature and society exhibit the same kinds of regularities (for any number of reasons), there should be a unified method applicable to both. Social naturalism, by contrast, conceptually subordinates society to nature: society is not "like" the natural world; the social and natural worlds are one and the same, and thus subject to the same laws and exigencies. For Polanyi this translated into the "stark utopia" that the market is driven by self-regulating natural laws and that this naturalistic "self-regulating" market mechanism should govern market society as a whole in the interest of social harmony and prosperity. For Arendt, it is the false security offered by the Rights of Man (natural rights) that is partially responsible for the abandonment of the Jews of Europe to their genocidal fates. For both Polanyi and Arendt, the cultural opposition between so-called natural and nonnatural institutions is at once the most important and the most dangerous aspect of classical liberalism's ideational infrastructure and knowledge culture.

Polanyi identifies the invention of social naturalism as the necessary factor in the birth of classical political economy – in many ways the forbearer of today's market fundamentalism. And like the science of political economy overall, social naturalism's significance for citizenship and rights was and continues to be in its far-reaching political implications. Since nature is a self-regulating system with which we would not think of interfering, social naturalists ask why then do we have so many laws and policies that interfere with the self-regulating entity of society? And why do we endeavor to help the poor? Scientific ignorance and rationalist hubris is the answer offered by Malthus and Ricardo, the pioneers of classical political economy. And they labored tirelessly in their efforts to convince politicians and intellectuals that institutional rules and political regulations inevitably sabotage the market.

Social naturalism has implications not just for how we think and know about society as a whole. It is also the basis of our perceptions of individual agency and (more accurately, in the language of social naturalism) of individual behavior. With the line between animal and humanity erased, social naturalism reduces people to their biologically driven instincts and needs for food and reproduction. It in turn takes on board the naturalist postulate that human society, like nature, is fundamentally constrained by the scarcity postulate – the constitutive and permanent condition of material scarcity. The combination of scarcity and biologization leads to the conclusion that the secret to societal order and prosperity is to maintain at all costs this condition of scarcity, for only the biological drive to eat can discipline the social masses into voluntarily taking up the bitter task of constant labor. Without scarcity the hunger-driven discipline to earn one's keep will also dissolve. The policy implications are direct: remove the threat of hunger from the poor by providing them with the moral perversity of poor relief (welfare), and so too the incentive to work dissolves. The moral of the story is that meddling with nature through state intervention and welfare relief will have perverse unintended consequences of worsening the very problem it was intended to solve.[42] No one has captured this ontology more brilliantly than Polanyi: "Hobbes had argued the need for a despot because men were like beasts; Townsend insisted that they were actually beasts and that, precisely for that reason . . . [n]o government was needed to maintain this balance; it was restored by the pangs of hunger on the one hand, the scarcity of food on the other" (Polanyi 2001: 119; emphasis in original).[43] In a stroke, social naturalism dissolves the

---

[42] When nature will govern and punish for us, it is a very miserable ambition to wish to snatch the rod from her hands, and draw upon ourselves the odium of executioner. To the punishment therefore of nature he should be left, the punishment of severe want. He has erred in the face of a most clear and precise warning, and can have no just reason to complain of any person but himself when he feels the consequences of his error. All parish assistance should be denied him; and he should be left to the uncertain support of private charity. He should be taught to know, that the laws of nature, which are the laws of God, had doomed him and his family to suffer for disobeying their repeated admonitions; that he had no claim of right on society for the smallest portion of food, beyond that which his labour would fairly purchase; and that if he and his family were saved from feeling the natural consequences of his imprudence, he would owe it to the pity of some kind benefactor, to whom, therefore, he ought to be bound by the strongest ties of gratitude. (Malthus 1992: 262–3)

[43] Joseph Townsend is usually attributed (including, eventually, by Malthus himself) as the inspiration behind Malthus's embrace of social naturalism and his battle to abolish all forms of welfare or poor relief.

Enlightenment tradition that distinguished humans from animals by their capacity for rational thought.

Social naturalism has further implications for the theories driving policy. As I demonstrate in chapter 7, as a conceptual schema it divides the world into a zero-sum logic and maps market liberalism's normative binary between natural and unnatural onto the categories of the social world. On the one side, grafted under the rubric of things "natural" is found the marketized version of civil society, which mirrors the freedom of the "state of nature" reorganized into the private sphere of market exchange. As part of nature, the market is in turn privileged with the self-regulation, certainty, autonomy, and the predictability of the laws of nature – a "spontaneous order" (Hayek 2007) constituted by the magic of Adam Smith's "invisible hand." On the other side, by contrast, are society's political and legal institutions, now grafted to the category of unnatural, arbitrary, and continuing threats to the "system of natural liberty" (Smith 1976). By this logic, state intervention in civil society violates the laws of nature and poses a clear and present political danger to the freedoms endowed to us by the power-free spontaneous order of the market. In the age of the scientific revolution, a cleverer way of achieving the shamelessly political goal of deregulating markets, abolishing poor relief, and creating a culture of antistatism could hardly be imagined.

This comprises a cultural logic and a goal that are still with us today. Postulating the market as a self-regulating natural system, today's market fundamentalism has inherited and nurtured social naturalism's claims to law-like necessity and naturalized policy mandates. It is easy to understand how important a cultural construct social naturalism is for market fundamentalism's efforts to delegitimate the political interventions of socially inclusive citizenship. The natural law that government interference always threatens liberty reinforces the default position that market solutions are in conformity with the laws of nature, and are therefore always the preferable ones.

It is the epistemic privilege that social naturalism endows to market fundamentalist social policies – its remarkable immunity to empirical disconfirmation, its claim to scientific veracity based on the hidden laws of nature, and its assumption of autonomy from social and political interference – that earns it special condemnation. Social naturalism has for two centuries been giving cover to a story about how marketization is a natural, necessary, and inevitable process beyond our control. If problems occur along the way, the argument goes, the fault cannot lie with market fundamentalism; after all, it is but a reflection of nature's design. Instead the problems are attributed to some interference with this design that has mistakenly shielded some aspect of the social order from the market's logic, thus impairing and violating the self-regulating market laws.[44]

Social naturalism was originally made up out of thin air, but that in no way mitigates either its capacity to influence social and political policies or its potentially catastrophic consequences for humanity. Among its most worrisome qualities, social naturalism makes institutions the enemy of rights and freedom, and bases human autonomy on the greatest degree of abstraction from politics and society. One of the central aims of this book is to expose just how dangerous for citizenship and rights has been social naturalism's antipolitical route to freedom, and just how much of a threat it continues to represent.[45]

Institutionalism

The cure for social naturalism is institutionalism, as it puts humanity, social action, and social artifice, rather than nature, biology, and natural laws, at the center of its epistemology and ontology. Institutionalism is thus the infrastructural stuff of citizenship. Institutions are organizational and symbolic practices that operate within networks of rules, structural ties, public narratives, and binding relationships that are embedded in time and space. To call something an institution is simply to say it is rule-driven. Institutionalism is the theory that most things are in part (not entirely) constituted and regulated by the rules that organize them, and thus to understand something it is necessary – though rarely sufficient – to identify and interpret the character and the effects of those rules. I especially like Friedland and Alford's (1991: 243) definition of an institution as "simultaneously material and ideal, systems of signs and symbols, rational and transrational ... supraorganizational patterns of human activity by which individuals and organizations produce and reproduce their material subsistence and organize time and space ... they are also symbolic systems, ways of ordering reality, and thereby rendering experience of time and space meaningful."

Rules cannot be found in nature; they can only be made by what Arendt (1979) calls human "artifice" – the activities and interventions

---

[44] This paragraph is drawn from Somers and Block (2005).
[45] Since it is the subject of chapter 3, this discussion of social naturalism neglects Arendt's (1979) critique of how the naturalisms of both the Rights of Man/natural rights and ethnic nationalism were major contributors to the conditions that made possible the Holocaust.

of real human beings. The institutions that comprise political, civil, and – yes, even economic – society are social (not natural) artifacts. To say that modern institutions are rule-driven, however, does not mean they are rational or logical, contra much of the writing of Max Weber. It simply means that they have social regularities that give them a likely continuity through time and space. But institutions can and do change, and those changes can only be caused by human activities. And anything that is human is as driven by the nonrational as it is by logical means–end thinking.

Institutionalism challenges the idea that markets and economies exist outside of institutional and cultural relationships, and so rejects social naturalism's conception of both society and individual action. Whereas social naturalism first imputes to economies and markets the self-regulating characteristics of nature, and then uses the market as the model for all of society, institutionalism, by contrast, rejects reducing society to the market, as well as reducing the market to the self-regulating ontology of nature. From the institutional perspective, for markets to function at all they must be embedded in regulations and institutions that define the rules of market interaction, even if the rules are "negative," e.g. legally protected free markets. But I take institutionalism even further. Rather than conceptualizing markets as distinct entities surrounded by or embedded in institutions, I believe that markets are socially, culturally, politically, and ideationally constructed artificial institutions. As an analytic construct, the idea of the market is indispensable; but empirically, it is a complex of rule-driven institutions.[46]

Historical institutionalism simply means that all institutions have histories. So too do their rules. It is thus necessary not only to identify but also to historicize institutions and their rules. For how something came to be tells us a great deal, though by all means not everything, about what it is now. The laws of nature, by contrast, cannot be historical; by definition they are outside of social time and space. This is not to say that theories of natural entities never change; the idea of gravity has a history, of course, but as a natural phenomenon gravity does not and cannot be affected by time and place. By contrast, historical institutionalism inhabits a knowledge culture that insists there is nothing human that is not historical, despite the many ideas about humans that make them appear not to be – to wit, social naturalism's claims about social biologization. Historical institutionalism and path dependence have an elective affinity

---

[46] This is what Fred Block means when he speaks of the "always embedded economy" (Block 2003).

with the Polanyite version of institutionalism I have been describing, as they all share a respect for the power of institutions to endure over time, such that the course of their development subsequently shapes the course of their future.

Outside of economic sociology, this conception of institutionalism is rarely included in general overviews of institutionalism, which tend to be limited to rational-choice institutionalism or sociology's "new institutionalism."[47] One reason might be that it has been more or less conflated with economic sociology more generally. But economic sociology is both much more, and much less, than institutionalism. It is more, because economic sociology covers a wide range of approaches to economic processes, including rational-choice theory and other microanalyses of social action, both of which are founded on neoclassical economics – the very theory that Polanyi developed his institutionalism to negate. But it is also less, because economic sociology has too commonly limited its focus exclusively to structural mechanisms of embeddedness, thus neglecting what Polanyi himself understood so clearly – that ideas, cultural beliefs, and practices, even rhetorical structures (such as naturalism) are just as powerful in shaping, constructing, and deconstructing markets.

Overview of the book

To catalyze my inquiries into the genealogies of citizenship, chapter 2 begins with an exploration of what we have come to call the disaster of Hurricane Katrina – the terrible Gulf Coast storm of August 2005, considered one of the greatest natural disasters in American history. This might strike some as an odd introduction to a work of historical sociology. But the tragedy of Katrina was neither an isolated instance of government mismanagement nor a natural disaster, as it has often been portrayed. Rather it was just one especially dramatic episode in a much longer narrative about what happens when market fundamentalism grafts its high-minded market discourse of universalism onto the deeply entrenched inequalities wrought by centuries of both legal and cultural racial exclusion. Long before the storm, market fundamentalism had been steadily delegitimating the work of redressing the wrongs of racial exclusion and replacing it with abstract principles of "color-blind" individual rights. The storm did not cause the terrible exclusions; it served

---

[47] See Thelen (1999) for one overview.

rather as the catalyst to expose and publicize what had so long been hidden – years of increasing economic inequality and social exclusion. That so many New Orleanians became the *left-behind* was thus the outcome of a previous story, not an anomalous fluke caused by the onset of a hurricane. Hurricane Katrina was viewed as a crisis because it exposed the terrible costs of market fundamentalism – costs that include the imperilment not just of citizenship rights but of human rights more generally, as large classes of humanity were demonstrably treated as disposable. In the course of the crisis the horrors of what we witnessed in the Convention Center, in the Superdome, and on the rooftops of New Orleans, were those of a people being refused the most basic right of all – that of recognition as moral equals.

Chapter 3 theorizes the social naturalistic roots of a society that is increasingly being rent asunder by internal borders that isolate our internally stateless citizens from the rest of us. These are the socially excluded who are citizens in name only, and thus have been robbed of their right to have rights – the right to be fully included in a social and political community, without which they cannot exercise any of the formal civil and political rights that they, in principle, still possess. Hannah Arendt's classic text on "The Decline of the Nation-State and the End of the Rights of Man" (1979) is the inspiration for this chapter's analysis, in which she demonstrates how interwar statelessness and the joint tyrannies of political naturalism and ethnic nationalism set the conditions for European genocide during World War II. While market fundamentalism does not engage in intentional genocidal practices, it is nonetheless the case that internal statelessness and the compensatory attachment to nation just as surely subvert the right to have rights – rights without which, as the story of Katrina so dramatically illustrates, the socially excluded have no more in the way of guarantees of the right to live than did Arendt's interwar stateless peoples.

Genealogies of citizenship must address the question of why we think about citizenship and rights in certain ways at certain times. In the context of its explosive reappearance in the late 80s and 90s, chapter 4 takes on citizenship as a conceptual object with T. H. Marshall as its most influential theorist. The chapter begins with the problematic of citizenship's long and puzzling absence from social research. I argue that much of the explanation for the strange career of the citizenship concept can be explained by a mix of the peculiarities of social science research in the post-World War II era with its focus on modernization theory, with what I call the "troubles of citizenship." These troubles are based inter alia on the contradictory and competing trajectories of rights-based versus citizenship-based genealogies. While the two can arguably be seen as constitutively incompatible, what they share may be even more important: both the liberal and republican traditions are organized by the zero-sum parameters of the great dichotomy between public and private, state and economy. This bifurcation negates the place of civil society as an intermediate third sphere. This absence of the "soul of the social" in citizenship's dominant traditions should be a source of great concern in the current climate of overbearing state power on the one side and the hegemony of market fundamentalism on the other.

Continuing in the vein of investigating the influence of ideas and knowledge cultures, chapter 5 examines the impact of the English translation of Habermas's *The Structural Transformation of the Public Sphere* (1989). The chapter begins by observing how the widespread embrace of Habermas's concept of the public sphere converged with the revival in the social sciences more generally of the *political culture* concept originally associated with Parsonian modernization theory of the 1950s and 1960s. Surprisingly, Habermas's Marxist-informed account of the Western bourgeois public sphere has much in common with the Parsonian political culture concept. In both cases they are used in ways that, paradoxically, are neither public, political, nor cultural. Instead, both political culture and the public sphere are appropriated by the private side of the public/private divide in political theory. To explain this peculiarity I suggest that the concepts themselves are both embedded in a historically constituted political culture, here dubbed a conceptual network, which I define as a structured web of cultural discourses that I call "Anglo-American citizenship theory."

In chapter 6 I examine the social science concept of social capital, so popular today among academics, policy makers, and the World Bank. I do so by looking at how social capital is used (both wittingly and unwittingly) to support market fundamentalism's assault on citizenship rights. Theories of social capital are especially attractive to sociologists, who see its use by economists as an acknowledgment that social relations contribute no less than economic factors to prosperity and market performance. I argue, however, that this sociological belief in the appreciation of the social on the part of economists is illusory. More likely, the social capital concept reflects economists' successful appropriation of the social to their own imperial aims (see especially Becker 1990).

There are also unfortunate political consequences of the widespread infatuation with social capital. Its advocates suggest that the productive utility streams attributed to networks of social relations greatly empower civil society against the state. But utility production is not the same as rights; and substituting the market-friendly work of social capital for the democratic rights-driven work of civil society devalues the public sphere. In fact, it is the rule of law, citizenship rights, compulsory associations, political institutions, and large-scale civic movements like Poland's Solidarity, not social capital policies, that are the real historical guarantors of individual freedoms and social prosperity.

Chapter 7 begins with the observation that despite its popular democratic references, the concept of civil society today seems to have been appropriated by the market. To explain this peculiarity I hypothesize that concepts are embedded in historically constituted epistemic cultures and networks. The chapter takes on the truly puzzling question of how the grand narrative of Anglo-American citizenship theory with its market fundamentalist subplot has, despite significant periods of retreat, survived and thrived well over a period of two centuries. To make sense of all this, I engage in the project of *unthinking* liberalism's knowledge culture by means of a *historical sociology of concept formation*. This entails developing a *historical epistemology* – the task of subjecting theories of truth to historical analysis. As a public discourse Anglo-American citizenship theory shares many of the naturalistic attributes of a paradigm – when confronted with inconvenient data, contradictory evidence suddenly loses evidential status. In practice, the approach entails coming to terms with how it is that so much of market fundamentalism has hardened into paradigms and knowledge postulates. I ask how it has been able to carve the social universe into public and private, market and state, such that the world appears to *actually be* divided into the spheres of private (market) and public (state). How and why does the market seem to really *be* part of the privileged domain of nature, while the sites of the social and the public sphere take on the character of being unnatural and thus devalued? Recognizing that these theories are historical artifacts rather than truths of nature is the key to their unthinking.

PART I

Citizenship imperiled: how marketization creates social exclusion, statelessness, and rightlessness

2

Genealogies of Katrina: the unnatural disasters of market fundamentalism, racial exclusion, and statelessness

> Sometimes noisily and sometimes sneakily, borders have changed place. Whereas traditionally, and in conformity with both their juridical definition and "cartographical" representation as incorporated in national memory, they should be at the edge of the territory, marking the point where it ends, it seems that borders and the institutional practices corresponding to them have transported into the middle of political space.
>
> (Etienne Balibar)

It is a pretty good bet that Hurricane Katrina is not the first thing one would associate with the subject of citizenship; nor would it seem to be a likely subject to which to turn in search of answers to some of the motivating questions I posed in my introduction. Indeed it may seem odd to begin a book on citizenship by bringing up a hurricane at all. But certainly more than all the chest-thumping speechifying about patriotism, flag burning, or political posturing over the war on terror, the story of the Katrina crisis is a social parable of citizenship in America today as well as for my theoretical account of the conditions that have brought us to today's imperiled state of citizenship and rights more generally.

In the "hulls of slave ships"

Consider first the government reaction to the hurricane. Thanks to global media exposure, the world was stunned by the callous indifference and utter ineptitude of all levels of government. Few could believe that it was exclusively the power of nature that explained the death, dislocation, and destruction. Even those most willing to give government the benefit of the doubt were not willing to believe that the director of the Federal Emergency Management Agency (FEMA) Michael Brown was doing a "heckuva job," contrary to President George W. Bush's "good ole boy" praise and back-slapping. Shock over this incompetence quickly turned into worldwide collective outrage: how could this happen in twenty-first-century America? What was wrong with federal, state, and local government that fiddled while New Orleans drowned?

Second, there was the overwhelming presence of those who can only be called the *left-behind*, which astonished and horrified even more than government ineptitude. As if the force of Katrina's winds had blown down a thick curtain of denial behind the Big Easy's jazz, culinary, and sexual cornucopia, suddenly we were exposed to a grimy backstage – a world never meant to be seen by the public, where toilets are cleaned and beds are changed, and in which a stunning 26 percent of the female population lived under the federal poverty line, almost double the national average. People who were kept invisible for so long now took center stage – the old, the sick, the poor, the disabled, the very young, the mentally challenged, the isolated, the single mothers, the African-Americans – all those who, well before Hurricane Katrina, had been the disposable and socially excluded of New Orleans. Night after night, we saw televised images of thousands calling for rescue from the watery deathtraps of flooded homes, from snake-infested streets, and precarious rooftops. We watched in dismay as more than 55,000 New Orleanians were packed, virtually caged, and abandoned in the Superdome and the Convention Center – sites of human containment that Jesse Jackson aptly characterized as "hull[s] of slave ship[s]."[1] We recoiled at the knowledge of how black New Orleans' citizens were blocked from walking across a bridge to safety from the flooding to a white suburb because they were caricatured as lawless rabble, an image that echoes Jacob Lawrence's print of a similar confrontation by armed whites against unarmed blacks in Selma, Alabama, forty years earlier (see cover image). Worst of all, we witnessed anonymous bloated corpses floating or lying unidentified and unclaimed. By the end, approximately 1,856 New Orleanians had died of dehydration, exposure, or drowning, or had been killed by the snake-and alligator-infested waters. A lot more were to follow (Brinkley 2006; Horne 2006). Yet these very realities were cynically denied for days by the Homeland Security politicians who had forsaken them.

---

[1] To be fair, it has been a long and successful government practice to temporarily house people in public buildings like schools during major storms for their protection. It is much cheaper, does not jam up the escape routes with traffic, and is less logistically challenging. In the case of Katrina, however, it is clear that using the Superdome and the Convention Center was less the result of rational thoughtful planning than last-minute desperate decisions on the part of beleaguered city, local, and state administrators (Brinkley 2006; Horne 2006).

A week later, sometimes longer, those survivors lucky enough to be plucked off their rooftops or liberated from the gigantic stinking cages were now corralled into the city airport where they were told they would soon be exported to unknown destinations. There was little effort to try to reunite those families that the wind and floods had blown asunder. And as the media swarmed in on the crowds now stuffed into airport lounges, things took a new twist: these New Orleanians, most of whose families had been American citizens for countless generations, now found themselves categorized as "refugees," as if they were unwanted immigrants seeking asylum. The shock at being so labeled was palpable. Surely they were due, at the very least, the basic right to social recognition accorded to all Americans? It appeared they were losing more than their homes; now they were being stripped of their very political and social identities. Perhaps it was the wind and water that physically had displaced them. But how could it have been so easy to displace them socially and culturally from their rightful identities as citizens?

The calamity of Hurricane Katrina was created from the intersection of these two phenomena – a multi-tiered government with dysfunctional rescue and emergency management capacities collided head-on with the fact of thousands who had been left behind, abandoned and helpless in a city that was otherwise evacuated. Alone, either one of these would have been terrible, but would not have amounted to a national tragedy of such proportions. Thousands of people left behind and unable to escape the hurricane would always be horrific; but had the city been fully prepared and organized to meet just such disasters, local, state, and federal government agencies could have prevented New Orleans from turning into a living death-trap.[2] There is a perfectly plausible scenario of an efficient city evacuation plan prepared to use buses and other means of transportation to collect and evacuate all those who had no means to leave on their own.[3] If *all* the people had been successfully evacuated, there would have been massive property loss but many fewer deaths.[4] At the same

---

[2] The lack of such preparation that both Brinkley (2006) and Horne (2006) report is truly chilling. In the course of writing this chapter, many new books on Hurricane Katrina have been published in addition to those already cited. See, for example, Brasch (2006), Brunsma *et al.* (2007), Dyson (2006), Hartman and Squires (2006), South End Press Collective (2007), Tierney (2006), and Trout (2007).

[3] Such a plan would have long in advance had a full listing of all those families and individuals who would have need of this assistance, including those in hospitals, jails, nursing homes, etc. Through phone trees, community networks, churches, and other associations of civil society, such an evacuation plan would have been eminently doable.

[4] Massive property loss is, of course, a tragedy for anyone when it involves one's home. Yet this is magnified a dozen times when it is the poor who are disproportionately affected,

time, a government that had fully funded the Army Corps of Engineers, and a city government that had made repairing and fortifying the levees a priority might well have stopped the most proximate source of the flooding.[5] But it was not done; thousands were left behind, and a tragedy of Shakespearian proportions did occur.

A broken contract?

What forces fueled this volatile conjuncture? One important answer to the puzzle is offered by Michael Ignatieff, a prominent public advocate for human rights (currently a Canadian MP). Writing in a modern version of what political theorists call the social contract tradition, Ignatieff argues that the government's treatment of New Orleans was nothing less than a violation of what he calls the *contract of citizenship*: "It was not blacks or the poor but *citizens* whom the government betrayed in New Orleans" (Ignatieff 2005: 15–17). In a brilliant disquisition on the state's obligations inherent in this "contract," Ignatieff accuses the Bush regime of breaking faith with the government's foundational contract to protect citizens from forces beyond their control, a trust that Herbert Hoover and the Army Corps of Engineers instantiated in their swift and effective response to the Mississippi flood of 1927. "[P]ublic authority has [since] been charged with this duty" to protect Americans against natural disaster, Ignatieff writes. "[T]his was the key element of the contract that seemed to have been ripped up like a roof shingle and cast into the infernal waters of New Orleans ... When the levees broke, the contract of American citizenship failed."

Ignatieff gives voice to the excluded. He observes that of all the players in the drama of Katrina, and of all the explanations for their plight, only the abandoned of New Orleans seemed to understand that their fate reflected the betrayal of citizenship's inclusive, universalistic, and egalitarian assumptions. They vociferously rejected being classified as "refugees" and indignantly reminded the nation that "We are Americans" with equal rights, not aliens begging for charity. Ignatieff is right to insist that this citizenly indignation cannot be called "sentimentalism" on the part

something that has been cynically borne out by the differential treatment of rich versus poor, black versus white, in post-hurricane compensation and reparations. My analysis, however, does not include the post-hurricane years of "reconstruction" and "repair."

[5] Both Brinkley (2006) and Horne (2006) report on the extent to which the predictions of real experts were completely ignored, indeed even suppressed, by politicians even while they proved remarkably exact in forecasting the devastating impact of such a hurricane on the infrastructure and population of New Orleans.

of those who had never come to grips with racism, class injustice, and the world of inequality in which they lived. The ravages of racism and the devastating impact of poverty that so many media voyeurs claimed to have been shocked – *shocked* – to have discovered in the wake of Katrina were hardly revelations to those suddenly displaced New Orleanians. Yet despite all that they had endured over the years in the way of racism and inequality, these Americans apparently still held closely to the ideals of American citizenship – so much so that they were traumatized to find they were treated not with the rights and recognition entitled to citizens, but as little more than superfluous population. Apparently, it still came as "bitter news" to the displaced and left-behind that "their claims of citizenship mattered so little to the institutions charged with their protection" (Ignatieff 2005: 16).

Ignatieff has offered a compelling rendition of citizenship's normative standards and the devastating consequences of its utter disregard. For him the human right to the dignity of social inclusion and recognition as full members of a political and social community *is* the normative ideal of citizenship.[6] He has uncovered the ethical core amidst the muck and detritus that the Bush regime's betrayal left in its wake. This makes it all the more disappointing that Ignatieff describes the nature of those normative and ethical principles by means of the *social contractual* metaphor, which inevitably evokes not the noncontractual reciprocal ties of membership and shared fate embodied in the ethos of citizenship, but rather the loosely interpreted Hobbesian/Lockean conceit of isolated individuals reluctantly coming together to sign a quid pro quo social contract for exclusively instrumental purposes.

To be sure, the idea of the social contract is capacious. For Hobbes, its intent was to provide security and justice only to those who can deliver a good equivalent in value to what is offered to them in the way of protection (or who can threaten to kill to get what they want); for Locke, the point of the contract was to secure their precontractual natural rights as free and autonomous individuals. For Hobbes the social contract was irrespective of gross inequalities in bargaining power, and meant that people in no position to deliver either benefits or harms to others – helpless children, the infirm, the severely disabled, the indigent,

---

[6] By normative ideal I mean the conceptual desiderata of citizenship and how it is defined as a set of principles. The reality is never coincident, even within citizenship's own terms. The normative ideal is not the same thing as an ideal type, which is meant to represent not a normative but an empirical standard – one with no implications as to its moral stature.

the socially excluded, etc. – have no rights. For Locke, the goal was to advance a self-regulating (free of the state) moral order of civil society, based on the peaceful exchange of property among equals, by constructing a *fiduciary* government to whom the people only *conditionally* turn over some rights in exchange for security. Liberalism as a political tradition discarded Hobbes's vision of the state qua benevolent dictator to whom the people give up their rights, and embraced Locke's version of the contract as consent to representative government. Hobbes's version of the contract as quid pro quo exchange, however, became essential moral law in economic liberalism's contractual tradition. With respect to citizenship, neither the Hobbesian nor the Lockean versions viewed their contractarians as a membership body of citizens. They were rather an aggregate collection of individuals acting together for instrumental reasons – for Hobbes it was to engage in quid pro quo exchange, while for Locke it was to resist the very powers of the public sphere upon which citizenship depends. Indeed so foreign is it to the original social contractarian tradition that, try as one might, no discussion of citizenship as such will be found in the classical liberal texts of Hobbes, Locke, or Smith.[7] There are only rights-bearing individuals who derive their rights not from each other or from the public sphere, but from the presocial and prepolitical abstraction of the state of nature. The empty promises of natural rights and social contractualism are unavoidably linked.[8]

Citizenship versus contract

I take issue with social contractarian approaches to citizenship like Ignatieff's. My quarrel is more than semantics. Words have powers; depending on who speaks them, they can create worlds, and one of the themes of this book is just how remarkably effective certain ideational and normative powers can be. As the people of New Orleans so poignantly understood, they were *citizens*, not "parties" to a contract. The

[7] With the exception of Hobbes's *De Cive* (1998) on medieval cities.
[8] A careful reading of Hobbes's and Locke's versions (not to mention Rousseau's) of the social contract would find even more radical and normative distinctions between them. According to Elizabeth Anderson, Locke was egregiously misappropriated by the libertarians (aka market fundamentalists), especially in the influential work of Robert Nozick (1974), in the mistaken belief that Locke allowed only property rights, defined in the narrowest possible material/market-based sense, to constrain the content of the social contract. There are conceptions of social contract theory that firmly reject these readings of Locke and deny that the basis of the social contract is a bargain made on the basis of grossly unequal bargaining power. Rawls (1971), for example, is considered a social contractarian, although he rejects any notion of rights as derived from hard bargaining or the manipulation of power differentials based on antecedent inequalities in personal or financial assets.

contrasts between citizenship and contract comprise a long list, but the basic difference is straightforward: citizenship entails reciprocal but *non-equivalent* rights and obligations between *equal* citizens; contracts entail market exchange of *equivalent* goods or services between *unequal* market actors. To be sure, the freedom to make private contracts has always been a foundational element of civil rights, just as (embedded) markets must always be part of a legitimate citizenship regime. But within a full citizenship regime, even freedom of contract is a right that has practical meaning only in the civil and public spheres where it is regulated by the practices and institutions of the rule of law. And, by contrast, while contractual rights have always been one among many citizenship rights, citizenship rights, by contrast, do not figure in contractual agreements.

To elaborate: contracts are the life-blood of markets – quid pro quo instruments of voluntary commercial exchange between equivalent goods, services, or monies. Citizenship, by contrast, is the life-blood of social solidarity in civil society and political communities comprised of noncontractual membership rights, relationships, and reciprocal responsibilities. Consumers make contracts as a private matter subject to civil law, as do employers and employees, contractors and clients, unions and businesses; in none of these cases is there an assumption of equivalence or equality between the actual parties to the contract. When acting as citizens, by contrast, we do not exchange equivalents among ourselves; rather we engage in reciprocal activities based on the principle that it is our fellow citizens – not people distinguished by social status, class, race, gender, and so on – who are equal under law.

Several caveats are in order. Because citizenship is a filing system by which people are distributed into and included in various political communities, this means they are excluded from others. Indeed, there are some people who are excluded from all political entities, for whom citizenship is nothing but an exclusionary hard line of demarcation. And these hard lines of demarcation are not merely at the national borders; internal divisions of class, race, gender, ethnicity, sexuality, etc. have always created gradations of *internal* citizenship, such that some are only "second-class citizens" while others are excluded altogether from even internal citizenship rights – even if by legal status they might be called "citizens" of this or that political entity. Thus while citizenship is the language of civil society, it is a language built as much on the dark side of exclusion and even dehumanization as it is on inclusion and solidarity.

Still, in its ideal-typical form, citizenship is the conservator of the common good, and as such it is supposed to mobilize the state to mediate between citizen and market where it protects against the full consequences of unmediated market exposure.[9] Contracts are built on utilitarian incentives that are designed to motivate people by their self-interest. Although the contracting parties are legally bound to exchange commensurate goods and services (no one gets "something for nothing"), there is no presumption of equivalence in the *outcome*, making social and class inequality the signature of market processes. Citizenship practices, by contrast, are constrained by principles of the legal (if not practical) equality of persons. Unlike in contractual transactions, the outcomes of these citizen activities cannot be measured by a monetary metric; at the finish of any particular citizenship practice people are just as morally and legally equal as when they started. It works this way if citizenship is adequately affirmed by institutional relationships and reciprocal obligations that operate not at the level of the self-interested free agent but at that of the civil, the social, and the public. Rather than create them *de novo*, individual citizens can only *participate* in these preexisting social and political structures, much as we participate in a language. In both cases there is some degree of individual freedom, but always within the parameters of preexisting structural constraints. Contracts, by contrast, are voluntary and revocable; the original terms of a contract can disappear for reasons of little more than pure venality because it is the contracting parties alone who create this instrument of temporary exchange.[10] In the contractual model individuals exist entirely prior to whatever voluntary arrangements they choose to construct – and deconstruct. Absent one party and it is over.

In the end I believe that the distinction between contract and citizenship is at root an ontological one. Because citizens are participating members of a relational political, civil, and social community that exists independently of any particular individuals, our very status and identity as rights-bearers is inexorably attached to that relational and public body. This makes citizenship not merely a bundle of rights, nor even just a status possessed by individuals – although it is both of those. Rather it is the *right to have rights* – the foundational public good for every person to be a member of a preexisting civil society and political community.[11]

---

[9] As the 1870 Bismarckian social policies demonstrate, public services and goods have existed in conditions without any meaningful citizenship, certainly not democracy. But the opposite is not true: to count as a citizenship regime, some kind of a public sphere is required.

[10] As I write today the airwaves are full of stories of growing numbers of large corporations simply dropping their contractual obligations to their employees to provide health care and retirement pensions – all with little more than a rubber stamp from the courts.

[11] The concept of the right to have rights is developed further below. It is also the subject of chapter 3.

Contract is the problem, not the solution

The analysis of citizenship I develop in this book sets a template for an alternative explanation for the tragedy of Katrina from that of Michael Ignatieff's social contractual one.[12] There is no question but that Ignatieff grasps the government's enormous violation of rights during the Katrina crisis. He errs, however, in suggesting that the remedy for repairing the breach is a healed social contract, because the crisis did not result from a broken contractual relationship in the first place. Rather, these rights violations reflected a breach of the noncontractualism of citizenship. The ethos of citizenship is Exhibit A of Durkheim's ([1893] 1984) famous stipulation that people are held together not by voluntary market-like contracts (as per Hobbes and Locke), but rather by the "noncontractual basis of contract." Durkheim, like Karl Polanyi ([1944] 2001) half a century later, and today's theorists of trust (Mizrachi *et al.* 2007), civil society (Alexander 2006), and moral economy (Block 2006), understood that for markets and contracts to function at all within the larger society, they depend on robust noncontractual relations of membership, mutual obligation, social inclusion, and reciprocity.[13]

There is, however, a surprising twist to my argument. While it was the ideals of noncontractual citizenship that the government so blatantly ignored in its response to the Katrina survivors, Ignatieff is right to say that contract did have a role in the tragedy. However, he is wrong to assign it the role of the noble citizenship contract that was violated by government incompetence and that now must be repaired. In my story, by contrast, contract is the *problem*, not the solution. The disregard for the lives of the African-American New Orleanians by FEMA is evidence of market fundamentalism's all too successful strategy to contractualize the relationship between the government and the people.

Over the last three decades market fundamentalism has been displacing and corroding the noncontractual bonds of citizenship and imposing those of contractual market exchange in their stead. Instead of being the solution (as per Ignatieff), then, it is the *contractualization of citizenship* that was the problem for the people of New Orleans – specifically, the transformation of the rights and obligations of citizenship from an ethic

---

[12] It is important to stress here that while Ignatieff uses the contractual metaphor, this does not suggest that he holds views compatible with market fundamentalism or neoliberalism more generally.

[13] Many argue that the Scottish Enlightenment scholars defined civil society in just this way – the noncontractual relationships without which capitalism could not function (see especially Wolfe 1989).

(if not always the reality) of noncontractual reciprocities based on the rights and responsibilities of equal inclusion, into one in which the right of social inclusion is conditional on being party to a market exchange of equivalent value. The rise of workfare epitomizes the contractualization of citizenship: the object of exchange is labor power in a quantity and quality equivalent to the lowest the market will bear (usually below the minimum wage), or that the government will accept, and the right earned in return is the right to independence from the "degradation" of government assistance, and to the new exercise of "personal responsibility." Under the terms of this increasingly hegemonic market morality, those unable to be a party to an employment contract, whether because of a lack of skills and education or, much more commonly, a lack of available jobs, adequate on-the-job training, or transportation and child care, or because of the need to care for an elderly parent, are treated – that is, blamed – as nothing less than contractual malfeasants.[14]

When measured exclusively by the contractual metric of labor market value, the unemployed or underemployed are stigmatized as lacking moral worth. Absent both contractual value and moral worth, poor urban minority populations such as those New Orleanians abandoned to Hurricane Katrina are characterized by scholarly analysts as an "underclass" – a term that explicitly conjures up an image of those who are "under," thus less than, the rest of the "regular" population, and which marks them as clearly excluded from membership in the mainstream of society. In effect, it characterizes them as outside the internal borders of the American political community, and thus no longer within the bonds and bounds of citizenly obligation. Unable to fulfill their side of the newly marketized exchange called citizenship, the left-behind of New Orleans, being contractual malfeasants, did not elicit much concern at any level of government because with their social exclusion they were no longer recognized as moral equals. They had become a surplus, superfluous, and disposable population.

For African-Americans, who made up the vast majority of the left-behind New Orleanians, exclusion from the body politic and civil society was hardly new, of course. Centuries of chattel slavery, followed by almost another century of legal (in the South) and informal (in the North) apartheid were never anomalous irrational inconsistencies

---

[14] It is popular to attribute unemployment among the poor to lack of human capital (education and skills), but there is evidence that this contributes only a small part – and increasingly contributes nothing at all – to the problem of disappearing jobs, even in the low-wage market. See especially Bernstein (2007), Frank (2007a), Handler (2004, 2006), Hacker (2006), and Uchitelle (2006).

with the more primary liberal and republican values of America's political culture, inconsistencies that were to be gradually overcome by the
progressive forces of the dominant liberal democratic ethos. Colonial
British Americans pursued "practices of racial and gender domination
long before they embraced ... liberal republican ideologies and institutions" (Smith 1993: 556) and the establishment of an independent republican nation with a partially liberal egalitarian constitution did nothing
to mitigate the racial paranthropoidism (subhuman status) of slavery or
the gendered ascriptive inegalitarianism that preceded it; nor did ending
slavery, overturning the legal exclusions of Jim Crow legislation, or even
the Great Society's belated attempt to right the wrongs the New Deal
inflicted on the backs of African-Americans (Katznelson 2005). As
Smith (1993; 1999) so powerfully demonstrates, American citizenship
was not only built upon but continues to embody what he calls an
"admixture" of multiple, however contradictory, coincident political
cultural ideologies, most prominently a "complex pattern of apparently
inconsistent combinations" of liberal, republican, and racial and gendered inegalitarian ascriptive forms of Americanism "accompanied by
recurring conflicts" but without any single one constituting it as a whole
(Smith 1993: 558). Contrary to wishful thinking, moreover, the path to
including the excluded has been anything but progressive; more accurately, according to Smith, it has been "serpentine." Thus, he warns us
that despite some genuine improvements "novel intellectual, political,
and legal systems reinforcing racial ethnic and gender inequalities might
be rebuilt in America in the years ahead" (1993: 558).

That not altogether novel system has been found in the rise of market
fundamentalism and the contractualization of citizenship. They have
radically worsened the conditions of African-Americans. I shall develop
this argument by first discussing what I mean by market fundamentalism,
by citizenship, and the contractualization of citizenship. I shall then
return to the genealogies of Katrina, elaborating on how I believe my
argument can help explain the phenomena that combined to create the
crisis of Hurricane Katrina.

Genealogies of "warring principles": egalitarian versus market precepts

Market fundamentalism

Market fundamentalism is the term popularized by George Soros (1998,
2000) to characterize the fervent conviction that all of social life should be
organized according to market principles. While some use the term as

merely an epithet, I approach it here as a comprehensive worldview and political movement.[15] As elaborated more fully in the rest of the book, market fundamentalism can be usefully divided into three parts: (1) it is a story built on a body of ideas, which can take any number of forms – a public discourse, a political narrative, an ideology or, when hegemonic, an ideational regime; (2) it is an organized political and social movement, well-funded, aggressive, and forcefully evangelizing in its global reach; and (3) it is a set of practices, legal interventions and rulings, political techniques, and "technologies."

As an ideational regime, market fundamentalism is the contemporary form of what Karl Polanyi (2001) identified six decades ago as economic liberalism's "stark utopia" – the idea that society as a whole can and should be subordinated to and governed by a system of self-regulating markets created by a multiplicity of incentive-driven individual choices. By "the market," market fundamentalists usually invoke an image of a system by which noncompulsive individual rationality is mystically coordinated (the "invisible hand") to produce both freedom and efficiency, and all without any need for political power or government coercion. It is the idealized process by which multiple individual actions on the part of rational utility-maximizers interact to determine prices and quantities. The market is the means by which supply and demand are balanced by the price mechanism in a way that transmits information and incentives so that the voluntary exchange of labor and goods among individuals produces the optimal use of productive resources. In its abstract idealized state of equilibrium, the market is conceptualized by market fundamentalists as organized around a system of material incentives. These incentives, for example, induce individuals to exchange labor and goods based on a balance of supply and demand, making markets the most efficient and optimal system of allocation under conditions of chronic scarcity.

---

[15] I use the term market fundamentalism, rather than neoliberalism, for several reasons. For one, I have been teaching sociology too long not to be sensitive to just how confusing the term liberalism can be for American ears. Not only is the word defined differently in the United States from the rest of world. To make matters worse, it is defined in exactly the opposite way – with American liberalism referring to a social democratic more activist government political philosophy and European or classical liberalism referring to a laissez-faire free market one. Another reason for preferring market fundamentalism over neoliberalism follows directly from the previous point. Neoliberalism, in large part thanks to its rhetorical strategies and media-oriented discourses, as well as its association with classical liberalism, conjures up images of small government antistatism. Neoliberalism and market fundamentalism, however, are anything but regimes of small *laissez-faire* government. They are, rather, regimes of *market-driven* big government, or big government conquered by market fundamentalism, as I discuss in some detail below. See also the Longview Institute website www.thelongviewinstitute.org.

According to market fundamentalists, this picture of the market is not only descriptive; it is also ontological and normative. Ontologically, market fundamentalists view the market through the prism of *social naturalism* – the conviction that the laws governing natural phenomena also govern human society. Social naturalism characterizes the market as a natural entity, rather than a social artifact, and as regulated by natural laws no less than other law-regulated natural phenomena like gravity and natural selection. Because it blurs the line between nature and society, social naturalism maintains that human nature is essentially constituted by biological drives and instincts. Society, like nature, is fundamentally constrained by the scarcity postulate – the constitutive and inevitable reality of chronic material scarcity – and the self-interested individual who responds primarily to material incentives. It is the incentive to overcome scarcity or to act on some other self-regarding interest that motivates the boundless transactions that constitute a self-regulating market. As an autonomous and spontaneous system, it is the social manifestation of nature's laws of scarcity-driven supply and demand, capable of responding to an almost infinite spectrum of price cues and incentive management techniques.[16] As most will immediately recognize, one of the hallmarks of market fundamentalism is its direct negation of its Keynesian predecessor, an economic policy based on a thorough-going institutionalism, in which markets are deemed to function best and capitalism saved from its own self-destructive impulses when embedded in publicly driven institutional investments and arrangements.[17]

Normatively, market fundamentalists believe that when left to its own devices, the market is not only efficient and optimal; it is also the only legitimate way to organize a free society characterized by universality, equality under law, freedom of contract, and voluntarism. By extention they also believe that state intervention, political regulation, "social engineering" and especially planning, are not only mechanisms of market impairment, inefficiency, perverse incentives, and inevitable impoverishment; they also see these forms of regulating capital as deeply immoral violations of the freedom and individual liberties endowed to people by virtue of their essential natural rights as human beings.[18] Political

---

[16] Any doubts about the appeal of market fundamentalism should be allayed by noticing the spectacular success of *Freakonomics* – an argument that the tools of economic analysis, especially that of incentive-management, can explain everything (Levitt and Dubner 2005; Frank 2007b). For the academic version see Becker (1976).

[17] See especially Block (1997), Hodgson (1988), and Kuttner (2007).

[18] To be sure, as I continually insist, the apparent simplicity of market fundamentalism does not represent the far more nuanced theories of neoclassical academic economists, let alone the antiorthodox economic scholars outside the mainstream such as the Nobel

and economic liberalism were born together in the late seventeenth and eighteenth-century English and Scottish Enlightenment. With the New Deal and the Great Society their ways parted, as democratic forces joined with political liberalism to tame the worst excesses of economic liberalism. As a result, economic liberalism in its purest free market/market fundamentalist expressions took up an alliance with political conservatism (and the Republican Party), even while still using political liberalism's language of individual rights and universal equality to discredit social-justice-inflected attempts to restrain the workings of an unregulated market or to redress past social inequities.

From this point of view, the work of market fundamentalism is restoration. For all its talk of liberal Democrats "living in the past," it is actually the market fundamentalists who see their project as removing the distortions put in place by New Deal and Great Society social programs, and thus restoring the market to what they argue was its natural state before the "socialized state" sent the "Constitution in[to] exile" (Rosen 2005; Epstein 2005).

It is useful to remember that post-tribal societies have always had markets, and as long as their scope is limited and they are embedded and regulated by civil, social, and political ends, they are essential (Polanyi 1977). Indeed, we have learned the hard way that markets are one prerequisite for a free and prosperous society.[19] In a socially inclusive citizenship regime, it follows that markets will be nurtured, but they must also be tempered by external rules as well as internal norms and ethics. In addition, scope restriction must be imposed between those kinds of production and allocation that lend themselves to market mechanisms, and those such as health care and other means of livelihood that must be organized by principles of equality and social inclusion – basic human rights, in other words. Of course, in reality no such sharp lines of distinction exist. "Boundaries" and "scope restrictions" are just handy metaphors for speaking of limits to what should be bought and sold for

Prize-winning Herbert Kahneman (see Kahneman *et al.* 1985) or Joseph Stiglitz (1989). And as is so often the case, those who call themselves followers of Hayek almost universally neglect Hayek's own caveats and complexifications. For example, with respect to the welfare state, Hayek (2007) himself wrote that "[t]here are common needs that can be satisfied only by collective action and which can be provided for without restricting individual liberty. It can hardly be denied that as we grow richer, that minimum of sustenance which the community has always provided outside the market, will gradually rise, or that government may, usefully and without doing any harm, assist or even lead in such endeavours." In this piece, he is arguing that the infringement on "freedom" comes from "state monopoly" not public provision, something not all that far from my own model of social pathology.

[19] Contrary to standard market fundamentalist dogma, the opposite is not true: capitalism does *not* automatically produce democracy.

private profit, and of what must be off limits to those aims. Keynesian macroeconomics, moreover, defines "the economy" to include the state's managerial role,[20] just as Berezin (2005) and Kahneman *et al.* (1985) remind us of the central role of emotions in even the most "efficient" of markets, and Fraser (1989) and Zelizer (1997, 2005) provide us with compelling portraits of the role of economics in the sphere of intimacy. For analytic and normative purposes, however, metaphors are necessary to represent a pluralism of separate spheres and activities – a market both regulated and contained in scope within a larger ethos of democratic socially inclusive citizenship.[21]

Market fundamentalists, by contrast, do not accept the viability of an ethical or practical pluralism of spheres. They cannot do so because they define nonmarketized sites of government and civil society as both coercive and inefficient, and thus as unfree and chronic threats to what they consider to be the natural freedoms of the market. Indeed market fundamentalism is fixated on dissolving the boundaries between the market and the domains of civil society, the public sphere, and the polity. Its goal is to privatize, to avoid all forms of regulation and above all to marketize those public goods and services such as health care, education, and pollution control that many of us believe should be insulated from the market and treated as noncontractual requirements of the common good (Levitt and Dubner 2005). Public goods and services are in particular not amenable to market methods of allocation.

The term market fundamentalism is intended to conjure up several kinds of association with religious fundamentalisms. One is the imperative to accept certain core beliefs based on nothing more than pure faith, despite – or sometimes even because of – any confirming or disconfirming "worldly" (scientific) evidence. With its roots in an appropriation of Adam Smith's "invisible hand," it assumes mystical, almost magical, qualities in its coordinating abilities. Another association is that both market and religious fundamentalisms rely on first or a priori principles, which, like the line in geometry or the foundational axiom in philosophy, are postulated as givens upon which whole systems are built. In philosophy, when something is postulated to be foundational, it means that it does not have to be proved or explained by a deeper cause. That which is foundational is taken on faith to be the only cause that matters. In this respect, foundationalism and fundamentalism are functional

---

[20] Tim Mitchell kindly reminded me of this.
[21] This image clearly shares much with Walzer (1983).

equivalents. Everything that flows from foundations and fundamentals are said to be effects, and these are usually richly illustrated – often creating the illusion of having "proved" the existence of the foundational entity by means of extensively illustrating what is said to be empirical evidence. Marx's postulated base of the mode of production, for example, is the foundation of his fundamentalism, since he claims it determines the nature of everything built upon it. Hence his famous aphorism in the sociology of knowledge: the ruling ideas of the time are the ideas of the ruling class. To say that market principles (including individual choice and the utility-maximizing self) are fundamental, then, is to say that they are taken as the starting point for understanding how the whole social world works. Like the foundation of a building, everything else follows from it, is modeled upon it, and is limited by its principles and parameters.

A third parallel between market and religious fundamentalisms is that neither of them can ever be in stasis. Rather, the essential disposition of all fundamentalisms is to expand and convert. Not to do so would be tantamount to leaving a newly built basement with nothing above it but open air. Like evangelical religious movements, market fundamentalism can never rest; it must always look to marketize greater areas of the social universe. In the case of market fundamentalism, however, this is a feat that can never be fully realized without destroying the very society it is trying to organize (Polanyi 2001; Leys 2003). Market fundamentalism is thus never finished in its pursuit of ever greater arenas to penetrate and convert. This is why market fundamentalists must be Evangelicals, always driven to convert to market principles all "nonbelieving" practices, institutions, and whole spheres of society. Indeed, even when it appears to be all but hegemonic, market fundamentalism is always in a state of expansionist desire, propounding ever more elaborate conversion narratives to conquer the last recalcitrant holdouts.

Because of this inherent expansionary drive to marketize nonmarket arenas, market fundamentalism is constitutionally unable to tolerate alternative noncontractual social phenomena. Market fundamentalism and the noncontractualism of citizenship cannot exist as "separate but equal" principles in a pluralist universe. Market fundamentalism's expansionist drive thus poses a constant threat to citizenship. Indeed the more successful it is in escaping its "proper" economic boundaries and subordinating noncontractual spheres of civil and political society to market-driven mechanisms, the more it threatens to become the very negation of citizenship.

Market fundamentalism should not be confused with the more nuanced arguments made by most mainstream academic economists, who recognize the pervasiveness of market failure and the need for the state to step in and provide public goods, as well as to insure against the big risks that the private sector cannot.[22] As an ideational program it is also very different from the complex mix of policies pursued by governments in actually existing capitalist societies. Capitalism as a functioning system resembles market fundamentalism not at all. Market fundamentalism thus presents many ironies and paradoxes. The zealous certainty of its free-market ideology is in direct proportion to the inaccuracy of its model of how existing capitalist societies and economies actually work. However regulation-free their theory-driven models of how markets should work, market fundamentalists know well that the "freest" of markets are in fact as deeply law-driven and institutionally embedded as any of the more "socialized" systems against which they rail. Whereas they propound the utopian idea that subjecting all domains of social life to the "spontaneous" and self-regulating market mechanism is both optimally efficient and imperative for a free society, fully functioning capitalist markets are in fact ensconced in multiplexes of legal rules, regulations, and institutions without which neither contracts nor property rights would function. Market fundamentalists are fond of protesting against corporate "over-regulation," "burdensome inefficiencies," and "over-taxation," which they define as "property theft." In reality, they understand perhaps even better than the rest of us just how critical it is that "free markets" are steeped in laws and public policy. As Polanyi (2001: 147) observed when demystifying the mythology surrounding the first epoch of market fundamentalism in nineteenth-century England, "*laissez-faire* was planned; the movements for social protection were spontaneous." What market fundamentalists worry about is not *whether* markets are imbricated in legal rules and political technologies of management, but rather *which* rules and techniques, and to whom will the benefits be conferred (Somers and Block 2005).

---

[22] There are exceptions of course to the rule that only nonacademic economists are dedicated market fundamentalists. The academic economist (and sociologist) Gary Becker, winner of the Nobel Prize in economics for his market fundamentalist theory of human capital (see chapter 6), and two other academics, Martin Feldstein and Mark Pauly, were all enormously influential in developing Reaganite social policy. Feldstein, for example, became Reagan's chief economic advisor and chair of the White House's Council of Economic Advisors (Hacker 2006).

The distance between market fundamentalism and the workings of actually existing capitalist markets underlines the degree to which it is a project driven primarily by an ideology, a grand narrative of market-driven human freedom based on nothing less than the laws of nature. It would be tempting, however, to mistake an ideational movement for one that is powerless to effect structural change. While not all ideas have causal powers, market fundamentalism is one idea that has demonstrated its powers to actually remake the world no less than the usual sociological suspects such as class structure, modes of production, state violence, social movements, law, etc. Through processes of what Fred Block and I call *ideational embedding*, and Pierre Bourdieu speaks of as the capacity "to make itself [neoliberalism] true," market fundamentalism uses its social naturalistic foundations to acquire an epistemic privilege, that in recent decades has been instrumental in transforming its worldview from a marginal argument outside the mainstream of political discourse into a full-fledged ideational regime with the capacity to withstand what for normal theories would be devastating empirical disconfirmation (Bourdieu 1998: 91).[23]

In its ongoing effort to convert, market fundamentalism deploys cultural images, discursive codes, "conversion narratives," and other ideational mechanisms, especially those that have operated successfully across times and places, such as Hirschman's (1990) three "rhetorics of reaction." Of these, Fred Block and I have identified "the perversity thesis" to be among the most effective in the project of dismantling social citizenship rights. The perversity thesis is a public discourse that criticizes social programs intended to help the poor through public transfers and social provisioning. It stipulates that these programs, however well-meaning, in fact create "perverse" incentives for welfare recipients *not* to overcome their own poverty through hard work. Rather, these incentives inexorably create a "culture of dependency," ultimately exacerbating the very problem they were designed to solve. According to the perversity thesis, therefore, welfare causes poverty; it is not poverty that generates the need for welfare assistance. As Malthus – the first to fully perfect the rhetoric of perversity – put it in 1803, by providing financial incentives for the poor to propagate and multiply "they [the Poor Laws] may be said to create the poor which they maintain" (1992: 100). As dependence sets in as a permanent feature of life, the perversity thesis leads us to believe that ultimately

---

[23] See Somers and Block (2005) for detailed discussion on market fundamentalism's epistemic privilege, which immunizes its basic precepts from empirical challenge.

there is no choice but to recognize that individual behavior is to blame for the distress of poverty.[24] As a subset of market fundamentalism, the perversity thesis thus preaches the virtues of personal responsibility, promotes a shame-based approach to poverty, and exhorts the exigency of restoring the "natural" incentives of hunger and shame. The perversity thesis is one of market fundamentalism's most successful ideational mechanisms. It works as an ideological wedge issue, which is intended to get the proverbial camel's (market fundamentalist's) nose under the social citizenship tent, opening the way for policy challenges and structural changes to follow.

Notwithstanding its ideational core, market fundamentalism is not merely a "reified structural force capable of acting without agents" (Peck and Ticknell 2002). For its second characteristic is that it is also an organized political and social movement, institutionally well-funded, involved in aggressively evangelizing neoliberal and market fundamentalist views of reality, and peopled by a wide range of advocates including financiers, global corporate elites, self-declared "Constitution in Exilers" (Rosen 2005), a conservative judiciary, public intellectuals, much of mainstream and conservative talk radio, TV, and print media, the lobbying industry, and Christian fundamentalists – to name just a few. Its organized political forces are channeled through networks of conservative and libertarian think tanks, funded through corporate wealth, and burgeoning with policy experts who are given extraordinary access to the media and to government.[25]

Market fundamentalism's third component is dedicated to implementation through marketization. Marketization refers to the processes, techniques, policies, and "technologies" (Mitchell 2002) used to convert into markets or pseudo-markets those areas of social life that are considered insufficiently marketized. It entails practical mechanisms and technical instruments of marketization that have been used repeatedly over the decades since market fundamentalism first made an appearance in the late eighteenth century. Part of this work entails turning previously noncontractualized goods and services into commodities so that they can be priced and sold. The motivations for producing, providing, or distributing these must also be detached from a noncontractual ethic of the public good to one of profit seeking and market discipline

---

[24] On the gendered nature of Malthus's argument, see especially Valenze (1995) and Gallagher (1986).
[25] See chapter 6 for an extensive engagement with this social movement aspect of market fundamentalism.

(Leys 2003; Lukes 2006a). At all levels of practice, perverse incentives must be eliminated and new ones instantiated to induce people – perhaps by psychology, perhaps by biologically driven hunger or desire, perhaps by utility-maximization and rational preferences – to participate in newly marketized exchanges, whether by creating new needs for things newly commoditized, or by supplying the requirements for a newly commoditized kind of self-exploitation, such as self-serve at gas pumps and check-out lines, or by succumbing to the marketized obligations of workfare and make-work imposed by the post-1996 welfare bill. High on the list of transformational tools is "deregulation," which, as I explain below, is actually more accurately described as a "takeover" of government agencies such as the Occupational and Safety Health Administration (OSHA), the National Labor Relations Board, and the Environmental Protection Agency; so is expanding the number of elected judges, passing bankruptcy and tort "reform," and shifting resources away from the public sector, degrading public schools, public services, and the institutions of the public sphere more generally. To fully understand this process, it is critical to examine a range of institutions that have been transformed through these processes of marketization. Few have done this more fruitfully than Colin Leys (2003) in his close-up examination of the British National Health Service and the British Broadcasting Company (BBC), as have Hacker (2006), Kuttner (2007) and Uchitelle (2006) for the United States.

Notwithstanding the significance of these institutional transformations, I concur with Peck and Ticknell's (2002) observation that it would be a mistake to minimize the power of ideas in comparison to structural changes. Empirical studies show that when major marketizing feats have been achieved, such as the successful passage of the 1996 welfare bill, they have been preceded by successful ideational conversions (Somers and Block 2005). I think they get it just right when they warn against reducing neoliberalism/market fundamentalism to techniques or empirical implementations while missing the crucial fact that "as an *ongoing ideological project* neoliberalism [market fundamentalism] is clearly more than the sum of its (local institutional) parts" (Peck and Ticknell 2002: 401).[26] Market fundamentalism is clearly an ideational movement, not an economic theory, for a capacious vision of market-generated societal freedom.

---

[26] Cited in Lukes (2004).

Historicizing citizenship's warring principles

I described above how market fundamentalism is constantly on the acquisitive move. What is aggressed upon, however, can in turn resist, and the genealogy of citizenship is very much a story of countervailing powers. Unlike market fundamentalism, which aims to negate citizenship as an alternative mode of social organization, citizenship does not strive to eliminate markets or contracts, for they are a constitutive element of the universal ideals of both freedom and the rule of law. It does need to contain the ever more centrifugal drive of marketization, however. In T. H. Marshall's classic account, this dynamic relationship between markets and citizenship began in the eighteenth century, and reflected citizenship's "warring principles." By warring principles, Marshall meant the conflict between market inequality and class divisions on the one side, and citizenship's egalitarian and universalistic legal principles on the other. In fact Marshall goes so far as to say that it was this permanent opposition between the internally warring principles of class versus equality that propelled citizenship from its origins as an instrument of landed property-owning gentry into a democratic institution of egalitarian universality. The outcome of this war, however, was neither predetermined nor static. The genealogies of citizenship are always historically contingent.[27]

In Marshall's account, the pioneers of citizenship rights were wealthy commercial English property owners struggling to gain independence from the crown. By challenging the crown's monopoly of public legal power, the gentry were able to institutionalize at the national level the first bundle of rights Marshall labeled as "civil citizenship" – the right to exchange property, to freely enter into civil contracts, and to defend these rights in courts of law. Their strategy was to use the preexisting universal discourse of English common law to claim that these rights were not exclusive to the crown but were natural and universal (universal exclusively to their class, that is). Their success created a paradox, however. The civil citizenship rights they gained were permanently inflected by both property-based market rights (hence divided by class inequalities) and the egalitarian universal ideals of the rule of law. Marshall tells a story of the dynamic historical conflict between these internally warring principles, in which the inequalities of markets inexorably excited protests based on the egalitarian promises contained in those same citizenship rights. In the British case on which he bases his story, these

---

[27] In Somers (1993, 1994a) I discuss both my appreciation and criticisms of Marshall's account, and present my alternative history of citizenship formation and rights.

protests led in the nineteenth century to political citizenship and in the mid-twentieth century to social citizenship and its grand expansion in the institutions of education, health, and welfare. Marshall's England of the 1950s was well on its way to establishing what from our vantage point today was clearly the apex of its social democratic "moment" when social citizenship had in fact become less contested and more institutionalized (although Marshall went out of his way to assert that Britain had by no means eliminated social inequality). And in the United States, thanks to labor unions in the 1930s and 1940s, the Civil Rights Movement of the 1950s and 60s, the women's movement, and the poor people's and welfare rights movements of the 1960s and early 1970s, citizenship was able to put some limits on the reach of the market. The forces of equality received a great boost with social citizenship and a rough balance of power between equality and class was temporarily achieved; it appeared that status equality (if not class equality) had finally found its institutional bearings. This was the highpoint of social democracy and Keynesian "mixed economies," a period that presents a challenging coda to Henry Maine's famous character-ization of the transition from "status to contract." In Marshall's idealized correction, the story of modernity no longer ends with contractual hegem-ony. Instead, social citizenship achieves the "invasion of contract by [equal] status" (Marshall 1992: 28). To invade, however, is not to conquer, and even social citizenship does not displace or eliminate contracts. Contractualism, markets, property rights (and the inequality they generate), and individual liberties continue to be essential elements of modern citizenship. But neither is contractualism able to rebuff its invader completely. Instead, the two exist in a condition of permanent contestation. In a kind of "return of the repressed," with the triumph of social citizenship, the universal and non-contractual precepts of equality and mutuality are positioned as counter-vailing powers against the expansionist drives and inegalitarian outcomes of the market.

It is easy to forget that Marshall's social inclusionary citizenship regime has never been an empirical reality; it is only an ideal type. The advantage of establishing an ideal type is that it allows you to compare citizenship regimes by measuring the distance between their actual arrangements and the standard set by that model. While there has never been any actually existing citizenship regime that achieves this empirical standard, there certainly are some that have been closer than others. The underdeveloped overly privatized American welfare state – roughly spanning the period of the New Deal through the Great Society while trailing off in the 1970s until its official demise with the 1996 welfare reform bill – is most commonly and correctly invoked as representing the furthest point away from the ideal socially inclusive citizenship regime that can be represented by a continuum bookended by democratic citizenship on one end, and a market fundamentalist regime on the other (cf. Fraser and Gordon 1997, 1998; Handler 2004, 2006; Katz 2001; O'Connor *et al.* 1999). One potential pitfall of the ideal-type method, however, is to confuse what is merely a label – a "social inclusionary" citizenship regime – for the actuality of a single uncontested ethos. Civil societies and political cultures always have multiple competing and usually contradictory public discourses, narratives, and institutional traditions. At any given moment it is the proportional dominance that each one holds in relation to the others that determines the character of the overall political culture. To associate the ideal-typical democratic citizenship regime with an ethos of solidarity, reciprocity, inclusion, and equality is only to say that in this kind of regime, the discourse of social inclusion has achieved (at least temporary) discursive dominance over its competitors in *naming* the political culture as a whole. It does not claim to represent an accurate empirical description of that political culture.

Racial domination, inequality and exclusion under an inclusionary citizenship

Of the many reasons for the distance between the actuality of American liberal citizenship and the ideal, perhaps none is more important than the competing traditions of what Rogers Smith (1993, 1999) calls the "inegalitarian ascriptive forms of Americanism" and Arendt (1979) characterizes as the "merely given," namely the illiberal exclusions from full rights-bearing membership in civil society and the polity based on race, gender, ethnicity, and nativism.

Of all these exclusions, most significant was the fate of African-Americans during the New Deal – the greatest American manifestation of Marshall's version of social citizenship. Katznelson (2005) gives us a chilling analysis of how social protections and retirement security for white males in the workforce was gained at the expense of African-Americans. In the 1930s, thanks to their disproportionate political power and their successful bullying, the Southern Congressional Democrats were able to force the federal government to accept their racial exclusions and the legalized terrors of Jim Crow. Succumbing to Southern opposition against an anti-lynching law, for example, was the price that Roosevelt paid to provide white Americans with the great social welfare and insurance programs that made up the core of the

New Deal – programs to insure old age, make good jobs available, acquire economic security, build assets, and gain middle-class status. All of these, according to Katznelson, constituted a "massive transfer of quite specific privileges to white Americans" (2005: 23). The worst offenses were inscribed into "racially laden" categories of work that were made ineligible for some of the most important New Deal policies (Lieberman 1998). For example, farm workers and maids constituted more than 60 percent of the black labor force in the 1930s and nearly 75 percent of those employed in the South. Yet agricultural and domestic workers were explicitly disqualified from the new laws that created modern unions, set minimum wages, and regulated the hours of work, and also from Social Security until the 1950s (Katznelson 2005: 22). Southern Democrats also prevented Congress from linking antidiscrimination provisions to a spectrum of new federally funded social programs, including community health services, school lunches, and hospital construction grants. Sympathetic to the cause, the *Pittsburgh Courier* summed up the situation in their editorial explanation for why they decided not to endorse FDR in his third run for president: "the Southern-dominated administration has worked assiduously to establish color discrimination and segregation as a policy of the Federal government, and to a distressing extent it has succeeded."[28] In sum, what Katznelson calls "affirmative action for whites" was achieved on the backs of African-Americans. Their exclusion from the New Deal's social rights was the deal cut with the South to achieve a new social regime that exclusively benefited white, mostly male, Americans.

With the arrival of the Great Society in the 1960s, many of the more egregious aspects of the New Deal antiblack policies came under scrutiny and began to be corrected through civil rights legislation and antidiscrimination Supreme Court decisions. But these improvements hardly erased the deep legacy of exclusion and inequality that the New Deal had so callously reinforced. Indeed the most that one could say is that in the 1960s African-Americans were able to move from complete exclusion to "merely" unequal membership. In many places, native people were not even recognized as persons in the 1960s, and to this day equal rights for women have never been constitutionally ratified. These deep exclusions should remind us that a truly socially inclusive citizenship regime in America has never been an empirical reality. Indeed, if we take the experience of exclusion seriously, we no longer can categorize the

---

[28] Cited in Katznelson (2005: 26–7).

New Deal, the GI bill, or other big US welfare initiatives under the unambiguous rubric of inclusive and equitable. Rather, these are all evidence of the continuous presence of multiple traditions – the illiberal primordial race-based political culture coexisting with the liberal egalitarian tradition in the peculiarly American story of citizenship. Recouping these practices of exclusion based on the fixed identities of race and gender forces us to qualify radically Marshall's optimistic reading of citizenship's progression, at least with respect to the United States. Clearly, Marshall's socially inclusive citizenship regime can be only an ideal. The actual outcome of the contest between citizenship and contract will always be indeterminate, contingent on the broader configuration of political, legal, ideational, and cultural forces and institutions, and especially on the varying powers of the state and the success or failure of social and labor movements. The historical dynamic Marshall recounts is only that; there is no justification to theorize in broader terms an inevitable progression from civil to political to social citizenship rights. These must remain, in the end, normative ideals.

From noncontractualism to the contractualization of citizenship

In the United States the invasion of the market by the forces of equality was not to last. Today, with the wind of market fundamentalism at its back, the principles and practices of contractualization continue to expand with all too little resistance. The contractualization of citizenship is the term I use to describe the process by which the government's relationship with its citizenry changes from noncontractualism to contractual quid pro quo market exchange. Noncontractual citizenship circulates rights and obligations among and between citizens and the government as they move through civil society, markets, and the state. With the large qualification of race and gender exclusion, the reciprocities of noncontractual citizenship include the kinds of programs embodied in the ideals of the New Deal and the Great Society, e.g. public health insurance, unemployment and disability insurance, Social Security, social provisioning, Medicare, protection from and rescue after natural disasters (FEMA). In return for these varying kinds and degrees of protection (e.g. against crime), benefits (e.g. education, the G. I. bill), and rights (e.g. voting), citizens are responsible for any number of duties, ranging from obeying the law to paying taxes, to serving on juries, to serving in the military, and so on. In return for these "entitlements," citizens qua workers are obligated to contribute specific taxes that the government putatively puts in reserve for when the entitlements come due.

Some call this circulatory process of rights and duties a citizenship "contract."[29] However, there is no contractual exchange in the strict market equivalence sense of the term, since the rights and obligations are not in a quid pro quo contractual relationship to each other. Current workers pay for current Social Security recipients, and the government actually uses the money "saved" for future entitlement programs for current budget demands. What distinguishes citizenship relationships from contractual ones is that there is no presumption of market or quantitative equivalence between the rights/benefits/protections on the one side, and the duties/responsibilities/obligations on the other. Instead, it is the citizens who are (ideal-typically) fully equal in their degree of moral recognition as fellow members of the political community. While we are by law required to respond to a jury summons, for example, it is nonetheless a diffuse kind of obligation which I may or may not ever even be called upon to fulfill. You do not get to be more or less of a citizen (except in a vague normative cultural sense) depending on whether or not you are called upon to serve on a jury. Nor is there a calculable exchange rate between the property taxes I pay for the public school system in the city where I have no children enrolled and the free public education I may or may not have received too many years ago to want to remember. Citizenship entails an obligatory circulation between rights and duties, but it is an exchange only in the metaphoric sense. Indeed it is precisely the noncontractual nature of the citizenship ethic that, for Durkheim (1984), stamps it with the quality of the "sacred," as something to be fiercely insulated from the "profanity" of quid pro quo market valuation.

Defining the ethic of citizenship as noncontractual can easily be misunderstood to suggest that citizenship relationships preclude the presence of contracts and market exchange. On the contrary, contract has never been a stranger to modern conceptions of citizenship, as the right to enter into private contracts is one of the foundational rights of the civil freedoms endowed by citizenship (Marshall 1992). But while they are constitutive of the citizenship ethic, contractual rights and practices occupy only one place and space among many other rights and practices that comprise the larger canvas of citizenship. Citizenship as a whole is not reduced to the presence of contractual right. It is only when this single right to engage in market contracts starts to expand and imperialize to the point where it occupies the entire canvas that citizenship inevitably

---

[29] For an alternative view that identifies citizenship as a contract even in its premarket form, see the brilliant work of Cowen (2008).

becomes pathologized. When citizenship has been conquered by contract, market fundamentalism has triumphed.

Recall that in the domain of the market, in contrast to the circulation of rights and duties characteristic of citizenship, commodities are produced for exchange (buying and selling) and prices are set not by moral obligation or by social need but by price mechanisms that are, theoretically at least, internal to the market. Vast numbers of these exchanges take place and each is underwritten by an implicit or explicit contractual agreement carried out on the "basis of quid pro quo obligations at a mutually agreed upon exchange rate" (Harriss-White 1996: 29, cited in Leys 2003: 241; see also Lindblom 2001). A contract, in the rights and duties of citizenship, involves an exchange of goods or services that must be equivalent in quantitative value between persons of whom there is no presumption of equivalence or equality. This is the meaning of quid pro quo – an exchange of equal market value. Contractualization aims to transform the noncontractualism of citizenship relationships to one of market-driven contractual quid pro quo exchange.

The transformative implications of the contractualization of citizenship are enormous. In a noncontractual relationship, as long as a citizen meets the required obligations, she is presumed an equal member of equal worth regardless of the market value attached to her citizenly responsibilities. But when citizenship has been contractualized, failing to provide a good or service of equivalent market value in exchange for what is now the *privilege* of citizenship, results in a reduction of the moral worth of the citizen. And depending on the degree and frequency and quality of such failures to meet contractual criteria, there will be an increasing refusal to recognize the citizen as deserving of membership altogether in the political and social community. When citizenship morphs into contractual morality the quid of government protection (e.g. protection from the scourge of unemployment or natural disasters) is only given in return for the quo of something of market value. Based on this Hobbesian-inflected conception of the social contract, people with nothing to offer or exchange in the way of useful labor or personal assets – the poor, the very young, the infirm, the severely disabled – have no rights because they have no worth; they become rightless and excluded. In a market society with increasing inequality of wealth and resources, the contractualization of citizenship sets into motion a mechanism leading inexorably to the social exclusion of many, and ultimately to a dystopian citizenship regime.

Like market fundamentalism, the work of contractualization is discursive, ideological, and facilitated by conversion narratives. But its sights are nonetheless set on institutional and legal conquests using legal interventions and rulings, techniques and technologies by which the institutions and organizations of social citizenship can be conquered, converted, transformed, or disrupted from primarily public and citizenship-oriented civil obligations to contractually conditional ones. The mandate is to remake the public institutions, services, and insurance policies of the social state from noncontractual foundations based on rights and responsibilities between government and its citizens into market-driven ones.

The contractualization of citizenship can take various forms, such as privatizing basic public needs like health care or retirement plans, which under a democratic inclusive citizenship regime would be either partially or fully provided under the protection of the government or a corporation. The drive to privatization is expressed in the movement to privatize Social Security (by individuals investing on their own in the stock market) and in the pressure to move to a system of individual health insurance contracts with private insurance companies, uncoupled from the workplace. In my view, the outcome will always be predictable. The numbers of people unable to afford private insurance, or just as likely denied insurance based on an "preexisting medical condition" (such as age) will increase, extending the consequences of poor health far beyond the poor up the ladder to the falling middle classes.

The paradigmatic case is the privatization of the employment structure, from government-assisted unemployment and retraining to personal responsibility for acquiring human capital. Perhaps the apotheosis of the new contractualization of citizenship is in the new workfare contract that forces the poor to accept any kind of work, no matter how degrading or low-paid, in exchange for the basic claims of citizenship. In many ways, according to Guy Standing, welfare-to-work represents "the end of the century of the laboring man."

It began with calls for the *rights of labor* – the right to improved social status, dignity, security and autonomy. It was a call for freedom *from* labor. By mid-century, in the wake of the Depression and a world war, there was the demand for the *rights to labor*, seeking to ennoble the drudgery of being in a job and hinging everything on "Full Employment", which was the full-time employment of men. The century is ending with the libertarians and others advocating and introducing policies to strengthen the *duty to labor*, the state-enforced obligation to labor to obtain entitlement to be treated as a citizen and receive state benefits. In the process, governments are making it harder to survive without labor, without being in a job. (Standing 1999: 337)

The problem with this new punitive *duty to labor* regime is in its collision with globalization and the restructuring of the economy more generally. There simply are no longer available the number and kinds of jobs to match the demands of citizenship's new contractualism. As I discuss below, moreover, the same process of restructuring means that the acquisition of human capital so favored by economists as the *deus ex machina* for unemployment no longer guarantees the right to earn (Bernstein 2007). As a result, many unable to succeed in the new citizenship regime of contractualization and workfare will fall completely outside the circle of any claims to membership (see Handler 2004). They become superfluous to a market-dominated society. In a culture marked by the contractualization of citizenship, unemployment becomes contractual malfeasance.

To effect this radical transformation in citizenship entails a series of practical and ideational conversions from the ideal-typical ethos of citizenship to one of contractual morality – conversions, which empirically do not flip from one to the other but which in fact change along a continuum:

- from an ethos of citizenship rights based in civil society membership and inclusion, to rights and inclusion made conditional upon market-driven quid pro quo contractual obligations;
- from a triadic balance of power in which the social state protects citizens-in-civil-society against full exposure to the market, into a dyadic instrument of unbalanced power pitting an alliance of state and market against individuals – now bereft of both state protection and membership in civil society;
- from the individual as citizen with moral worth based on human recognition and membership, to the individual as a measure of human capital whose worth is conditional on her market value;
- from civil society as the ontological site of individual identity, to the "death of the social" ("there's no such thing as 'society,'" said Margaret Thatcher) and the collapse of the civil sphere into a market auxiliary in the form of social capital;
- from the democratic rule of law, to the "laws" of markets;[30]

---

[30] This is not to suggest that the "rule of law" ever represented a pure and impartial entity that existed outside of the social and political, nor that we are witnessing for the first time the "contamination" of neutral law by the market. Clearly, the law has always been deeply implicated with social and economic power. Rather, I am suggesting that it is the *normative ideal* of equal justice independent of market power that is transforming into a normative ideal that links liberty and justice to the free market model. On the complex meanings of the "rule of law," see, for example, Cass (2003), Fitzpatrick (1992), Karst (1989), and Tamanaha (2004). I thank Diana Yoon for discussing this point with me and directing me to these references.

- from government- and corporation-based assumption of social risks, to "personal responsibility" for the inevitable risks of modern capitalism;
- from the boundaries of inclusive citizenship marked primarily by nation-state borders, to *internally* exclusive borders within nation-states, which establish internal divides between now stateless and right-less citizens and the rest of the "personally responsible" population;
- from the dominance of sociology and social knowledge, to the rule of economics and market-modeled knowledge of society and human agency (see Frank 2007b; Levitt and Dubner 2005);
- from a political culture that allows different degrees of membership (e.g. "second-class citizenship" for pre-civil-rights era African-Americans) to one divided between full members and those peoples expelled altogether from any level of political or social membership;
- from the struggle against commodification, to a new employment structure in which there are no jobs available to commoditize a growing surplus population.

Marketizing and contractualizing New Orleans

I turn now to exploring the role that market fundamentalism and the contractualization of citizenship as general phenomena contributed to the specific crisis of Hurricane Katrina. At the beginning of this discussion, in considering the combination of factors at work, I posed two questions: (1) how to explain the failures, ineptitude and utter incompetence of all levels of government?; and (2) how it was possible that thousands of New Orleanians were left behind, left alone to face deadly flooding while the majority of the population took safe refuge outside the city. As I have already indicated, the problems that led to Katrina are deeper and of longer duration than can be explained by market fundamentalism or contractualization alone. No proposition makes sense without considering the legacy of chattel slavery, more than six decades of legal exclusion, a hypocritical New Deal that worsened the "old deal" of race-based exclusion, and a stigmatizing system of welfare that was stamped with the aura of a young black pregnant female (Katznelson 2005).[31] Nonetheless, if there is validity to my argument that much of the fault lies with the noncontractual bonds of citizenship being forcefully displaced over the last four decades by the contractual conditionality of

---

[31] See especially Dyson (2006) and Powell *et al.* (2006).

market exchange, when coupled with the story of racial exclusion in the South, my argument should be able to provide some convincing answers to these questions.

Starving the beast – the era of big (market-driven) government is back

First, the state. "Failure of government" at all levels is common parlance in explaining the slow, inadequate, and negligent response to the hurricane. But evaluating government performance cannot be done using abstract assumptions but by whether the performance fails or succeeds according to a particular yardstick of standards and values. Judging from media reports and public opinion polls, most Americans were personally outraged by the government's failures. But however morally indefensible we may believe its conduct to have been, failure can be ascribed to the government *if* and *only if* it counts among its values and principles the citizenship ideals of shared risk and solidarity, and the belief that it is the government's job to protect and rescue its citizens irrespective of their personal behavior or ascribed moral worth. These are not, as we know well by now, the standards and values of market fundamentalism; indeed, they represent everything the ownership society and the "personal responsibility crusade" aims to overturn. However counterintuitive it may seem, then, the administration's ineffectiveness during (and since) the Katrina crisis is evidence *not* of failure but of just how *successful* market fundamentalism has been: in its determination to restructure the institutions of governance along market lines; to make clear that the government is no longer in the business of rewarding those who fail to take personal responsibility for their own well-being; and in its reorganization of incentives to forcefully "dissuade" people from seeking help from the state and the public sphere. The message that was not conveyed in words, but in (in)action, was that whatever minimal human rights to life and livelihood that a poor African-American community might have once believed were their rightful due as American citizens were no longer available. The community had become expendable.

"Starving the beast" is the Heritage Foundation's contribution to market fundamentalism's linguistic arsenal.[32] It is a tribal code that prescribes cutting taxes so much that the ensuing budget deficit

---

[32] See the Heritage Foundation website (www.heritage.org) for the fullest elaboration of this strategy. See also Krugman (2003b).

inexorably "starves" the government of its capacity to continue funding "discretionary" social programs, regulative agencies, and whatever protective institutions of social insurance and the minimal social state may still be in place from the New Deal and the Great Society. At first glance the "starve the beast" metaphor appears to be a new market fundamentalist rhetorical flourish on conservatism's age-old "anti-big government" mantra, which was best expressed by two of Ronald Reagan's most quotable quips: "The nine scariest words in America: 'We're the government and we're here to help you' "; "The government is not the solution to the problem; it *is* the problem." But market fundamentalism's narrative of antistatism is not a new version of "trickle-down economics," a conservative strategy popular during the Reagan years that focused on shrinking the government and cutting taxes for the rich. Both the Reagan and the current G. W. Bush administrations' unprecedented budget deficits make clear just how deceptive is market fundamentalism's antistatist discourse, which includes rhetorical excesses such as Grover Norquist's famous exhortation to shrink the state so much that it will be small enough to be "washed down the bathtub drain."[33] In fact, market fundamentalists do not object to the existence of big government per se, but only to the specific use to which "big government" is put in servicing the New Deal and Great Society social programs. Indeed, just a glance at recent transformations in the tax codes, or in the Medicare drug policy, reveals that the government is market fundamentalism's necessary best friend. The state is the critical instrument for appropriating power. Under market fundamentalism government institutions once dedicated to social, regulative, and redistributive policies have been steadily conquered and reorganized to support marketization and contractualization. So while public conversion narratives still rail against the "the problem of big government," what market fundamentalist regimes *actually* do is use big government as the solution for their marketizing ambitions.

The new narrative is instead intended to mislead and distract from the spectacular growth of the American government under the conservative administrations of Reagan and especially Bush II.[34] Part of the confusion stems from the conflation into one of what are actually two separate institutional complexes of the state – one, the executive-driven military and security state; the other the bureaucratic organization of government

---

[33] Norquist (2004).
[34] This growth has also been carefully organized to aid and abet the war on terror and the systematic reduction of individual liberties and civil rights.

agencies designed to regulate commerce through market oversight, to protect food, drugs, and the environment, to levy taxes, and above all to administer the social programs that fall under the rubric of the "social state," including Social Security, Medicare, welfare, etc. "Starving the beast" always refers to the second social state; the first, by contrast, is always the object of bipartisan fiscal beneficence.

Even if market fundamentalism has taken this distinction between political rhetoric and actually existing market-driven government to new heights, it would be a mistake to think of even "big-government conservatism's" commitment to conquering and enlarging the state as a new twist of strategy. Just as nineteenth-century market fundamentalists understood that the road to laissez-faire was paved by active state intervention and government power, today's Washington lawyers, lobbyists, judges, and party apparatchiks know all too well that the road to market fundamentalism is paved by market-driven government (Block and Somers 1984; Polanyi 2001). So invested are they in the deception, however, that when it comes to revealing this secret, apparently it takes a brave pundit to speak this truth about power. For rather than a big Republican party luminary, it was simply the relatively unknown Joseph Goulden (1972) from the conservative think tank Accuracy in Media, who observed that "the Republicans" have over the years "directed a counterrevolution ... Their mission was not to destroy the New Deal, and its successor reform acts, but to conquer them, and to leave their structures intact so they could be transformed into instruments for the amassing of monopolistic corporate power."[35] Goulden illuminates the hypocrisy in the triumph of an antigovernment narrative on the part of an administration that created in Homeland Security a bureaucracy more bloated than even the entirety of the Great Society's social state. As a central part of the state bureaucracy that has been almost entirely outsourced to the private sector, Homeland Security is a good example of not only market-driven governance but also governance-driven marketization. Clearly, big-government conservatism is bigger than ever. The myth of antistatism dissolves against the reality of the market-conquered state (Block 1997; Kuttner 1997; Leys 2003; Mitchell 2002; Sunstein 2004).

FEMA as moral hazard

Count the hollowed-out condition of FEMA as a prime example of how a government agency performs when a state has been successfully starved of the necessary resources for its citizenship functions and reoccupied

[35] Cited in Frank (2006).

instead for market-driven aims. FEMA's performance was so horrific that it prompted the New Orleans *Times-Picayune* to proclaim its failings "so extravagant, outrageous [that] one wanted to say fabulous except that they were also deadly" (Horne 2006: 88). After decades of what can only be called rather dicey attempts to produce a federal disaster agency, FEMA was created under the Carter administration in 1979 in response to the pleas of individual state governors, and as a former governor he well understood that local resources are not equipped to cope with large national disasters. In its original mandate, then, FEMA was never intended to be the agency of last resort, to be mobilized only after local efforts proved inadequate for disaster relief; it was designed to protect its citizens in the *first* instance.[36]

The realization of FEMA's citizenship norms was short-lived. While the radically conservative John Birch Society attacked FEMA at its founding as a covert attempt to create an authoritarian national state, it was the Reagan administration that quickly turned what the President called a "socialist welfare money-drain" into a patronage post for large campaign contributors almost entirely without experience in disaster relief.[37] There was an exceptional period in the 1990s of rather heroic achievements under Clinton's appointee, James Lee Witt. But beginning in 2001 President G. W. Bush once again began starving FEMA of funds targeted for rescue and emergency management, and he turned it into a haven for corruption and business cronyism. Contrary to Carter's original mandate to keep FEMA a completely independent agency, moreover, he essentially buried it under the jurisdiction of the bureaucratic behemoth of the new terrorism-focused Department of Homeland Security. Undoubtedly, there was an advantage to FEMA's new low profile, as it masked the agency's increased level of patronage.

In addition to "starving the beast," the ideational weapon of choice in the conquest of FEMA and its conversion into an instrument of contractualization has been a variation on the perversity thesis. In keeping with the dominant role that private insurance plays in market fundamentalism's vision, the affiliated idea is that of "moral hazard," a term invented by insurance agencies to refer to the "morally compromising" incentives they believe are built into all government insurance policies. The assertion is that when people are insured by the government (i.e. FEMA)

---

[36] On the origins of FEMA, see Haddow *et al.* (2008).

[37] Thanks to Allen Hunter for the information about the John Birch Society. In response to FEMA's performance during a Reagan-era South Carolina disaster, then Senator Fritz Hollings lambasted FEMA employees as the "sorriest bunch of jackasses I've ever known" (cited in Brinkley 2006: 247).

against costs that they could avoid (in theory) by exercising more personal responsibility (e.g. by not living in New Orleans), insurance acts as a perverse incentive to engage in exactly the risky behavior they have insured themselves against – i.e. "choosing" to live in cities like New Orleans that are hurricane-prone. Proponents of the moral hazard discourse rhetorically ask why anyone would take the trouble to move to safer locations when they know the government (aka the taxpayers) funds an agency dedicated to nothing but rescuing them from disasters and restoring their property. To these critics of social insurance, by encouraging expectations of entitlements from a "nanny" government, FEMA embodies the worst kind of moral hazard and supports perverse incentives at the expense of the vast majority of responsible taxpayers. FEMA is the perfect scapegoat; after all, from the perspective of market fundamentalists, FEMA is the embodiment of the moral hazards that created expectations of caretaking and rescue, thus robbing Americans of self-initiative, independence, and personal responsibility (Hurd 2005; Kotkin 2006; Poranski 2005; Tracinski 2005). Indeed, the discourse of contractualizing citizenship demonizes the institutions of citizenship across the board as moral hazards: in the absence of market incentives, all forms of social insurance can be accused of harboring perversity.

To break the addiction to this kind of entitlement mentality, market fundamentalists developed what Hacker (2006) dubs "the Personal Responsibility Crusade," a public relations campaign aimed at shaming people into avoiding association with public insurance or government assistance. Its motivating message? "Government should get out of the way and let people succeed or fail on their own" (2006: 52). Most of this is being accomplished through the "great risk shift," which, in Hacker's (2006) terms, entails nothing less than an "assault on American jobs, families, health care, and retirement" by government and corporations. Under market-driven governance, the state assumes only a conditional relationship to individuals and families, now forced to become parties to the marketized contractualization of newly commoditized public services.[38] To market fundamentalists a well-funded, bureaucratically autonomous, and effective mechanism of social insurance such as FEMA entails nothing less than a menace to the goal of making individuals personally responsible for their own safety and emergency management (Horne 2006). Thus the "plan" delivered to the vulnerable population of New Orleans was, in the words

---

[38] It is now the government that exclusively sells flood insurance, and for a high price, without which a mortgage cannot be acquired for homes in government-certified flood zones.

of one journalist: "In the event of a major hurricane, you're on your own" (Nolan 2005: 1, cited in Brezina 2008: 2). This Orwellian construal of Katrina would surely have the effect of dispelling ideational or cultural doubts about the virtues of "personal responsibility" and of teaching the poor not to look to the government for rescue.

All too transparent were the crocodile tears and begrudging apologetics the Bush administration eventually conjured up for the clearly expendable population of New Orleans. As in so many other aspects of market fundamentalism, the implications of FEMA's performance are as instructive as they are harsh: some (disposable, surplus) human lives may have to be sacrificed to this morality tale, but the benefits of teaching this "lesson" outrun the costs. Political embarrassment and a touch of bad press are a small price to pay for how much the Katrina debacle bolstered the market fundamentalist narrative that social insurance and public protection rest on morally hazardous foundations. As the visual media spotlighted ever more stark images of abandonment, the interpretative voice of market fundamentalism controlled much of the public narrative that "explained" the meaning of it all: however well-meaning in intent, promises of emergency management no less than welfare entitlements put into place a set of incentives that lead inevitably to *more* – not less – of the very disasters FEMA was intended to solve. Whenever the government "meddles" in the natural workings of markets, incentives become perverse. The failure of FEMA to respond to Katrina demonstrates how marketization serves as structural disciplinarian in the crusade for personal responsibility.

In short, as fraught with cognitive dissonance as it may be, FEMA's abandonment of thousands of poor African-Americans reveals how successful the contractualization of citizenship has been. Rather than a failed response to the hurricane, FEMA's behavior marked a great success in the transformation of the social state from a body of institutions organized by the ethic of citizenship to one conquered by the marketization of citizenship. To wit: the government that produced this hapless FEMA and betrayed New Orleans was no longer the government of FDR and the Great Society. Nor was it a government structured to meet the public and moral obligations of protection that strong citizenship regimes in social democracies impose on the polity. Nor was it a state positioned more or less to accommodate the demands and expectations put forward by strong social movements from civil society – what Polanyi (2001) calls the "counter movements" for social protection that act as countervailing powers to unchecked market forces, or what Alexander (2006) calls the social movements for "civic repair."

To be sure, neither were the actual New Deal and Great Society administrations the same as the mythologies surrounding the governments of FDR and the Great Society; in reality, the New Deal especially fails to live up to its image, since it institutionalized as many new varieties of race and gender inequalities as there were programs of redress for the typical male employee. Still, however imperfect and unrealized were the quasi-social democratic regimes of the New Deal and the Great Society, they nonetheless represented an ethic of addressing and ameliorating the inevitable insecurities and risks associated with modern capitalism.

By contrast, the FEMA of late August 2005 embodied the tattered, bedraggled, market-driven, and corrupted skeleton of a once regulative social state, now barely hobbling along after almost forty years of regulatory degradation, privatization, tax codes shifting economic burdens from wealth to work, and manichaean rhetorical vilification by market fundamentalism's conversion narratives of "romancing the market, starving the state" (see chapter 7 below; Block 1997). When a state agency has been conquered and degraded (by cronyism and corruption) to the point where it cannot carry out even minimal protective functions, then not only does it signal the success of market-driven governance; it also signals that more Katrinas are inevitable.

The left-behind: civil society and internal borders of social exclusion

However accurate my explanation for government behavior during the hurricane, a full understanding of the Katrina tragedy still requires an answer to the second question – why were so many people left behind to face a deadly hurricane on their own? The dominant conservative answer to this question shows just how influential the perversity thesis continues to be even a decade after welfare reform. Even by market fundamentalist standards, this argument seems especially heartless when applied to the context of Hurricane Katrina. It's called "blaming the victim" or, in more academic terms, the welfare dependency theory, and it goes as follows: years of welfare dependency under Aid to Families with Dependent Children (AFDC) created a class of psychologically and characterologically damaged people with perverse "entitlement mentalities" and a "culture of dependency" on the government (Somers and Block 2005). Nor was it a new argument reserved for conservatives. Readers may be familiar with Daniel Patrick Moynihan, the long-term Democratic senator from New York, who was the first to put the "cultural failure of the black family" on the public agenda. His analysis of the "degrading culture of dependency" put blame squarely on the failure of black men to perform patriarchal gender roles, especially that of married man. This still informs both liberal and conservative discourse and policy today.

The Katrina-inflected version of the story alleges that even after the 1996 national welfare reform bill, the poor of New Orleans had managed to manipulate the system so that few recipients were actually kicked off the rolls and forced to go to work, thus further entrenching a culture of entitlement. According to the welfare-dependency thesis, these New Orleanians were "so dependent on others that they [became] powerless and unable to care for themselves ... having no responsibilities [they] look[ed] to the federal government for survival ... waiting on *others* to behave responsibly" (Poranski 2005). It was a population so drugged by "the narcotic of welfare" that they were unable and/or unwilling to be self-reliant in the face of impending disaster. The very existence of FEMA exponentially worsens this attitude of entitlement by reinforcing expectations that the government would take care of them, would rescue them, would do for them what they had long ago forgotten how to do for themselves (Hurd 2005; Kotkin 2006; Poranski 2005; Tracinski 2005). From this perspective, the crowds crammed in the Superdome should have been "a dispeller of illusions, a revealer of awful truths ... Honest observers will recognize that this natural disaster ... was set by the man-made disaster of a counterproductive welfare state" (Kotkin 2006: 29).

Despite the appeal of this theory to those who sat comfortably through the hurricane on dry and well-heeled ground, it has the inconvenience of being contradicted by the facts. Thanks to the survey of Hurricane Katrina evacuees (Brodie *et al.* 2006) we now know that with regard to employment status and "dependency-relevant" characteristics (indicators of motivation, initiative, self-reliance, etc.) there was little difference between those who evacuated and those left behind.[39] The data show that of the survivors housed in the Houston Astrodome 66 percent had been employed before the storm and 52 percent were employed full-time (Brezina 2008: 19). No wonder they demonstrated "independence, self-reliance" and "high levels of self-reliance and initiative," according to the survey. One would hope this would put an end to this new twist on the old canard of welfare dependency and the perversity thesis. It is unlikely to

[39] Taken between September 9 and September 12, 2005 from New Orleanians living in Houston's Astrodome and designed by the *Washington Post*, the Kaiser Family Foundation, and the Harvard School of Public Health (Brodie *et al.* 2006). For the wealth of eye-opening data compiled by this survey, see the superb introduction to it by Brezina (2008).

do so, however, as it is an essential element in the narrative of contractualizing citizenship.

By contrast, most sociological analyses of the tragedy of those left behind in Katrina's wake point to the culprits of race and class. This is with good reason, as according to the Brodie *et al.* (2006) survey, those unable to evacuate in advance of the storm were 93 percent African-American, and in comparison to New Orleans residents overall they were disproportionately from lower-income households (despite so much full-time employment), and had less education (Brezina 2008: 15). Without automobiles or transportation expenses, they simply did not have the means to evacuate (2008: 20).[40] My argument builds from these analyses, but adds a twist. It seems to me that why so many African-Americans were abandoned to Hurricane Katrina can in part be accounted for by racism and class prejudice. But the problem with making these the exclusive culprits is that these scourges have been constants in the lives of black communities since America's inception. We all recognize, however, that something qualitatively more terrible was at work in those scenes of abandonment and terror, something even more than the inflictions of racism's second-class citizenship. This was an entire population being excluded from the rights of citizenship and civil society. Even more, however, what the world witnessed in those horrific weeks was the denial of moral recognition, and hence the wide-scale violation of human rights.

In light of racism's ugly legacy, it is clear that market fundamentalism cannot alone be blamed for so many New Orleanians being abandoned to fend for themselves while the rest of the city evacuated. But when it converged with the fabric of the long and deeply entrenched wrongs of American racism, market fundamentalism inflicted something qualitatively different, and even worse. It robbed a people of their due recognition. It was this that truly distinguished the left-behind from the pre-storm evacuees: well before the storm they had long suffered the invisibility characteristic of a socially excluded surplus population unrecognized as moral equals by the mainstream of civil society. This was the common thread that knit together all of the left-behind – primarily African-Americans, women and children, but also the old, the sick, the disabled, the mentally impaired, the young, the hospitalized, the isolated, the

---

[40] Because of the proportion of the black male population that is incarcerated on a semi-permanent basis, female-headed families make up the vast majority of the poor (Gault *et al.* 2005; Jones-DeWeever and Hartman 2006). I am very grateful to Tim Brezina for allowing me to cite this survey which he reviews in his then unpublished manuscript (now Brezina 2008). His manuscript contributed greatly to this and the previous paragraph.

homeless, the car-less. These were the rightless, the stateless, and the socially excluded who existed on the wrong side of deeply entrenched internal borders – borders not at the edges of nation-states designed to keep out noncitizens, but boundaries deep within the heartland of the nation, where those who are well served by the market are protected from those who aren't (Balibar 2004b; Bosniak 2006).

Social exclusion

As I discuss in chapter 3 of this volume, the term *social exclusion* began in Europe as a way to describe and theorize poverty by placing it concep-tually in a larger social structural context, and by viewing the poor in relationship to society as a whole. Standard approaches to poverty look at individual or family resources in isolation and designate as poor those whose total income falls below a statistical threshold. Long-held pre-Malthusian social understandings of poverty squarely laid the blame on structural systemic problems, such as trade downturns leading to widespread unemployment, or in distorted distribution methods, as Amartya Sen (1982) has so importantly observed. On the basis of this kind of structurally induced poverty, a recognition of the social right to livelihood made poor relief or (later) social welfare available for the under- or unemployed. This was of course the same causal logic invoked in both the New Deal and the Great Society social programs for relief.

Today, economists have "captured" the poverty turf, and social prob-lems are increasingly explained by economic models rooted in the rational utility-maximizing agent. As a result, the classical sociological analysis of poverty has been turned on its head. The market model focuses not on systemic problems but on the individual agent or family, and identifies personal behavioral, cultural, and moral failings such as dependency, sexual promiscuity, and outright laziness (see especially O'Connor 2002). According to the logic of market analysis, these behaviors are complemented, even induced, by the perverse incentives built into the very system of welfare that is supposed to be the cure for poverty. In a direct echo of Malthus, market fundamentalists argue that the "cure" is really the cause, and make the mantra that "welfare causes poverty" (rather than vice versa) the leading banner of the idea-tional assault on social welfare that culminated in the 1996 welfare reform bill.

The concept of social exclusion bypasses this focus on the perverse attributes either of social welfare institutions, or of individuals and families (characterological, cultural, or material) – attributes which allegedly distinguish them from of the rest of us. It also moves beyond the classical sociological model, which still focuses on the individual impact of poverty in terms of a series of socioeconomic deficits. Instead, it concentrates on the consequences and reproduction of poverty in relational and societal terms, namely a life of exclusion from the mainstream of society as a whole, which in turn precludes recognition as fellow humans who inhabit the same social and moral universe. Even more than C. Wright Mills' (1959) famous injunction to look at personal troubles as public problems, social exclusion stretches the meaning of poverty from a focus on either the socioeconomic or the characterological pathologies of individuals to the lack of recognition by others as moral equals due the same level of respect and dignity as the rest of the community, and treated according to the same standards and values. Fifty years ago, Marshall captured this broad deeply social understanding when he argued that poverty and inequality must be addressed not by income transfers but by a form of citizenship that he called social citizenship – which refers less to any specific entitlement or social benefit than to the foundational socially necessary right of membership in society and recognition by others. Marshall writes:

By social citizenship, I mean the whole range from the right to a modicum of economic welfare and security to the *right to share to the full in the social heritage* and to live the life of a civilized being *according to the standards prevailing in the society* ... which in turn means a claim to be *accepted as full members of the society*, that is, *as citizens.* (Marshall 1992: 6, 8, emphasis added)

Marshall goes on to describe social rights as "necessary requisites of civil freedom" (1992: 16). In other words, civil rights, with which human rights are usually associated, are already dependent on prior full inclusion according to the standards of civil society, foremost of which he identifies as universal rights to quality health care and public education – rights that endow the kind of equal social recognition that means-tested poverty programs can never do. The implications are clear: if social *membership* is the solution, then social exclusion is the problem. Deep and durable inequality entails deep and durable exclusion, which in turn means nothing less than the collective loss of the right to have rights.

Still, this is but an intermediate answer that begs a further question – why and how could one segment of a population have been subjected to such social exclusion in the first place?

The story behind the socially excluded of New Orleans parallels that of starving and conquering the social state, but this time seen from the bottom-up view of a primarily poor African-American population

whose precarious lives and patterns of social exclusion long predated the
rise of market fundamentalism, even while deeply exacerbated by it. My
narrative of how so many New Orleanians found themselves left behind
on the eve of Hurricane Katrina has several intertwining threads – one
built on an intractable legacy of slavery, misrecognition, paranthropoidism, terrorism, exclusion, and legal rightlessness; another based on exclusion from New Deal policies crafted exclusively for whites and at the
expense of African-Americans; and another spun from market fundamentalism's ability to delegitimate and displace the Great Society's
limited efforts at social inclusion and political redress for the wrongs of
history.

Recall market fundamentalism's discourse of ontological and normative
freedom, universality, and equality. While the association of this language of
political liberalism with market domination is characteristic of liberal capitalist democracies, it is distinctly prominent in the United States.[41] The
blending of market fundamentalist discourse into the discourse of political
liberalism has been essential not only to market fundamentalism's rise to
ideational prominence over the last several decades. It has also been critical
to its ability to delegitimate America's briefly prevailing social citizenship
regime, which from the mid-1950s to the early 1970s had begun to redress the
past wrongs of racial and gendered exclusions based on ascribed or "primordialized" identities. As modest as were these corrections, a frenzied
cultural backlash nonetheless ensued. Market fundamentalism, by riding
its winds, was able to take advantage of the backlash and in a few years to
bring a halt to the momentum to redress race-based inequities – but before
policy and law were able to make deep and substantial enough inroads into
reducing the wrongs inflicted by primordial and ascriptive-driven exclusions.
In its most recent and successful challenge to *de facto* separate and unequal
school segregation, for example, the conservative majority of the Supreme
Court recently ruled that even voluntary efforts to achieve integration
violated the high-minded and abstract constitutional principles of a "color
blind" society based on individual rights (*Parents* v. *Seattle* and *Meredith*
v. *Jefferson*, decided June 28, 2006). Market fundamentalism thus grafted
its universalistic discourse onto the substance of a society that was still
deeply segregated and rent with historically inflicted inequalities. In effect,
the discursive triumph of market fundamentalism has the effect of freezing
in place the identity-based inequalities, and historical exclusions, and

---

[41] However, as the cases of China today or Pinochet's Chile in the 1980s so vividly demonstrate, liberal democratic political cultures are by no means inevitable outcomes of what
are often called "free-market societies."

then worsening them through deepening market-based class inequalities. The result is nothing less than total social and political exclusion from membership in the human community.

The earlier primordial discourses were notable precisely because they existed alongside, often seemingly unaffected by, the official public liberal universalistic and egalitarian discourse of the American polity – a discourse based on universality and individual rights that without irony claimed to represent the nation as a whole. Some argue that this illiberal exclusionary discourse of ascription is an entirely separate tradition from the mainstream liberal discourse of individually based merit and achievement, one which coexists (however uneasily) with the "multiple traditions" of America's political culture (Smith 1993, 1999). Others view exclusionary practices and discourses as simply the flip side of the structural binary code of civil society, and thus indivisible from liberalism's inclusionary precepts of citizenship (Alexander 2006; Shklar 1991). Whichever approach one takes, and there are of course many more, there is no way to prove objectively which is true, as these are analytic, not empirical distinctions.[42] What *can* be demonstrated empirically is that the long-term active and influential presence of these primordially driven traditions was still very much evident in the unequal membership characteristic of African-American citizenship in the years preceding the full-scale emergence of market fundamentalism.

Because the public narratives and mythologies of political liberalism have a kind of default monopoly of legitimacy, by appropriating a vocabulary which denies the influence of ascriptive discourses of exclusion, market fundamentalism was remarkably successful in its efforts to claim that historical race exclusions happened too long ago to justify violating the principles of universality, individual rights, and color blindness by such redressive policies as affirmative action. To some extent, it has even been able to simply erase from memory the long-term significance of slavery and the legal exclusions of Jim Crow. Instead, any inequalities that might exist today are attributed exclusively to the individual failure to acquire the skills and education, the human capital, necessary to succeed in the employment market. These failures are in turn treated as personal problems with economic consequences, rather than social problems amenable to sociological analysis. In reality, however, two different systems of inequalities and exclusion – one based on immutable particularistic and arbitrary

---

[42] My approach to competing discourses, as demonstrated in chapter 7, is structural and binary. The idea of universality, for example, cannot be comprehended without a concomitant idea of particularism, and the same is true for inclusion/exclusion.

race-based attributes, the other based on market-driven class inequalities – have been grafted together to create a previously unmatched level of almost total exclusion from civil society, an exclusion that is much greater than the sum of its parts as it amounts to nothing less than nonrecognition. So while income inequality and the wealth gap have affected the entire American populace, racial minorities, especially African-Americans, have suffered to a degree both quantitatively and qualitatively greater than any other sector of the population.[43] This qualitative difference made itself visible in New Orleans during the last week of August, 2005. But long preceding Hurricane Katrina lies the legacy of chattel slavery and its enduring role in the meaning of American citizenship.

We are all familiar with the bizarre sense of cognitive dissonance experienced from reading the declamation that "all men are created equal" in virtually the same sentence that permits slavery, excludes blacks from full personhood and women from independent citizenship. Racial and gendered exclusions based on ascribed or primordialized iden-tities – attributes not based on any actual *actions* on the part of the excluded but on what Arendt (1979) called "merely given," such as race, gender, and ethnicity. These policies and practices, in place in various legal and cultural forms and degrees since the founding of the American republic, attributed inferior, dependent, and only partial per-sonhood to women, and subhuman status to African-Americans. They were then used to justify gender and race-based exclusion from full or even partial membership in civil society and the body politic. In an attempt to overcome not only this but also the legacy of the hypocritical New Deal, a liberal-dominated Supreme Court and a Democratic con-gress in the 1950s through the early 1970s began the work of redressing radical inequalities. One result was the Great Society's increase in AFDC in the 1960s and 70s. For reasons of structural demographic change, migration patterns, and deindustrialization, the welfare rolls increased steadily during these years. Unlike the universal (though fictional) prin-ciple of worker-based contribution programs of Social Security and Medicare, potential welfare recipients were subjected to means-testing. By itself this required a kind of self-selection, which stigmatized and degraded.[44]

---

[43] See data collected by and presented by Mishel *et al.* (2006); see also Kuttner (2007).

[44] Fraser and Gordon (1997, 1998) emphasize how much the stigma was based on the degrading status of "charity" and "dependency" versus the dignified attitude toward the quid pro quo of contract; see also Lindblom (2001).

In the late 1970s, an ideational assault began against the so-called urban underclass – the contemporary codeword for widely unemployed poor blacks – who were accused of exploiting the redistributive generosity of middle-class taxpayers in the interest of living culturally pathological lives of dependency, sexual promiscuity, and moral degeneration. For market fundamentalists the real target was the government programs. They focused their ire on welfare's "immoral" violation of contractual quid pro quo exchange.[45] Why were they getting "handouts" when they were not working for a living? The attack rhetoric was filled with stories about lazy "welfare cheats" and parasitic "welfare queens." It increasingly targeted poor black single mothers for getting pregnant only to increase the amount of their welfare checks. In 1980s America, stigmatizing the culture of dependency of those who exploited the system was an easy sell. Welfare recipients increasingly were differentiated from the "deserving" recipients of Medicare and social security, and they were branded the "undeserving" morally compromised poor who were to blame for their own fate. By providing subsistence without an exchange of labor, welfare actually encouraged laziness, dependency, sexual promiscuity, and morally compromised subjects (O'Connor 2002).

During the Reagan presidency, the ideological war on the poor was coupled with a steady progression of antipoverty and social program cuts, which achieved its zenith long after Reagan with the 1996 Clinton welfare reform that ended AFDC and replaced it with Temporary Aid to Needy Families (TANF) – a punitive new program forcing beneficiaries to move from "welfare to work."[46] After years of ideational assault, the 1996 Personal Responsibility and Work Opportunity Act (PRWOA) represented the most significant advance in the contractualization of citizenship – the crowning achievement of a thirty-year campaign against the poor's violation of contractual morality. To gauge the influence of the contractual ethic in effecting this change we simply have to look at the document that accompanied the 1994 "Republican revolution" in the US

---

[45] For the sake of simplicity, in my discussion of welfare I knowingly take the risk here of conflating libertarian market fundamentalism with traditional conservative views that foreground the responsibilities and duties of citizenship. The conservative view, which is paternalist and inegalitarian rather than libertarian, deviates from straight market logic in that conservatives believe the rich have some obligation to the poor, although the poor are still required to work if they can. This patriarchal approach still privileges the market in many ways, but it also differs from the straightforwardly contractual quid pro quo exchange of market fundamentalism and libertarianism. For a full and fascinating discussion of these differences, see Elizabeth Anderson www-personal.umich.edu/~eandersn/workfare.pdf.

[46] Elsewhere Fred Block and I have analyzed the causal mechanisms that drove that bill to legislative passage (Somers and Block 2005).

House of Representatives. This was the Contract with America, which made its centerpiece the abolition of all support for (handouts to) the poor, both working and otherwise. Notice this was not a "covenant" or even a "compact" with America, which would have gestured more toward moral obligations, reciprocal rights, and distributive justice. These were *contractual* principles and, proving the bipartisan appeal of contractualization, they were reprised in the remarkable moniker attached to the 1996 Clinton welfare bill – the Personal Responsibility and Work Opportunities Reconciliation Act (PRWORA). Surely the title captures – one might say it almost caricatures – the bill's essential message that unemployment results from personal irresponsibility and dependency rather than any shortage of good jobs or opportunities.

It should not be surprising that ending welfare was the first real institutional accomplishment in the long struggle to defeat the social state. Ever since the Lockean thought experiment first linked individual liberties, property rights, and political representation to the "workmanship ideal" gained by "mixing toil with the soil," the right to sell one's own labor power in exchange for a wage became the archetype of contractual freedom. In the United States, it also expressed an extra contemptuous distance from slaves who were forced to labor, but did not have the concomitant right to earn (Shklar 1991). It was an easy step from there to reach backwards to valorize and appropriate St. Paul's famous aphorism that morphs this putative right to work into the *obligation* to work, such that those who do not work should not eat. Under the contractualization of citizenship, it would no longer be acceptable to receive something for nothing.

From citizen to contractual malfeasant: the human capital myth

With the end of welfare one of the last vestiges of social protection by the state dissolved into the market-driven politics of contractualizing citizenship. According to market fundamentalism, this should have restored the equilibrium to the labor market that welfare had derailed by its system of perverse incentives. For most of modern economic theory, the natural condition of humanity is that of material scarcity, which serves as a constant incentive for people to seek paid labor. Using naturalist assumptions about the social world, classical economists argued that by keeping people hungry scarcity has the biological advantage of spurring people to labor by natural rather than by coercive means. To be able to keep oneself and one's family from starving, biology will drive people to work. Remove that compulsion of nature by providing "free, unearned" food (i.e. welfare relief), and the incentive to labor dissolves. The converse, of course, is also true: remove that unearned food, and scarcity will once again restore the biological incentive to work. In theory, then, restoring the natural condition of scarcity-driven biological hunger and removing the perverse incentives of welfare dependency should drive people back to work and restore economic equilibrium.

There is only one problem with this contractual utopia: in a world in which contract has crowded out the citizenship ethic, two things are necessary to participate in the labor market: (1) what economists call human capital – learned skills, primarily education, that give added value to labor power and make someone attractive enough for an employer to be willing to pay a price for her time, skills and labor; and (2) available jobs that pay a living wage. As for the first, ex-welfare recipients had few skills that were treated as worthy of any significant marketable value in today's global economy. They were thus backed into the degradation of workfare or into trying to support a family on a minimum wage that is hardly enough to support a single person. As for the second, it was the lack of jobs, not just a shortage of education and skills, that kept the labor market beyond reach for so many New Orleanians. Whereas deficits in human capital have long been the favored explanation for unemployment, it is becoming increasingly difficult to claim that with the right training and education, success on the job market will follow. Moreover, just as it was once only manufacturing jobs that were "lost" to globalization, today it is white-collar middle-class and professional skilled work, such as computer technical support, accounting, and many medical functions, that are being outsourced. The human capital thesis flounders upon the rocks of the well-known problem of disappearing jobs: across the spectrum of employment, jobs are disappearing as fast as the seeming inevitability of layoffs and outsourcing (Uchitelle 2006; Hacker 2006). In short, human capital has become increasingly irrelevant to escaping financial woes through employment (Bernstein 2007). As Uchitelle (2006) puts it, this is the era of "the disposable American."[47]

The results are unequivocal. Market fundamentalism and the contractualization of citizenship have today created levels of inequality unmatched since the Gilded Age (Uchitelle 2007; Gross 2007; Lowenstein 2007; Frank 2007a;

---

[47] Barack Obama, Democratic senator from Illinois and candidate for the 2008 presidency, recently made the point that "even those who followed the standard advice for coping with a globalized economy – get more education for higher skilled jobs – were losing out. People were told, you've got to be trained for high-tech jobs," Mr. Obama said, "and then it turned out that some of those high-tech jobs were being outsourced. And people were told, now you need to train for service jobs. And then it turned out the call centers were moving overseas" (cited in Toner 2007).

Mishel *et al.* 2006). According to Larry Summers, former Treasury Secretary under President Clinton, since 1979 the share of pretax income going to the top 1 percent of American households has risen by seven percentage points to 16 percent, while the share of income going to the bottom 80 percent has fallen by seven percentage points (Leonhardt 2007). "It's as if every household in that bottom 80 percent is writing a check for $7,000 every year and sending it to the top 1 percent" (Leonhardt 2007). To no one's surprise, market fundamentalism has not distributed its inequities at random. For African-Americans, their long history of social exclusion and second-class citizenship means that disposability came earlier, was deeper, and had more devastating consequences. Blacks now hold less than one-tenth of the wealth of the white population and are disproportionately represented among the poor and the working poor. For many of the faces we saw at the New Orleans Superdome and Convention Center, the "American dream" has been "turned into a nightmare by its maddening unattainability. A two-parent family working full-time at the minimum wage earns less than half of what is needed to realize the dream at today's prices" (Block *et al.* 2006: 15–16). Under a contractual regime, those with little or no market value are considered fortunate if they are hired by the tourist industry to clean toilets and change bed sheets, even though the wages for this kind of work still leave them steeped in poverty. For the rest, even those options are not available. Until the 2006 Democratic Congressional victory, this was met with indifference by those who represent the business community. For ten years they managed to keep the minimum wage from being raised. But welfare reform is a bipartisan project. In mobilizing support against welfare, no one promised to end *poverty* as we know it, but only "to end *welfare as* we know it." Apparently, if the price of restoring the ethic of contract is poverty and even hunger, so be it.

Even beyond the African-American population, the social exclusion that linked together the left-behind of New Orleans was a particularly lethal kind of exclusion, characteristic of citizens in a civil society that has been conquered and recalibrated from a solidarity-driven moral metric to a contractually driven one based on market principles. The solidaristic normative ideal, as we know, makes social inclusion in civil society a universal moral right, thus insulating it from the effects of successes or failures accrued in the noncivil spheres of market and state. To be sure, in reality wealth and property almost always win out when it comes to being *more* included and *more* valued than others. But as long as the power that wealth confers is limited to market power, and is contained within the sphere of the market, it has some degree of legitimacy. This rarely happens, however. When the market currency of wealth and property, and the power it confers, transgresses and violates market boundaries, it becomes an imperial power and imposes a market-driven moral metric on civil society. By displacing the civil ideals of universality and the equal worth of citizens irrespective of their wealth or power, people become defined, valued, and accorded the "privilege" of social inclusion based exclusively on their contractual value. Those whose knowledge, skills, or contributions are not assigned significant market value are not recognized by others to have equal moral worth. And because contractualism is built on the principles of voluntarism and individual choice, those unable to get work – whether from a lack of marketable skills or because of global outsourcing – are accused of not taking personal responsibility and being in their situation by choice. This is the process by which the structurally unemployed become contractual malfeasants. Clearly, this is an exclusion marked by the lethal stigma of imputed moral unworthiness.

Exacerbated by the success of the personal responsibility crusade, as contractual malfeasants they find themselves outside the boundaries of the gated communities behind which are safely harbored only those people and things defined as honorable and worthy according to the terms established by the new market morality. But many saved their special brand of normative abuse for those affected by the toxic mix of racism and market fundamentalism. Right-wing television commentator Bill O'Reilly, in effect, acted as the spokesperson for those norms when he demonized the Katrina victims as "thugs, crack addicts who didn't want to turn off their drug supply," and found the "moral" of Katrina to be "if you don't work hard you will be stranded on a roof top and no one will help."[48] In a world in which social inclusion is contingent on meeting contractual obligations, those without assets are inevitably degraded and dehumanized. When contractualism invades and transforms the normative standards of civil society, where citizens once stood we now find little more than metrics of human capital.

From civil society to social capital

So far I have argued that the left-behind – those New Orleanians who were not evacuated before Hurricane Katrina – were victims of a prior invisibility characteristic of moral, social and racial exclusion. It was an exclusion driven by market principles grafted onto preexisting ascriptive

---

[48] To which a blogger on his web page replied: "I didn't know being poor was a crime and that the sentence was death." I believe it's a safe assumption that O'Reilly's moralizing censure shares with that of the academic and professional devotees of the 'welfare-dependency' thesis the advantage of never having had to confront either empirically or experientially the inside of a welfare office or that of a soup kitchen.

discrimination. However, this was only the first of a two-part process of loss because the marketization of civil society does more than transform the worth of individual citizens into market valuations. The second part is redolent of Polanyi's (2001) discussion of the inexorable destruction of civil society that results when those relationships and goods that should be protected are instead marketized. Markets cannot provide and allocate necessary human services in a universal and egalitarian manner. Health care in America, which is distributed almost exclusively through a market-driven insurance sector, is already out of economic reach for 47 million people. As corporations and employers increasingly rid themselves of employee health care expenses, individuals and families are being left to fare on their own in the insurance market. Market logic dictates insuring only the young, the healthy, and the "cherry-picked," leaving millions uninsured. The reduced lifespan shown to be characteristic of the uninsured is a direct effect of a private health care system.

The insecurity generated by widely publicized mass layoffs (now characteristic of jobs across the class divide), accompanied by the fear of poverty and degradation associated with minimum wage work, all contribute mightily to deep collective despair and a virtual public mental health crisis as both Uchitelle (2006) and Hacker (2006) demonstrate so well.[49] Colin Leys evokes with particular poignancy the desolation of it all in his recent study of marketization in Britain. "There are also accumulated psychological costs; rising rates of mental illness linked to unemployment and loneliness, insecurity and family breakdown caused by casualization, and the emergence of a new 'underclass' of unemployed young people with high rates of drug abuse and crime" (Leys 2003: 217–18). This represents a civil society in crisis. As the crises deepen, the cultural and ideational powers of market-driven and contractual morality deploy the language of universality, individual merit, and personal responsibility to prohibit interventionist social policies and programs.

There is another dimension to the collapse of civil society: in parallel with the transformation from citizen to unit of human capital, contractualization aims to transform civil society into *social capital*. Social capital refers to the utility-generating market value that networks of social relations potentially produce. As an alternative to government support, social capital represents an attempt to put the burden of economic development directly on poor communities. Individuals are also encouraged to use their social capital (social relationships) as a means of

---

[49] See Uchitelle (2006) for a harrowing discussion on the psychiatric effects of "disposability."

building human capital – again, as an alternative to state support. But evaluating communities and social relationships primarily for their economic value dissolves the very reason for civil society's existence as a site insulated from market logic. Transformed into social capital, civil society becomes an appendage to the market. For those communities which have little or no utility-generating value, they are often used simply to absorb the market's externalities (such as being used as a site for toxic waste), and other social costs that the poor have always borne to keep the rich in their comfort.[50] For the left-behind of New Orleans, the utility-generating potential of their communities was bleak long before the hurricane. Decades earlier, before market fundamentalism had arisen from the ashes of the 1970s, excluded African-American populations had strong communities that provided a considerable degree of material, cultural, and spiritual support. However, years of the state's abdication of its citizenship obligations inevitably led to the steady degradation of civil society, especially the social bonds of those communities most in need. One would have been hard pressed to find much social capital in what had become impoverished and broken communities, thus exacerbating their moral and market unworthiness in the eyes of mainstream civil society. And with moral unworthiness comes increasing social exclusion, invisibility, lack of recognition by others, and ultimately greater expendibility.

Conclusion

I began by suggesting that Hurricane Katrina was a parable of citizenship in America today. Deconstructing Katrina – excavating the hidden stories of what came before, exposing the unseen assumptions and the well-guarded practices that belie the public alibis for so many lost and abandoned lives – reveals much about citizenship rights and the costs of their erosion. Of all the ways in which Hurricane Katrina should strike us as instructive, however, the most notable is how dramatically this one great tragedy illuminates the conditions currently endangering a socially inclusive democratic citizenship, conditions that inevitably led to the catastrophe of so many people being abandoned – first by the contractualization of citizenship, then by a hollow and corrupt federal agency that had been conquered and cronyized by market-driven politics. Most dramatically, thanks to Katrina, we now know what is entailed when an entire segment of civil society has so disintegrated that its people have been robbed of their ontological rights to membership and inclusion, and with it their

---

[50] This is the subject of chapter 6 on social capital.

recognizable humanity – without which no other rights are possible. Katrina thus shows us *in extremis* what social exclusion and expendability look like. It does so by presenting us with a dystopian state of citizenship, embodying so many of the violations and displacements that contribute to democracy's imperilment.[51]

As the tragedy of Katrina unraveled, it placed in stark relief the fullness of the citizenship ideal being violated. We learned that citizenship is not primarily about the benefits it confers – although it certainly includes these. The protests voiced by the Katrina survivors were not about losing their rights of free speech, assembly, or their rights of habeas corpus, let alone their rights to property, legal representation, the vote, or to public education. There was no reason to protest over those rights because they had not lost them in any formal sense of the law. Yet they understood all too well that their citizenship had been denied them by all levels of political governance. They were no longer in any meaningful sense citizens; they were now, in effect, stateless people.

In 2005, after years of marketization and contractualization, the groundwork had been laid for thousands of New Orleanians to be transformed into contractual malfeasants. In the context of centuries of racism and internal colonialism, we recognize that market fundamentalism is hardly single-handedly responsible for creating the numbers and kinds of social exclusion we observed in Hurricane Katrina. But market fundamentalism and the contractualization of citizenship have radically worsened and transformed the afflictions of racism. They have intensified the color of poverty, inequality, and superfluousness by grafting the high-minded language of the market – universalism, color-blindness, individual rights, and merit – onto still very much existing race-based inequalities. They have thus managed to derail programs such as affirmative action that were intended to redress the past wrongs of racism.

The structural effects of racism and market fundamentalism have created a surplus population concentrated in the African-American community. Attributed with little of contractual value, they have become the socially and morally excluded – invisible, dispensable, and forgotten. Human beings treated this way become surplus, not worthy of social or moral recognition by others. Long before the storm, public culture and policy changes had effectively made the poor of New Orleans internally stateless, rightless, and unworthy of recognition as fellow humans by the mainstream of society. As stateless people, they were excluded from

---

[51] See Dershowitz (2004) for discussions of how conditions of rightlessness help us understand what is necessary for achieving rights.

membership in a political community, and in practice, from access to the legal rights of citizenship.[52] We have also learned that full inclusion clearly requires membership in both an organized polity and a functioning civil society. The abandoned New Orleanians clearly inhabited the wrong side of civil society's internal borders – excluded from meaningful membership in the larger civil, social, and political community.

If social naturalism justifies government inaction under normal social conditions, an actual natural disaster is its ideal alibi. "No one could have predicted that the levees would break," dissembled President Bush in late August 2005, feeling secure in hiding behind the inevitabilities of nature. It was not nature, however, but market fundamentalism that set the stage for calamity before the levees actually broke. The Army Corps of Engineers had long been underfunded despite widespread knowledge of just how inadequate the levees were to protect the city of New Orleans against powerful hurricanes (van Heerden and Bryan 2006). With government's denial of global warming, the protective wetlands in the coastal regions were slowly but inexorably eroding. But it was above all the drumbeat of deregulation, marketization, and privatization that contributed most to degrading and contractualizing the noncontractual institutions, rules, and practices meant to protect people and public goods. And in perhaps the most perverse logic of market fundamentalism, the response of market-driven governance to this most extreme case of natural disaster aimed to teach the lesson of how to shift incentives away from the moral hazard of social insurance, towards the personal responsibility imposed by social naturalism and market forces.

Nothing represented this moral hazard more than FEMA – its very existence considered a monument to the perverse incentives embodied in the wrong-headed policies of government protection. As long as people felt entitled to government protection and restoration in the event of natural disaster, they would fail to take personal responsibility for their own financial well-being and continue to be dependent parasites on the state. Letting people take personal responsibility for dealing with the forces of nature and (the private insurance) markets is to respect the

---

[52] Statelessness, however, does not make for freedom from police harassment. Social exclusion means losing one of the most important citizenship rights, the right to protection by the police. Equally, however, it means losing protection *from* the police. Just as Arendt (1979) points out about the externally stateless in the twentieth-century interwar period, the socially excluded during Hurricane Katrina found themselves immediately subject not only to unchecked policing but also violence and harassment from the National Guard, both of which showed up a full five days before a peep was heard from FEMA.

biological will to survive, the social naturalist claim goes. By contrast, political interventions taken to fortify the levees along with guarantees that the state will provide emergency relief inevitably instantiate the perverse incentives to dependency. There was nothing natural about the disaster of the hurricane, the flailings of a corrupt federal agency, and least of all about the myth of social naturalism itself. In short, the failure of FEMA during Hurricane Katrina was a testimony to the market-driven state having successfully delegitimated and defanged what market fundamentalism considers to be the moral hazard of social insurance. By the time of the hurricane, social naturalism had long worked its way into the heart of social policy and political will, destroying the administrative capacities of FEMA and leaving it as little more than a perch of cronyism.

Just as FEMA's failures registered market fundamentalism's success in starving the state, so too the poverty revealed when the winds of Katrina blew away the curtain on the marginalized populace of New Orleans confirmed just how successful the contractualization of citizenship has been in the decade since the passage of the PRWOA. The more solidified this displacement of citizenship by contract has become, the more civil society is appropriated by the market to absorb the externalities that markets leave in their wake – in this case, by providing a space where the poor remained contained and invisible, and where they cannot tarnish the image of the efficient marketplace. In the process, the principles, practices, and institutions of solidarity inevitably decomposed and frag-mented. With their civil society in ruins, the citizens of New Orleans were cut loose from their status as members embedded in mutual relationships with each other and with government at all levels. The wider political culture tolerated with averted eyes the tragic consequences that years of social and political exclusion had wrought on a vast swath of the pop-ulation of one of America's large urban areas. It should not surprise us that when Hurricane Katrina hit, the cries of New Orleanians for help and rescue would go unanswered for days. Katrina simply confirmed their status as surplus, disposable, and unrecognized. Katrina briefly opened a window onto the socially excluded. Small wonder the world found it so easy and appropriate to label Katrina's survivors as "refu-gees." They had lost their right to have rights.

Karl Polanyi (2001) wrote about the tragic consequences of the Industrial Revolution's commodification of humans into labor during the nine-teenth century's epoch of market fundamentalism. But the tragedy for the urban poor who have little of value to exchange in today's contractual regime is not the misery of commodification; it is that they are considered of so little value that few even *want* to commodify them. Yet in a market fundamentalist regime in which contractualization rules, it is precisely gainful employment that makes possible recognition by others – and with that, inclusion in a political, civil, and social community (Shklar 1991). Historically, when this kind of market-driven quid pro quo require-ment has displaced one of rights based on inclusionary civil membership, more often than not it has amounted to some kind of indentured labor, or perhaps confinement to a poor/work house (Marshall 1964). For the person who has little to exchange, the standard pound of flesh is usually one's rights and with them, one's moral recognition (Liptak 2007). This is the formula for producing expendable people. And this is the thread that linked together the socially excluded of New Orleans.

On the last page of *The Great Transformation* (2001: 268), Polanyi writes a remarkable final paragraph:

Resignation was ever the fount of man's strength and new hope. Man accepted the reality of death and built the meaning of his bodily life upon it. He resigned himself to the truth that he had a soul to lose and that there was worse than death, and founded his freedom upon it. He resigns himself, in our time, to the reality of society which means the end of that freedom. But, again, life springs from ultimate resignation. Uncomplaining acceptance of the reality of society gives man indom-itable courage and strength to remove all removable injustice and unfreedom. As long as he is true to his task of creating more abundant freedom for all, he need not fear that either power or planning will turn against him and destroy the freedom he is building by their instrumentality. This is the meaning of freedom in a complex society; it gives us all the certainty that we need.

By "society," Polanyi means what we today call civil society or the social. He thus passionately distinguishes it from the spheres of the market and the state, and locates civil society as the site without which there can be no hope for citizenship and human rights, social justice and individual freedom. As remarkable as it might seem in today's culture of market fundamentalism, Polanyi truly believes that the noncontrac-tual relations of reciprocity, solidarity, and redistribution are not only necessary characteristics of a robust and rights-centric civil society; he also stipulates that they are on the same existential plane as death and freedom. The implications are clear: civil society's ability to resist market fundamentalism and state coercion is not the optional fantasy of sociologists and socialists; it is necessary for the survival of democracy.

3

Citizenship, statelessness, nation, nature, and social exclusion: Arendtian lessons in losing the right to have rights

The revival of attention to Hannah Arendt's discussion of statelessness in her magisterial *The Origins of Totalitarianism* ([1951] 1979) has added enormously to our current understandings of migration, citizenship, and ethnos in the context of globalization (see especially Benhabib 2004, 2001; Power 2004). In this chapter, I bring Arendt's analysis to bear on a very different kind of statelessness (to date less recognized) – one that characterizes Americans who hold *de jure* citizenship but who nonetheless are being expelled from the rights-bearing terrain of the rule of law, from protection by the social state (usually called the welfare state), and from access to the public sphere. These are the socially excluded. My argument is that increasing numbers of people have lost meaningful membership in civil society and political community – that which confers recognition and rights – through a process of the contractualization and commodification of citizenship. Systematically degrading the public sphere and subjecting the institutions of the state to conquest by market fundamentalist regimes are transforming the foundations of citizenship from social and noncontractual to contractual and market-driven ones. As both Arendt and Karl Polanyi (2001) understood, governing through contractualism returns civil society and the public sphere to the tyranny of social naturalism, disintegrates civil society, and produces the stateless "freedoms" of natural rights. In short, it steals the "right to have rights," the precondition for citizenship and social inclusion.

In "The Decline of the Nation-State and the End of the Rights of Man," Arendt recounts how the stateless refugees of interwar Europe became little more than the "scum of the earth" – her shocking words for the dehumanization inflicted upon those whose loss of membership in a political community transformed them into an expendable surplus population (Arendt 1979: ch. 9). Her association of "scum" and "statelessness" derived from her basic political and moral conviction that human personhood is distinguished from biological life by membership in an organized political body and full citizenship in a nation-state. Three-quarters of a century after Arendt's tale of statelessness, which she links to the tyranny of ethnicity over the rule of law and the hypocrisy of the "Rights of Man," a similar dynamic is occurring today through a not altogether unrelated historical decoupling of the two entities that have historically made up the tenuous unity of the nation-state – that unstable marriage of ethnos and demos that has, at least since the early modern era, served as the mechanism for the distribution of peoples into one or another political entity. But what the robustness of *de jure* citizenship promised in Arendt's mid-century era of burgeoning social states is being denied today by the increasingly expansive regimes of neoliberal market fundamentalism. The status of formal citizenship can no longer by itself endow the *social* membership necessary to claim the bundle of rights due to all citizens.

The thesis of this chapter is that while today's stateless citizens are also losing the right to have rights, in this case by losing the protections of a social state, in contrast to Arendt's mid-century Europeans they are not landing in a political vacuum. Instead, a large majority are being compensated for their loss of demos with an alternative identity of ethnos and nationalism, which has propelled them full force into the political culture of the *nation*. This large group of Americans – mostly white, mostly working classes, often Evangelicals, often the working poor – have become *stateless citizens* in the guise of militant patriots. The last thirty years of neoliberalism and market fundamentalism in tandem with the new post-9/11 security state have produced this new regime, which is remaking the political identities of a broad swath of the public by increasingly turning them into stateless nationals who take comfort in the compensatory identity of cultural, rather than social, inclusion.

Those familiar with Arendt's work may question my applying to the internal conditions of a nation-state the theoretical arguments and conceptual vocabulary she developed in the context of interwar Europe to explain genocide on a massive scale. But as has become increasingly clear over the years, *Origins* is a great deal more than a brilliant historical analysis; it is equally a political theory of the conditions necessary for enabling human survival. Stripped down to its most basic infrastructure, the story of statelessness and the futility of the Rights of Man is a robust theory about the constitutive preconditions for the destruction of a people – and by the logic of inversion, for preserving civilization and human rights. As Arendt herself wrote in the 1953 second edition, *Origins* is a work of politics as much as one of history (Kohn 2002).

In what follows I reprise Arendt's story of Europe in the years from the end of World War I and the Treaty of Versailles through the political practices and decisions that made genocide inevitable. From this narrative I distill concepts, relationships, and causal mechanisms to construct what can be characterized as an Arendtian matrix made up of two binary and normative oppositions – between nation and state on the one hand, and between the Rights of Man and the rule of law on the other. Both, I believe, fall under a single more all-encompassing "great dichotomy," one that Arendt shares with other great thinkers of her generation such as Karl Polanyi, namely the opposition between *social naturalism* and *political artifice*. Arendt, like many other philosophical veterans of the great horrors of the first half of the twentieth century, believed passionately that the more committed we are to the side of artifice, the safer humanity will be. With these intellectual tools in hand, in the second part of the chapter I return to contemporary American society to construct a social and political hypothesis about a populace that is once again losing its right to have rights while gaining an ever thicker fictive ethnic nationalism and the cultural exclusion of others.

Narrating Arendt on the triumph of the nation over the state

Chapter 9 of *Origins*, "The Decline of the Nation-State and the End of the Rights of Man," divides into two sections. The first, "The 'Nation of Minorities' and the Stateless People," begins with the signing of the peace treaties at the end of World War I, when the victorious Western allies engaged in a project to reconfigure the political, social, and ethnic geography of Eastern and Central Europe. The breakup of the Austro-Hungarian and Czarist empires had created new "successor states," such as Hungary, Poland, Yugoslavia, and Czechoslovakia. The question the Allies confronted was the future of over 100 million people who, under the empires, had been contained as relatively autonomous ethnic and religious clusters. Thanks to the new political map of Europe, the minorities now found themselves residing in countries ruled by majority ethnicities other than their own. Arendt recounts the so-called Minority Treaties – a stupefyingly arrogant (my words, not hers) set of treaties imposed on the successor states by the League of Nations to address this problem. The treaties specified that the new states were to be governed by the majority ethnic group – "state peoples" they were to be called – regardless of the large numbers of ethnic minorities, such as the Croats in Yugoslavia, the Ukrainians in Poland, the Sudeten Germans in Czechoslovakia, and the Jews everywhere. The League decided to designate these ethnic minorities as official "Minorities," for whom an explicit series of protective measures and rights were created. Intended to guarantee civil rights to the minorities in the context of their subordination to majority ethnic rule, these rights included religious toleration, the right to practice one's own religion, to learn and teach Hebrew for Jews, as well as other cultural and economic protections. Notably, the right to political representation was not among them.

The successor states signed under protest, pointing to the double standard in which the Western powers did not put themselves under the same set of requirements. At first the minority groups were treated as merely "second-class citizens," but citizens nonetheless. It was a condition that Arendt called "half stateless" – while they were *de jure* citizens who still held passports, their minority status meant that they were excluded entirely from governance. Ironically their national passports actually guaranteed far greater political recognition abroad than in their home countries (Arendt 1979: 76). In their own nations they were vulnerable to whatever political decisions were made by the "state peoples," including that of being denaturalized and expelled by majority rule.

In 1934 Germany instituted the Nuremberg Laws stating that only those of Aryan descent could be German citizens. Long before the Nazis thought up the idea of the final solution and the gas chambers, they understood that the first step in the destruction of the Jews would be to systematically strip them of their citizenship and turn them into stateless peoples. Germany had not been subject to the Minority Treaties, and Hitler interpreted this neglect of assigning protective rights to minorities as implicit permission. Inspired by the success of the German Reich, in short order the dominant ethnic governments of the successor states began a domino process of expatriation – the instrument of choice for solving their minority "problem." So began the first burst of widespread statelessness in the interwar period. As the states insisted on their sovereign right of expulsion and withdrew all political and legal protections, millions who had been promised civil and other juridical rights were now thrust outside the pale of law and turned into refugees. When the states abrogated all formal national documents, the minorities became *apatrides sans papiers*. One might have thought they would have found refuge in the West. But instead, they found themselves unwanted everywhere, including in the Allied nation-states in which they sought refuge. The newly stateless found themselves reviled as nothing less than the "scum of the earth," left only to beg for entry into the very countries that had created this disastrous state of affairs.

This was the genius of fascism's denaturalization policies, which was mimicked by the successor states that followed the German example. They understood that people outside of a political community would no longer induce social recognition, and thus would provoke repulsion in even the most liberal of states. In Arendt's words, those whom "the persecutor had singled out as scum of the earth – Jews, Trotskyites, etc. – actually *were* received as scum of the earth everywhere; those whom persecution had called undesirable became the *indesirables* of Europe." The official SS newspaper stated explicitly in 1938 that "If the world was not yet convinced that the Jews were the scum of the earth, it soon would be when unidentifiable beggars, without nationality, without money, and without passports crossed their frontiers." This kind of "factual propaganda," Arendt continues, "worked better than Goebbels' rhetoric" (1979: 269).

Nation versus state/law

Nation-state creation, according to Arendt, had historically required a whole list of prerequisites including homogeneity of population and rootedness in the soil. Without these conditions, the Allies' attempt to "regulate" the "nationality problem" by the Minority Treaties and their project of nation-state building was "simply preposterous" (Arendt 1979: 270). That minority rights guarantees were recognized as even necessary in the first place was in itself an acknowledgment that the dominant ethnic nationalities were the only ones who could expect real protection by political and legal institutions of polities no longer ruled by law but by nationality. The Allies should have known that it was unlikely that the majorities would ever accept as full citizens those minority people who "insisted" on maintaining their own separate nationality (i.e. ethnicity). Turning over political rule to the resident ethnic power inevitably conflated demos into ethnos. Arendt declares that as soon as the treaties were signed, and even before the mass expulsions began, the *"transformation of the state from an instrument of the law into an instrument of the nation* had been completed; *the nation had conquered the state, national interest had priority over law* long before Hitler could pronounce 'right is what is good for the German people'" (1979: 275, my italics).

This is the first of Arendt's normative oppositions – nation versus law, ethnos versus demos, instruments of nation versus instruments of state, prepolitical identity versus political agency, who you are versus what you do, nationalism versus citizenship. These are theoretical principles abstracted from the specificity of the particular story Arendt tells of interwar Europe, principles that serve as the foundation of her more general theory of politics and ethics:

For the nation-state cannot exist once its principle of equality before the law has broken down. Without this legal equality, which originally was destined to replace the older laws and orders of the feudal society, the nation dissolves into an anarchic mass of over- and underprivileged individuals. Laws that are not equal for all revert to rights and privileges, something contradictory to the very nature of nation-states. The clearer the proof of their inability to treat stateless people as legal persons and the greater the extension of arbitrary rule by police decree, the more difficult it is for states to resist the temptation to deprive all citizens of legal status and rule them with an omnipotent police. (Arendt 1979: 290)

The failure of the Rights of Man

But what about the rights guaranteed by the Minority Treaties? Did they not include the promise of civil rights intended to protect the "non-state people" from the tyranny of the ethnic majority? Indeed they did promise to do so. When the League of Nations signed the treaties they assumed that as long as the minorities were guaranteed the basic jurid-ical-civil rights the problem of safeguarding rights would be solved. There was only one problem. The rights specified in the treaties did *not* include the most important right of all – the right without which no other rights would have any meaning, the right without which there would in effect be no legal self to which the other rights could be attached. This foundational right of *citizenship* Arendt calls "the right to have rights." She describes it this way:

We became aware of the existence of a right to have rights (and that means to live in a framework where one is judged by one's actions and opinions) and a *right to belong to some kind of organized community*, only when millions of people emerged who had lost and could not regain these rights because of the new global political situation. (Arendt 1979: 296–7, my italics)

The right to have rights, in other words, is nothing less than the right to membership in an organized political entity. And without legal and political membership qua citizenship, there would not be an agent capa-ble of claiming the bundle of rights that *were* included in the Minority Treaties.

How was it that the signatories of the treaties could have forgotten something as basic as citizenship when they calculated how to protect the minorities in the new successor states? Arendt argues that (without framing it in quite this terminology) it was an inevitable legacy of classical liberalism. For the liberal democratic nation-states of the League of Nations, conceptualizing a right of membership as a funda-mental ontological necessity was outside the boundaries of liberalism's political and normative lexicon. In the liberal worldview the need for citizenship is precluded by a different set of rights, the Rights of Man or natural rights, which had long served as the symbol of liberation from tyranny. In Arendt's words, "the secondary category of rights springs immediately from the nature of Man – Man in *nature*, not God, not history, is the source of Law, independent of the privileges granted by Sovereign or Estates." Thus "[citizenship] was never even mentioned among the human rights [because it] cannot be expressed in the categories of the eighteenth century because they presume that rights spring imme-diately from the 'nature' of man" (1979: 297).

The Lockean fiction imported into the treaties by the League of Nations was that individual freedom is the ontological human necessity, specifically freedom from all political and social domination. It is our *natural* rights that confer this freedom. Natural rights by definition are autonomous of social relationships and institutional foundations. Individuals have rights simply because they are human beings: "no special law ... [had been] deemed necessary to protect them because *all laws were supposed to rest upon them*" (1979: 291, emphasis added). For the European minorities who found themselves expelled by the very governments the treaties had assigned to be their protectors, these nat-ural rights were of course useless. Their very promise of freedom is conditional on their being *pre*political; there was no written positive law that acknowledged them, no constitution or international agreement that recognized them, and the Covenant of the League of Nations had never even so much as mentioned them. These were rights that led a "somewhat shadowy existence as an appeal in individual exceptional cases for which normal legal institutions did not suffice" (Arendt 1979: 280–1). The only guarantee of the rights promised by the treaties was the "guarantee" that human ontology is rooted in the natural rights of the presocial, prepolitical individual. As the final arbiters of human freedom, no other authority could be invoked to support them:

The decisive factor is that these rights and the human dignity they bestow should remain valid and real even if only a single human being existed on earth; they are independent of human plurality and should remain valid even if a human being is expelled from the human community. (Arendt 1979: 297–8)

Natural rights can also be viewed from a slightly different angle. They also require the explicit *absence* of political authority and positive law.

If we have Hobbes to thank for the first claim for the existence of natural rights, it is Locke who created the revolution in conceptual space that gave liberalism its permanent foundations. Motivated by the need to find the roots of human freedom in a safe refuge from the coercion of the absolutist state, Locke created a narrative based on imaginary human existence prior to all social and political appurtenances. In his narrative thought-experiment people were born in a state of nature, in which they were rights-bearing solely by virtue of being human – and clearly not by reason of any act of law, government, or national sovereign. To be sure, on the grounds of these originating natural rights, Lockean persons eventually emerged from the state of nature to contractually agree to a civil society and a fiduciary government. But a fundamental conflict ensues: because perfect human freedoms can *only* exist in the state of nature, they cancel out any justification for institutional foundations or political support. With natural rights now defined as alternatives to positive law, for two and a half centuries liberal discourse invoked human rights "whenever individuals needed protection *against* the new sovereignty of the state and the new arbitrariness of society" (1979: 291). And yet, when put to the test, it was precisely against arbitrary state power that these "inalienable" and "indefeasible" rights were utterly unenforceable: "the moment human beings lacked their own government and had to fall back upon their minimum rights, no authority was left to protect them and no institution was willing to guarantee them" (1979: 292). This was true not only in the successor states where nationalism had conquered the rule of law. As became clear in short order, wherever refugees appeared on their doorsteps asking for admittance, liberal states which based their own constitutions upon the indefeasibility of human rights displayed total disdain for the stateless. France, the United Kingdom and the United States were no more interested in protecting the putative human rights of the now stateless minorities than were the original expelling states.

That the rightless and stateless would be perceived and treated as the "scum of the earth" reflected the ontology driving the political decision to expel and denaturalize. Outside of political community, it was well understood that humans lose the very qualities that make them human. It is here that the awful hypocrisy of natural rights achieves its most tragic consequences: "[S]tateless people could see ... that the abstract nakedness of being *nothing but human* was their greatest danger. Because of it they were regarded as savages ... It seems that a man who is *nothing but a man* has lost the very qualities which make it possible for other people to treat him as a fellow-man" (1979: 300). The Nazis understood this best. Long before they herded Jews and other unwanted people into the gas chambers, they had found "to their satisfaction" that by first depriving them of their citizenship, and thus of all legal and political status, "no country would claim these people" (1979: 296). Ontological dehumanization brought forth by statelessness and the loss of citizenship was the precondition to extermination on a mass scale.

In Arendt's schemata, statelessness invoked not only rightlessness, but more profoundly it made people indistinguishable from the the scum of the earth. Clearly these are words she uses to provoke alarm at the association of humans with "scum" – worms, slugs, and other filthy creatures of the biological world. Arendt's association of "scum" with "statelessness" derived from her basic political and moral belief that the only source of human personhood – mutual recognition – is membership in an organized political body. To explain how people could be so dehumanized and biologized, she introduces the concept of the right to have rights. Creating a lexical ordering of rights in a single phrase allows Arendt to explain the apparent paradox that the minorities of interwar Europe could have been guaranteed their civil and civic rights by the Minority Treaties, but still have found themselves utterly rightless when it mattered. Her argument is that the promised juridical-political rights of the Minority Treaties were meaningless without the *first* right to the right to have rights. In the context of massive European expulsions, losing that primary right meant losing or never being given citizenship. Arendt, of course, was making a more general existential and ontological point about human personhood: humans become least recognized when they are stripped of everything and forced to live "bare lives" (Agamben 1998) as "nothing but human" (Arendt 1979: 297). Conversely, the precondition for exercising any rights is the *prior* right of inclusion, membership, and mutual recognition – i.e. citizenship.

Arendt calls this section of her chapter "The perplexities of the Rights of Man." I interpret this to mean that natural rights are perplexing – and tragically ironic – because statelessness, the condition of not belonging to any political organization, *should be* the ideal liberal utopia, where people should find themselves at the very apex of their freedoms and sovereign rights. History put the theory to the test: cut loose from government and political community, the stateless achieved the very telos of natural rights theory: "If a human being loses his political status, he should, according to the implications of the inborn and inalienable rights of man, come under exactly the situation for which the declarations of such general rights provided. *Actually exactly the opposite is the case"* (1979: 300). The theory failed.

Arendt points out with irony that those "outside the pale of law" had more "freedom of movement" than an imprisoned criminal and "more freedom of opinion in the internment camps of democratic countries than they would in any ordinary despotism" (1979: 296). But history showed that "neither physical safety ... nor freedom of opinion changes in the least their fundamental situation of rightlessness. *The prolongation of their lives is due to charity not to right,* for no law exists which could force the nations to feed them; their freedom of movement, if they have it at all, gives them no right to residence which even the jailed criminal enjoys ... and freedom of opinion is a fool's freedom for nothing they think matters anyhow." Here Arendt truly points to the empty abstractness of rights rooted in a "place" called the state of nature.

The fundamental deprivation of human rights is manifested first and above all in the deprivation of a place in the world which makes opinions significant and actions effective. Something much more fundamental than freedom and justice, *which are rights of citizens,* is at stake when belonging to the community ... is no longer a matter of course and not belonging not a matter of choice ... This extremity and nothing else is the situation of people deprived of human rights (1979: 296, emphasis added).

Thus Arendt insists that human rights are only viable within an organized political community, and that it is only through citizenship that the right to have any rights at all can be guaranteed. Liberalism's antistatist utopia turns out to be a dystopia: the rightless and stateless did not just suffer the loss of their own governments; they were turned away by all governments in all countries. "The calamity of the rightless ... is not that they are oppressed, but that nobody even wants to oppress them" (1979: 296). Absolute "freedom" incites repulsion, not protection: "The world found nothing sacred in the abstract nakedness of being human" (1979: 299).

Nature versus political artifice

Beneath the thick brush of Arendt's chapter on statelessness, there is an elegant design made up of two sets of oppositions:

1. nation versus juridical state; ethnos versus demos; national identity versus political identity; blood descent versus civil society; biology versus agency;
2. the Rights of Man versus the public sphere; natural law versus the rule of law; state of nature versus citizenship; contract versus membership.

Arendt's theory, framed here in its starkest form, is that whether the future bodes more genocide or a culture of human rights depends on our consistently choosing the far side of both dichotomies – that is, the side of political artifice, the rule of law, and a pluralistic political community. The mutual exclusivity between citizenship rights and natural rights is at the heart of Arendt's normative oppositions – that between the state of nature and the nature of the state, between natural rights and legal citizenship rights, between naturalism and institutionalism, between nature and political artifice. Whereas the first dichotomy contrasts the rule of law with national and ethnic identity, the second contrasts law with the abstraction of nature.

Although these are two separate oppositions, in Arendt's account they worked in sequence with each other – the collapse of the state into the nation prepared the way for the collapse of law into nature. In the first phase, only those who belonged to the imaginary biologized nation were worthy of inclusion. Once thrust outside the only nation to which they could make even formal claim to belonging, the minorities of the successor ethnic nations were thrust outside the framework of any organized polity. Viewing it in this sequence demonstrates that the two sets of distinctions actually amount to the single more encompassing one between nature versus artifice. Both a nationalism depleted of law and a liberalism depleted of an organized political community amount to the same thing. They are two kinds of naturalism set in opposition to the rule of law, to rules of equality, and to the political construct of citizenship rights.

At first glance, this may seem puzzling. While liberalism's natural rights and the Rights of Man are of course derived from the fictive state of nature, we are more accustomed to thinking of nationalism and ethnicity not as products of nature and biology but of culture and community, both of which apply to collectivities rather than to biologically defined individuals. Indeed the very idea of national identity seems to be constitutively based on "groupness," a very long distance from the individualism of Man in the state of nature. Yet identity based in the nation, ethnicity, and culture is ultimately no less driven by the seduction of naturalism's epistemic privilege than is liberalism's naturalistic ontology.

Ethnic and national identities are derived from stories about the essential nature of persons. To be sure, it is in the context of families of origin and descent that individuals usually come to awareness of this identity. But while communities, even families, come and go, ethnic identities do not; they are treated as ascribed, natural, and primordial, rooted in the very "blood and soil" of the nation. Identity myths are thus based on vertical lines of descent which inscribe individuals with their biological natures. These identities do not originate from horizontal cultural relations with others. Nor are they the result of political or social actions. Instead they are part of the "mere existence that is mysteriously *given to us* by birth." As such they are rooted in the "whole sphere of the merely given" (Arendt 1979: 301). Nationalist and ethnic groups are simply aggregations of these primordial identities. The illusion of nationalism as a collective cultural construct, rather than a naturalistic and biological one, derives from this secondary moment in which individually defined naturalized identities create imagined communities. In the first instance, however, identities are defined by "blood and soil," rather than by horizontal ties constructed in communities.

Tragic evidence of how ethnic and national identity is biologized comes from the case of Sarajevo in the early 1990s, one of Europe's most cosmopolitan cities before the Bosnian war in the former Yugoslavia. Despite decades of intermarriage and a culture of deep pluralism among Serbs, Bosnians (Muslims), and Croats, once the Serbs declared a nationalist war of ethnic cleansing, these culturally constructed horizontal ties among families, friends, neighbors, civic groups, and political cultures dissolved in an instant. Instead, the Bosnian Serbs responded to the cries of hate and violence issued from their "blood" relatives of Serbia against their fellow non-Serbian citizens of Sarajevo. To the Bosnians, Serbia was by and large a land of complete strangers, which the vast majority of Bosnian Serbs had never so much as visited. Yet the vertically defined naturalized identities of nation and ethnicity proved to be the foundational catalyst that incited the Bosnian Serbs to genocidal action. In the context of Arendtian theory, Sarajevo's collapse is all the more tragic because in its prewar conditions, Arendt would have recognized the city as her exemplary site of conscious political action and social artifice. Naturalized nationalist and ethnic identities are imposed against the will of a people in equal proportion to their being embraced. German Jews under the Nazis were the classic victims of passive biologization of Jewish national identity over and against their actively chosen assimilation through German citizenship. Generations of German citizenship had convinced many Jewish families that they did not need to flee the country under Hitler; as Germans first and foremost they were surely not at risk of expulsion. State-sponsored genocide (prefigurative of Bosnia fifty years later) followed when the tragic optimism of the Jewish citizens was felled handily by the tyranny of biology over political community. Until very recent changes in citizenship laws, Germany was emblematic of how naturalized "blood" ties were used to negate those of citizenship (Brubaker 1992).

The naturalism of natural rights theory is of course more straightforward. As the central mechanism of liberalism's great thought-experiment, social naturalism underlies all of its philosophical tenets. At the root of liberalism's social naturalism is the stipulation that the inexorable powers of nature and its laws – made conceptually available for the first time by the scientific revolution – are the only conceivable source of countervailing power to that of the state. This created an alliance between prepolitical freedom and nature – or, put more to the point, between freedom and antistatism. The mapping of social naturalism's binary divide between the natural and the artificial onto liberalism's divide between freedom and tyranny sealed this alliance for the next three centuries (Block 1997; see also chapter 7 below).

It follows readily that natural rights became liberalism's core mechanism to preserve human freedom against what was categorized as the ever-menacing threat of state coercion. As the bearers of natural rights born free in the state of nature, humans are ontologically presocial and prepolitical, defined only by their solitary relationship to nature itself, and not by relations with others. The concept of natural rights is thus militantly antirelational; only grudgingly do these natural-rights-bearing persons enter into contractual relations with others to create a civil society modeled on nature's laws. As a mirror image of the state of nature, civil society is the next best refuge from the chronic tyranny of the state.

Arendt's view of liberalism, then, is that it is as biologically driven as nationalism. "Man," ontologically a product of nature, can preserve freedom only to the extent that she preserves her ties to the imaginary state of nature: "From the beginning the paradox involved in the declaration of inalienable human rights was that it reckoned with an abstract human being who seemed to exist nowhere, for even savages lived in some kind of social order" (1979: 291). It is not by accident that Arendt uses the disturbing allusion to "savages" to argue that humanly constructed political entities are universal necessities. By treading on the naturalistic terrain of her conceptual opponents, she is demonstrating that social and political rules are necessary, even among those who may appear most "primitive" to us in that they live as "natural" an existence as conceivable while still being human. And just as it is their humanity, however distant from our "advanced" civilization, that illustrates the value of political membership and social organization, it is the *absence* of those products of human endeavor that marks the divide between the recognizably human and those not recognized as such: "The loss of home and political status became identical with expulsion from humanity altogether" (1979: 297).

Arendt's metaphor of the stateless as the "scum of the earth" is thus hardly accidental. They were biologized, reduced to their animal needs, which, as we know from Marx (1977c: 77–86), expels them from our human species-being, making them no longer subjects for human empathy and mutual recognition.

For Arendt the "abject freedom" of statelessness reduces people to beasts, a situation in which "rightless people are indeed thrown back into a peculiar state of nature" (Arendt 1979: 300). The mark of what she calls the "dark background of mere givenness," what I'm calling naturalism, means that "they have lost all those parts of the world and all those aspects of human existence which are the result of our common labor, the outcome of the *human artifice*" (1979: 300–1). Here we arrive at the clearest statements of Arendt's alternative to the naturalism of both nationalism and liberalism. More is required than merely the institutions of laws and states, and even more than the fact of citizenship itself. It requires collective political action toward the goal of human justice:

Equality, in contrast to all that is involved in mere existence, is not given to us, but is the result of human organization insofar as it is guided by the principle of justice. We are not born equal; we become equal as member of a group on the strength of our decision to guarantee ourselves mutually equal rights. Our political life rests on the assumption that we can produce equality through organization, because man can act in and change and build a common world, together with his equals and only with his equals. (1979: 301)

The inability to act or make any impact on the world, by contrast, results from the "background of mere givenness, the background formed by our unchangeable and unique nature." The stateless and rightless refugees were "persecuted not because of what they had done or thought, but because of what they unchangeably *were* – born into the wrong kind of race or the wrong kind of class" (1979: 294). Whether by expulsion or denial, losing citizenship means finding ourselves in a world of social naturalism in which we cannot act in the social world. It is this inability to *matter* through agency that pushes people to the edge, if not over the edge, of humanity. The stateless "are deprived not of the right to freedom, but the right to action; not of the right to think, but of the right to opinion . . . blessings and doom are meted out to them *according to accident and without any relation whatsoever to what they do, did, or may do*" (1979: 296). Nature, in short, "the merely given . . . is a permanent threat to the public sphere" (1979: 301). In the end, a people's right to have rights is most threatened by expulsion from the public sphere and by being thrown back "on their natural givenness or their mere differentiation" – by nation and ethnicity. No longer citizens of a polity, "they are no longer allowed to partake in the human artifice, they begin to belong to the human race in much the same way as animals belong to a specific animal species."

Arendt's republicanism and her focus on the importance of political membership has led some to worry about her having too great a trust in the state, with too little recognition of civil society's need to preserve freedom (Cohen 1996; see also chapter 1). As I read her, however, she has no love for the state in and of itself, nor absolute trust in the law, and certainly not in political entities as such. Hers is a dualistic vision: only states can commit genocide, but at the same time only states have the potential to prevent it. This makes it also a tragic vision: cosmopolitan citizenship and human rights are the ideal, but they are as yet unrealizable in an international global universe still driven by nation-states. Despite much hand-wringing over the demise of the nation-state in a global society, little has changed in the interceding half-century to give us any greater optimism about the possibility of a truly democratic international human rights regime (Power 2004).

Statelessness today

Arendt forces our attention to the macro processes of interwar Europe by the striking name she gave the chapter that is the subject of this article – "The End of the Nation-State and the Decline of the Rights of Man." Was she justified in making such definitive declarations of demise regarding two of liberalism's most foundational precepts? Certainly hers was a brilliant insight that the nation-state as we knew it was threatened and transformed when the League of Nations installed ethnic governance over the rule of law in the successor states of Central and Eastern Europe. Given that Germany's Nazi era represented the virtual perfection of the subordination of law by nation, at the time of her writing she was surely right about both the demise of the nation-state and the ineffectiveness of the Rights of Man. But in the post-World War II period of prosperity and social democracy, nations and states appeared to have seamlessly conjoined once again into a universe of nation-states.

Arguably, however, it was a unity that lasted only a few decades. With the beginnings of neoliberalism in the 1970s and the phoenix-like revival of market fundamentalism in the 1980s, the nation-state's ambiguous unity once again began splitting into its two component parts. Over the last few decades, and radically intensified in the post-9/11 years, the culture of the nation has been disarticulating from the institutional entities of the political and we are once again seeing the same binary divide – on the one side the naturalized "imagined community" of the nation; on the other the institutional and legal foundations of the state. From these have emerged two competing spheres of belonging and participation: one associated with a militant security-driven nationalism inflected by conservative moral social control and a radical free-market ideology; the other with the rule of law, democratic commitments, and citizenship rights – civil, political, and social, as well as democratic participation and a socially embedded market. Across this chasm (often characterized as "red" and "blue" states in the case of the United States), it is arguable that the populace is allied exclusively with either the nation or the state – but not both.

This renewed disarticulation of nation from state frames the context of similarity between Arendt's Europe and the early twenty-first century. We again live in a world in which refugees, *apatrides*, victims of human rights violations, superfluous people, and genocides are becoming the norm rather than the exception. But it is the interior of American society to which I now want to draw attention – not in a search for empirical anachronisms, but to bring attention to the analytic similarities that emerge by mapping the implications of Arendt's theoretical work onto the pattern of nation-state uncoupling today.

Using the analytic dichotomy that I developed from Arendt's narrative, I argued above that the minority peoples of Europe became surplus people subject to genocide at the point at which they found themselves on the wrong side of the opposition between nature and human artifice, between social naturalism and the rule of law. Today, the binary of nature versus artifice, nationalism versus citizenship, is forging similar analytic dynamics along different historical and empirical axes. The dominance of natural rights today is taking place not in the interstices of nation-states, but in the rise of market-driven states. The result is increasing numbers of stateless citizens – socially excluded people who hold formal *de jure* citizenship, but no longer *de facto* citizenship. When the state no longer carries out its role of constraining capitalism, people are left fully exposed to the unmediated market. With no meaningful participation and with only the thinnest of connections to civil and legal rights, they are, in effect, left stateless and rightless. The state, however, has not shrunk away; it has been transformed into an instrument of market-driven governance.

Unlike in Arendt's story, being expelled from the public sphere and cut loose from the state has not propelled these stateless nationals into a vacuum of identity. Instead, they have been symbolically "relocated" into the zone of the nation and its thick identity-endowing patriotic and religious culture of belonging and participation. In today's post-9/11 nation, the rise of ethnos provides the internally stateless and excluded with an alternative ontology to that of demos. They have become nationalist patriots – a symbolic garb that compensates for the loss of rights by cultural and symbolic identification with the dominant political culture. This is a curious inversion of the pattern of events in the Arendtian story, yet the logic at work is the same. In the case of the European Jews, nationalism and natural rights worked in tandem to expel them from the human community. Today, while it is natural rights that are responsible for social exclusion, nationalism is not amplifying but compensating for statelessness, providing an alternative source of human identity – one that allows them to be at the very heart of the *included*, this time not as rights-bearing citizens but as free-market patriots.

Losing the right to have rights through the contractualization and naturalization of citizenship

Over the last thirty years, and sharply accelerated over the years of the G. W. Bush administration, the programs, pensions, health care, and tax breaks designed to help the middle class and working poor have been steadily disappearing. This "Great Risk Shift" (Hacker 2006) from corporations, government, and social insurance schemes onto the vulnerable shoulders of those least able to bear it is the modern form of what Polanyi called "disembedding the market," referring to another era of "great transformation." The effect is that people are no longer protected from the inevitable risks of market society either by the government or by employment-based benefits. The once triadic configuration of government, market, and workers/families has been reduced to a deeply unequal dyad. This is leaving vast numbers of Americans "stateless" – by which I mean a condition of pure market exposure no longer mediated by the now absent government.

The poor and low-income members of this ever enlarging group experience statelessness in a particularly virulent way, lacking the usual markers of middle-class respectability such as education, good health, and cultural capital. They are the segment of the stateless that has become today's socially excluded. As such, they no longer have meaningful membership in civil society – that which confers recognizable human identity. The process by which this is happening is that of the contractualization of citizenship. Unlike in Arendt's time, market society today requires more than formal, legal citizenship to sustain the right to have rights. Market embeddedness is necessary, as well as an autonomous public sphere and a civil society independent of market invasion. What the robustness of Arendt's *de jure* citizenship once provided is being denied today by regimes of market fundamentalism. Systematically degrading the public sphere and conquering the social state, these market regimes are transforming the foundations of citizenship from social and universal to contractual and conditional. Put slightly differently, the noncontractual relations of citizenship are becoming contractualized and driven by market principles. Unemployment was once recognized as the responsibility of the commons. Today, that unemployment check has dissolved into a moralizing chant about taking personal responsibility for life's hardships. The journey from the public to the private, from the social to the natural, entails moving from an at least partially rights-driven civil society with some degree of market embeddedness to one with full exposure to the discipline of the market.

Market fundamentalism is the term popularized by George Soros to capture the religious-like certitude of those who believe in subordinating all dimensions of social life according to market principles. Today, just as in Polanyi's early nineteenth century, for most people the years of ever increasing market fundamentalism have led to a modern dystopia, generating levels of inequality not seen since the Gilded Age. This contractualization of citizenship is a process driven by the withdrawal of the state from social and market embeddedness, accompanied by the systematic dismantling of civil, political, and social citizenship rights. In this process, statelessness is both the end and the means of exclusion. "Starving the beast" (as per the Heritage Foundation) is the mechanism by which political expulsion is accomplished while it is also the outcome of that accomplishment.

There is no need to reprise the rise of market fundamentalism and privatization. Here I want only to highlight the conquest by market powers of the state's institutions of inclusion, protections, and rights. Freed from the "interference" and "inefficiency" of the state, excluded from the institutional fetters of law, justice, and public goods, a large segment of society has been catapulted into social exclusion. The end of interference with the freedom of contract, the end of the minimum wage, the end of restrictions on hours of labor – these are only some of the achievements and the desiderata, some accomplished already and some still in planning, of market fundamentalism.

In market societies, as we know from T. H. Marshall (1992), the measure of inequality and exclusion is directly proportionate to the degree of market embeddedness by the egalitarian institutions of citizenship. And, from Polanyi, we know it is proportionate to the degree to which the marketizing processes can be resisted by protective counter-movements. In today's culture of market fundamentalism, the few weak movements that struggle over the proportional balance between the drive to expand market principles versus the attempt to restrict marketization to its appropriate sites are increasingly being defeated as public services and public goods from education to health care to citizenship itself, are succumbing to privatization, degradation, and stigmatization.

Social exclusion and losing the right to have rights

To reorient our thinking from Arendt's story to the market-driven mechanisms of exclusion prevailing today, it is helpful to introduce the term "social exclusion." Europeans use the concept to refer to poverty. Replacing poverty with social exclusion is bracingly clarifying. It gives the lie to the current trend of attributing poverty to individual behavioral character traits and substitutes a framework of social institutions and relationships to account for market outcomes. Whereas poverty levels are usually constructed from malleable statistical measurements of government-defined income levels, social exclusion points to the consequences of poverty – exclusion from the mainstream of society. The great achievement of the concept of social exclusion is to turn a narrow economic term regarding income and behavior into a political category signifying relations of power and powerlessness that are codified in social policies.

T. H. Marshall (1992), an Arendtian contemporary, clearly understood the difference in the meaning of poverty between income levels on the one hand, and questions of social inclusion and exclusion on the other. In his well-known triptych of citizenship rights – civil, political, and social – Marshall dismisses the usual association between social rights and the stigmatized means-tested welfare schemes or income redistribution policies. Instead, he defines social citizenship as the universal right to quality health care and public education – rights that endow the kind of equality that poverty programs could never do. By social citizenship, Marshall writes, "I mean the whole range from the right to a modicum of economic welfare and security to the *right to share in the full in the social heritage* and to live the life of a civilized being *according to the standards prevailing in the society* . . . which in turn means a claim to be *accepted as full member of the society*, that is, *as citizens*" (Marshall 1992: 6, 8, emphasis added). Then, as if to anticipate and/or echo Arendt directly, Marshall goes on to describe social rights as "necessary requisites of civil freedom" (1992: 16). Civil rights, in other words, are already dependent on prior full inclusion according to the standards of civil society.

Marshall then makes the same point from another angle. Civil rights, the first of his three types of citizenship, include the economic and civil freedoms characterized by freedom *from* the state – the right to property, to liberty of the person, freedom from habeas corpus, freedom of speech and assembly, and so on. But it is the last clause in Marshall's definition of civil citizenship that is often overlooked, namely what he calls the "right to justice." This he defines as a "different order" from the other civil rights "because it is the right to defend and assert all one's rights *on terms of equality* with others and by due process of law" (1992: 8, emphasis added). All the rights in the world, Marshall is saying here, mean nothing without full access to the rule of law; but formal rights to access are meaningless without the inclusionary resources necessary to create the kind of person capable of accessing and acting on those rights. This is what he means by terms of equality – it is another way of once again invoking full social inclusion as the prerequisite to substantive, not merely formal, access to the system of justice. Although the last of his three citizenship rights, its relative importance is clear: social citizenship is "a necessary prerequisite of civil freedom" (1992: 16).

Today both equality and due process are threatened by market-driven exclusions. The loss of rights that these entail parallels Arendt's nationalist and naturalist-driven interwar exclusions. Marshall's prioritization of full membership and Arendt's ontological postulate of political belonging both make membership *as citizens* the foundational necessity of human personhood and identity. When market-driven inequalities and social exclusions deny adequate ontological foundations for access to the universal services of civil society and the public sphere – quality public education, adequate health care; in short, all the aspects of life necessary to live the life of a "civilized" being – the consequences are people without that primary foundational right of recognition and personhood.

The links between social exclusion, statelessness, and losing the right to have rights demonstrate that the formal legal citizenship held by today's socially excluded has no more *de facto* meaning than did the civic rights guaranteed by the Minority Treaties of yesteryear. By formal law they may be citizens, but today's socially excluded are no longer rights-bearing citizens. By default they have become mere denizens who reside in the country but are for all intents and purposes stateless and superfluous people (Hammar 1990). The borders demarcating citizen exclusion and inclusion that form the periphery of states, have in the twenty-first century migrated to the center of our social world (Balibar 2004b).

From market externalities to social inclusion

Market externalities is the term used by economists to capture the "imperfections" that result from "interferences" with what under ideal circumstances would be a balanced equilibrium of market forces. Included among such externalities are environmental decay, air pollution, shortages of flu vaccines, "sticky" levels of unemployment and underemployment, lack of public health, and wage levels below a living wage, to name just a few. When Karl Polanyi, who had no patience for euphemisms, addressed the similar consequences of the early nineteenth-century commodification of land and labor, he saw them as more than imperfections but as threats to the fabric of the social body. As he unearthed earlier episodes of unsustainable levels of inequality and poverty that were ripping apart communities, Polanyi introduced the idea of a "double movement" to characterize the various social groups and movements that coalesced to counteract the social dissolution. These included trade unions and working-class mutual societies, as well as cross-class alliances that fought for factory legislation, resisted poor relief repeal, and sought extension of the franchise. But market fundamentalism soldiered on despite these movements by at once subjecting ever greater dimensions of society to market principles while in time intensifying nationalist policies. By the early twentieth century, massive failures to recognize what Polanyi calls the "reality of society" led to fascism and totalitarianism. Only the embedded markets of the American New Deal and British social democracy managed to avoid these latter fates.

Given the extent and kinds of today's market externalities, one might expect a similar upsurge in Polanyi's double movements of resistance. Indeed if we lived in a different political universe, it would not be unreasonable to expect real social unrest, massive working-class protest, or at least widespread demonstrations. There are, of course, no such double movements in sight, at least in the Anglo-American world. Instead, the very people most victimized by social exclusion – the stateless, the rightless, the working poor and blue-collar classes, the déclassé middle classes – have embraced something that apparently fills a much deeper need than social revolution, namely the identity of the nation and the ethnos of America.

Nationalism is often treated as a phenomenon in which the objects of inclusion and exclusion are marked by the boundaries of nation: "we" are Americans, "they" are foreigners. And to be sure, there is no shortage of xenophobia and American chauvinism passing under the banner of

American patriotism (one need only remember how French fries morphed into "freedom fries" after France refused to join in the invasion of Iraq). Moreover, 9/11 so galvanized the patriotic impulse of Americans that for a while the nation as a whole embraced nationalist identification. But at root, accusations of questionable patriotism and loyalty are always more directed against fellow citizens than actual foreigners, for it is by "othering" internal dissenters and the socially excluded that the included are able to distinguish themselves as true patriots ready to defend the nation against the threats from without or within.

Recall that, in Arendt's story of interwar Europe, the processes of exclusion began with ethnic denaturalizations. The expelled were those who by choice or coercion were deemed to be by nature alien from the dominant ethnic nationals. As the polluted *within* the national body, denaturalizations were incited by nationalist purification narratives and carried out in the name of national survival (Alexander 2006). "Pure" national identity depended on the ability of the included to distinguish themselves from the cancerous growth within the body of the nation, making national survival dependent upon ruthless expulsions of the nonbelongers.[1] While the weapons of purification may be of a different order today, the foundations of national identity are much the same. Despite the temporary lull of patriotic unification following 9/11, the *real* enemies to the nation are the outlaws within the social body – immigrants, nonwhites, nonheterosexuals – or those insufficiently aligned with the dominant ethnos of American nationalism and patriotism.

National identities are thus dependent on the internal differentiation of "us" versus "them." Rather than the relatively weak identification with the constitutionally-defined government, it is this attachment to a naturalized *prepolitical* internally differentiated national community that fills the vacuum left by social exclusion and statelessness. Essential to this self-identification is the contradictory proposition that while "real" Americans are by far the majority of the population, they are nonetheless the victims of those who do not share the same love and identification with country. Any potential resentment they might feel is quelled by the oldest salve known to political rulers – the balm of fictive belonging by virtue of one's authentic and natural roots in the national soil in tandem with a fervent stigmatization of the internal others who threaten the

---

[1] Often subjected to the metaphor of cancer in the body politic, the case can be made that if another person has cancer one feels pity but not fear; but when the cancer is inside your own body, one will take any means necessary to destroy the disease.

survival of the true nation.[2] Thus without so much as a peep from the media, Anne Coulter, one of the right's most visible public intellectuals had no trouble finding a publisher for her best-selling book on the "treason" of American liberals (Coulter 2003).

Some may object that evangelical right-wing religion more than nationalism has become the driving force of internal exclusionary identity politics. But this confuses the direction of the causal arrows. Religious and values-based litmus tests, conflating political differences to wars against "people of faith," and the use of biblical injunctions as political wedges in the culture wars, are proxies for the inclusions and exclusions of the nation. Criticism of evangelical Christianity, indeed support for the separation of church and state, are markers of "anti-Americanism," and threats that need to be purged. For Evangelicals, blurring the line between church and state provides a mechanism of national social belonging and identity. For their political leaders, by contrast, blurring that line is a means to mobilize "the base."

Free-market patriots

While national identity is rooted in a naturalistic story of American ethnos it always contains within it a set of cultural commitments and practices. Among these, religious orthodoxies are more often than not the first among equals. But conflating nationalist loyalty with a zealous commitment to the idea of the free market is surely one of the great peculiarities of American nationalism. From the perspective of the long tradition of populist anticapitalism in Europe and the United States, one could almost call it another puzzle of American exceptionalism. In my view, the secret of free-market patriotism is in the concept of *freedom* which, more than any other, is the dominant trope of American nationalism. That a passionate antistatist conception of freedom from government tyranny is the flip side of freedom of property from state interference is of course not an American peculiarity but a particularity of liberalism *tout court* (Block 1997). It is nonetheless quite exceptional that the long tradition of American nativism's antistatist right-eousness and its demand to "get government off people's backs" has almost seamlessly grafted onto a three decades long movement by the privileged to restructure the tax system by eliminating taxes on wealth and shifting the losses onto income from labor. The truly breathtaking

---

[2] The post-9/11 Bush regime declared that "those who are not with us, are against us," just as anyone who raised any criticisms of the government "aided and abetted the terrorists."

achievement of American nationalism is that the current regime of market fundamentalism supports government of the rich, by the rich, and for the rich – *which is being voted in by people who are not rich*. Indeed one of the most remarkable findings in Thomas Frank's best-selling *What's the Matter with Kansas?* is just this passionate willingness on the part of the socially excluded to take whatever actions necessary to ensure that the largest possible tax cuts go to the wealthiest and most privileged Americans (Frank 2004, 2005). Today's peculiar form of nationalist identity formation is one that reproduces the very economic policies that cause those most victimized by them to be expelled into the "freedom" of statelessness.

The zealous but often puzzling ardor of the socially excluded toward the kind of free-market capitalism that does most harm to their livelihoods can perhaps be explained in part by the association between the façade of cowboy capitalism and the peculiar American obsession with absolute freedom. Inversely, it might also explain the vitriol directed by "hardworking patriots who love their country and are persecuted for it" toward liberals, intellectuals, and rich "Hollywood types" who are "either highborn weaklings or eggheads hypnotized by some fancy idea [and] *always* ready to sell their nation out at a moment's notice" (Frank 2005: 47).[3] The social exclusion produced by losing the social protections attached to citizenship leads to a powerful sense of class resentment among today's stateless nationals, while attachment to the nation compensates with cultural inclusion and a passionate belief in the free market.

There is some degree of uniqueness in this. It is not always possible for the socially excluded to be compensated for their loss of status and rights by being "allowed" into the culturally exclusive portals of the nation. Jews and all the millions of other dehumanized *apatrides* had no such option in the 1930s and 1940s. Whether national inclusion is available to the rightless "detritus" of society is thus entirely dependent on the prevailing distribution of power. Because today power flows in the opposite direction from that of interwar Europe – the stateless move from the exclusions of citizenship to the inclusions of nationalism – today's socially excluded find themselves in a very different position from the European Jews and others stateless peoples. Today, those who dominate political governance have every reason to encourage those excluded from

---

[3] It does seem to explain the fierce loyalty of African-Americans to the Democratic Party. As the victims not only of social exclusion but of the association between national identity and whiteness, they have no trouble understanding the true consequences of being stateless in a market fundamentalist regime.

the rights of citizenship to identify themselves more strongly than ever as the patriotic included.

Alliances between the politically powerful and the powerless are hardly new in the history of politics. Yet the kind of alliance held together between the white working classes and the kind of power represented by the currently hegemonic market fundamentalist regime is unprecedented in American history. The patriotic fervor in the hearts of those most victimized by marketization is guaranteed to at once obscure the source of their exclusion and rightlessness while turning their potential rebellion into nationalist pride and righteous anger directed toward the vilified others. The result is a coalition held together by political expediency. Whereas the state defines, concedes, enforces, or endows citizenship *rights*, the nation demands and receives *duties*. As a prepolitical naturalistic identity, nationalism invokes the duty to die for – and vote for – the regime that has taken on the pious mantle of true patriotism.

Those who take comfort in their cultural inclusion are unlikely to become victims of the Patriot Act or other forms of political policing. But it is more than likely, in fact inevitable, that their social exclusion will only increase, as all the righteousness of national inclusion and identity cannot erase the fact that they have lost the right to have rights. Identity tied to ethnos – without the accompanying right to have the membership rights of citizenship and civil society – is an identity reduced to biology and to the state of nature. The site of the nation is the space of rightlessness. Whereas nation-states have always distinguished themselves from others by means of a thick exterior boundary on the perimeter of a territorial "container," they have also maintained the illusion of an *interior* without borders, a national space kept open by the political public sphere where differences are subordinated by the constitutional state. With the rise of the contractualization of citizenship, an interior border now duplicates that of the exterior. Only those who have borne the burden of internal social exclusion for centuries – first from slavery, then through racial apartheid – are immune from the compensatory allure of the nation.

We learned from Arendt that statelessness reduces human beings to nothing more than the scum of the earth. Because they were no longer recognizable by others as fellow humans worthy of empathy, their annihilation seemed legitimate. With little resistance from the outside world, the Nazis were able to exterminate the stateless and rightless of Europe in record time. Whether the world will take notice of a similar process taking place today by natural means (malnutrition, untreated illness and disease, reduced life expectancy, infant mortality, permanent jail time, etc.) is still an open question. What is clear is that today's story has a very different twist to it. Instead of the deadly meaninglessness of natural rights, today naturalism has converted to nationalism and has changed the face of politics in the United States. With the exception of those being extinguished by serving as cannon fodder in the "war on terror," it is likely that today's socially excluded will die slowly of exclusion from what Arendt, Polanyi, and Marshall all understood to be the prerequisite of social recognition – full membership in civil society and the universal rights of citizenship that attach to this membership. This is the foundational and primary right in the right to have rights, without which there is no mutual recognition between equals that full human identity requires. History discloses that losing the right to have rights entails losing the inclusion necessary to be recognized as part of humanity itself.

PART II

Historical epistemologies of citizenship: rights, civil society, and the public sphere

4

Citizenship troubles: genealogies of struggle for the soul of the social

> When philosophy paints its gray on gray, then has a form of life grown old, and with gray on gray it cannot be rejuvenated, but only known; the Owl of Minerva first takes flight with twilight closing in. (G. W. F. Hegel)

Generations of conceptual knowledge

Perhaps only the Owl of Minerva would have predicted it: just when so many of the egalitarian ideals T. H. Marshall so brilliantly theorized in "Citizenship and Social Class" ([1950] 1964) had been all but completely betrayed, his historical sociology of citizenship suddenly achieved canonical status. Forty-five years after its initial appearance and out of print for decades, the now legendary essay reappeared – and with it a virtual explosion of interest in citizenship studies (Marshall and Bottomore 1992; Isin and Turner 2002; Shafir 1998). Across all the disciplines, from law to comparative literature, from sociology to public health, the concept of citizenship seems to have overnight become one of the central categories of public life. As the increasing momentum of interest is rapidly producing a truly enormous body of literature, citizenship also has become one of those rare academic topics properly claimed by scholarship and the political public sphere alike (Archibugi and Held 1998; Blair 1996, 1998; Commission of the European Communities 1997; Eder and Giesen 2001; Fierlbeck 1991; Freedland 2001; HM Government 1991a, 1991b, 1991c; Lewis 1993; Marcella and Baxter 1999; Straw 1998; Tritter 1994; United Kingdom Commission on Citizenship 1990).

Citations to *Citizenship and Social Class* can be used to track this expanding literature, as figure 4.1 demonstrates. The number of citations to Marshall reported by the *Social Science Citation Index* (SSCI) from 1950 through 2002 underlines the point: after four decades of what are roughly steady rates of citation, in the early 1990s there is an upward

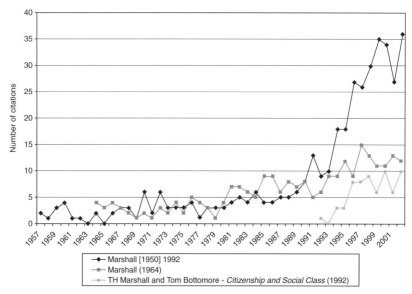

Source: Social Science Citation Index at ISI Web of Science

4.1 T. H. Marshall citation rate 1957–2001

spike that ends in a citation rate about thirty-seven times greater than that of the previous decades.[1]

Such a sudden eruption of interest in citizenship over the course of a little more than a decade makes the "rediscovery" of citizenship in the 1990s a true phenomenon of our time. This has been much commented upon. Indeed sometimes it seems to be unwritten law that no article or book on the subject is allowed to begin without this observation. Surprisingly, however, what have been virtually absent from the literature are engaged efforts to account for the many years of silence. The premise of this chapter is that developing such an account is a matter of compelling importance for both historical sociology and social theory more generally. For despite the topic's current prominence, history shows us that citizenship has been only an occasional concern to social analysis, with the strange habit of being discovered, forgotten, and rediscovered yet again. One does not have to be a sociologist of knowledge to puzzle over such an oddity. Here is one of modernity's great signifiers – touching as it does on virtually every dimension of life from identity and the self to social provisioning and gender

[1] For social science citations on citizenship theory before Marshall, see Bain (1933); Branford (1906); Eldridge (1928); Hertz (1941); Hover (1932); Lancaster (1930); Mekeel (1944); Scruggs (1886); Sherwood (1923).

discrimination – making a significant appearance only once every fifty years. How do we explain this strange career of the concept of citizenship in scholarship and the public sphere more broadly?

One way of thinking about it is through the eyes of Minerva's bearer of wisdom. Hegel used the legend to forewarn that the owl would not bestow true knowledge of the world we live in until that world had become "a form of life grown old." This is a view that gives meaning to what today seems tragic: much of the social justice made possible by the twentieth-century democratization of citizenship rights had to be left in shambles "with twilight closing in" before philosophy could "paint its gray on gray" and put citizenship rights back at the center of social thought. To be sure, depending on one's angle of political geographic vision, there will be different perceptions of just how much social provisioning Western Europe and the United States have successfully dismantled – the usual continuum of demise puts Anglo-American societies at one pole, moving all the way to Scandinavian at the other, with continental Europe spreading out in between. But despite once convincing arguments for the welfare state's institutional durability (Leibfried and Pierson 1995; Pierson 1994), a decade later there can be no gainsaying the effects of market fundamentalism's global assault on what Marshall most famously dubbed social citizenship (Crouch 2001; Eder *et al.* 2001; Esping-Andersen *et al.* 2002; Freedland 2001; Huber and Stephens 2001; Pierson 2001; Procacci 2001).

It would be a mistake, moreover, to think that the "form of life grown old" is limited to social provisioning. Just as significant, especially in the United States, is the radical transformation of the federal judiciary over the last quarter century. With the exception of the rights of property and a commercially oriented interpretation of freedom of speech, a successful assault has been launched against virtually all the civil rights that Marshall made foundational to the very possibility of democratic citizenship rights. According to one of today's most acclaimed legal scholars "[t]o a degree that has been insufficiently appreciated, and is in some ways barely believable, the contemporary federal courts are fundamentally different from the federal courts of just two decades ago" (Sunstein 2003: A2). And because they have a causally reciprocal relationship to each other, these challenges to civil and legal rights can in no way be separated from those of political and social rights. Today's attacks on welfare and other forms of entitlement (Mead 1997; Murray 1984; Olasky 1992) also place the blame on an "excess" of democracy for the reckless spread of a system of "handouts" (Somers and Block 2005).

Hegel would not have been all that off-base in other ways as well. After all, it was history itself and not an autonomous, self-propelling burst of enlightenment that spurred the academic community to wake up to the significance of citizenship as an object of study. The spectacular appearance in Eastern Europe and Russia of new possibilities for political organization and processes of democratization made it impossible to any longer ignore an ideal and an institution that had once again become a central driving force of history. That the decline of the welfare state and the rise of democratic movements in Eastern Europe coincided with the rediscovery of citizenship (and its associated vocabulary of civil society, the public sphere, and democratic political culture) is a story familiar enough not to require my reprising it here. Instead, my goal in this chapter is to go beyond Hegel's theory of the twilight of history to a deeper understanding of the long absence of citizenship from the sociological agenda, including during the period of historical sociology's greatest strength in the 1970s and 1980s. This is in many ways unexplored territory.

Two themes will take center stage in my investigation: first, the peculiarities of twentieth-century social science and, second, what I am calling the "troubles of citizenship." With respect to the former, the history of nineteenth- and twentieth-century social science reveals deep and recurring blind spots regarding the subject of citizenship. Much of the explanation for these lies with the genealogy of the social sciences in the context of political liberalism and the academic division of labor among the disciplines. In a struggle entailing the politics of epistemology, sociologists recognized that to establish a turf of their own, separate from those of political science and economics, a conceptual site centered on the social that is independent of state and market would have to become emblematic of the sociological imagination. The long-standing hegemony of political and economic liberalism, however, consistently superimposed on this triadic view the binary of public/state versus private/market, thus completely effacing the site of the social. As a sociological institution rooted in civil society, rather than a formal legal category, with this effacement citizenship was too easily eclipsed from social thought.

Not all of the blame can be placed on disciplinary troubles, however. Equally responsible are the deep and seemingly intractable troubles of citizenship inherent in the concept itself, a concept and a practice that is at once normative and deontological while also aspiring to full empirical status as an institutional mechanism of governance and national sovereignty. This epistemological conflict between the normative and the empirical is itself a product of the concept's deeper ontological troubles between citizenship and the rights to which it is attached.

To understand this conflict, we need to begin with the troubled genealogies of both halves of the citizenship concept. While they form a conceptual pair, *citizenship* and *rights* have different and deeply conflicting ontological meanings rooted in their different genealogies and conceptual mappings. For citizenship is a concept born of the republican tradition, thus constitutively of the public sphere – governmental institutions as well as those of civil society. Rights, by contrast, are the hallmark of liberalism, the private sphere and the prepolitical beings who bear them. Citizenship is a political and institutional artifact of civil society and the law that evolved to overcome the dangers inherent in unregulated markets, power-centric states, and deracinated free agents. Rights, by contrast, are said to be natural to individuals in the original "state of nature." This attaches rights to a kind of governance produced not by civil and political institutions, but by a fictitious social contract consented to precisely by deracinated presocial and prepolitical men and women. Citizenship is deeply bound to the particularism of place, time, and membership, which makes it site-specific and void beyond the bounds of the polity. Natural rights, by contrast, are bound to no place at all but are universally natural to all humanity and thus are utterly portable and indefeasible regardless of anything as arbitrary as political boundaries.

For much of its life course citizenship as a potential object of study has been trapped in these conflicting genealogies of republicanism and liberalism, which I believe goes a long way toward explaining the puzzle of its recent long absence. But there is also a moral to this story of genealogies that has meaning for the history of the present. That it was historical events, rather than spontaneous intellectual developments, which catalyzed the recent citizenship epiphany suggests that our enlightenment was gifted undeservedly, without our having to even acknowledge or engage directly these blind spots and conceptual troubles. This in turn forebodes that as long as these inherent conceptual irritants are still with us, the field of citizenship studies is at risk. After all, if they once fueled its disappearance, there is no reason not to believe that these same troubles could do it again. We cannot always rely on the Owl of Minerva to stir our collective consciousness.

These, then, are the issues that frame this chapter. Several stipulations are in order before proceeding, however. The first concerns the relationship between T. H. Marshall's *Citizenship and Social Class* and the topic of citizenship more generically. This is not an essay on T. H. Marshall, and it should not be read as such. But a central point of my argument is that from the moment that Marshall first delivered his famous lectures in

152   Genealogies of Citizenship

1949, *Citizenship and Social Class* and citizenship as a social science concept became virtually one and the same. It is hard in today's context where a thousand concepts bloom to remember that in the absence of any serious preceding sociological heritage, Marshall essentially invented the social approach to citizenship. And once he did so, he became until recently its sole "owner."[2] To be sure, there was Reinhard Bendix's masterful *Nation-Building and Citizenship* (1964), and Bendix undoubtedly ranks higher than Marshall in the pantheon of sociology's greatest scholars. Nonetheless, Bendix's work on citizenship never came close to Marshall's in gaining the almost hard-wired association between the man and the subject.[3] Thus from the time of the original publication of *Citizenship and Social Class* at mid-century until a new generation of scholars finally came onto the scene at the century's end, T. H. Marshall and citizenship were inexorably yoked together.[4]

The second stipulation concerns Marshall's relationship to welfare state studies. There is no question that 1970s/1980s scholarship on welfare state policies used both Marshall and the concept of *social* citizenship extensively (Orloff 2005). This literature on social citizenship, however, was not the same as today's citizenship studies (nor, not incidentally, did it define itself as such). In some respects it may have been precisely the influence of this only partial aspect of citizenship that precluded attention to the concept as a whole. Be this as it may, welfare state studies and their association with Marshall's famous social citizenship should not be mistaken for citizenship *tout court* as theorized either by Marshall himself or as it has developed today.

The troubles of citizenship: genealogies and contradictions

When Marshall paired citizenship with rights, he was quietly challenging three centuries of conflict between political liberalism's foundational concept of rights with its exclusive valorization of the private sphere of the individual, and classical republicanism's foundational concept of citizenship with its exclusive valorization of the political. In classical republican citizenship theory there exists no concept of rights. Conversely, and beyond

---

[2] This is ironic since Marshall himself did not continue the work on citizenship but shifted almost exclusively to public service and scholarship on social policy. He came back to it only later in life. See Marshall (1981).

[3] A quarter-century after Marshall, Ralf Dahrendorf – a sociology student of Marshall's at the London School of Economics and a towering intellectual figure in his own right – briefly engaged Marshall's theory of citizenship (Bulmer and Rees 1996; Dahrendorf 1996).

[4] Examples of other such "ownership" relationships are few, but would include, for example, Marx and capitalism, Smith and the market, Weber and the Protestant ethic.

rhetorical flourish (such as in that of the *Declaration of the Rights of Man*), there is no substantial presence of citizenship in classical political liberalism. None of this should surprise. The genealogy of citizenship and the genealogy of rights entail two distinct streams of thought, each with very different origins and processes, each with a different relationship to institutional developments, and each with different degrees of influence in shaping history. Yet, as is so often the case, it is precisely because they developed in direct opposition to each other that their histories are so deeply intertwined. Indeed once the discourse of rights entered the public sphere in the seventeenth century, the two streams of thought soon developed in explicit opposition, each refining and sharpening its own ontologies and epistemologies in an ongoing relationship of *agonistes*. If we are to understand the interrupted career of the citizenship concept, then, we have to begin by recognizing this deep fissure at the very heart of the idea of citizenship rights.

Republicanism and citizenship

The idea of citizenship was born with classical Greece's mode of governance and social organization. Through the institution of the polis human freedom was attached to the privilege of citizenship, which was defined as collective (male and elite) participation in public life. Its political ideal – "to rule and be ruled" – meant that to be meaningful, social action had to take place in the site of the political. Outside of the polis was the nonpolitical site of the *oikos* – the private domain in which economic life and intimacy took place under the control of the familial household. Considered little more than a (gendered) place of material and biological reproduction, the nonpolitical *oikos* could never achieve a standing higher than that of mere "necessity." So demeaned was this dimension of human life that its activities were ontologically discounted, as social identity existed only in the context of the public forum and in the active exercise of participatory political agency. To be a republican citizen was exclusively to be a political being.

Other aspects of the citizenship tradition should be noted. Like the rights tradition that followed, republican theory conjoins the normative and the empirical. On the one hand, citizenship is a normative ideal; to gain membership in the public forum is not a right but a privilege and an honor that endows virtue on those who earn it. Moreover, that its promise to rule and be ruled stands on a foundation of slavery and gender oppression only strengthens the importance of its normative status – its empirical failures have had the effect of motivating subsequent republican thinkers all the more towards bringing citizenship ever closer to its ideal state of political equality. At the same time, theorists of republicanism also refer to citizenship as a straightforwardly institutional mode of governance – privileged, exclusive to be sure, but nonetheless amenable to empirical analysis (see e.g. Oldfield 1990; Pocock 1998). The problem is that because no such republican mode of governance has existed since the celebrated Italian city-states of the Renaissance, it is exclusively the normative dimension that has survived in modern political thought – but survived in the hands of its fiercest critics as much as in those of its advocates.

As republicanism ebbed and flowed over time – Rousseau was of course one of its greatest theorists – we see the first instance of a binary vision of the social world and its unhappy consequences for the possibility of a sociology of citizenship. Entirely missing from republicanism's split into the mutually exclusive spheres of public honor versus private necessity was anything in between – specifically, a sphere of the *social*, or civil society. And republicanism had other troubles. Its single-minded valorization of the political in tandem with its demeaning of the private sphere made it vulnerable to accusations by conservative and liberal critics of responsibility for the Terror of the French Revolution. Almost two centuries later it would also be blamed for Soviet totalitarianism (although by then communism had replaced republicanism as the favored scapegoat). Still, an indelible link was established in Anglo-liberal political culture between theories that prioritized the political, and threats to individual freedom. Combined with the absence of a "third sphere" of the social, all of this added up to an inauspicious forecast for a republican-based sociological appropriation of citizenship.

Citizen to subject to Man: liberalism and rights theory

Surely it is one of the strangest aspects of our modern knowledge culture that one searches in vain to find the words *citizen* or *citizenship* in political liberalism's founding texts.[5] In fact, in what in chapters 5 and 7 I call *Anglo-American citizenship theory*, there are no citizens. Instead, there are only rights-bearing individuals who are ontologically fierce opponents of the very idea of human identity being embedded in any political processes, regardless of any putatively associated honor or institutional empowerment. The "rights" in the couplet of citizenship rights are therefore in many ways the mirror image of "citizenship." Its Lockean genealogy reveals the same dichotomous foundation that excludes the social

---

[5] See Locke ([1690] 1961) and, with some caveats, Hobbes ([1642] 1998).

from its theory of both human freedom and political governance. Locke can be seen, moreover, as having both engendered and then dashed sociological hopes. On the one hand, he was truly revolutionary as the first to invent the idea of a self-regulating civil society autonomous of state power, and which replaced the political as the site of action and identity formation. On the other, the disappointment comes when he immediately hijacks civil society away from its promise as an autonomous site of the social, and instead transforms it into a presocial private sphere of commercial exchange (see Taylor 1990 for a philosophical approach to this issue, and chapter 7 of this volume).

At first glance Locke's promise appears simply to echo that of Hobbes (1973), who had already changed the terms of discourse by locating the origins of human identity not in political authority but in the state of nature. But Locke's treatise on political rights was actually both a recognition and a deep criticism of Hobbes's sleight of hand. For Hobbes takes a revolutionary stance against traditional absolutism by rejecting the notion that rights can only be granted by the positive law of the state, a position that relegates people to subjects rather than citizens. Instead he insists that people are born free and equal, and endowed with natural rather than conferred rights. But what he gives with one hand, he then steals back with the other. Deeming individuals to be ontologically predisposed to anarchy and violence for the sake of their own survival, Hobbes's rights-bearing individuals agree by social contract to *forgo* those very rights and relinquish them into the hands of an all-powerful political ruler. With that reversal, Hobbes relegates once free individuals back to the status of subjects, a move he has them choose voluntarily out of rational self-interest.

Hobbes clearly had a leg in both worlds. On the one hand, he wants to start from a position of natural rights over and against the tradition of politically conferred arbitrary governance. On the other hand, or leg, he thoroughly mistrusts people in their natural condition, and believes that only the artifice of political power can ensure order and security. But rather than endow his solitary individuals with the capacity to act together politically by creating regulative social institutions, he summarily demotes them back to rightless subjecthood by housing them, quite literally, in the belly of the Leviathan.

Locke challenges this argument by reversing Hobbes's ultimate source of authority from the "benevolent" state back to the natural rights of individuals in the state of nature. From there Locke's individuals agree by means of a social contract to construct not a state but a naturalized version of civil society. But although Locke does not return Hobbes's subjects to domination by state power, he still has not freed them to become citizens. For the true state of humankind is neither political nor social, but based on the capacity to produce and exchange private property in civil society, which he defines not as social, but as a civilizing sphere of private interaction and commercial exchange. In contrast to the state, it is harmoniously self-regulating, as it has been designed to mirror the norms of the state of nature. As such, however, there can be no social membership in civil society, but only unencumbered, detached, rights-bearers who have chosen to constitute themselves as an independent aggregate of free agents. "To understand political power aright, and derive it from its original, we must consider what state all men are naturally in, and that it is a state of perfect freedom to order their actions and dispose of their possessions and persons as they see fit, within the bounds of the law of nature, without asking leave, or depending upon the will of any other man" (Locke [1690] 1952: sect. 4).

So while Locke refuses Hobbes, he equally refuses the social relationality of citizenship. No conception of political or social membership is possible in a presocial marketized conception of civil society and an exclusively tyrannical state. For Locke, these are not men and women but abstract Man – and thus rights-bearing by virtue of a universalistic, naturalized individualized free agency. Each individual is constitutively autonomous vis-à-vis all other people and all relational entities.

This leads to a difficult question: When people are endowed with rights simply by virtue of being universal abstract Man, rather than an English, French, or Athenian woman or man, by what means can these natural rights-bearers defend themselves against violations by the state? The answer given by Locke is famously simple. It is yet another right with no institutional foundations – the natural right of the individual to resist the tyrannical artifice of the political, a mandate Americans used to justify the Declaration of Independence a century later.

Citizenship and the French Revolution

So much for the hope of finding the social site of citizenship in the origins of liberalism. But surely citizenship and rights come together in the *Declaration of the Rights of Man and the Citizen*, one of history's most famous assertions of the natural rights of citizens? After all, it was the French Revolution that for "about two centuries constituted the ideal model for those who fought for their own emancipation and the liberation of their people" (Bobbio 1996: 81). And it is the principles of the

Rights of Man that constitute, "whether we like it or not, an obligatory reference point for the friends and foes of liberty" (Bobbio 1996: 81. See also, Balibar 1994; Hunt 1996).

But when we turn to this founding document of modern citizenship, things turn out to be not what they seem. Although every schoolchild associates the terms *citoyen* and *citoyenne* with the French Revolution (forever seared in memory by Dickens's sinister Madame Defarge and her infamous knitting needles), in fact the terms *citizen* and *citizenship* appear only a handful of times in the *Declaration*. Where they do appear in the text, they are subordinate to abstract universal Man, who is free by natural right and not by membership in any social of political entity. It was Locke's state of nature in the *Second Treatise*, Thomas Paine's *Rights of Man*, and Rousseau's "noble savage" that inspired this revolutionary statement – certainly not Aristotle or Machiavelli.

The "doctrinal nucleus" (Bobbio 1996: 82) of the *Declaration* can be found in the first three articles. The first asserts that individuals are born free and equal in rights as their natural condition, which thus precedes any formation of civil or political society; the second states that the sole purpose of political society, which is an outcome of individuals' consensual social contract, is the "preservation of the natural and imprescriptible rights of man" – namely, liberty, property, security, and resistance to oppression; and the third asserts that all "sovereignty rests essentially in the nation," which is explained to be the embodiment of the aggregate of the rights-bearing individual.

Not until one has read over one-third of the *Declaration* does the word "citizen" even make an appearance, in Article 6, and there only as a marker for abstract Man (Hunt 1996: 78). Thus rather than republican citizenship it was in the Lockean language of naturalistic, presocial, prepolitical, and property-protecting Man that the famous *Declaration* defined the terms of political identity, individual liberties, and popular governance.[6]

Paradoxically, it was the reactionary rhetoric of conservatism (Hirschman 1990) that launched what was arguably the most republican-sounding criticism of the rights-based tradition. "I've never met Man," thundered Edmund Burke, "only English, French, Italian men" (cited in Arendt 1979: 299). But Burke's commitment to free markets eventually overruled his traditionalism, and from J. S. Mill through the great liberal thinkers of the

---

[6] No one has written more brilliantly than Balibar on the *Declaration*'s use of the conflicting concepts of "rights/liberty" and "citizenship/equality" (see, especially Balibar 1994: 39–69, 205–25; 2004a, b).

twentieth century, not until Arendt ([1958] 1998) and Wolin (1960) did any serious competition from republicanism arise.

In its exclusively binary depiction of the universe, the rights tradition has no place for the intermediary sphere of the social. Just as in republicanism, liberalism's public/state versus private/market dichotomy exhausts the spectrum of governance and human agency. The difference between liberalism and republicanism is thus almost entirely normative rather than analytic. Liberalism maps a privileged epistemology of social naturalism onto a fictive aggregate of rights-bearing individuals. It thus spins a metanarrative that invokes a "fear and loathing of the political" while it valorizes the private and "romances the market" (see chapter 7). Republicanism collapses identity into political citizenship and demeans the economic practices of reproductive necessity. For liberalism, human identity in natural rights is not only prepolitical and presociological; its vision of tyranny is rooted in the very political bodies celebrated as the realm of freedom by the republican tradition. To be a rights-bearing "citizen," then, is not to be a member of any political or social entity. Rather, it is to be an isolated individual whose self-interest alone induces a contract with others – reluctantly and contingently. Political liberalism's contractualized conception of citizenship is one without membership, built only from an aggregate of individual rights.[7]

The sociological implications of the rights tradition hardly make it fertile ground for a sociology of citizenship. Instead liberalism fashions a causal argument for the primacy of both the prepolitical and the presocial. Even the famous "social" in the social contract is not social in the sociological sense of the word. Rather, it consists of temporary, voluntarily aggregated individual action from which the right of exit is at all times present. How different this is from intuitively sociological notions of citizenship in which rights are held by virtue of membership in an entity that exists prior to the individual.

Like republicanism, liberalism is at once normative and institutional, with the normative usually trumping the institutional (thus suggesting why its scholarship prevails in political and legal-constitutional theory rather than the empirical social sciences). Just as in republicanism's political ontology of human agency, liberalism's state of nature is an appeal to a solely normative commitment that cannot be used to analyze the conditions that support or disable human freedoms. This makes liberalism no more a foundation for a sociology of citizenship than its theoretical rival.

---

[7] L. T. Hobhouse (an important influence on Marshall) for an example of how liberalism directly addresses issues of citizenship (Hobhouse [1911] 1964).

Marxism and the critique of bourgeois citizenship and rights

As it happens it was not republicanism but Karl Marx who left us with the most enduring and influential critiques of political liberalism. To be sure, in his early vision of the fundamentally relational nature of human "species-being" and in his various articulations of a post-capitalist world, Marx follows Hegel in setting up a *triadic* social universe. He thus holds out the promise of laying the groundwork for a sociological perspective. Unfortunately, he also follows Hegel in making civil society the site of market exchange and economic production, thus fully conflating civil society with the private site of the public–private binary. So Marx disappoints the hope for a fundamental destabilization of the public–private dichotomy. But he has other fish to fry, namely to pierce the "illusions" of bourgeois citizenship and to leave the liberal idea of rights in shambles. Rather than Burke's concern for the abstraction of natural rights, for Marx the rights-bearing Man of Reason and individuality born in political liberalism's state of nature is too particular. While it exhibits a specious universalism, the only "natural" rights-bearers in real capitalism were none other than the very particular bourgeois men who make up society's ruling class. Reflecting in the 1840s on the new constitutions produced by the American and French Revolutions, in "On the Jewish Question" Marx makes clear how he perceives the true meaning of modern "political equality" in a liberal constitutional state:

Nevertheless, the political annulment of private property not only fails to abolish private property but also even presupposes it. The state abolishes, in its own way, distinctions of birth, social rank, education, occupation, when it declares that birth, social rank, education, occupation, are non-political distinctions, when it proclaims, without regard to these distinctions, that every member of the nation is an equal participant in national sovereignty, when it treats all elements of the real life of the nation from the standpoint of the state. Nevertheless, the state allows private property, education, occupation, to act in their way – i.e., as private property, as education, as occupation, and to exert the influence of their special nature. Far from abolishing these real distinctions, the state only exists on the presupposition of their existence; it feels itself to be a political state and asserts its universality only in opposition to these elements of its being.[8]

In *Capital*, Marx later extends the critique to the labor process by once again fiercely and polemically puncturing the specious "equality" endowed by bourgeois law and political rights, and especially the "voluntary"

---

[8] See www.marxists.org/archive/marx/works/1844/jewish-question/index.htm.

contract between "equal" individuals in the labor market. Urging us to leave this world of "egalitarian illusion and rights" and to follow him "below," where the *real* causal mechanisms of bourgeois society are at work, he points to the one underlying truth of bourgeois law. There, behind a door that reads "only those here on business should enter," and in contrast to the "fair" labor market contract that makes its appearance "above," we see the tyrannical and all-powerful capitalist employer striding forcefully, while behind him slinks in subordinated and meek powerlessness the putatively equal rights-bearing working person.

In order that our owner of money may be able to find labour-power offered for sale as a commodity, various conditions must first be fulfilled . . .. [The worker] and the owner of money meet in the market, and deal with each other as on the basis of equal rights, with this difference alone, that one is buyer, the other seller; both, therefore, *equal in the eyes of the law* . . . Accompanied by Mr. Moneybags and by the possessor of labour-power, we therefore take leave for a time of this noisy sphere, *where everything takes place on the surface and in view of all men*, and follow them both into the hidden abode of production, on whose threshold there stares us in the face "No admittance except on business." This sphere that we are deserting, within whose boundaries the sale and purchase of labour-power goes on, is in fact a *very Eden of the innate rights of man. There alone rule Freedom, Equality, Property and Bentham.* Freedom, because both buyer and seller of a commodity, say of labour-power, are constrained only by their own free will. They contract as free agents, and the agreement they come to, is but the form in which they give legal expression to their common will. Equality, because each enters into relation with the other, as with a simple owner of commodities, and they exchange equivalent for equivalent. Property, because each disposes only of what is his own. And Bentham, because each looks only to himself . . . and no one troubles himself about the rest, and just because they do so, do they all, in accordance with the *pre-established harmony of things*, or under the auspices of an *all-shrewd providence, work together to their mutual advantage, for the common weal and in the interest of all.*

On leaving this sphere of simple circulation or of exchange of commodities, which furnishes the "Free-trader Vulgaris" with his view and ideas, and with the standard by which he judges a society based on capital and wages, we think *we can perceive a change in the physiognomy of our dramatis personae.* He, who before was the money owner, now strides in front as capitalist; the possessor of labour-power follows as his labourer. *The one with an air of importance, smirking, intent on business; the other, timid and holding back, like one who is bringing his own hide to market and has nothing to expect but – a hiding.* (Marx 1978: 337–42; italics in original)

In light of this long quotation it may be surprising that Marx rejects the idea that modern bourgeois rights have achieved nothing. Instead, he sees them as "a big step forward," albeit a judgment he bases on the "limits of current conditions." "Within the prevailing scheme of things," bourgeois rights are the best that can be hoped for. This small concession is consistent with Marx's over-the-top admiration for capitalism as a necessary step toward communism. Expressed lyrically in *The Communist Manifesto*'s famous encomium to the heroic emergence of capitalism out of the slavery of feudalism, this nod to bourgeois rights is very much in line with Marx the ultra-modernist, indeed a pioneer of classical modernization theory with its teleological progression from "tradition" to "modernity," and from feudalism to capitalism.[9] Right up to the last decades of the twentieth century, it is Marx's enduring image of the illusory quality of political rights that leaves the most lasting impression on the social sciences.

Where does this leave us?

It is time to take stock. Modern ideas of rights derive from natural law and are attached to people not as citizens of any particular political entity but as abstract Man with natural rights. As Locke first conceived them in the state of nature, these ethereal individuals exist independently and prior to any political or social body. Today's human rights movement finds its roots in this understanding of indefeasible natural, universal rights. But history has shown us that the normative idea of the rights-bearing subject is tragically abstract, for this is a subject whose very identity is rooted in the "state of nature," where no political power can actually *enforce* these rights and protect the bearer. On the basis of the sovereign power of nation-states to control their own borders and population movements, untold numbers of stateless people – Jews, "Gypsies," and other ethnic minorities expelled and denaturalized by their own governments – have been served up to genocidal regimes while sovereign liberal nations have stood by and refused asylum. These stateless peoples, as Arendt ([1951] 1979) so brilliantly reminds us, were in full possession of their natural rights as they entered the gas chambers in Nazi Germany.

Citizenship, by contrast, is available only to those with the privilege, not the right, of membership in a specific political body existing prior to and independent of any particular human beings. Looking from the outside in, citizenship is discriminatory and exclusive; but once inside, it is a force for equality and inclusion. Still, in one important respect, the two traditions have much in common. When considered on their own terms both genealogies have been forged through an erasure of the social.

---

[9] See also his "Private Property and Communism" and "The Meaning of Human Requirements" in Tucker (1978).

It is this that goes a long way to explaining the silence of a serious sociological engagement with citizenship in the years before Marshall first makes an appearance.

Inventing a sociological citizenship

By the time of T. H. Marshall's *Citizenship and Social Class* (1950), the intellectual landscape had been transformed. The singular conflict between liberalism and republicanism was a distant memory. The intellectual and political fray now was characterized roughly by three competing political approaches to public life and social policy. Economic and political liberalism were still very much alive in the Conservative Party, but republicanism largely had been replaced by two versions of Marxism: Britain's postwar Communist Party and Fabian social democrats in the Labour Party who adhered to the ameliorative model of Marxism (or reformism, as it had been called since the German Social Democrats in the first decades of the twentieth century).

It was the social democrats who won the debate in mid-century Britain. The governing Labour Party had remarkable success instituting a social welfare state unprecedented in the breadth of its interference with the market in public goods and services (e.g. health and education), without threatening capitalism as a system of governance (Eley 2002). Marshall, who in 1950 was one of Britain's leading social scientists, was an important friend of these social democratic policies (Halsey 1982). Thus when he transformed the idea of citizenship from a purely juridical status to a full-fledged causally dynamic institution extending from contract and property to law to political participation to social policy, it is not surprising that his innovative concept of *social* citizenship, with its valorization of social and economic rights, gained the most attention. In the heated debate over the value of reformism in modern capitalist society, *Citizenship and Social Class* was read as the theoretical imprimatur to the social democratic regime.

The association was well deserved. Marshall was a man who dedicated more than half his adult life to public service in the interest of egalitarian social policy.[10] He explicitly intended his interventions to give a political

---

[10] Although Marshall was a sociologist by degree, he spent the bulk of his time in the academy in the London School of Economics' Department of Social Policy (Marshall 1981).

and moral legitimacy to public policy in the interest of social needs that would be equal to that held by property rights, individual civil rights, and those of participation (Barbalet 1988; Marshall 1981). *Citizenship and Social Class*, moreover, was organized around the central political debate of the day – namely, were there any measures short of Marx's revolution that could fundamentally improve the condition of the working classes in a modern capitalist society rent by class inequalities? Marshall's answer was yes, and provided much support for the claims of a fit between the modern capitalist world and reformist social democratic governance. Like the original Fabian sociologists who served as the intellectual shop of the Labour Party, Marshall divided history into tradition versus modernity, localism versus the nation-state, particularism versus universalism. Like them, he allowed only that which could be found on the modern side of history to count as real causal factors in the progression toward greater egalitarianism. And like theirs, his position was dismissive of any causal status attributed to "premodern" working-class social movements and artisanal organizations such as guilds and proto-trade unions.

Yet it is the differences between Marshall and the social democratic Labour Party that best helps us understand why Marshall's theory of citizenship was not sufficiently recognized as either an original social theory or one that laid the ground for a new field of social science, as well as why the prevailing intellectual and political culture more generally had negative implications for the reception of *Citizenship and Social Class*. One of these differences was the now familiar problem of the "missing site of the social" across the entire spectrum of public discourse. It was an absence driven not by the obvious differences among liberalism, social democracy, and Marxism, but by what they had in common, namely that the default institutional and normative political landscape had been invented, shaped, delimited, and dichotomized by liberalism's manichaean "great dichotomy" (Bobbio 1992) between the private market and the public state. While for Marxists and Labourites the normative terms of debate were inverted from those of liberalism – the private, not the public, was the sphere of coercion and unfreedom – theirs was no less a manichaean dichotomy between the mode of production and the state without an intervening social site.

In this dichotomized pre-Marshallian world, the idea of citizenship as a social institution had not been invented. Instead it was still conceived as a basic legal status defining nationality. For liberalism, the source of rights was not primarily political membership but the long heritage of English liberties enshrined in common law – the legal and symbolic apparatus of individual protections against the state. For Marxists and

Labourites, by contrast, rights were capitalism's cunning trickery. Yet, like liberalism, the direction of power and authority in the distribution and nature of rights flowed entirely from the private to the public.

We should now be beginning to make sense of how *Citizenship and Social Class* was received in the context of mid-century British politics and political culture. As a novel theory of citizenship, it was ignored not because it was evaluated as bad history, bad theory or even because it was ruled out of epistemological court for being nothing more than a speculative hypothesis unsupported by evidence. Rather, it simply did not fit into the prevailing categories of knowledge at the time of its debut. In this knowledge culture of the absent social, there was no conceptual vocabulary available for Marshall's particular project of redefining citizenship through the social. Instead he was read through the prism of a political discourse that pitted reformist social democracy against more radical Marxism on its left, and laissez-faire free-market theory on its right. It is thus not surprising, then, to find that his provocative work did not provoke a following, nor did any major texts on the subject of citizenship and capitalism appear that implied a Marshallian influence. In the 1950s British sociology was busy emulating American postwar quantitative social science, and Marshall's text appeared old-fashioned in its qualitative and deceptively easy historical style (Marshall 1964; Lipset 1964). An American edition of *Citizenship and Social Class* was hardly considered at the time.

By the 1960s the world had become a very different place, both politically and in scholarship. Over the course of the 1950s Marshall's prodigious talents as a teacher had produced a group of young sociologists that included some of the leading British and American social scientists of the postwar generation.[11] This, as well as his coterminous role as a leading public intellectual, led to a new appearance of the essay "Citizenship and Social Class" thirteen years after the first edition, and fourteen years after his famous (Alfred) Marshall lectures of the same name. But it would be wrong to take this as a long overdue recognition of Marshall as a pathbreaking theorist of citizenship or of the sociology of citizenship as an important new field of scholarship. In fact the new volume bundled the essay with a collection of his essays and lectures on other topics, and was tellingly renamed *Sociology at the Crossroads* (1963). Less an effort to

[11] John Goldthorpe, Ralf Dahrendorf, and Seymour Martin Lipset are among the most well known (Bulmer and Rees 1996).

foreground a new approach to citizenship, the repackaging was clearly marketing Marshall as a leading academic salesman for the infant discipline of British sociology. Perhaps for just this reason of legitimacy, in 1964 Seymour Martin Lipset (himself one of Marshall's crop of remarkable student protégés at the London School of Economics in the 1950s) convinced an American publisher to produce an American edition of the new volume (Marshall 1964). The story of this transmigration turns out to be a critical episode in the story of the long absence of a sociology of citizenship.

Twentieth-century American social science was notable for its denial of political power. Yet, while very true of the post-World War II generation, a longer view of American social science suggests that this antistatism was less characteristic of the beginning of the century. American social scientists from the end of the nineteenth century well into the interwar era focused extensively on the state (Ciepley 2000). Many sought to engage policy and government, having studied in Germany where they had come under the influence of the German Historical School, a group of economic historians and sociologists who theorized the rise of capitalist modernity through the prism of the state.[12] The pragmatist movement in philosophy and its political commitment to a "workable" society was also an influential part of this knowledge culture.

This explicit attention to the state came to a roaring halt with the emergence of European fascism and the outbreak of war in 1939. Totalitarianism came to dominate the conceptual approach to Germany and the Soviet Union, purging any potentially neutral consideration of the state in postwar scholarship. Instead, liberalism's foundational view of the menacing state chronically threatening individual freedoms quickly came to dominate the Cold War political and knowledge culture.[13]

This was the context of that generation of American postwar social scientists who rebelled against the statism of the prewar social scientists. But why, then, would Lipset have adopted T. H. Marshall into their fold? After all, Marshall's theory considers the market-intervening state as a

[12] The Historical School dominated the German academy at the turn of the century and exercised enormous influence on those important English economic historians who founded the institutionalist *Economic History Review*. The most significant of these were W. J. Ashley and William Cunningham.

[13] Emblematic of the age was a review of Polanyi's *Great Transformation* ([1944] 1957c) by Hans Morgenthau, one of the foremost political scientists of his time. In direct reference to the Prussian state, Morgenthau dubbed Polanyi's argument that political power was a necessary component of freedom as manifesting "the heavy hand of Hegel."

necessary and positive good for citizenship rights. The answer is that in a period in which the concept of totalitarianism had redesigned the conceptual map of American social science, Lipset read Marshall as a variant of *modernization* theory – an essentially stateless, developmental story about self-propelling industrialization and democratization. In this climate *Citizenship and Social Class* was read as an argument less focused on rights and more on the stability that Marshall argued can be achieved in an unequal society as long as class differences are mitigated by political inclusion and public services.

In his introduction, Lipset explains the publication of an American edition of a fifteen-year-old book by arguing that Marshall deserved a wider social science audience than he had as yet received (Lipset 1964; Marshall 1964). Yet Lipset does not celebrate Marshall's path-breaking sociological contribution to a historical theory of political rights and social justice, or to his exploration of the balance of power between the inequality of capitalism and the equalizing status of citizenship – as Marshall himself characterized his own work. Instead, Lipset defined Marshall as first and foremost a pioneer in the then current (early 1960s) "renewed interest in historical and comparative sociology." And it is in these terms that he explained the long delay in the appearance of an American edition, stating that when *Citizenship and Social Class* was first published in 1950, the social science community was fixated almost exclusively on "quantitative techniques and methodological rigor." In that atmosphere, according to Lipset, Marshall was dismissed as an "example of the old-fashioned type of sociology that had characterized European scholarship before World War II . . . which regarded such men as Max Weber, Emile Durkheim, and Robert Michels as outmoded representatives of the prescientific era of sociology." A decade or so later, "far from being a representative of the past, Marshall had proved to be a precursor of the future" (Lipset 1964: vi–vii; see also Steinmetz 2005).

As a theorist of citizenship rights whose discovery of Marshall and his citizenship theory in the 1970s went on to shape my entire intellectual outlook, I find this to be heady stuff. And as a historical sociologist who came of age in the 1970s, I find it to be puzzling stuff. Not only do we *not* associate the revival of the field of comparative-historical sociology with the 1960s (with the exception of Barrington Moore [1965]); but here is Lipset – among the most prominent targets of attack by the 1970s generation for his advocacy of modernization theory – sounding a siren for T. H. Marshall in exactly those terms. According to Lipset, the book should have become one of the founding texts of a new historical sociology. Yet it very definitely did not.

The puzzle is perhaps solved by a closer look at the new moniker under which Lipset introduced T. H. Marshall to an American audience. In contrast to the British title of *Sociology at the Crossroads* (1963), the American title was *Class, Citizenship, and Social Development* (Marshall 1964). It was Lipset's third term – "social development" – that eclipsed the others in its significance for how the work was received on the American side of the pond. For it was this concept of development that Lipset put at the substantive core of the historical sociological approach he was anxious to revive. "Comparative historical sociology," according to Lipset, "is a body of inquiry which, lacking a better label, has been called the sociology of development ... sociologists interested in problems of societal modernization and nation building in Africa and Asia have come to recognize that the 'old states' of the world have much to tell us about these processes" (Lipset 1964: vii).

So social development was a more general variant of "modernization theory," which in the 1960s had become a prestigious and influential field of social science. And Lipset was among its most eminent and powerful practitioners. But to the next generation of rebels it was perceived as a kind of intellectual imperialism – whether under the guise of development or modernization – by which modernization theorists imposed the yardstick of advanced Western industrial (capitalist) society as the measure against which to evaluate (and influence policy in) Third World countries around the globe – and inevitably to find them wanting.[14] Modernization theory, like the "empirical theory of democracy" with which it was associated, conflated what was actually a normative "ought" with a putatively empirical "is." It shied away from Western capitalist inequalities and racisms (among other failures) and instead held up for the rest of the world to emulate a universal standard that was really an American model of national success – a model characterized not by political ideologies but by a democratic "political culture." This, too, was a term of art, defined as a set of psychological values committed not to any single vision of the good, but to an all-encompassing political moderation and the procedural rule of law (see chapter 5 below).

Modernization theory was about to meet its demise in the late 1960s, first under the unparalleled assault of Barrington Moore's comparative

---

[14] The critique of modernization theory is too enormous to even consider representing here. But among the most significant and influential discussions are Bendix (1964) and Grew (1985).

and class-based attack on its universalizing premises, and then under a stampede of the 1970s generation of political and historical sociologists. Mistakenly aligned with Lipset's consensus-driven modernization theorists, Marshall's star was extinguished virtually overnight. Surely there is a cruel paradox in the consequences of Lipset's endorsement of T. H. Marshall as a pioneer in comparative-historical sociology. By reducing the field to "social development" and modernization theory, Lipset made Marshall a "marked man," and his sociology of citizenship was lost for another two generations.

The 1970s generation of historical sociology: a new knowledge culture is born

The generation of 1970s historical sociologists was shaped by a combination of its historical context and the requisite ritualistic patricide of dominant mainstream scholarship. Opposition to the Vietnam War and other perceived forms of imperialism shaped their revulsion for a government waging war against peoples of the Third World. To be sure, they embraced the demand for participatory democracy that emerged from the famous Port Huron Statement by Students for a Democratic Society (SDS). But it was the coupling of the critique of capitalism with a passion for political activism that informed their outlook toward scholarship. Living in a time of prosperity at home, and with no premonition of the rise of market fundamentalism yet to come, citizenship had little more meaning than its association with the privileges of an American passport – hardly comparable with Marshall's driving passions for social equality and justice.

The rejection of Lipset's definition of comparative-historical sociology may be best represented by a conference hosted at Harvard in 1980. The gathering was organized by Theda Skocpol, one of the pioneers in the state-centered version of historical sociology, and included many of her generation's leading lights. Most interesting about both the conference and *Vision and Method in Historical Sociology* (Skocpol 1984), the book that followed, was that they were not organized around major sociological themes but around a number of social science's greatest twentieth-century figures (e.g. Barrington Moore, Marc Bloch, Karl Polanyi, E. P. Thompson, Reinhard Bendix). Each of these figures in some way had inspired this new generation to bring history and comparison back into the heart of the social sciences.

Notably absent from these figures/mentors was the preceding generation of self-proclaimed comparative-historical sociologists, including

Lipset and other modernization theorists.[15] Another surprising feature
of the volume was the minority status of Marxism. Out of nine chapters,
each dedicated to a different scholar, only two subjects (Perry Anderson
and Edward Thompson), at most three (Immanuel Wallerstein), could
by any stretch of the imagination have been called Marxists. Even they
were involved in one form or another of a deep revisionism away from
standard Marxism – toward the state (Anderson), the market (Wallerstein),
and working-class culture (Thompson).

One factor that triggered the link between the revival of comparative-
historical sociology and the rediscovery of the state more generally was
the confrontation with governmental power in the context of the Vietnam
War. The view of the state that these pioneers of historical sociology
brought into comparative-historical focus was staunchly Weberian
and Hintzean, defined almost exclusively as the site of the monopoly of
force, violence, coercion, and extraction – a considerable stretch from
Marshall's view of the state as the site of those equalizing institutions
of citizenship designed to mitigate the excesses of the market. While
Bendix's *Nation-Building and Citizenship* (1964) was read by this new
generation as a great critic of structural functionalism and modernization
theory, Bendix himself was admired as one of the lone American sociologists who recognized Weber's tough-minded focus on domination and
the state. Despite attention to the book overall, however, little was
directed to his work on citizenship.

In my view, the state-centric approach of 1970s comparative-historical
sociology contributed (albeit inadvertently) to the invisibility of citizenship. At issue was that chronic problem of the impossible "fit" – or
lack thereof – between a sociology of citizenship's necessary "third
sphere" of the social, and the now familiar binary between the mutually
exclusive domains of market and state. "Bringing the state back in"
was a reaction against both the "society-centered" reductionism of modernization theory and the socioeconomic reductionism of Marxism.
In this context, a return to the social was entirely off the agenda. When
the state displaced the mode of production and took center stage in

---

[15] This perceived slight did not go unnoticed. With the publication of *Vision and Method* in
1984, I received a note from David Landes, the great Harvard economic historian, con-
gratulating me for my chapter on Karl Polanyi (Block and Somers 1984), but pointedly
observing the absence of a long list of scholars from the generation associated primarily
with modernization theory and the "end of ideology" and an eclectic group of other
"elders." Landes's list of the missing included Lipset, of course, but also Bell, Homans,
Schumpeter, and Gerschenkron.

scholarship, moreover, it did not have the effect of destabilizing the dichotomy. Rather, it just switched analytic allegiances from the economy to the state, and reversed the causal arrows from reductionism to "relative autonomy." It would take the rediscovery of civil society for the real shakeup to occur.[16] But this is the subject of the chapters to follow.

[16] Before we leave this period in the story of the sociology of citizenship, it would be amiss not to call attention to the one great exception to its more general neglect in the 1970s and 1980s – the enormous body of work on the welfare state that flourished in Europe and the United States. In its initial phase this research was framed very much in Marxist terms as analysis of the contradiction between "legitimacy and accumulation," in the influential language of the day. The "legitimacy" at issue was modern capitalist society's ideology of equality and justice for all; the "accumulation" was the reality of capitalism's unending need to accumulate, which inevitably produced such great class inequality. For an extended discussion, see Orloff (2005).

5

What's political or cultural about political culture and the public sphere? Toward a historical epistemology of concept formation

> Concepts are words in their sites. Sites include sentences, uttered or transcribed, always in a larger site of neighborhood, institution, authority, language. If one took seriously the project of philosophical analysis, one would require a history of the words in their sites, in order to comprehend what the concept was ... One conducts the analysis of the words in their sites in order to understand how we think and why we seem obliged to think in certain ways. If one embraced more specific conjectures about the ways in which the condition for emergence and change of use of a word also determined the space in which it could be used, one would be well on the way to a complex methodology.
>
> (Hacking 1990b: 360, 362)

Political culture is a rejuvenated concept with what many consider a shady past. It first dominated the horizon of political science and political sociology in the late 1950s and 1960s in the context of a flourishing postwar political sociology focused on replicating the conditions of Western democratization. Now that democratization again dominates the world agenda, the concept has been revived by political scientists and sociologists in the late 1980s and 1990s (see, e.g. Alexander 1991, 1992a; Alexander and Smith 1993; Eckstein 1988; Laitin 1988; Lipset 1990; Putnam 1993; Tarrow 1992; Wildavsky 1987). Attributions of its shady character come from the company it kept in its first life. The political culture concept was associated originally almost exclusively with modernization theories, Parsonian-influenced political sociology, and the behaviorist revolution of the 1950s and 1960s. Soon much was made of its inherent conservatism (Buxton 1985), and it was effectively felled by the more radical social science critiques of the late 1960s and 1970s (see e.g. Tilly 1975: especially 603–21). Yet the recent publication of

171

an English version of Habermas's *The Structural Transformation of the Public Sphere* ([1962] 1989) suggests that it was wrong to blame Parsons, modernization theory, or ideological conservatism for the problems of the political culture concept. Habermas's Marxist-Weberian account of the rise and fall of a liberal democratic public sphere has more in common with the original political culture concept than it has differences. Understanding the sources of these deeper similarities and their restrictive consequences is the goal of this chapter.

My central claim is this: whether called political culture or the public sphere, in both its Parsonian and its Habermasian forms the political culture concept is used in a way that is hardly political or cultural. In the case of political, although it is oriented to public affairs, these thinkers' concept of political culture is shaped fundamentally by the antipolitical, private side of political sociology's "great dichotomy" (Bobbio 1992) between the public/state and the private/society spheres of social life. In the case of cultural, their concept refers more to what is naturalized than to what is recognizably cultural. What accounts for this peculiarity of the political culture concept? And what difference does it make?

I hypothesize that the Parsonians and the early Habermas use the political culture concept in this curious antipolitical and naturalistic way because the concept itself is embedded in a political and cultural structure. This particular 300-year-old political cultural structure (Hall 1992; Rambo and Chan 1990) is Anglo-American citizenship theory. To understand the peculiarities of the political culture concept, the internal logic of this theory can be made visible by viewing it as a conceptual network and by developing a historical sociology of concept formation. Fortunately, many of the analytic tools for developing this methodology are already available in a body of rich scholarship that can be grouped loosely under the rubric of the "new" political culture project. Under this heading I include recent work in cultural history and sociology, the history and sociology of science, the new institutionalism, and network and narrative analysis. By examining the original political culture concept through the lens of this broadly conceived approach to political culture, we can use the political culture concept as its own reflexive instrument, thereby turning the concept back on itself.

Social scientists in recent years have come increasingly to recognize that the categories and concepts we use to explain the social world can themselves be fruitfully made the objects of analysis. The work of turning social science back on itself to examine the often taken-for-granted conceptual tools of research – fundamental categories such as agency and order (Alexander 1982a, 1992c), structure (Sewell 1992), gender (Scott 1988), person (Carrithers, Collins, and Lukes 1985; White 1992), and society (Tilly 1984) – falls under the rubric and the mandate of practicing a reflexive sociology (Bourdieu and Wacquant 1992; Collins 1988; Woolgar 1992). The work of reflexivity is above all historical: it challenges us to explore the historicity of our theoretical semantics as well as our epistemological foundations (standards of knowledge), usually to discover that they themselves have histories of contestation, transformation, and social conflict. Such histories are not unlike the more straightforwardly social phenomena that sociologists are used to examining. When aimed specifically not at whole disciplines or even theories, but toward our presuppositional conceptual vocabulary, this task entails what I dub a historical sociology of concept formation (Canguilhem [1966] 1978; Foucault [1966] 1978; Gutting 1989; Hacking 1988; Stinchcombe [1978] 1982; Tilly 1984; Wallerstein 1991). The method points to a way of practicing social research based on the principle that all of our knowledge, our logics, our theories, indeed our very reasoning practices, are marked indelibly (although often obscurely) with the signature of time, normativity, and institution building. Like other such ideas in the sociology of science, such as paradigm (Kuhn), episteme (Althusser), doxa (Foucault), and "style of reasoning" (Hacking), a historical sociology of concept formation emphasizes what we now find to be relatively uncontroversial – the historicity of thinking and reasoning practices. A historical sociology of concept formation differs from the classical approach of Mannheim's or Marx's sociology of knowledge in that it does not seek the deep social interests from which theories are derived. Nor does it seek any particular set of beliefs, ideologies, or truths. Rather it looks for the conditions of possibility, or the conceptual networks within which concepts are framed and constrained. It aims to explain how concepts do the work they do, not why they do so in terms of interests, by reconstructing the histories of their construction, resonance, and contestedness over time. Empirically exploring such histories can help us work through many basic impasses in theoretical and empirical social science.

   The conceptual network surrounding the political culture concept is Anglo-American citizenship theory. First formulated in the seventeenth century by John Locke, and more generally expressed in political liberalism, this theory is actually a story of the sociological foundations for preserving "English liberties" and the liberal democratic institutions to which those liberties gave rise. The foundational elements of the Anglo-American citizenship story have survived intact over three centuries and continue to shape the political culture concept today.[1] A major reason for the tenacity of this story is that it was mapped onto a sophisticated modern social science epistemology in which nature provided the criterion for evaluating knowledge. When these two features were combined – that is, when the narrative was grafted to the epistemology of social naturalism – the narrative became naturalized. The outcome is what historians and social scientists recently have come to call a metanarrative. Metanarratives, as we will see, are among the most enduring, most flexible, and most troublesome of social science cultural schemas.

Following March and Olsen's (1984: 747) similar complaint that "what we observe in the world is inconsistent with the ways in which . . . theories ask us to talk," my concern about Anglo-American citizenship theory is not philosophical but an "empirical prejudice" generated by research into the historical processes of English democratization and citizenship rights. This research has produced a view of the meaning and making of political cultures of democratization which does not conform to the Habermasian model or to the dominant political sociological paradigm. But the subject of this chapter is neither that historical evidence nor my alternative reconstruction of citizenship formation; rather, it is a prolegomenon to a full exposition of that alternative story. A prolegomenon is needed because the dominant approach is not susceptible to direct empirical criticism based on competing evidence. Rather, when such evidence is presented, it is ruled inadmissible by the gatekeeping role of the prevailing metanarrative of Anglo-American citizenship theory. Like a paradigm, a metanarrative not only provides the range of acceptable answers; it also defines both the questions to be asked and the rules of procedure by which they can rationally be answered. No alternative empirical approach to the roots of an Anglo-American political culture of democratization can be considered seriously until the gatekeeping power of the dominant metanarrative is challenged historically. On this point, both Tilly (1984) and Wallerstein (1991) have written elegantly and convincingly.

From the outset, the political culture concept has occupied a prominent place in the story of this metanarrative. Its seventeenth-century task was to provide cohesion for the domain of civil society (soon simply

---

[1] Of course, it is an empirical question just how stable and how durable the metanarrative of Anglo-American citizenship theory has been under any given circumstances. To be sure, it has never been without competitors; the primary one is that of civic republicanism, as Pocock (e.g. 1985) and others have demonstrated so spectacularly over the last twenty-five years.

society), the newly discovered site of market exchange believed to provide the foundation for English liberties. Although defined as part of the private sphere, the political culture concept was assigned the critical job of adjudicating and guarding the boundaries between public and private. Once it was embedded in such a deeply naturalized metanarrative, it could not be destabilized easily by competing evidence or routine empirical investigation. But as a result, political sociologists' research in political culture has been constrained empirically across the ideological spectrum. Both Parsons and Habermas correctly understood the importance of political culture's normative role in mediating between state and market/society. Both understood that in principle this normative dimension should be given a sociological significance of its own as a third site mediating between markets and the administrative state. Yet when Parsons and Habermas engaged with the political culture concept, they were engaging with a hardened cultural network of which the single concept was an inseparable component. As a result, the political culture concept came to be reduced to a functional requisite of an autonomous private market society.

To understand this dynamic, I first look more closely at the Parsonian and Habermasian political culture concepts; second, I examine the new political culture project as it has been used recently by social historians and cultural sociologists; and third, I outline the principles of a historical sociology of concept formation. In chapter 7 I will use this historical sociology of concept formation to explore the place of the civil society concept in the deep structure of Anglo-American citizenship theory and, finally, to show how the metanarrative of this theory continues to constrain the political culture, public sphere, and civil society concepts in contemporary political and social research.

Political sociology and the political culture concept

The social sciences discovered the political culture concept in the late 1950s and 1960s. Almond's (1980: 26–8) recent revisiting of the different accents placed on the concept by (for example) Almond and Verba (1963), Beer (1962), Converse (1964), Dahl (1966), Lipset ([1960] 1981), and Pye and Verba (1965) reads like a *Who's Who* in American social science and indicates the centrality of the concept in the 1960s. The idea of political culture resonated with several preoccupations of postwar American social science. These included the general concern about communist upheavals and postcolonial Third World independence movements; a shift in the social sciences away from the study of formal institutions and toward a focus on political attitudes and voting practices; and the self-defining project of political sociology to distinguish itself from political science by its focus on the social conditions for democracy.

This last preoccupation was not new. Following the lead of Tocqueville, Schumpeter (1943: 297) set the intellectual agenda for postwar political sociology: "Democracy in the sense of our theory ... presided over the process of political and institutional change by which the bourgeoisie reshaped, and from its own point of view rationalized, the social and political structure that preceded its ascendancy."

As figure 5.1 indicates, this statement contains the presuppositions on which modern political sociology came to rest – the basic dyadic causal model of political sociology with the following components. First, the dichotomization of state and society as the point of departure; a clear analytic distinction had to be established before the relationship between the two could be examined (Alford and Friedland 1985; Pizzorno 1971; Runciman 1969). Second, the explanatory basis of political sociology's scientific project was distinguished explicitly from the traditional orientation in political science toward formal institutions: "Political sociology starts with society and examines how it affects the state"

5.1 Political sociology's dyadic political culture model

(Bendix and Lipset 1957: 79).[2] Finally, Schumpeter's statement reflected what came to be a presupposition: that Western European democratization was the political outcome of the rise of bourgeois capitalism in the nineteenth century and would continue to be so in the tumultuous twentieth. Each of these presuppositions was to be incorporated fully into the political culture concept.

Political culture in the Parsonian tradition

The obvious empirical problems of this monocausal and unidirectional link between society and politics set the stage, in part, for the turn to the political culture concept in the late 1950s. Political sociologists observed that similar industrializing processes were producing varying levels of stability in the leading Western industrial nations of Britain, the United States, France, Germany, and Italy – a problem that Jessop (1978: 12) later called the "obstinate fact that capitalism is not universalistically associated with formal political democracy" (also see Therborn 1977). Unmediated macro processes of industrialization clearly were not sufficient to explain the wide empirical variation in political outcomes among industrialized and (especially) industrializing nations. The logical solution was to examine the intervening variables. Many were introduced. Among the most influential were regulated industrial and political conflict (Dahrendorf 1959), "cross-cutting social cleavages" (Lipset and Rokkan 1967), and a highly developed set of social conditions ancillary to economic development, such as literacy, legitimacy, education, and technological appurtenances (Lipset [1960] 1981). Yet it was Talcott Parsons' towering position in the social sciences that suggests why the predominant reaction was to adopt a more normative perspective that emphasized the intervening cultural orientations conducive to democratization.[3]

Talcott Parsons had long grappled with the enduring problem of "meaning and moral order" (Wuthnow 1987), and he argued forcefully for distinguishing between culture and society in social systems (Kroeber and Parsons 1958). Whereas society should refer to the system of

---

[2] The state, in this usage, meant the political system – for example, democracy or totalitarianism (Tilly 1975). This provoked Sartori's (1969: 92) exasperated blast that "political sociology is often a misnomer, for what goes on under its name is often a 'sociological reduction' of politics" – an observation that contributed to the trend toward "bringing the state back in" which swept the social sciences in the 1970s and 1980s.

[3] Parsons wrote his own version of democratization and modernization after the defining works in political culture had been written (see Parsons 1967, 1971).

interaction between individuals and collectivities, culture should address only "values, ideas and other symbolic-meaningful systems" (Kroeber and Parsons 1958: 582–3). Addressing the dilemma of how normative action could coexist with a law-like social system, Parsons argued that sociological theory had to attribute meaning as well as instrumentality to action (also see Parsons 1937). It made sense that political sociologists should be especially motivated to balance normative with social explanations; after all, political processes such as movements for democratization inevitably involve both systemic macro phenomena – e.g. wars, depressions, industrialization – and social actions to which humans assign meaning and sometimes even devote their lives. To this end Parsons developed his tripartite schema, which differentiated analytically between three systems: the social, the cultural, and the psychological. Parsons believed that these distinctions captured the deep analytic truth that all social interactions included aspects of all three: indisputable rootedness in the social system, meaningful reference to the cultural system, and causal influence by psychological motivations (Parsons and Shils 1951).

Parsons thus created the major alternative both to the (then) reigning anthropological definition of culture, which dated back to E. B. Tylor's view that culture included all human practices beyond the biological, and to the Marxist and sociologists of knowledge subordination of culture to material forces, the social environment, and class interest. In moving away from both of these positions, Parsons took the first step toward what sociologists began to call a "normative theory of culture" – so called because the idea distinguished between ideals and meaning, on the one hand, and the more all-inclusive anthropological "way of life," on the other (Jaeger and Selznick 1964; Swidler 1986). This was an enormous move forward for the social sciences, and Alexander (1990, 1991, 1993), Cohen and Arato (1992), Smelser (1992), and Wolfe (1989) are among those who most recently have reminded us of the significance of this achievement.

Parsons, however, then made a consequential decision in his approach to culture – one which implicitly reflected his disciplinary commitment to establishing firm epistemological boundaries for the foundations of sociological knowledge.[4] He was concerned that if cultural codes and

---

[4] I owe this formulation of Parsons' "consequential decision" regarding culture to Alexander (1988, 1989b, 1990). More important than any single publication, however, is the message that can be read in the personal intellectual trajectory Alexander forms with Parsons' work. Although the casual reader no doubt associates Alexander with the first major attempt of

symbolic systems were conceived as independent free-floating symbolic systems, culture would not be regarded as a legitimate part of sociology. If, however, the notion of culture were treated as the socially institutionalized norms and subjectively internalized social values of a social system (Swidler 1986), the social sciences would undergo fusion rather than fission.

This shift from the analytic autonomy to the internalized reduction of culture was an unfortunate move for Parsons and for sociology. The tremendous advances in the Parsonian attention to culture were canceled out with one stroke – ironically, the same stroke he had used initially to define a sociology of culture. If a conception of culture was to contribute to (and, indeed, count as) *social* knowledge, Parsons argued that it would have to be attached to the subjectivities of socially inculcated individuals and collectivities. Yet although this position gave the culture concept the promise of a central place in social analysis, in research practice it acquired only a functional role in the social system (Alexander 1990: 5; Camic 1986: 63–9; DiMaggio and Powell 1991: 17).

On this Parsonian foundation, then, postwar political sociologists and political scientists introduced the political culture concept as a critical intervening variable for explaining democratic political outcomes (Almond 1980: 26–7).[5] Following Parsons' conception of culture more generally, these thinkers defined political culture as the "subjective feelings, attitudes, and consequent behaviors" believed to characterize individual and collective "political orientations" – that is, values – across a political system (Rosenbaum 1975: 4). A political culture consolidated the "underlying psychological forces" and the political "attitudes"

the post-Parsonian generation to uncritically rehabilitate Parsons, the picture is actually a great deal more complex and historically developmental. Originally drawn to Parsons (Alexander 1983b) in an attempt to ground a "nonrational" conception of agency in culture and meaning (something that he demonstrated was missing in Marx, Durkheim, and Weber alike [Alexander 1982b, 1983a]), Alexander quickly came to distance himself from Parsons' overwhelming cultural reductionism. Through an immanent critique of Parsons, he helped to create the version of post-Parsonian (one could say anti-Parsonian) semiotic sociology of culture first represented in his Durkheim collection, (Alexander 1988; also see especially Hunt 1988), worked out most systematically in Alexander (1989a), elaborated in Alexander (1990), and demonstrated empirically in Alexander (1992a, 1992b, 1994) and Alexander and Smith (1993). As I discuss later in this chapter, this approach uses structural linguistics to demonstrate the benefits to be gained for sociological analysis in recognizing the analytic – although not the concrete – autonomy of codes and structures in cultural research.

[5] Among the best-known classics of the period for political sociology are Almond and Powell (1966), Almond and Verba (1963), Banfield (1965), Black (1966), Deutsch and Foltz (1963), Eckstein (1964), Lipset (1960 [1981]), Pye (1962, 1965), Pye and Verba (1965), Smelser (1959), and Verba and Nie (1973). The recent revival of the concept that follows loosely in the same tradition includes Eckstein (1988), Huntington (1975), Thompson *et al.* (1990), and Wildavsky (1987).

believed to shape much of civic life and political behavior. This definition combined broad issues of cultural affect with the specific issues connected to democratic stability. Thus conceived, the political culture concept opened a window to a deeper understanding of numerous political events and processes, from coups and revolutions in Africa and Latin America to civil war in Northern Ireland.

In applying the concept, social scientists specified its dimensions as following a continuum from "integrated" to "disintegrated," representing the degree to which "most people" have "similar, or compatible political culture orientations" which are "congenial" to their political institutions. Congenial values and orientations were used to explain degrees of accommodation to a society's stability. Dysfunctional values were invoked to account for disruptive behavior such as strikes and protests against government actions (Almond and Verba 1963; Pye and Verba 1965). In combination, these core elements of a political culture were perceived as the fundamental variables explaining "the creation and maintenance of a society's fundamental political order" (Rosenbaum 1975: 6).

Political sociologists thus were poised to take advantage of Parsons' normative schema for bringing together social and political cohesion. The political culture concept was precisely the variable they were seeking to intervene between what they assumed to be the independent variable of capitalist industrialization and the varying cross-national outcomes in degrees of democratic stability. Although Almond (1980: 19) later insisted that "political culture is not a theory; it refers to a set of variables which may be used in the construction of theories," it certainly functioned as a theoretical model that spoke directly to the search for a modulated normative connection between a definite conception of society and politics, and as a mechanism to "bridge the micro-macro gap in political theory" (Almond and Powell 1966: 51–2; Almond and Verba 1963: 32; Pye 1965: 9). The dependent variable reflected the need to state clearly how political democracy was to be defined – namely, as a system of high political stability under a representative government. The independent variable of economic development firmly grounded the political culture concept in social science knowledge. Most important, as an intervening variable, political culture addressed the empirical and normative dissatisfaction with "vulgar" economistic explanations.[6]

---

[6] Much the same kind of "intervening variable" argument continues into the present to be used in empirical research, even though the original use of the political culture concept has become somewhat less prominent in this research. See, for example, Bollen and Jackman (1985); for contrast see Eckstein (1992).

The model can be illustrated in the most celebrated representation of the genre, Almond and Verba's *The Civic Culture* (1963). There the authors introduce political culture as a "linking" concept designed to connect the social structural basis of politics to its institutional outcomes: the political culture concept serves as "the connecting link between micro- and macropolitics" (1963: 1–3, 33). They suggest that all political systems have legitimating symbols and that these systems exhibit a greater or lesser degree of popular consensus regarding those symbols. In a democratic political culture, or a "civic culture," citizens contribute to the maintenance of the democratic system by three kinds of "internalized aspects" or orientations toward legitimating symbols – cognitive, affective, and evaluational (1963: 15). Repeating his debt to Parsons, Almond (1980: 26–7) reflects on the original political culture concept as one "adapted to the analysis of the cultural properties assumed to be associated with democratic stability," which led them to stress "political knowledge and skill, and feelings and value orientations toward political objects and processes."

In another classic of this genre, Smelser (1959) posits that early nineteenth-century English working-class social movements were the result of a transitional conflict between the "traditional" values attached to a domestic artisanal division of labor and the alienating "role strain" produced by conflicts over new values demanded by the industrial factory labor process. Similarly, Lipset (1967) suggests that "extremist" French trade unions were the result of the particularistic values of French employers (attached to a premodern economic system), which "lagged behind" the universalist values necessary to modern capitalist markets.[7] The only epistemological status granted to the actual codes and meanings of a political culture was the argument that "social progress" could be impeded by "backwards" values which lagged behind long after traditional societies had been transformed into modern social systems. According to Banfield's (1965) famous theory, for example, the political culture of southern Italy contained values and practices so "morally backwards" that it left the region in no condition to receive the benefits, or take on the responsibilities, of Western economic progress.[8]

What, in retrospect, were the strengths of the Parsonian political culture concept, and why has it seen such a strong comeback of late? The first strength was its empirical methodology. Because cultural

---

[7] Examples can be found in Alexander and Seidman (1990).
[8] See Putnam *et al.* (1993) for a stunning revisitation of Italian political culture that owes more to Tocqueville than to Parsons.

attitudes could be aggregated and empirically translated into a range of variables, this work became known as "the empirical theory of democracy" (e.g. Barry 1970; Duncan and Lukes 1963; Pateman 1980). A political culture is the empirical pattern formed by the social distribution of these attitudes (Almond and Verba 1963: 12–14). Almond (1980: 26) continues to celebrate the idea that "the explanatory power of political culture variables is an empirical question, open to hypothesis and testing." By making the political culture concept empirical, one could counter Parsons' often-criticized abstractness.

Second, and more relevant to this chapter, the political culture concept – and Parsons – should be praised for giving the previously neglected intervening normative/cultural sphere of civic culture a critical and well-deserved centrality in macrosocial explanation – an explanation whereby both political and social life were mediated inexorably by normative cultural dimensions.[9] By transposing culture into societal norms, Parsons (1967) acquired the analytic variable with which to argue for the normative cohesion of society. This theoretical combining of culture with politics became increasingly prominent in Parsons' work as he became convinced that the normative element was most significant with respect to the polity. The importance of this triadic model, and the reason for the current appeal of the political culture concept, was made strikingly apparent by the drama of the late 1980s and early 1990s that unfolded across Eastern Europe and the former Soviet Union – for example, the explosive impact of Poland's famous Solidarity movement. Similarly, the intellectual significance of an independent sphere of political culture is underscored by the flood of literature in the 1990s in political theory and sociology addressing the newly "discovered" sphere of civil society (e.g. Alexander 2006; Alexander and Smith 1993; Calhoun 1992, 1993; Cohen and Arato 1992; Keane 1988; Kennedy 1991, 1992; Putnam *et al.* 1993; Seligman 1993; Somers 1993; Taylor 1990; Walzer 1991; Weintraub 1992, 1995; Wolfe 1989).[10]

Ultimately, however, the broad array of criticisms overwhelmed the strengths. Criticism was leveled at the rational individualist explanation of political structure (Rogowski 1976); at the "individualist" fallacy

---

[9] The current resurgence of interest in culture attests to the enduring quality of this insight.

[10] This theoretical combining of culture with politics became increasingly prominent in Parsons' own work as he became convinced that the normative element was most significant with respect to the polity (Wolfe 1989: 205). The importance of this triadic model has been underscored by (e.g.) Alexander (1991, 1992a, 1993), Alexander and Smith (1993), Bell (1989), Calhoun (1993), Cohen and Arato (1992), Keane (1988), Walzer (1990), and Wolfe (1989).

(Schuech 1969); at the unitary culture of consensus embodied in the idea of a single national political culture (Mann 1970; Thompson *et al.* 1990); and at the anti-institutional abstractness of the values constituting the political culture concept (Rueschemeyer *et al.* 1992). The most influential critical discussions at the time included Barry (1970), Fagen (1969), and Tucker (1973), all of whom took issue with the political culture literature for attributing the production of political structures to the cultural domain (Almond [1980: 29–32] and others [Liphart 1980] argue vehemently that this position is attributed wrongly to the political culture concept).[11]

The preoccupation with a "continuum of political integration," however, most sharply defined the political culture concept and located it in a historical period and a Cold War intellectual culture overwhelmingly concerned with rapid global disequilibrium and political violence. The hegemony of this intellectual culture, as we now know, was to end abruptly. When political scientists and sociologists, using new macro-structural approaches, launched a full-scale assault on the paradigm in the late 1960s and 1970s, the political culture concept, not surprisingly, was one of the first casualties. Moreover, in the midst of an explicit search for the causes of political stability in the postwar world of nation building and decolonization, it is plausible that the fate of the political culture concept was sealed by its utility in addressing what had become the overriding social science concern – obsession, one could say – with societal equilibrium and political instability characteristic of the political climate of the 1950s and 1960s.[12]

Influenced by various versions of Marxism, Weberian theories of bureaucracy, and the Braudelian *Annales* school, the new structural approaches rejected theories of "backwards" cultures and values as explanations for social change or stability. Instead, the new analyses stressed class domination and emphasized developed nations over underdeveloped nations, core over periphery, states over societies. Insofar as political culture was addressed explicitly in any of the influential

---

[11] Citing the original book (Almond and Verba 1963: chs. 1 and 15), Almond (1980: 29) asserts that political culture is treated simultaneously as both an independent and a dependent variable, as "causing [political] structure and as being caused by it."

[12] The concept also was tied to a massive research methodology that was cross-national and global and entailed highly quantified survey research techniques. The monumental growth of US research technologies, most of which were government-sponsored, was both cause and consequence of this context. US scholars were sent all over the globe to survey world populations in the belief that analyzing and comparing the global data would provide explanatory links between individual attitudes and behaviors and the very survival of political regimes (see especially Almond and Verba 1963: ch. 1).

structural theories of this period, it was usually addressed for purposes of criticism and rejection.[13] In light of the way in which social scientists constructed pre-modern or non-Western cultural practices as primitive and constraining forces on economic progress, political culture was an idea that a new generation of social scientists was only too happy to abandon.

Barrington Moore's (1965) comparative historical analysis of the varying routes to the modern world was the text that set the terms for revisionist scholarship. Moore provided a monumental challenge to the antihistorical premises of political culture and modernization theory – that there exists a single "normal" developmental path to the modern world and that departures from this pattern are deviant and dysfunctional rather than alternative routes. By problematizing variation rather than assuming deviance or "lags," Moore demonstrated how comparative historical methodology could be used to address issues of social change and class analysis to a very different effect than that of modernization theory. In the 1970s Moore's mantle passed to Wallerstein (1974) and to Anderson (1974) with the publication of the first volumes of each of their projected multivolume recastings of the making of the Western capitalist world. Tilly's (1975) *Formation* should be regarded as the third point in this early triad of second-generation influences (if we consider Moore and E. P. Thompson [1963] the first generation) on the shape of the historic turn in macrosociology (see Skocpol's [1984] edited collection on historical sociology for the best summation of these influences).

The demise of the political culture concept thus can be explained in part by the emergence of a more radical 1960s social science. It would be a mistake to leave it at that, however, as its epistemological vulnerabilities were a deeper reason for the demise. The first sentence of the preface of *The Civic Culture* may be the most revealing: "This is a study of the political culture of democracy and of the *social* structures and processes that sustain it" (Almond and Verba 1963: vii; emphasis added). Although virtually all of the contemporary criticism focused on the question of which variable – political culture or political system – should be granted the status of independent variable, this lucid declaration reminds us that three variables were at issue: the independent variable (the social system), the intervening variable (the political culture), and the dependent variable (the political outcome – in this case, democratic stability). Yet for actual research purposes, the independent variable (economic development) was taken as

---

[13] Moore (1965), Tilly (1975), Wallerstein (1974), and Skocpol (1979) were among the most influential critics.

given, and was not subjected to critical scrutiny, while empirical research focused exclusively on the relationship between political culture and political systems. Thus, despite its acclaim as an empirical theory, the most important weakness in the model is that its causal theory is not posited as an empirical question in which cause and effect are presented as a connection to be explained. Rather, the causal analysis is already inscribed in the concept itself, or (in slightly different terms) the independent variable (social system) is inscribed at the outset in the intervening (political culture) and dependent variables (democratic stability). In the laudable effort to bring together society and culture, the latter is collapsed into the former.[14]

Although the ultimate independent variable "society" received the least attention from critics at the time, in retrospect it is the most significant for the concerns of this chapter. Where did the political values of a political culture come from? How could variations in such values be explained? How do we explain democratization? Numerous mediating factors were presented as partial answers (e.g. political socialization and psychological internalization), but the basic assumption – which never was subjected to empirical research – was that political culture was a product not of the cultural or the political system but of the social (market) system: cultural attributes were "the product of socialization experiences" – a position "sustained by much evidence" (Almond 1980: 29).[15] The independent variable "society" became at once the most important explanatory component of the theory and the least scrutinized. The payoff, however, was clear. The foundational place of "society" allowed the political culture model to be rooted firmly in social science logic, thus avoiding risking its credibility by association with speculative notions of culture as artistic or symbolic systems. The irretrievable loss was that we were left with an enduring conundrum: what is cultural about this political culture concept?[16]

---

[14] For this reason scholars described it as a "sociological approach" (Barry 1970) in which liberal democracy is treated as a social system used to specify the relationship between the political and civic culture and the political structure.

[15] Again, this can be traced to Parsons' functional reductionism, in which he tried to create a complex interplay of different subsystems. Unlike Marx (and to some extent, as we will see, the early Habermas), Parsons' problem was not economic but functional reductionism (and, in his later work, his evolutionary frame), and a failure to understand social movements and social action in their own cultural terms (Alexander 1983b). As stressed recently by Cohen and Arato (1992), Parsons placed great emphasis on the independence of the legal sphere and the institutions of parliamentary government.

[16] Alexander's (1989a, 1990, 1992b) immanent critique of Parsons has made it possible to retain the cultural impulse while moving beyond Parsons' reductionism through the incorporation of an approach to political culture rooted in language as an analytically autonomous cultural system (also see Alexander 1992a; Alexander and Smith 1993).

If the culture component of Parsons' political culture concept is more social than cultural, what about the concept of politics? What, after all, is the meaning of the term political? Cicero called the commonwealth a *res publica*, a "public thing" or the "property of a people." What is political has always been identified with what is public – that is, common to the whole community, such as the system of dispensing justice, the power relationship between ruler and ruled, national policing, and economic regulation (Wolin 1960). Yet the political culture theorists defined the very essence of such political concerns as belonging to the antipolitical domains of private society. Moreover, even the reference to "political" is misleading. These are not beliefs associated with the practices, discourses, and institutions of democratization, but beliefs about the most appropriate regulation of private life. The impetus to make the political culture concept a third and intervening variable between state and society was forcefully overdetermined by the power of the deeper foundational divide between public and private. Surely it is a paradox that the political culture concept is defined as a people's antipolitical identity.

Habermas's public sphere: political culture as bourgeois rationality

The recent translation of Habermas's *Transformation of the Public Sphere* ([1962] 1989) has made his discussion of the public sphere one of the most celebrated of new approaches to political culture. Yet the connection between Habermas and the Parsonian version is actually surprisingly close. Habermas originally published his book in 1962, just one year before the publication of *The Civic Culture*. The topic of these works, moreover, is virtually the same – the impact of public opinion on liberal governments. Habermas's reflections thirty years after he wrote his book reveal his own ambivalence toward the (then) prevailing Almond and Verba school of the political culture concept. He recalls, on the one hand, that when he set out to address the subject in 1960, the sociology of voter behavior was only beginning in Germany, and there was a "glaring absence" of studies under the heading of "political culture." On the other hand, Habermas recalls that as late as 1963 Almond and Verba had "still attempted to capture the 'civic culture' by means of a few attitudinal variables" – a methodology he clearly set out to prove deficient by way of historical analysis (Habermas 1992: 438). These recent reflections underline just how much distance thirty years has put between Habermas's recent work and this earliest expression of his political sociology. An assessment of the contributions his entire body of work has made to democratic theory and political sociology would look very different from the one presented here, and would demonstrate the many reasons why Habermas is rightly considered among the most important and influential democratic thinkers of the twentieth century (see, for example, Cohen and Arato 1992). In this chapter I address only his 1962 book, however, because it is this work that has become the source of current discussions over the public sphere concept.

Habermas (1989) uses the term public sphere to denote both the social space and the rational discourse that constitute free and open democratic public opinion. For him, this is the normative precondition for a democratic polity: "by 'the public sphere' we mean first of all a realm of our social life in which something approaching public opinion can be formed. Citizens behave as a public body when they confer in an unrestricted fashion about matters of general interest" (Habermas 1974: 49). In this formulation, Habermas reveals the degree to which his work on the public sphere is simultaneously a normative theory and a sociological analysis of democratic political cultures (Calhoun 1992). Because the public sphere is the social space in which "the public organizes itself as the bearer of public opinion," Habermas perceives it to be one of the central organizational and normative principles of the modern liberal political order: "It is apparently more and other than a mere scrap of liberal ideology that social democracy could discard without harm" (Habermas 1989: 4). And, like those who studied civic culture, Habermas views the study of this complex of political culture as a sociological window into "our own society from the perspective of one of its central categories" (1989: 4–5).

Habermas has been criticized for limiting his conception of rational public opinion to that of a bourgeois practice (Calhoun 1992; Eley 1992: 325–31; Fraser 1992; Somers 1993), for his economism and his exclusion of religion as a source of democratic political culture (Zaret 1992), and for his unawareness of the gendered nature of bourgeois reason (Eley 1992; Fraser 1992). (Recently, however, he has addressed the issue of gender exclusion in a particularly intriguing way, formulating his reinvestigation of the issue by examining whether women were excluded from the bourgeois public sphere in the same fashion as workers, peasants, and the "people" – that is, as men lacking "independence" [1992: 427]). As important as these issues are, they are not my concerns here. Rather, I wish to address the assumptions underlying Habermas's argument, for despite some obvious differences they share significant strengths and limitations with the Parsonian one. (It is important, however, to emphasize just how much Habermas has refined his ideas about the democratic political process in the thirty years following the publication of the early book.)

The most obvious difference between this early Habermasian and the Parsonian political culture concept is Habermas's Marxist slant and his more strongly structural and historical conception of political culture. It is generally accepted that in his early writings, Habermas was still rooted deeply in his Marxist inheritance from the Frankfurt School. Although the Parsonian political culture concept is ultimately defined as internalized norms/values, Habermas's public sphere constitutes a quasi-institutional sphere. I say "quasi" because it is institutional in the literal sense of referring to public coffeehouses, newspapers, and other material expressions of public opinion, rather than to something that is subjective, or composed only of people's thoughts and ideas – and yet still does *not* consist of public sector institutions. This dramatic difference from the Parsonian notion explains some of Habermas's current appeal in that the term "sphere" serves as a metaphor for a structural locale supported by institutions and discursive networks, which gives the realm of culture its institutional and discursive due (e.g. Calhoun 1992; Eley 1992; Zaret 1992).[17]

More significant than their differences, however, are the underlying similarities shared by the two approaches. The major strength of Habermas's public sphere concept parallels the most important strength of the Parsonian approach and accounts for much of its well-deserved current appeal, namely the attempt to describe and structurally locate a sphere interstitially between public and private. It thus represents Habermas's effort to resolve the problematic public/private split inherited from political sociology. His concept of the public sphere, therefore, is based on a triadic rather than a dyadic model, one that explicitly recognizes the normative zone between the state and the market as well as between the micro and the macro. Like the Parsonian political culture concept, Habermas's public sphere is at once distinguished from, even while it is linked on both sides to, the market and the state. It demarcates at once the end of the strictly private realm of civil society (here understood solely as the market) and the beginning of the "official" public domain of the state.

This emphatic structural distinction between the interstitial public sphere – creating a third space between the public and the private – and the official, institutional bureaucratic state of the public side of the model explains the resonance of Habermas's concept with today's

---

[17] Wuthnow (1987), for example, places Habermas in the structuralist category.

political celebration of civil society as it emerged during the 1980s in Eastern
Europe and the former Soviet Union. Scholars generally agree that it is
from this "third sphere" – whether called the public sphere, civil society (in
the broad, associational sense of the term), or political society – that the
Eastern European revolutions of 1989 were launched (see e.g. Cohen and
Arato 1992; Kennedy 1991, 1992).[18] From this perspective, civil society is
a zone of civic life oriented toward political issues and public life but free of
the direct control of the official state and its coercive mechanisms.
Embedded within civil society, the discourse of the public sphere focuses
on political matters. Hence the attribution "public" sphere: "We speak of
the political public sphere . . . when discussion deals with objects connected
to the activity of the state" (Habermas 1974: 49). Like the Parsonian
concept, however, Habermas's political culture is not part of the political
sphere in any governmental or institutional sense: "Although state activity
is so to speak the executor, it is not a part of it" (Habermas 1974: 49).

The problem, it turns out, is that Habermas cannot synchronize his
innovative depiction of the triadic structural location of the public sphere
with his substantive analysis. His triadic structural model cannot hold its
ground against the ontologically prior and more deeply entrenched public versus private dichotomy: "It [the public sphere] was specifically a part
of 'civil society' . . . the realm of commodity exchange and social labor
governed by its own laws" (Habermas 1989: 3). Habermas's substantive
notion of the public side of this division is limited to the official bureaucratic state and its administrative apparatus – about which he is deeply
wary as a source of democratic ideals. And although Habermas's public
sphere is an arena for political discourse, he argues that the citizens who
conduct this debate must be fully formed by private life in advance of
their political participation. Political identity, including fundamental
commitments to democratic practices, is formed not in the public arena
but in the private world of "socialization" and market society. In conceptualizing the public sphere, therefore, Habermas "presumes that the
private sphere provides it with fully formed subjects with settled identities
and capacities" (Calhoun 1994: 23).

Habermas's public sphere and the identities of the citizens who people
it are thus not constituted by the participatory practices, legal discourses,

---

[18] Social historians – even before E. P. Thompson – influenced by anthropology (e.g. John
and Barbara Hammond, R. H. Tawney, Karl Polanyi) have long recognized the importance of analyzing an independent zone of a participatory democratic political culture as
central to popular and bourgeois contributions to the overall transformation to national
democratic political institutions. (For a review of similar literature by German social
historians, see especially Eley 1992: 294–306.)

or processes of democratic activity that take place within it. Instead, as in the Parsonian model, the people enter the public sphere to advance their private interests in a public context: "The bourgeois public sphere may be conceived above all as the sphere of private people come together as a public; they soon claimed the public sphere regulated from above against the public authorities themselves, to engage them [state authorities] in a debate over the general rules governing relations in the basically priva- tized but publicly relevant sphere of commodity exchange and social labor," in particular, with regard to matters pertaining to the working of national markets (Habermas 1989: 27). Rather than practices of democratization, these are rules which organize social life and the econ- omy. This, in other words, is Marx's bourgeois democracy – one that serves as an instrument not of the ruling class but of the bourgeois representatives of society. The similarity in theoretical location of Habermas's public sphere to the Parsonian political culture concept is immediately noticeable: the democratic public sphere of public opinion – although it may be oriented to "public" issues – is situated firmly on the private side of the deeper public/private divide. Although this notion of a democratic political culture is not literally "in the heads" of private people in the form of individual values, as in Parsons' approach, none- theless it is firmly tethered to the private realm of market society. That tether prevents Habermas's political culture concept from floating over the divide into a truly independent third sphere between the economy and the administrative state.

Craig Calhoun suggests that Habermas is more ambiguous as to whether his public sphere concept falls on the public or the private side of the great dichotomy, and states that my characterization seems "half true but not altogether accurate" (personal communication). I would argue that the ambiguity lies precisely in the coexistence of Habermas's explicit desire to locate his public sphere in an intermediary triadic location between public and private with the deeper, more foundational, ultimately determining binary public/private division. Habermas's (1989: 30) own diagram (see figure 5.2) demonstrates this ambiguity, and makes clear his prioritizing of the dyadic over the triadic model. There is a set of double lines between the "private realm" and the "sphere of public authority," locating the "public sphere in the political realm" on the *same* side of those lines as "the private realm," separated only by a single, weaker line from the "realm of commodity exchange and social labor." Habermas's intellectual influences in part explain these choices. Like American political sociologists, he was influenced by Schumpeter's famous declaration that the new phenomenon of capitalism was the

Private realm		Sphere of public authority
Civil society (realm of commodity exchange and social labor) Conjugal family's internal space (bourgeois intellectuals)	Public sphere in the political realm Public sphere in the world of letters (clubs, press) (market of culture products) "town"	State (realm of the "police") Court (courtly– noble society)

5.2 Habermas's dyadic model (1989: 30)

first "private sphere ... born as a distinguishable entity in contrast to the public" (1989: 19). Habermas also draws from Hannah Arendt's under-standing of the "public relevance" of this new private sphere of civil society, in which market activity for the first time was "of general inter-est" (1989: 19). The market aspect of the private sphere assumes "public relevance" and makes possible the birth of the early political culture of democratic public opinion. Concomitantly, it is the "stratum of 'bour-geois' ... the 'capitalists,' the merchants, bankers, entrepreneurs, and manufacturers" that was the "real carrier of the public." In opposition to state authority, the bourgeoisie was the "public of the now emerging *public sphere of civil society*" (1989: 23; emphasis in original). The only thing that made possible the critical free discourse of the public sphere, according to Habermas, was the fact that it was private people who related to each other in civil society.

Like the Parsonians, Habermas was also influenced by traditional political sociology, liberal political economy, and the Scottish moralists, as well as by Hegel and Marx. This legacy is most apparent in Habermas's historical analysis: "The social precondition for this 'developed' bour-geois public sphere was a market that, tending to be liberalized, made affairs in the sphere of social reproduction as much as possible a matter of private people left to themselves and so finally completed the privati-zation of civil society. The public sphere depended on developmental processes occurring in the realm of social relations" (1989: 15). Here Habermas is unambiguous that the public sphere emerged from deep socioeconomic transformations, specifically early finance and trade cap-italism, new commercial relationships, and the "traffic in commodities and news created by early capitalist long-distance trade" (1989: 15). In this argument Habermas postulates a causal homology of political dis-course and the market. It is a model in which the expressions of what

would become the grounds of democratic discourse "appear as the
excrescence" (Eley 1992: 292) of an accumulating set of transformations
that clearly fit under the rubric of industrialization and modernization.
An additional suggestion in Habermas also ends in disappointment.
Insofar as the content of the public sphere is formed by sources outside
the market, it is formed by the "intimate" sphere of family. Yet even the
family appears to be a function of market relations: "The privatized
individuals" who made up the public sphere "entered into it" from a
"space" that was "the scene of psychological emancipation that corre-
sponded to the political-economic one. Although there may have been
a desire to perceive the sphere of the family circle as independent ... it
was ... dependent on the sphere of labor and of commodity exchange"
(Habermas 1989: 46). In fact, the closer we look, the more clearly it
appears that the public sphere is represented as a transmutation of
personal and market privacy into the domain of "public" issues regarding
the management of socioeconomic life – something Habermas refined
dramatically in his subsequent work.

In Habermas's early theoretical and causal model, as in the Parsonian
political culture concept, the causal variable of society (understood var-
iously as social institutions by Parsons, as levels of economic development by Lipset, Almond and Verba, and as the market by Habermas) is
inscribed a priori in the public sphere/political culture concept. If, on the
one hand, the public sphere is the grounds for democratization, but, on
the other, the conditions for the possibility of a public sphere reside in the
private realm of the market, ultimately we are left with the same question:
what's political or cultural about the political culture or public sphere
concept?

With regard to the political dimension, and inferring from his own
discussion, Habermas might give an answer that points to the public
sphere's addressees as constituting the "political" – that is, "the agents
of the state and their policy makers" to whom the private individuals
address their concerns. Yet this answer can hardly be adequate in view of
the overriding and more troubling assumption that the public sphere's
political and democratic ideas appear to be spontaneously constituted by
market forces.[19] As to the cultural dimension, we are at an even greater
loss. As in the Parsonian notion, events in the public sphere appear to
have no cultural meaning on their own terms; rather, they are norms that
summarize the actual activities of society. The "medium" of the public

---

[19] Although Craig Calhoun did not claim that this was an adequate answer, he suggested it as
one possibility (personal communication).

sphere, moreover, is "peculiar and without historical precedent: people's public use of their reason" (Habermas 1989: 27). As becomes much clearer in his later work, Habermas's treatment of discourse is not rooted at all in the realm of culture, as we usually think of that term, in either the sociological or the semiotic sense. Rather it is based on speech act theory and pragmatism, very much the opposite of the cultural tradition, which comes from Durkheim, Saussure, and structuralism. (See especially Alexander [1989b, 1992b, 1993] for convincing critiques of Habermas's hyperrationalism, and Calhoun [1992] on the influence on Habermas of speech act theories of discourse, rather than of more recognizably cultural theories.) Parsons' functional reductionism has not yet substantively been challenged by this early version of Habermas's public sphere concept.

A new political culture concept

The new cultural history

An alternative view of the relationship of political culture to democratization has recently developed among social historians influenced by symbolic and structuralist anthropology and linguistics, mixed with elements of Marx, Foucault, Bourdieu, and Hayden White, resulting in what Hunt (1989a) and Bonnell and Hunt (1999) have consolidated under the "new cultural history."[20] In its incarnation among social historians, the political culture concept only occasionally has been defined explicitly (see e.g. Baker 1990; Chartier 1991; Hunt 1989b; Sewell 1993). To give a schematic summation, practitioners of the new political culture concept insist, first, that historical actors' practices, activities, and

[20] The best known of these include Chartier (1982, 1988, 1991), Furet (1981), Hunt (1984), Lacqueur (1991), Sewell (1980), and those writers represented in Hunt's (1989a) collection *The New Cultural History*. The primary development of this alternative conception is structuralist: it comes from intellectual and social historians; cultural and literary theorists influenced by European social theorists; philosophers and linguists, notably Saussure, Derrida, Foucault, and Habermas (variably interpreted); cultural and structural anthropologists such as Bourdieu (1977), Douglas (1966), Geertz (1973, 1983), Lévi-Strauss (1969), and Sahlins (1976, 1981); and anthropologically oriented social historians such as Natalie Davis (1975) and E. P. Thompson (1963). From Geertz (1973) comes the idea of politics as culture; from Saussure ([1916] 1959), politics and culture as linguistic systems; from Foucault (1979), power and domination at the micro level. This discussion is not intended to be a complete review of the cultural studies literature on political culture. Rather, it is limited to a selected set of social historical works relevant to historical and political sociologies of citizenship and democratization. From the standpoint of cultural studies overall, there are obvious important exclusions such as the "Birmingham school" of cultural studies, or works dealing with class and status distinctions in contemporary American culture.

political ideas must be viewed as symbolic systems with their own histories and logics; and, second, that these symbolic logics themselves are modalities of politics and power as much as they are cultural expressions. Much of this new cultural history is directed to studies of popular rituals and ceremonies (e.g. Aguilhon 1981), of how cultural representations in republican revolutionary practices disempowered women in the years after the Revolution (Landes 1988), or of contests over the language in which political issues were articulated (Furet 1981; Hunt 1984; Sewell 1980). These studies have transgressed the boundaries long prevalent in social history dominated by Marxism and the *Annales* school between the "materiality" of social relations, the "ephemera" of politics, and the merely "ideal" relevance of culture (Sewell 1993).

Much of the historical work on political culture focuses on the French Revolution, using the structuralism of Lévi-Strauss and the semiology of Saussurean linguistics. The hallmark of the structuralist and semiotic approach to culture and meaning is its rejection of the singular "speech-act," which Lévi-Straussians and Saussureans believe to be a voluntarist and misleading ideal-typical theory (Stinchcombe 1982). Instead, structuralism emphasizes that cultural expressions must be viewed not as subjective meanings randomly "experienced" by social actors, but as elements embedded in systems of signs, symbols, and linguistic practices organized by their own internal rules and structures (Alexander 1990, 1992b, 1992c; Lamont and Wuthnow 1990; Saussure [1916] 1959; Stinchcombe 1982; Wuthnow 1987). Social actors engaged in speech or action are thus interpreters of culture who are both constrained and enabled by these sign codes and their internal relationships. Studies based on this approach suggest that social processes are intelligible only in the context of their cultural mediation.

There are several prototypical examples of the new political culture concept from French social history and the work on the French Revolution. Using semiotics as his intellectual weapon, François Furet (1981) launched one of the first and most influential assaults on the long-reigning social interpretation of the French Revolution. Instead of class struggle, demographics, or Braudelian materialism, Furet argues that the autonomy of politics and culture is the driving force behind the causes and consequences of the Revolution. Furet's explanation eschews any form of interest-based analysis. Instead it focuses on the impact and meaning of the new democratic republican political language of the revolutionary struggle. Instead of analyzing political forms in Mannheimian or Marxist terms – as ideologies or as aggregated effects of values or interests – Furet conceives of political forms in cultural terms as discourses possessing their own internal systems of logic. Rather than deriving from the social, Furet's "new political culture [is] driven only by its own internal logic of democracy" (Hunt 1984: 11).

In *Politics, Culture, and Class in the French Revolution*, Lynn Hunt (1984) also developed an influential and path-breaking cultural explanation. Although she broadens her use of political culture to emphasize conflict and the role of revolutionary actors, Hunt, like Furet, insists that social actions and political outcomes are unintelligible unless one decodes the internal systems of political culture and the political forms at play in the revolutionary process. Her theory rejects the analytic subordination of political cultures to social values or deep economic processes as such, thus allowing her to look beyond the traditional social science concept of the societal arena for sources of popular political consciousness, meaning, and action. As she argues reflectively, this perspective allows her to determine that the ideology of democratic republicanism was not merely a "vehicle for the rise of capitalism, the rule of notables, or the establishment of a strong central state" (Hunt 1989b: 2). By exploring topics such as the icons used in local parades, the changed content of the revolutionary calendar, and how language facilitated the creation of new forms of revolutionary address, Hunt's work expands the notion of political culture. All of these elements, according to Hunt, must be viewed as political, and politicizing, forms of life – as important in making sense of the revolutionary process as classes, social interests, and the state (Hunt 1984, 1989b).[21]

Keith Baker (1982, 1990) and Roger Chartier (1982, 1988, 1991), fourth-generation *Annaliste* historians, also build on, but go far beyond, any strict structuralism. Baker and Chartier deploy Foucault's (1972, 1973) historical epistemological systems and Bourdieu's linkage between cultural representations and structures of power and stratification, as well as critical and selective appropriations of Habermas's (1989) theory of the public sphere (for his critique, see Baker 1992). The result of this intellectual recombination is an interpretation of the cultural origins of the French Revolution that overturns the traditional evaluation of the

[21] Hunt explicitly acknowledges (and her work is exemplary for this acknowledgment) the broad range of influences on her work, including Geertz, Durkheim, Tilly, and Marx. In addition, as an anonymous referee pointed out to me, Hunt's book can be seen as exemplifying the difficulty of the cultural structuralist project of integrating the cultural with the societal "level." As was noted widely when it was published, Hunt's text abruptly and uneasily combines her cultural structuralism with her historical sociology. The book is divided into two parts – the sociological and the semiotic, the Tilly and the post-Tilly. This difficult problem is not solved by the new political culture concept (Archer [1988] tries to do so in *Culture and Agency*), and it is important not to gloss over this point or to suggest that this is no longer much of an issue.

influence of Enlightenment philosophy on the revolutionary rupture. Baker and Chartier, by challenging the dichotomization between principles and cultural meanings on the one side, and "underlying" political and social realities on the other, have shown how cultural and ritualistic meanings combined with practices of sociability and association to form a new and revolutionary political culture. Rather than serving as a dominant ideology merely imposed on a public, these new cultural forms and practices allowed Enlightenment thought to be interpreted in multiple ways, often contradictory, but always revolutionary. Baker demonstrates the structuring power not of particular ideas but of the "field of political discourse, a set of linguistic patterns and relationships that defined possible actions and utterances and gave them meaning" (1982: 212). Bringing together the social and the representational worlds through the political culture concept, Chartier shows how "discursive associations" directly challenged the authority of the Old Regime – whether through the democratizing impulses of literary sociability or through the emergence of a modified version of Habermas's new eighteenth-century public sphere (Chartier 1991).

A new cultural sociology

In their interest in ritual and symbolic codes, cultural historians have been joined by a new generation of sociologists of culture. While social historians were turning to structuralist notions of culture to launch their assault on rigid versions of Marxist and *Annaliste* history, American sociologists began to address their own frustration with the prevailing macro and micro approaches to social life – both of which seemed to leave out too much and explain too little – by developing a renewed approach to culture (for an overview see Mukerji and Schudson 1991). But whereas the social historians formulated alternatives to interest-based cultural notions, sociologists primarily addressed the limits of Parsonian value-based cultural sociology as the baseline for the new thinking (e.g. DiMaggio 1990; Griswold 1987, 1992; Hall 1987, 1992; Lamont 1992a; Lamont and Wuthnow 1990; Sewell 1992; Swidler 1986, 1987; Wuthnow 1987).[22] Moreover, many cultural sociologists have used some implicit notion of a political culture to demonstrate the degree to which culture itself exists within symbolic systems and relational practices (e.g. Alexander 1992b,

---

[22] Many of them have combined French semiotics with the post-Parsonian work of Geertz (1973, 1983) to create what Alexander (1990, 1992b) calls a "late-Durkheimian" approach to the culture concept.

1992c; Alexander and Smith 1993; Lamont and Fournier 1992; Mukerji and Schudson 1991, Wuthnow 1990).

The new generation of cultural sociologists are motivated by the attempt to avoid two blind alleys. The first is the danger of confusing analytic autonomy with historical/phenomenological autonomy, something that the new cultural historians appear to stray dangerously close to. In arguing for the autonomy of culture, for example, the historians open new avenues of investigation such as the conceptual languages of politics, complex forms of power embodied in public and civil associations, and the rituals of public social life. Yet even as they open some avenues for investigation, some of these cultural historians have closed off others. In their eagerness to abandon the long-reigning determinism of the social sciences and to assert the autonomy of culture, for example, the semiotically inclined cultural historians at times have tended to locate society on one side of an analytic divide, with culture on the other.

Dangers exist in claiming an absolute autonomy of culture from material life. In the first place, this claim precludes examining the role of cultural life in constituting the material realm – and we should all know by now that economic life is too important to be left to the economists. Moreover, even in asserting that cultural and social analysis are "separate but equal," cultural historians risk reinforcing the false dichotomy and the epistemological hierarchy between the material and the ideal that they seek to transcend. To define culture as a separate sphere without examining the hierarchical distinction between a social life that is deemed "natural" and a cultural life that is deemed (merely) "constructed" or "symbolic" ultimately reinforces the privileged place of the social system as a natural object, free from "the mediation of cultural codes" (Alexander 1992b: 294). Thus unless we call into question what is and is not construed as a "natural object," cultural historians will ultimately naturalize society over culture and find themselves back in the reductionism that they sought to escape in the first place.

The second blind alley the cultural sociologists attempt to avoid is the argument for the mutual constitution of culture and society. This approach leads to what Archer (1988) calls a "central conflation," which makes it impossible to disentangle and "untie" the constitutive elements. "The intimacy of their interconnection denies even relative autonomy to the components involved ... [I]n the absence of any degree of autonomy it becomes impossible to *examine* their *interplay*" (1988: 80; emphasis added). (For a similar discussion of Archer, see Emirbayer and Goodwin 1994.)

Many of the post-Parsonian sociologists of culture, such as Alexander (1988, 1989a, 1990, 1992b), Alexander and Smith (1993), Archer (1988),

Emirbayer and Goodwin (1994), Griswold (1987, 1992), Kane (1991), Rambo and Chan (1990), and Sewell (1992), elaborate an approach that avoids these blind alleys of absolute autonomy and conflation. They avoid these impasses by distinguishing between analytic autonomy and concrete/empirical autonomy. The distinction means that for research it is important to treat cultural structures as analytically distinct from material forces, exploring their internal logic and history apart from other domains of social life. In the analytic dimension, the "current arrangement of its units can be understood primarily in terms of the earlier traditions from which they have evolved" rather than expressing material social forces or interests (Alexander 1990: 9). The approach "assumes that both [symbolic and material forces] are always present as analytical dimensions of the same empirical unit" (Alexander 1992b: 297). Yet although cultural structures first must be treated as analytically autonomous, in concrete instances the two domains are intertwined. Precisely how the symbolic and the material are intertwined and to what degree they overlap are empirical questions to be investigated rather than stipulated a priori. The cultural dimension "overlaps, but is not contiguous with, the society" (Alexander 1992b: 298).

Sewell has elaborated on this theme with his ingenious working-through of the confusion surrounding the term structure. He characterizes the problem as one in which mainstream – and especially macro – sociologists typically contrast "structure" with "culture": the "semiotically inclined social scientists [e.g., anthropologists and anthro-historians] ... regard culture as the preeminent site of structure ... the term structure is assumed to refer to the realm of culture, except when it is modified by the adjective 'social.'" As in the analytic/concrete distinction, Sewell introduces a virtual/actual distinction between schemas and resources. Schemas are "fundamental tools of thought" as well as the "various conventions, recipes, scenarios, principles of action, and habits of speech and gestures built up with these fundamental tools"; resources are nonhuman material objects as well as "observable characteristics of real people who live in particular times and congregate in particular places" (Sewell 1992: 8, 10). Like Alexander and others, however, he insists that a complete sociological analysis must recognize that this separation is only analytic and that "sets of schemas and resources may properly be said to constitute structures only when they mutually imply and sustain each other over time" (Sewell 1992: 13).

With the assumption that culture is both dependent on and autonomous from social life, sociologists are vigorously comparing, conceptualizing, and documenting the relationship rather than defining the problem in terms of the society/culture dualism. This tendency is evident in Alexander's (1992b) and Alexander and Smith's (1993) work on the variable distribution of social events across a relatively stable set of cultural codes in American civil society; in Brubaker's (1992) work on the varying political cultures of citizenship across France and Germany; in Collins's (1981, 1988) comparative work on gender and class distribution, marriage, and property relations across cultural systems; in DiMaggio's (1992) work on the distribution of cultural capital across groups; in Griswold's (1987) arguments that in the post-Parsonian approach to culture the things to be explained are first the cultural object itself and then – with great caution – the properties of a group or individual that engages with that object; in Lamont's (1992b) study of French and American cultural practices, in which she problematizes and empirically compares, case by case, the variable relationships between culture and its "determinants"; and in Swidler's (1986) empirical application of her "tool kit" theory to different degrees of "settled lives."

Analytic assumptions

From this rich literature in history and sociology can be garnered some basic shared assumptions on which the new political culture project is being constructed.[23] It is worth the inevitable risk of oversimplification to clarify these assumptions in order to identify the differences between the new and the old, to suggest how the new political culture concept provides alternatives to the problematic theoretical traditions in the earlier versions, to build a bridge between the new and the old, and to clarify the epistemological implications it offers for a historical sociology of concept formation.[24]

Definitions

Whereas both the Parsonian and the Habermasian approaches to political culture relegated cultural beliefs to expressions of social and economic interests generated by the properties of the social system, the new concept

---

[23] Cultural studies in general, especially those of popular culture, have become totally interdisciplinary; as a result, the assumptions at work can baffle students from any single discipline (Mukerji and Schudson 1991: 5).

[24] Again, a caveat: these assumptions are not introduced as the basis for a claim that this new work has "solved" the problems of theorizing the place of political culture in society and in social analysis more generally. All of these assumptions have weaknesses, such as the "dearth of theoretical propositions" concerning the source of some of the structuralist's binary codes (e.g. "deep neurology," Wuthnow 1987: 339). Rather, I take these assumptions to be relevant to the specifically epistemological benefits of the new political culture concept, and to its ability to help us understand the limits of the old.

defines culture as a structure in its own right constituted autonomously through a series of relationships among cultural elements (Baker 1990; Chartier 1988; Hunt 1986, 1989a; Sewell 1993). Although cultural systems may be viewed in part as the "accretion of innumerable social acts," they cannot be understood as internalized values or exteriorized interests (Alexander 1990: 8). Rather, these political discourses exist as independent relational structures in such forms as legal doctrines, political or civil societies, and symbolic systems of moral distinctions in politics or people (see especially Sewell 1980, 1985, and Stinchcombe's 1982 discussion of moral categories in structuralist analysis). These works thus pose profound challenges to the prevailing essentialism of social analysis, in which the meaning of something is believed to be established by defining its essence. In these newer works, meanings are conceived as relational. Relationality of meaning moves the references of a cultural element away from representing a "real" social object with "essential" attributes. Instead, individual meanings are activated only in relationship to other meanings and narratives. In incorporating books into social history, for example, Natalie Davis tells us that "a printed book is not so much a source of ideas as a carrier of relationships" (Mukerji and Schudson 1991: 10).[25]

Causality and autonomy

Much of the criticism among contemporary social historians and cultural sociologists is directed toward traditional Marxist, *Annaliste*, and Parsonian approaches to culture. This criticism is leveled at the reduction of cultural representations to epiphenomena of the material or social world – if not in the "first" then eventually "in the last instance." The new culturalists thus have vigorously challenged the claim that political cultures are determined, a priori, by the social system and/or its stages of socioeconomic development. By contrast, the more structuralist-influenced political culture concept is not caused by the social but develops and changes on the basis of its own internal rules and processes – as well as in historical interaction with other domains of life. Such political practices and discourses have meanings and histories partially internal to

---

[25] In recent works on the French Revolution, the array of topics addressed under the rubric of political culture – and thus thought to represent various forms of cultural rules and codes – includes ongoing coffeehouse associations and reading societies (Chartier 1991); political symbols, festivals, and revolutionary rituals (Hunt 1984; Ozouf 1988); journalistic techniques; the languages of politics (Furet 1981); Enlightenment categories of thought; republican conceptions of Reason (Baker 1990); the daily life of the sans-culottes (male and female); and the gender dimensions of republicanism (Landes 1988). (For a deeply sociological definition of "representations," see especially Chartier 1988.)

their own relationships and dynamics. Such causal autonomy in turn allows, even mandates, a central role for culture in structuring political outcomes. The structuring power of cultural discourses and codes permits political action to be understood in an entirely different way than that of a "fit" of political ideas with a social or political system, and irretrievably calls into question the causal power of a social world independent of its cultural mediation.

More Geertzian approaches posit that the meaning of the cultural system is constituted not only by its own roles but also by the social activities that surround it, and that actors create the meanings "as they go" in interaction with the structural forms (e.g. Sewell 1980, 1985). These, however, are still considered forms of cultural activities. In this "dramaturgical" approach to the political culture concept, cultural patterns are "assumed to play an expressive role in dramatizing and affirming the moral obligations on which social interaction depends – the moral order" (Wuthnow 1987: 332).

Of course, causality and autonomy have always had at least two separate aspects. The first rejects the claim that culture is determined by society or the economy in favor of the claim that culture is autonomous. The second asks whether the inverse is true – are society and the material world caused by the cultural? The influence of structuralism, symbolic anthropology, Bourdieu, and the poststructuralists on the new cultural historians has led them to argue that social relations can be perceived only through interpretive grids – cultural logics – rather than existing as "natural objects" in their own right. Cultural, symbolic, political, and social relations are mutually constitutive (see especially Sahlins 1976). Hence empirical investigations emphasize questions of how aspects of political culture are variably appropriated and used, made and remade, and to what effect.

The power-culture link in political culture

The political in the political culture concept, as used by Parsons and Habermas, refers more to values and rational ideas about politics than to either classical or cultural meanings of "political." By contrast, the political in the new political culture concept rejects the excessively social approach, which derives explanations for political ideas, symbols, and events from deeper social and economic phenomena, in favor of "the analysis of the political as such" (Baker 1990: 1, 2–11; Hunt 1989a: 1–22).[26] There are differences of degree in how the "political" in the

---

[26] That Carr was one of the preeminent historians of the twentieth century notwithstanding, this quote is too good to pass up as representing the social approach that the social

political culture concept is elaborated, even among the cultural historians. Baker defines political culture as a "set of discourses or symbolic
practices" by which "individuals and groups in any society articulate,
negotiate, implement, and enforce the competing claims they make upon
each other" (1990: 4–5). In this sense, and drawing from Pocock's (e.g.
1985) work on how English political discourse embodied and structured
political historical events, "political authority is . . . a matter of linguistic
authority: first, in the sense that political functions are defined and
allocated within the framework of a given political discourse; and second,
in the sense that their exercise takes on the form of upholding author-
itative definitions of the terms within that discourse" (Baker 1990: 5).

In this conception of politics, Baker emphasizes how available political
languages serve as the public symbolic frames in which historical actors
convert their immediate "private" experiences into political interpretations.
He argues that the very notion of "interest" – which governs traditional
approaches to politics – is itself inherently "a political one . . . a symbolic
and political construction, not simply a preexisting social reality" (1990:
5–6). The latitude of outcomes and analytic contingency made available to
social scientists in this struggle over the "power to define" is apparent in the
problem that Baker sets for himself: "to show how the revolutionary script
was invented, taking on its power and its contradictions, from within the
political culture of the absolute monarchy" (1990: 4).

For cultural historians influenced more by Gramsci, Bourdieu (e.g.
1984), and the later works of Foucault, the power/culture link is built
into the very nature of the symbolic logics, boundaries, differences, and
demarcations (e.g. the "Birmingham School" in Grossberg *et al.* [1992]).
These analyses tend to follow the lines of Marx's "dominant ideology
thesis" to analyze the "control of subjectivity in everyday life through the
shaping of common sense and the naturalization of social relations" –
indeed, through the very capacity to "impose a specific definition of reality
which is disadvantageous to others (e.g. Bourdieu's 'symbolic violence')"
(Lamont and Wuthnow 1990: 294–5). Foucault's later works in particular
analyze culture through the "prism of the technologies of power," which
exist not only in the state but also in the everyday cultural interactions
of social life – visits to the doctor, sexual relationships, love, schooling, and
so on. In this approach "power is ubiquitous in social life, operating in

historians were rejecting: "Since the preoccupation with economic and social ends represents a broader and more advanced stage in human development than the preoccupation
with political and constitutional ends, so the economic and social interpretation of history
may be said to represent a more advanced stage in history than the exclusively political
interpretation" (Carr [1961] 1965: 164–5, cited in Hunt 1989a: 6).

micro-level . . . and at the macro levels" (Lamont and Wuthnow 1990: 295). Perhaps not surprisingly, this overarching view of the culture/power relationship, which provides little room for exploring competing appropriations of cultural symbols, has taken root primarily among studies of cultural hegemony, and less so among French social historians analyzing the popular revolutionary overthrow of the *ancien régime* (one of the reasons, I believe, for the deserved excitement about the publication of Habermas's work on the public sphere).[27]

In sum, the most distinctive quality of the rejuvenated political culture concept is definitional: rather than a collection of internalized expressions of subjective values or externalized expressions of social interests, political culture is now being defined as a configuration of representations and practices, which exists as a structural phenomenon in its own right. It bears little resemblance to the Parsonians' social psychological approach or to the dominant-interests approach of traditional Marxism. And while the new political culture concept has points in common with Habermas's public sphere, overall it rejects his overly social, rationalist, and economic interpretation of political cultural developments. Independent of both the economy and the state, this rejuvenated political culture shapes the outcomes, the meanings, and the very course of political action and social processes. These changes not only challenge traditional answers to the question "What causes culture?" They also point to entirely new ways of analyzing political and social life as a whole.

Turning the political culture concept back on itself: toward a historical sociology of concept formation

Having examined the new political culture project, I am now better positioned to ask what this work implies for the problem I posed at the outset of this chapter: why do political sociology's political culture and public sphere concepts appear to be neither cultural nor political? My answer is that sociology's political culture concept is itself constrained by a newly defined political culture structure. In abstract terms, this structure takes the form of a conceptual network because it is a structured relational matrix of theoretical principles and conceptual assumptions. As a relational concept the sociological meaning of political culture is produced, organized, constrained, and contained by its embeddedness in this conceptual network. To decipher the ambiguities of the concept, the

---

[27] For important critiques see Sherwood *et al.* (1993), Lamont (1989), Lamont and Wuthnow (1990).

internal logic of this network must be made visible. This is a project that requires a historical sociology of concept formation. Here I sketch the outlines of this research program in programmatic terms. In doing so, I draw implications from the new political culture project discussed above and augment these by appropriating from theories that sometimes have been engaged in heated combat: cultural sociology, science studies, network and institutional analysis, structuralism, and poststructuralism.[28]

A historical sociology of concept formation

A historical sociology of concept formation is comprised of three dimensions. First, it directs us to take a reflexive approach to concepts; second, it defines concepts as relational – that is, they exist not as autonomous categories but in relational patterns; and, third, it treats concepts as historical and cultural artifacts, rather than as labels for preexisting external objects.

Reflexivity

The new political culture concept makes it possible to engage in a self-conscious conceptual reflexivity. Reflexivity – literally, turning back on the self – makes the original political culture concept itself the object of inquiry (the problem to be explained) rather than an unproblematic category of sociological inquiry (Zimmerman and Pollner 1970). Parsonians use the political culture concept to label those values they theorize to be the chief factors in determining political systems. Habermas employs the political culture concept as an analytic label for a set of communicative practices and rational institutions expressing bourgeois political interests. Making the political culture concept itself the dependent variable – that is, changing it from explanatory tool to problematic-to-be-explained – generates a new set of questions: why and how and to what effect have social scientists believed that the social world contains something significant called a political culture? To answer these questions, I use the new political culture concept to explain the old. A reflexive inversion, in short, makes it possible to examine the old political culture concept through the analytic lens of the new.

---

[28] The excuse for such shameless scavenging is that, despite numerous differences among approaches, they overlap around *relational* themes and assumptions that together provide the foundations for a historical sociology of concept formation.

Concepts as relational objects

Once we have turned the political culture concept back against itself to make it the object of explanation, we can formulate and specify *how* we want to look at it. A traditional approach might assume that first we observe something, then we form a concept to label its attributes, and then we discover other objects that have those same attributes and can be cited as other examples of the concept. More fashionable in our post-positivist theory-driven social science culture is the assumption that the concept is formed first and then determines what attributes are gathered under its rubric. In practice, however, Hacking (1988) argues it does not work in either of those ways because we would not, in the first place, have "grouped individuals or actions had we not produced knowledge connecting the class with other classes" (Hacking 1988: 54). A historical sociology of concept formation adopts a relational rather than a categorical approach to the political culture concept. As Habermas and the Parsonians use it, sociology's political culture concept is an autonomous social science category to which we ascribe a set of attributes, which then are specified in their empirical contexts. There are two different arguments about what the concept really is – that is, two answers to the question "What attributes of the political culture concept should be included in the category?" The question represents an implicit theory of concepts that Karl Popper ([1934] 1959) called "essentialist" – a philosophy that looks to the *essence* of things for information about their true nature.

In contrast to this essentialist approach, or what recently has been called the "categorical imperative" (Emirbayer and Goodwin 1994), a historical sociology of concept formation rejects the importance of asking what the political culture concept *is*. Instead it examines the political culture concept as embedded in a relational configuration of concepts – a conceptual network consisting of a multiplicity of signs, codes, and concepts. Building from the new political culture's legacy in structural linguistics, one can conceive a conceptual network as the matrix or the "field" (Bourdieu and Wacquant 1992; Brubaker 1985) in which concepts are embedded. It is a web or a structured configuration of relationships among concepts that are linked to each other by virtue of sharing the same conceptual net. The network concept directs us to look for the matrix of ties between the conceptual nodes and to discern the relational patterns they form. Concepts have relational identities because they are embedded in structures and histories composed of configurations and coordinates of ideas, epistemological rules of validity, and cultural logics.

That concepts have relational identities does not suggest that conceptual networks are holistic, consensual, or noncontested entities. Rather, it suggests the influence of the Foucaultian notion of the historically contingent but nonetheless internal integrity of a cultural pattern or logic, such that pragmatic choices within this pattern are regulated by the pressures of meaningful consistency. Moreover, this pressure for patterned consistencies within conceptual networks does not translate in any way into a coordinated, systemic integrity in the larger domain of culture as a whole, which itself is composed of numerous, often competing conceptual networks, mediated by a multiplicity of power relations. This larger domain is not subject to any single logic. Nor does this idea signal what may appear, at first glance, to be a shift from the subjective to the objective conception of culture. As we are reminded by Stinchcombe (1982: 78–80) and Alexander (1992b), if a phenomenon is indeed a form of culture – that is, a modality of meaning – it will have "mental," moral, and normative as well as structural dimensions. Stinchcombe urges us to recognize that "a socially instituted category makes use of human mental capacities, whatever they are" (1982: 80). Alexander (1990: 26) similarly emphasizes this point: "We cannot understand culture without reference to subjective meaning, and we cannot understand it without reference to social structural constraints." More than the (probably) false distinction between subjective and objective, the most important definitional shift in a historical sociology of concept formation is away from thinking about a concept as a singular categorical expression to regarding concepts as embedded in complex relational networks that are both intersubjective and public.[29]

The most notable implication of this idea is that concepts in a conceptual network are not only related to each other in the weak sense of being contiguous; they are also related ontologically. That is, concepts cannot be defined on their own as single entities, but only deciphered in terms of their "place" in relation to the other concepts in the web

---

[29] Indeed, this focus on culture as an attribute of a particular category of person (e.g. an *homme bourgeois* and a capitalist, a Protestant, an American) joins most closely the Parsonian with the Marxist model of political culture. Neither model denies that cultural spheres exist independently of subjective minds. For Parsons, for example, introducing the tripartite view of the cultural domain was a major contribution; similarly, Habermas's concept of a public sphere gives us an "objective" handle on culture. Each of these approaches presumes, and the relational approach calls into question, that at the level of ontology (that is, what is the essence of this thing called culture?) the cultural sphere, like cultural values, is an expression of categorical attributes.

(Lévi-Strauss [1964] 1969; Polanyi [1944] 2001; White 1992).[30] What appear to be autonomous categories defined by their attributes are reconceived more accurately as historically shifting sets of relationships that are contingently stabilized.[31] Thus, instead of employing a language of categories and attributes, a historical sociology of concept formation substitutes a language of networks and relationships to support relational thinking.

Concepts as historical and cultural objects

In the third dimension of a historical sociology of concept formation, the political culture concept is recognized as a historical and cultural object rather than what Durkheim called a "natural object" – by which he meant simply an abstract name for what appears to be a given external social object. To clarify, I contrast this again with the approach taken by political sociology. Both Parsons and Habermas approach political culture by attempting to arrive at a conceptual definition that reflects most clearly the actual facts they are trying to represent. Then they evaluate the quality of their definition by the goodness of fit between the label and the external social reality. Recall that the new political culture project challenges this method by arguing that social practices and political ideas must be reconceived as historical and cultural objects in and of themselves, rather than as reflections of external social phenomena. Yet practitioners of the new political culture concept do not always follow through on its most radical epistemological implications. The new political culture concept is still a label for something else – in this case, political ideas of (say) French workers, expressed through linguistic systems and ritualistic practices. And although they offer a new version of what political culture is, these cultural historians do not break completely with essentialism. Their work stops short of a thoroughgoing reflexivity that would make the political culture concept itself a cultural object subjected to critical scrutiny.

A historical sociology of concept formation builds on the foundation laid by the new political culture project to argue that just as political ideas and social practices are not abstract reflections of external social attributes, so must our own theoretical concepts be understood not as given

---

[30] I take the term "place" in relational terms from Polanyi ([1944] 1957); for empirical application see Somers (1993). Another similar expression is that of "positions" in a "field" (see e.g. Bourdieu and Wacquant 1992).
[31] The similarity of this idea to White's (1992) relational theory of identity is discussed in Somers (1998).

phenomena with natural attributes but as cultural and historical objects embedded in symbolic and historically constructed cultural structures, and assigned meaning by their location in those structures. Recognizing social science ideas as cultural objects is hardly new, of course. It began with Durkheim and continued with his students and descendants Mauss, Lévi-Strauss, and Halbwachs. In a move that far foreshadowed Foucault, Durkheim recognized that our most primordial logical categories of time, space, and causality are social creations (Durkheim and Mauss [1903] 1963). In doing so, Durkheim also produced a socialized version of Kant's famous distinction between noumena and phenomena, often recognized in philosophy as nominalism. More recently, ethnomethodologists have made problematic the discourse and practice of the human sciences, finding that "scientific accounts of human behavior are themselves permeated by rich, subtle practices and assumptions which are typically ignored and unrecognized" (Pollner 1987: ix).

Here the theoretical links become explicit between cultural historians and sociologists, on the one side, and structural and network sociologists and institutional analysis, on the other (Emirbayer and Goodwin 1994; Powell and DiMaggio 1991; Wellman 1983; Wellman and Berkowitz 1988; White 1992). Tilly, for example, reminds us of the depth of the relationality of identity when he tells us, perhaps having in mind the famous story *The Return of Martin Guerre*, that "the ability to simulate or reconstruct . . . relationships . . . in fact allows imposture: by falsely claiming the same set of relationships, one organism can assume the identity of another ... *Eventually we must find the means of placing relationships rather than individuals at the very center of the analysis*" (1984: 27, 32). The new institutional sociology suggests that cultural structures join together different elements into what DiMaggio and Powell (1991: 14) call "loosely coupled arrays of standardized elements." Once cultural patterns are recognized as such, and are recognized to have some rule-bound existence outside individuals' minds and social practices, they can be understood sociologically as deeply implicated in our understanding of how institutions work (DiMaggio and Powell 1991).

Above all, the extensive work that has flourished recently in science studies has contributed enormously to the approach suggested here, with its emphasis on the historicity of knowledge (Canguilhem [1966] 1978, 1988; Foucault, e.g. 1972, [1970] 1973, 1977, [1966] 1978; Geertz 1973, 1983; Gutting 1989; Hacking 1979, 1990a; Kuhn 1970; Shapin and Schaffer 1986), epistemological reflexivity (Knorr-Cetina and Mulkay 1983; Woolgar 1988, 1992), and network approaches to social science knowledge (Latour 1993; Pickering 1984, 1992, 1993). Science studies practitioners define as historical and cultural much of what has long been taken to be natural. Following Latour (1988: 68), a historical sociology of concept formation takes it that a concept "never survives beyond the narrow networks of practices and circumstances that define its validity." Unlike Latour, however, I am far from convinced that such networks of practices are always so "narrow." On the contrary, the relationships that I examine in this historical sociology of concept formation are very wide and deep historically – the kinds of structures that Sewell (1992: 24) defines as having "high depth" and so much "durability" that they appear almost to be second nature (see chapter 7).

In sum, three aspects of a historical sociology of concept formation can be identified – its reflexivity, its relationality, and its recognition of social science concepts as cultural and historical objects. This sociology weaves together two distinct strands in the human sciences. The first tradition – that of the history and sociology of culture, structuralism, and network analysis – finds that cultural objects must be understood in relation to other objects. The second tradition – that of science studies – extends this observation to the concepts of the human sciences themselves. A historical sociology of concept formation is inspired by both the structural and the reflexive traditions, and assumes a form that resembles neither in its entirety. From this perspective, the political culture concept and all social science concepts lack natures or essences; instead they have histories, networks, and narratives.

PART III

In search of civil society and democratic citizenship: romancing the market, reviling the state

6

Let them eat social capital: how marketizing the social turned Solidarity into a bowling team

Setting what is surely an all-time record, in less than a decade the concept of social capital has shot with meteoric speed through the epistemological fast track to become one of the reigning ideas of our time. Even in the rarified air of conceptual superstars, social capital is notable for a charismatic appeal unmatched in recent memory. Few ideas have been projected into such an array of protean forms, displayed such remarkable theoretical promiscuity, or been endowed with such seemingly unlimited powers and capacities for good. From east to west, north, and south, from postmodern capitalist hegemons to struggling postcolonial regimes, the global reach of its ascribed value and applicability is stunning. Society, economics, politics, medicine, anthropology, psychology, epidemiology, ethnicity, history, economic development, marriage, child-raising, international relations, sexuality, institutionalism, law, community, education, race, gender, family, civic affairs, democracy, and global poverty – these are just some of the arenas and concerns to which the social capital concept has been applied in the role of what the World Bank Program on Social Capital calls "the missing link" in the effort to end poverty in the developing world (Grootaert 1997).[1] The breadth of its resonance is equally astonishing. From economists to public health scholars, from public intellectuals to peripatetic health care workers, from World Bank and IMF financiers to NGOs across the globe, from New England town meetings to C-SPAN TV – everyone, it seems, has fallen under the epistemic spell of social capital.[2]

---

[1] See the World Bank Web site on social capital at: www.worldbank.org/poverty/scapital/whatsc.htm.

[2] "It is difficult to think of an academic notion that has entered the common vocabulary of social discourse more quickly than the idea of social capital" (Dasgupta and Serageldin 1999). For a random sampling of the recent social capital literature, see Adler and Kwon

This is a phenomenon that puzzles. For one thing, the actual term social capital is not new, having been in circulation for almost three-quarters of a century since it first appeared in Hanifan (1920), followed several decades later by J. Jacobs (1961), brought into economics and public policy by Coleman *et al.* (1966) and Loury (1977), into sociology by Bourdieu (1986), and finally becoming a foundational concept of rational-choice theory by Coleman ([2000] 1988, 1990) and neoutilitarianism by Becker (Becker and Nashat 1997; Becker and Murphy 2000). For another, that socioeconomic prosperity is dependent on nonmarket, noncontractual social relations can be readily traced back to Aristotle, Adam Smith, Marx, Tocqueville, Durkheim, Weber, Malinowski, and Karl Polanyi, again to name only some of the most obvious. The implication that it is a new discovery and, moreover, that cooperative social practices and mutual associations are critically important for successful social movements, would certainly amaze many a social historian and social movement theorist. Legal historians would be equally provoked by such a claim, even those only minimally familiar with the preambles, statutes, and rule books characteristic of medieval and early modern guilds, apprenticeship regulations, tramping associations, eighteenth-century artisanal credit unions, or nineteenth-century friendly societies. And as for its being news that strong reciprocal relationships and associational networks are valuable cultural resources – well, one does not even want to imagine the bemused reaction of an anthropologist.

This, then, is the conundrum that needs to be engaged: how and why has social capital come to represent a new form of social knowledge? Even more significant, why does the term have such crowding-out power that it is quickly becoming the sole occupant of the conceptual space once filled by a multitude of competing, jostling, and differing ways to characterize the value of social relations? Clearly, it appears to have become an object of our culture's political imaginary. Onto it has been projected an idealized realization and long-yearned-for solution to a multiplicity of problems. But if social capital has been anointed as the object of a remarkable collective cathexis, why and how and to what effect has it

---

(1999), Baron *et al.* (2000), Arrow (2000), Becker (1996), Becker and Murphy (2000), Body-Gendrot and Gittell (2003), Bowles (1999), Bowles and Gintis (2002), Dasgupta and Serageldin (1999), Edwards *et al.* (2001), Evans (1996), Fine (2001), Fukuyama (1995a, 1995b), Gambetta (1988), Glaeser *et al.* (2002), Grootaert (1997), Grootaert and Van Bastelaer (2002), Krishna (2002), Lesser (2000), Lin (2001), McLean *et al.* (2002), Munch (2002), Ogilvie (2004), Orr (1999), Portes (1998), Putnam (1993, 1995, 1996, 2000, 2002), Putnam *et al.* (1993) Stewart-Weeks and Richardson (1998), Warren (1999), Taylor and Leonard (2002), Straw (1998), Rose (2000), Robalino (2000) Rotberg and Brucker (2001), Saegert *et al.* (2001).

come to assume this position still puzzles. What is the theoretical and – more important – the political work social capital is performing? What need is it fulfilling?[3] One does not have to be a sociologist of knowledge to be intrigued with the significance and implications, the causes and consequences of such a phenomenon.

In what follows I use the metaphor of a "perfect storm" to diagnose and account for the social capital phenomenon. A perfect storm is not one, but a collision of multiple storms. In many ways, the most important of these was the publication of several works by Robert Putnam in 1993.[4] *Making Democracy Work* (Putnam *et al*. 1993) produced the counterintuitive finding that what makes democracy work in Tuscany is best explained not by the state's well-known campaign of institutional anticorruption reforms and public policies, but by the local participation of civic groups such as choral societies and church associations. Marking Putnam's achievement as a crossover success from academia to the global public sphere, the *Economist* magazine celebrated the book under the caption "Civic Lessons" (1993). Almost simultaneously, *The American Prospect*, a journal of the liberal intelligentsia, published "The Prosperous Community: Social Capital and Public Life" (Putnam 1993), in which he admonished and forecasted the dangerous condition of American society, which has been increasingly "bowling alone." Bowling, of course, serves as metaphor and microcosm of the fact that "every year over the last decade or two, millions more have withdrawn from the affairs of their communities" (Putnam 1993: 68). No less than the future of democracy, Putnam forewarned, in what became a series of articles and books, hangs in the balance of whether or not the nation's solitary bowlers would once again become team players (Putnam 1993, 1995, 1996, 2000).

The second of social capital's catalyzing storms itself represented a collision of dynamic historical processes – intellectual, epistemological, and scholarly, but also cultural, economic, sociological, religious, and political. Four of these are of interest to my story: (1) neoliberals looking for solutions to market externalities and transaction costs; (2) neoconservatives advocating a new site of moral restraint and cultural alternatives to the "handouts" of the welfare state and the "excesses" of democratic participation of the 1960s and 1970s; (3) sociologists, political scientists,

---

[3] In psychoanalytic terms, one would almost have to call it a fetish, although I prefer *totem* as a more Durkheimian approach to the way that inanimate objects, even social categories, can take on the characteristics of collective desiderata.

[4] It is entirely arbitrary to name 1993 as the "takeoff" year of social capital's perfect storm. I do so only because one must register some kind of a beginning, and because of Putnam's central place in the popular discovery of the social capital concept.

rational-choice theorists, and economists (many of whom doubled as public intellectuals) competing over the disciplinary turf of how to best include social relationships in prevailing economic models; and (4) the World Bank's search for a "post-Washington consensus" in dealing with global poverty and economic development (under the influence of Joseph Stiglitz).[5]

Call these the multiple streams and trajectories of social capital, each starting from different origins under different conditions and each with different political aims, but eventually all cascading toward the same point where (to painfully mix metaphors) upon colliding with Putnam's emergence into the public sphere, they erupted into the perfect storm of social capital. Most significantly, despite their radically competing political goals and ideologies, these many social capital trajectories all had the same epistemological agenda, namely, to develop a new theory and vocabulary that would name, explain, and "make true" for political knowledge a source of value that would serve as an alternative to the power of the state. For most, this was economic value, but for others it was moral, and for still others, it was political. But what they all shared was the search for a social mechanism independent of the state to enhance economic prosperity and solve social problems. The goal was to switch from state-centered models of development and entitlement-based solutions to social problems, to market-centric ones which would be resolutely joined to civil society as a whole. With each social capital trajectory driving toward the same epistemological desideratum, their collision was inevitable. When it happened it triggered an enormous opportunity structure to capture, fulfill, and control this space. In the event, social capital possessed the powers to seize the prize.

In parallel development to the four social capital streams was a fifth trajectory, separate from the others yet perhaps the most important for the political dimension of the social capital story. This was the democratic left's "civil society" movement. Civil society is a concept that in large part was "rediscovered" and put in recirculation during the 1980s in Eastern Europe by Poland's Solidarity, the GDR's New Forum, and Czechoslovakia's Charter 77 (to name the best known), as well as by the new social movements in Western liberal democracies. Advocates of the new civil society concept saw it as both a normative ideal and a social site for autonomous democratic practices, self-organization, and citizen participation, with the goals of contributing to public deliberation in the

---

[5] The World Bank's adoption of the social capital concept deserves its own story to do justice to the quantity and innovative quality of this work.

public sphere and influencing public policy and the state.[6] But above all, these civil society movements were organized to fight the tyranny of the communist states by establishing flourishing zones of social relations autonomous from the political regimes that for so long had successfully been able to repress them (Arato and Cohen 1984; Cohen 1985; Kitschelt 1993; Offe 1984). Civil society was the capacious rubric to which these movements were both dedicated and attached.

At first glance it would appear that there was little difference between these movements and the social capital streams, as they both shared the passionate goal of establishing and normalizing an antistatist site of the social. But there was one distinction between the civil society movement and the others, a distinction so great that the social capital concept would come to represent a deep and abiding oppositional threat to that of civil society. Whereas the motivational logic behind the social capital movements was to identify an antistatist site of the social, with perhaps the single exception of the "Putnamites" this was a utility-generating view of the social that put it in firm alliance with the market. The vision of civil society carried by the democratic left was also deeply antistatist. In contrast, however, their conception of civil society equally demanded autonomy from the market. They vigorously challenged as false liberalism's standard dichotomy between state/public and market/private, arguing that this represented not the empirical world but rather liberalism's normative binary epistemological landscape. Breaking apart the dichotomy to make room for a third sphere of the social was initially triggered by the widespread currency of Poland's Solidarity. But to effect a permanent change in the distribution of conceptual space required a contest of epistemological politics. Would the social be liberated from the manichean binary between public and private to become civil society – a third sphere of autonomy from the predations of both market and state? Or would social capital capture the civil society ideal and subordinate it to the role of handmaiden to the market?

In what follows, I have grouped these phenomena, processes, streams, and trajectories under two broad, interweaving causal narratives – one primarily intellectual and scholarly, the other political and event-driven.

[6] Although the civil society concept was equally a phenomenon of South American anti-authoritarian politics in the 1980s, I leave that aside in this chapter. On the history and rediscovery of civil society, see, among many sources, Alexander (2006), Arato (1981, 2000), Barber (1996), Calhoun (1993), Cohen and Arato (1992), Cohen (1999), Edwards and Foley (1998), Edwards *et al.* (2001), Ehrenberg (1999), Foley and Edwards (1996), Geremek (1992), Giddens (1998), Hall (1995), J. Keane (1988), Kennedy (1991, 2002), Rosenberg and Post (2002), Seligman (1992), Somers (1995a, 1995b, 1999), Taylor (1990), Walzer (1991), and Wolfe (1989).

Combined, they make up a larger canvas of multiple intersecting needs and resources, processes and powers, and causes and effects of the epistemological politics behind the social capital concept. The academic/intellectual story is that of the complex relationship between economics and sociology for control of the soul of the social. Because sociology is the discipline that has contributed the most to bringing social capital into the mainstream, this is by necessity a tale of sociological self-deception. Sociologists believe that after years of "sneering contempt" (McCloskey 1994), economists have finally accepted the social dimension of markets. In adopting the social capital concept, a small group of neoliberal economists qua public intellectuals appear to be offering an olive branch of respect to sociology. But it is just that – appearance. Blinded by desire for recognition by economists, sociologists have taken appearance for reality. In so doing they inadvertently collude with the neoliberal project of appropriating, domesticating, transforming, and evacuating the social from public knowledge. Sociologists feel pride in their belief that the social capital concept finally has sociologized knowledge of the economic. But it is actually the inverse. Through a Trojan horse of social capital, the social is being successfully marketized.

The political story is one of the relationships in the 1990s between neoliberal and neoconservative movements on the one side, and the democratic left in Europe and the United States on the other. This story takes us from the revolutionary democratic shipyards of the Polish Solidarity trade union movement in Gdansk, to the recent US trend of substituting "faith-based organizations" for public services once provided by government, to the current nostalgia for the bowling leagues and neighborhood church groups of 1950s America. This is also a story of appropriation and domestication. Powerful neoliberal and conservative public intellectuals of the 1980s and 1990s were drawn to the antistatist and anticommunist impulses of the civil society concept, and at first they eagerly appropriated the idea from the Eastern European revolutionaries. However, once they recognized it as a site peopled by trade unionists, new social movements, and participatory rights-driven politics, they quickly turned to taming and transforming its unruliness. In a truly Pygmalion achievement, civil society became but a shadow of its former identity as, at the hands of conservatives, it morphed into social capital, becoming politically manageable, tamed, respectable, domesticated, and bustling with bowling leagues, church picnics, home schooling, family values, moral regulation, backyard barbeques, volunteer labor, and faith-based soup kitchens. For those committed to market solutions, social capital answered a different need from that of the democratic left's civil society activists. It was the ideal antistatist solution to the externalities and the imperfections that emerge inevitably from an overly rapid marketization and displacement of public services and social-safety-net regimes at home and abroad. Like civil society, social capital is antistatist; unlike civil society it perches not in between but on the market side of the entrenched dichotomy between private and public, market and state.

These are, in brief, the dynamic narratives that produced the perfect storm of social capital. But before turning to my causal stories, let me put my own cards on the table by delineating my view of social capital's immanent incoherences and the fundamental threat it poses for "the soul of the social."

Social + capital = the evacuation of the social

The social capital literature is riddled with competing definitions. Still, at the most general level, most would agree that social capital refers to the economic value produced by social relationships (Åberg and Sandberg 2003; Arrow 2000; Becker 1976, 1996; Becker and Murphy 2000; Bourdieu 1986; Coleman [1998] 2000; Fukuyama 1995a; Grootaert and Van Bastelaer 2002; Putnam 1993, 1995, 2000; Putnam *et al.* 1993). By creating and maintaining social and normative cohesion over time in durable networks and communities these relationships are said to generate a kind of streaming utility that the market either cannot or will not produce but on which capitalism depends for reducing what economists call transaction costs. Thus the World Bank's definition of social capital: "Social capital consists of a set of horizontal associations between people, consisting of social networks and associated norms that have an effect on community productivity and well-being. Social networks can increase productivity *by reducing the costs of doing business*. Social capital facilitates coordination and cooperation" (World Bank 2004; italics added).[7]

At the heart of social capital theory is the thesis that capitalism depends on what Durkheim (1984: 215) famously called the "non-contractualism of contract," specifically trust, mutual reliability, and the reciprocal norms and networks of noncontractual social relations. Absent these attributes,

---

[7] To be fair, the paragraph following this reads: "Social capital also has an important 'downside': communities, groups, or networks which are isolated, parochial, or working at cross-purposes to society's collective interests (e.g. drug cartels, corruption rackets) can actually hinder economic and social development" (World Bank 2004).

there could be no meaningful contracts but only an aggregate of multiple "spot" markets, a condition in which societies cannot endure.[8] A harmless and unobjectionable reprise of an old idea? Maybe. Still, there are onto-logical, methodological, and epistemological reasons why pairing social together with capital actually threatens the very social relations upon which social capital depends. Parsing social capital into the two separate concepts of social and capital demonstrates just how much is compromised in their coupling.

What is capital?

Standard neoclassical economics defines capital as any kind of resource (physical or otherwise) capable of producing streaming utility resources, that is, with the capacity for economic value over time.[9] Capital is also something that must be owned and thus is also a form of property. But if capital must be property, the inverse cannot be true; the vast majority of one's possessions do not produce economic utility over time. This may be obvious in some cases: automobiles most famously lose value overnight. But is the difference always so evident? We take for granted that whether or not something counts as capital is empirically inherent in the object itself, even if the capital in question is "human capital," because even mental skills must be manifested in an educational credential or certifi-cate of training. But is the important distinction between property and capital always so easy to determine by having empirical access to the object?

Consider the case of two apples I have brought home from the grocery store. Both are my property, but, as it happens, only one of them is a form of capital. But how to tell which is which? After all, they look virtually identical. Examine them as I might, the answer will not be found in the apples themselves, for the status of capital is not inherent to the object. Rather, the distinction must be found in my mental state of intention-ality. Here is why. I bought each apple for different purposes: one to eat,

---

[8] See Block (1990) for a discussion of spot markets versus contracts. There is also an enormous literature on the role of trust in social capital; see especially Fukuyama (1995a), Gambetta (1988), Warren (1999).

[9] A Marxist or even an institutionalist definition of capital would be very different. A coherent Marxist perspective could not take on board the notion of social capital in the first place because Marxism and institutionalism begin from the premise that capital is constitutively social in the first place (see e.g. Block 1990; Fine 2001). For Marxism, the term social capital is thus redundant. For social capital to make sense, capital would have to first be depleted of its social nature only to be a feeble conception of social, now conceived as the aggregate of individual actions, choice, and decision theoretics.

the other to extract the seeds to start an apple orchard. Being hungry, I gobble up apple number one, seeds and all. Alas, unable to defer gratification, apple number one is no more. As planned, however, I extract the seeds of apple number two and plant them in my apple-orchard-to-be. The two apples were identical when I unpacked the groceries and put them on the kitchen counter. But even before I ate the first one, only the second counted as capital. Why? Because I bought the two apples already intending not to consume them both, but to invest one of the apples. It was my intention that determined the different status and fates of the two apples.

My argument is that there is nothing inherent in apples, machines, skills, culture, or computers that make them inherently recognizable as capital. Capital is not an objective attribute but a mental state that resides in the heads of individual agents.[10] It represents a decision to defer the immediate gratification of consumption, enjoyment, utility, and exploitation in expectation of greater future rewards. At the theoretical level, the only thing that distinguishes capital from other commodities is all in the mind.

What is social?

If we start from the assumption that what is social is that which pertains to society, the sociological method tells us that that which is social is by necessity relational. Whether one reads Hegel, Marx, Tocqueville, Durkheim, Bourdieu, or Giddens, sociology's foundational a priori is the social as a "social fact," what Durkheim (1938) defined as social relations external to the mind, a mechanism of relational constraint, irreducible to its individual agents. Subfields as far apart as contemporary actor-network theory and critical realism share this same foundational premise that society exists outside the mind of any individual agent (though not necessarily of a collective agency). Call it a social formation, a social structure, a network, even a society of two, as the Victorian novelists liked to do. However unstable in a poststructuralist age, the social is still performatively relational. In Geertz's (1973) famous formulation, the social is irreducibly relational "all the way down."

---

[10] By external I include the educational skills of human capital. They do not count as capital if they are simply knocking about in your brain while watching television, not being put to any productive use. Only the intention to invest them endows them with the status of human capital.

Sociology, however, has never had exclusive rights to the study of the social. As much as they tried to hold it at bay, there is a competing approach that lays equal claim to the study of society even while resolutely rejecting its relationality. This is utilitarianism, today often used interchangeably with rational-choice theory. Although not dubbed as such until Bentham in the nineteenth century, utilitarianism properly begins with Hobbes's utilitarian man and becomes a full-fledged social theory with Locke's invention of civil society, a fully self-regulating social entity independent of the state and functioning as a countervailing source of power and social organization (Somers 2001). Locke's contractual vision of civil society could not be less relational. It is peopled by ontologically isolated, separate individuals who, in their presocial "state of nature," are constitutively autonomous vis-à-vis any and all others and relational entities: "[W]e must consider what state all men are naturally in, and that it is a state of perfect freedom to order their actions and dispose of their possessions and persons as they see fit, within the bounds of the law of nature, without asking leave, or depending upon the will of any other man" (Locke [1690] 1952, ch. 2, section 4: 4).

This methodologically individualist view of the social steadily developed from Hobbes, through Locke, to Smith, Bentham, Mill, and Spencer. It was above all Malthus ([1798] 1992) who, beginning from the individual utility-maximizing agent, was the first to fully realize the utilitarian project of theorizing society as a market. After lying dormant from Spencer to the mid-twentieth century, it again manifested itself, first in Homans's and Coleman's "social exchange" theory, then in today's thriving neoutilitarian rational-choice theory.[11] The celebrated social contract notwithstanding, a less relational approach to the social would be hard to find. Yet the problem utilitarianism has always posed for sociology is that this ontologically contractual social theory is nonetheless a theory of society. It is its shared object of study in the social, rather than in a common relational method, that makes utilitarianism a full-fledged alternative approach to that of sociology. To be sure, sociology's commitment to the constitutive and irreducible relationality of the social does not deny that individuals have purposeful mental states. But these *mentalités* are not presocial and utilitarian but social and relational. However it is spun, a social state of purposefulness is ontologically and irreducibly at odds with utilitarianism's competing conception of the social as an aggregate of presocial intentionalities. Utilitarianism's

---

[11] Consider that in its second edition, Randall Collins's widely used *Three Sociological Traditions* (1985) became *Four Sociological Traditions* (1997) with the addition of utilitarianism.

methodologically individualist view of the social always trumps the idea of a relational entity.

And social + capital = ?

These are two fundamentally opposing approaches to the social: the relational and the utilitarian. The marriage of social to capital thus poses the question of which view of the social is the one coupled with social capital. If we take the sociological perspective, social capital becomes a concept evacuated of its constitutive sociality. This incoherence results from trying to conjoin sociology's relational view of the social with a definition of capital inexorably tied to a conditional intentionality. The effort to attach the relationally social to the intentional agent turns both into something else entirely. Social capital cannot have it both ways: it cannot be both externally relational and internally intentional. It simply does not hold. There is an advantage its advocates gain from this incoherence, however. It gives social capital the kind of capaciousness that readily provides it with the appearance of relationality.

By contrast, the meaning of social capital becomes entirely coherent if we accept the utilitarian view of the social as an aggregate of contractually interacting individual agents. When this version of the social is linked to capital, the two methodological individualisms become compatible. The social aggregate becomes a utility-generating economic asset, while the social is transformed from a relational entity into an agent's personal property. From this perspective, anyone can have access to social capital as long as she is willing to convert her social relationships into capital by choosing to "invest" in them, rather than to immediately "consume" or exploit these connections. In so maximizing the utility function (future value) of the social network qua social capital, she might decide to prepare meals for a sick family member or to provide useful financial advice to a neighbor. From the point of view of social capital theory, however, these are instrumental choices made in the expectation that at a future point these investments of time, money, or friendship will produce far greater utility returns (i.e. provide far more valuable individual gain and profit) than they would have had if she simply had "used" the connections right away (to get a job, advice, emotional support, etc.). Social capital thus becomes a utility-driven "Rolodex" theory of social connections – one that the individual metaphorically carries around in a briefcase ready to access as she or he sees fit. The ontological and methodological postulates of utilitarianism convert relationships into utility functions.

Both rational-choice theory and modern economics define the fundamental unit of social analysis as the utility-maximizing individual agent.
But the postulate that all social and political analysis must be built on
microfoundations has two overwhelming difficulties: one is the long-
standing difficulty of the externalities and free riderships that result
from rational actions applied to public goods. The other is the problem
of basing a positivist theory of causal mechanisms on the empirically
unobservable quality of mental states. Both of these problems stem from
the postulate that the individual agent's mind, and consequent behavior,
makes no distinction between market exchange and social interaction.
Perhaps it is precisely this appeal to self-interest that endows social
capital with its ideational appeal and promiscuity.

The social approach to society, by contrast, is one with an infrastructure built on the practices and performances of social membership.
Social membership is practice-driven, not agent-driven. The relationships are not constructed upon trust (one of the foundational postulates
of rational-choice theory's approach to the social) because trust is a
mental state exhibited by individuals. Relationships do not trust, agents
do (or do not). Relationality makes the foundational unit of analysis
an interaction, never individual mental states or an agent's investment
choices.

More struggles for the soul of the social: sociology and economics

As social capital fills so many intellectual and political needs, it is no
surprise that, as almost all the literature on the subject complains, there
exists no single definition. Nonetheless, all seem to agree that social
capital is, by virtue of the term capital, something that produces value.
At the same time, because it is social, it is value that is in some way
generatively connected not to standard market value (as in mainstream
neoclassical economic theory), nor to state-expenditure value (as in
Keynesianism), but to something distinctively social. How paradoxical,
then, that it was neither Coleman (1990), the rational-choice sociologist,
nor Becker (1990), the self-designated "imperialist" economist, but Pierre
Bourdieu, the sociologist, who first gave social capital its superstar
status.

The protean shape of social capital: Pierre Bourdieu

In "The Forms of Capital" (1986), Bourdieu discusses the concepts of
cultural and symbolic capital, which he was already well known for

having made the central theoretical elements of his theory of class reproduction, especially in the educational system. In this essay Bourdieu introduces the fungibility of capital: the idea that market value and economic
power, while always produced by capital, are not necessarily produced by
standard monetary or economic capital. It is just as likely to be the cultural
or symbolic capital of prestige and knowledge that generates value. Yet in a
paradoxical response to his own success with cultural and symbolic capital,
Bourdieu expresses concern that too much attention to discourse and
culture is threatening to efface the reality of actual market power. In an
effort to navigate a delicate balance between economism and "culturalism,"
he thus adds social to his other forms of capital. Although he explicitly
distinguishes social capital from economic capital, he develops the idea of
social capital to capture the economic value produced by nonmarket social
connections and relations. The family is his primary exemplar, but the
social connections holding corporations together also demonstrate the
value-laden resources produced by group membership, cooperation, and
coordination: "Social capital is the aggregate of the actual or potential
resources which are linked to possession of a durable network ... The
volume of the social capital possessed by a given agent thus depends on
the size of the network of connections he can effectively mobilize and the
volume of the capital ... possessed by a given agent, or even by the whole
set of agents to whom he is connected" (Bourdieu 1986: 248–9).

This succinct definition reveals much about Bourdieu's ambiguous
place in the social capital genealogy. On the one hand, he did not focus
on or theorize about social capital in any great depth beyond this one
path-breaking essay. Instead, he turned back to a deeper exploration of
symbolic capital, and to a direct assault on the power of economic and
financial capital in constituting the hegemony of neoliberalism (Bourdieu
1998). And although the term does play a significant role in *Distinction*
([1979] 1984), he nonetheless never produced a body of social capital
literature comparable to these other kinds of capital for which he will be
primarily remembered.

Nonetheless, the contribution that Bourdieu made to social capital
theory is unique. Unlike any of the social capital theorists to follow, his
interest in social capital was to synthesize phenomenological and structural analysis. His Marxist roots spurred him to explain the reproduction
of class power, and he found social capital useful for this purpose. At the
same time, his commitment to hermeneutics ensured that interpretative
meaning would be as important as that of class structure. Bourdieu
pioneered this mix of structure and agency as interrelated poles of a
single theoretical approach. The conceptual apparatus he uses is the

term *habitus*, where structure and agency are always in mutual play. In this, Bourdieu differed radically from all the social capital theorists to follow, indeed from the very utilitarianism with which he has often been wrongly associated.

To be fair, however, Bourdieu makes getting right his use of social capital not at all simple. In the above quotation, for example, where he uses some form of the term "possession" three times in a five-line statement, his social capital seems eminently compatible with utilitarianism. The possessor, moreover, is a "given agent," or a "whole set of agents," for whom the "volume" of social capital, and thus its potential value, is determined by the "size" of her or his network of connections. This begins to sound suspiciously like what I dubbed earlier the Rolodex theory of social capital. But this reading derives from wrongly attempting to understand Bourdieu's theory of social capital apart from his master concept of habitus. By integrating the social capital and habitus concepts, he produces a theory less about how social connections can be owned, than about how one is more commonly owned by, that is, possessed by, social capital. He differs from utilitarianism, according to Bourdieu himself, not just because he links actors and structures; but also because he does not theorize agency and strategy through utility-maximization and intentional choice. Bourdieu's agents, rather, are social actors who both act and are acted upon, by their unconscious and their practice-driven habits.

In the end, Bourdieu's social capital is a great distance from the dominant utilitarian and rational-choice approach. And if he has been read by some as too economistic in his use of language, he certainly compensates by his numerous and explicit critiques of the very notion of agential ownership that he sometimes appears to be embracing (Bourdieu 1986). Does this explain why many of today's social capital theorists have mysteriously forgotten their debts to one of sociology's greatest thinkers of the twentieth century? It is hard to know. At a University of Chicago conference James Coleman stated that his social capital theory differed from Bourdieu's insofar as Bourdieu was on the side of the "underdog" – Coleman's way of pointing to Bourdieu's Marxist and structuralist influences. And in fact there are many who believe that Bourdieu's ideas have not been incorporated more broadly into the mainstream of social capital literature because he did not separate his mainly structural analysis of inequality from his own political commitments. I have a different view: the diminishment of Bourdieu's contribution to social capital is the direct result of the rise to prominence of Gary Becker and James Coleman.

Sociology and social capital

For most sociologists, social capital refers simply to the value inherent in the networks and/or norms (values) that shape the quality and quantity of a society's social interactions. With the qualifying terms "networks and norms" always paired, it appears that even in this minimalist definition there is an internal contradiction. A network is a structure of relationships irreducible to but not exclusive of its individual components. Network theory, which has contributed mightily to the growth and appeal of social capital, is fundamentally relational, and much of its own growth is a product of its opposition to methodological individualisms of all stripes. From this perspective, social capital is not just an aggregate of the individuals and institutions that underpin a society; it is the relational glue that holds them together.

The sociological concept of norms, by contrast, is a social psychological approach to social organization. Variably associated with the Parsonian "political culture" paradigm of the 1960s, modernization theory, and the quantitative study of "empirical democracy," the approach focuses on the psychological values and attitudes that citizens hold with respect to a host of measures of political and socioeconomic life (see chapter 5). Using a normative yardstick modeled exclusively on an idealized Anglo-US political culture, only certain measures of political norms added up to a "healthy" society. These included belief in democratic pluralism (not democratic outcomes but procedural neutrality), in modern industrial capitalism and its ancillary technologies of progress (Fordism), in the transcendence of all forms of traditionalism (familialism, clientalism, and nationalism), and in "the end of ideology" and class conflict. In these empirical studies of democracy, it was the summation of these values that bore the burden of explaining whether societies were deemed healthy and modern or potentially totalitarian and authoritarian.

Like social capital theory more generally, this norm-centric approach diverts attention away from economic inequalities, unemployment, race and gender discrimination, and public sphere activities, and toward aggregates of attitudes held by individuals. The incompatibility of the network and norms-based version of social capital is hard to reconcile. The latter presupposes a methodological individualism that is not only at odds with network analysis; it also brings it perilously close to economic theory.

The economists

Although the giants of mainstream academic economics (e.g. Arrow 2000; Akerlof 1984; Solow 2000) have criticized social capital vigorously, there are those who find it eminently compatible with the discipline's foundational precepts. From the perspective of what Glaeser *et al.* (2002) call the "economic approach," the sociological method violates the very logic of capital, namely, its methodological individualism. Accordingly, they develop a "model of optimal individual investment decisions" (Glaeser *et al.* 2002: F438) and explicitly oppose it to "group-based analyses, which emphasize institutions, norms, conventions, social preferences, and aggregate/group outcomes rather than the investment decisions of individual actors" (2002: F438). Their definition of social capital equally rejects anything sociologists would recognize as social, building instead on a modified version of human capital theory with its incentive-driven and agent-centric understanding of market optimality: "Social capital [is] a person's social characteristics – including social skills, charisma, and the size of his Rolodex – which enables him to reap market and nonmarket returns from interactions with others. As such, individual social capital might be seen as the social component of human capital" (2002: F438).[12] The economic approach thus simply expands Becker's (1975, 1976, 1993) original human capital theory to include skills oriented to other people: personal skills, educational achievement, and individual character attributes (e.g. work discipline) are analyzed in the aggregate to determine the success or failure of optimal market outcomes.[13]

Information-theoretic economics

A different definition of social capital derives from the recent disciplinary "revolution" of information-theoretic economics associated primarily with Joseph Stiglitz (1989, 1994, 2000). Social capital, from this perspective, is composed of the nonmarket relationships that individuals bring to bear to cope with the inevitable risks of market imperfections associated with asymmetrical knowledge between contracting agents (Stiglitz 1989). Strictly speaking, the very virtues of the information-theoretic conception of social capital prevent it from being considered an exclusively economic approach. Like Becker's theories of how the economic can be extended to explain social behavior, Stiglitz's incorporation of social variables as endogenous to market behavior violates the "rules" of

---

[12] I have long caricatured social capital theory as a Rolodex approach to social relations and social action, but always in irony, playfulness, and even parody. Imagine my surprise to find that reality – without a trace of irony – now imitates the art of caricature: "We assume that individual social capital includes both intrinsic abilities ... and the results of social capital investments ... e.g., a large Rolodex" (Glaeser *et al.* 2002: F438).
[13] See Bowles and Gintis (2002) for a brilliant critique of the "economic approach."

mainstream neoclassicism, with its strict boundaries between endogenous market preferences and exogenous social context. Both are more properly grouped with the rational-choice/utilitarian approach in which social capital refers to the aggregate of social control behaviors that individuals use to address negative market externalities, especially those associated with public goods (e.g. Coleman 1990). Positive market externalities, by extension, are also a product of social capital, in this case not merely aggregate sanctions but, most importantly, the value generated by strong principles of trust among individuals (Fukuyama 1995a; Gambetta 1987, 1988; Dasgupta and Serageldin 1999; Pharr and Putnam 2000; Åberg and Sandberg 2003).

The Neoutilitarians: economic "imperialism" at play in the site of the social

Despite their common interest in social capital, the information-theoretic economists differ substantially from the real revolutionaries of social capital theory. These latter are a distinct interdisciplinary breed of social scientists-cum-economists, public intellectuals, and policy advocates one could also dub the rational-choice neoutilitarians (the academic school) or in political parlance, neoliberals. James Coleman and Gary Becker, sociologist and economist respectively, have done more than any others to advance rational choice's utilitarian principle of analyzing all of society as a market. At its analytic core neoutilitarianism is built squarely on the foundations of the neoclassical utility-maximizing rational actor. Where it differs from standard economics, however, is in the society-wide scope to which it applies these utilitarian precepts and in transgressing the firm boundaries between the economic and the social set by the neoclassical paradigm (Becker 1976, 1986, 1990, 1993, 1996; Becker and Murphy 2000). For them, the work of social capital is an "imperial" project (Becker 1990: 39).

In a radical challenge to the neoclassical paradigm, rational-choice utilitarians extend the postulate of utility-maximizing human action to the entire social and political universe. In so doing, they violate the exacting rules established by the discipline more than a century ago, which mandate the proper scope of economic analysis to a strictly bounded definition of the economic. In going off the disciplinary reservation, however, the neoutilitarians are going forward to the past; their approach is no less than an explicit embrace of the eighteenth- and nineteenth-century epistemological regime of classical utilitarianism, the most capacious approach to society ever claimed by a single theoretical tradition. Classical political economy was not a single discipline but an entire moral philosophy. Ridiculous to Malthus, Ricardo, or Bentham would have been the idea that they should limit their analyses to what a bunch of academics later claimed to be the legitimate boundaries of the "economy." For the very hallmark of utilitarianism was its claim that the self-regulating laws of nature drive not only the market, but society as a whole. Society was, in effect, a large market (Bell 1981; Malthus [1803] 1992; Polanyi 2001).

It was not until the 1870s that utilitarianism was cut down to size by what we now recognize as neoclassical economics. Only then did the marginalist revolution for the first time establish strictly defined limits to the proper scope of economic analysis. A Rubicon could not be crossed from the "outside" – the noneconomic terrain of the sociological, historical, or anthropological others – to the "inside" – the terrain of the economy proper, where the operative principles of market equilibrium and utility-driven preferences were treated as given: "What most economists would classify as non-economic problems are precisely those problems which are incapable of being analyzed with the marginalist paradigm" (Heilbroner and Milberg 1995: 7).

The marginalist revolution was the symbolic catalyst for years of sociological exile in the wilderness of exogeneity. There sociologists cultivated an exquisite resentment toward economists. Cast out from the only social science turf with actual power and influence, sociologists duly turned their attention to the social detritus, the "nuts and the sluts," the non-utility-maximizers. But a small faction was not ready to walk away without a fight for recognition and inclusion. A subgroup of economic sociologists launched a long-suffering guerrilla war from without, shooting missiles across the bows in the form of intellectually indignant theoretical assaults: what about the social? where do preferences come from? what about embeddedness? and what about the noncontractual basis of contracts? Inquiring sociologists demanded to know. Such assaults were brushed off easily as so many flies by the powerfully situated elephant of modern economics, and insult was only added to injury with Milton Friedman's (1953) influential reinforcement of the outside/inside boundary regime as set forth in his classic article on positivist economics.[14]

But we should all know by now that the favorite game of the gods is to inflict the most perverse of curses – namely, to give us exactly what we

---

[14] The image of elephants "brushing off flies" in reference to the contempt economists have long held toward their sociological challengers was given to me by Robert Solow (personal communication, 1990).

want. Thus, in the last third of the twentieth century a new breed of economist was born in Gary Becker, dedicated to violating the marginalist rules of the game in favor of an entirely new set of rules. These mandated that economists pay a lot of attention to that social world outside the previously insulated sphere of the strictly economic. Becker first converted the once sociological topics of education and skills into economic human capital theory, then quickly enlarged his scope of attention to everything social, from drugs to sex, to welfare, war, and marriage, and so reinvented social capital: "Social capital [is] crucial not only for understanding addictions . . . but also for most other behavior in the modern world, and probably in the distant past as well" (1996: 6). And lest anyone doubt the literalness of Becker's reference to "most other behavior," *Accounting for Tastes* (1996) reveals that fitting appropriately under Becker's rubric of issues to be explained by human and social capital theory is no less than everything – from jogging to government propaganda, with child abuse and deception falling somewhere in between (see also Becker and Nashat 1997; Becker and Murphy 2000).

This is a project Becker proudly calls one of "economic imperialism" (Becker 1990: 39): "From a methodological viewpoint, the aim . . . is to show how [what] is considered important in the sociological and anthropological literature can be usefully analyzed when incorporated into the framework provided by economic theory" (1990: 194). Once colonized by the imperial power, variables once recognizable as sociological (such as power and politics) and thus exogenous to the market, are now reframed to be newly analyzed and made intelligible by treating them as market variables. Becker's arguments for social capital's breathtakingly wide reach are mirrored by the broad spectrum of concerns for which scholars, politicians, public intellectuals, and institutions have found it beneficial, most notably the World Bank's familiar use of the social capital concept to theorize the social conditions for sustainable development (www.worldbank.org/poverty/scapital/whatsc.htm).[15]

Neoutilitarian social capital theory has thus cycled back through time to display the startling hubris of classical utilitarianism's long-rejected imperial project. In addition to physical, natural, financial, and human capital, economists and rational-choice theorists have coupled the social in an intimate embrace with capital. Whereas the prevailing neoclassical orthodoxy has long disdained and dismissed the social, neoutilitarians recognize the far greater advantage in hijacking the sociological paradigm

---

[15] There is a vast literature on social capital and development. See especially Evans (1996), Fine (2001), McMichael (1998), and Woolcock (1998).

and commandeering it into an appendage to the market. For this, social capital is the perfect Trojan horse.

Social capital, sociology, and the Trojan horse

Sociology is besotted with social capital, besotted with the belief that the "discovery" of the concept represents the surrender by economists to the constitutive role of the social. The belief is that after years of exile in the wilderness of exogeneity, extra-market social relations have at last been anointed with the status of a valued source of streaming utility. The long-desired marriage between sociology and economics has at last been consummated. But this marriage has more the whiff of romanticized puppy love than a real union between equals, for there is a glaring imbalance in the distribution of desire and power between the two putative lovers. Whereas neoliberal economists have a purely instrumental and, well, utilitarian relationship to the social, sociologists are breathtakingly, disproportionately, and recklessly infatuated. Social capital has become a totem animating deep-seated desires for academic *inclusion* into the privileged circle of power so long occupied exclusively by economics, the "queen of the social sciences." Surely social capital's success signals nothing less than a great sociological achievement – the triumph of *recognition* (or so the argument goes) by the economists?

But this social capital-philia is more worrisome than simply an embarrassing case of "utility-envy." Nothing better illustrates the wrong headedness of the infatuation than the parable of the Trojan horse, which in this version tells the tale of a specious peace-offering bearing the "gift of recognition of the social." Beguiled by a few economists and rational-choice theorists who appear to traffic in the social, sociologists eagerly interpret social capital as an olive branch from those who have finally surrendered to the need to "sociologize" the market model. The real story, of course, reveals just the opposite: this is a Trojan horse bearing not a sociologizing of the market model, but a *marketizing of the social*. And marketizing the social signals nothing less than a full-scale threat to the irreducibility of relationality at the heart of the social.

Robert Putnam: the promise and the disappointment

I turn now to the work of the political scientist, Clinton advisor, and celebrity of C-SPAN, the *New York Times*, and *People* magazine, Robert Putnam. While Bourdieu, Becker, and Coleman may have been the theoretical pioneers of the revival of the social capital concept, there is no question that Putnam triggered its real takeoff to fame among the broad public of academics and policy intellectuals. It was Putnam who brought social capital into circulation as a solution to what he and others saw as long-standing empirical problems of modernizing development in southern Europe and the developing world, as well as for the "malaise" of civic culture in the United States.

Robert Putnam first impressed the public intelligentsia and political classes with his now famous articles on "Bowling Alone" (1993, 1995, 1996), in which he argued that current ills in the United States were caused by a precipitous decline in the life of civil society, specifically in the sharp drop in the character of associational life, in communal trust and neighborly cooperation, and in civic commitments more generally. But true academic stardom first came to him with his adventures as "Tocqueville in Italy" in *Making Democracy Work* (1993), a comparative historical study of Italian regional governance coauthored with several Italian colleagues over the course of the previous twenty years. In this study Putnam's aim is to compare the causal significance of different variables in making democracy work. His focus is on a series of nationwide institutional reforms aimed at sustained modernizing development, greater governmental transparency, and increased democratic participation (the elimination of corruption, cronyism, and patronage). More than a decade after their implementation, the outcomes were puzzling: real developmental success and genuinely reformed local governance (measured by quantifying civic practices) were in evidence, but exclusively in the northern Italian regions, and not in the southern.

Using macroanalytic comparisons, Putnam tests several explanatory hypotheses. Because the institutional reforms were nationwide and regionally uniform, he effectively rules out any causal role for the Italian state and its local political institutions in explaining the regional variations. More generally, Putnam interprets the defeat of this hypothesis to exclude altogether the influence of political power. That leads to his now famous and controversial finding: the success of the northern regions could be attributed almost exclusively to their singular four-hundred-year histories of deeply embedded horizontal ties and community associations characterized by attitudes of trust and normative reciprocity. As the embodiment of social capital, it was these horizontal ties and norms of trust that served as the lifeblood of prosperous liberal democracies. Thus, social capital became the analytic and theoretical foundation of a new social theory of democracy.[16]

---

[16] Among the universe of "Putnamian" literature on his Italian research, especially important are Levi (1996) and Tarrow (1996).

Crossing the pond to the late twentieth-century United States, Putnam turns to what he defines as a quarter-century of increasing malaise in civil society. Once again he concludes that it is social capital that explains this phenomenon, but in this case it is due to social capital's dramatic decline and virtual disappearance over the past several decades, most famously manifested in the decline of bowling league membership, church choirs, community barbeques, and the decay of other kinds of associational and community involvement. Among other empirical evidence, he finds that the number of Americans who attend public meetings on community or school issues dropped between 1973 and 1993 by more than a third (Putnam 1995: 68). Here Putnam gives a lengthier exposition on the nature and limits to what can justifiably fall under the rubric of social capital. Included are horizontal social ties in local communities driven by cultural values and attitudes of trust and reciprocity among "joiners": bowling leagues, neighborhood barbeques, church choirs, the Girl Scouts. Explicitly excluded, just as in Italy, is any causal role for the decline of such political institutions or programs as federally funded job training, entitlement rights, and community social programs, as well as participation in politics, political parties, and political citizenship institutions more generally, and, most alarming, the decline of the power and membership strength of trade unions. Neither the exercise of power, nor even basic struggles over the institutions of rights and civil liberties, have any causal significance in Putnam's findings. But he goes even further. Not only are politics, power, and the condition of the public sphere missing in his explanation for the decline of civil society; so too is any attention to the dramatic restructurings of the economy and the market over the same period of time (e.g. the privatization of public goods and services, the radical restructuring of firms and corporate downsizing, newly restrictive labor market rules and regulations, the systematic weakening of trade union institutional power). "Bowling Alone" (1995, 2000), the canonical text for the theory and empirical application of social capital, summarily dismisses sociology's usual suspects, most prominently the collapse of the welfare state and its social safety nets, the neoliberal restructuring and privatization of the economy, and a newly regressive tax system that has been systematically shifting the tax burden from wealth to work. The weakened condition of citizenship rights and political participation, a degraded public sphere, and the dictates of market forces have all been taken off the agenda. Instead, we are implored to go bowling.

There are other concerns about Putnam's thesis. As others have noted, not all relational entities are positive and healthy phenomena. What Portes and others call the "dark side of social capital" has all too often been exhibited in fascist youth associations and Nazi brown shirts, in today's skinheads, urban gangs, and populist and racist evangelical churches, among others (Portes 1998). Before any sanguine theories of social capital continue on their present tack, empirical work is necessary to determine the conditions lending themselves to this dark side of social capital. Not to do so is tantamount to eliminating half of the human record of history and society.[17]

There can be absolutely no doubt that Robert Putnam is a committed civic democrat in search of the foundations of social justice, for whom building a democratic egalitarian civic culture is a consuming passion. He is explicitly not an apologist for the neoliberal or market fundamentalist project. In this commitment, however, I believe his use of the social capital concept is misapplied and wrongheaded. He excludes the entire spectrum of the very institutions of governance, rights, and power without which civil society could not be sustained against the corrosive effects of unregulated market forces. These absences, moreover, are not presented as empirical findings of this or that case (e.g. Italy), but as the very essence of the theoretical work that he wants social capital to perform. Putnam never comes to grips with the fact that the theory of social capital extends market principles to those noncontractual arenas of social life where utilitarian ethics will do nothing less than corrode the very social ties and civic practices he so celebrates. To achieve the practices and institutions of trust, communication, and reciprocity that Putnam tries to represent in the social capital concept requires abandoning its constitutive postulates of localism, acquisition, individualism, the market model of efficiency, the marketization of the social, and the radical autonomy from power and politics. Success with these revisions, however, would leave us not with an improved version of social capital; instead, it would return us to the primacy and the irreducibility of the social where, ideally, we should have started in the first place. And this would take us back to the conceptual site and the normative ideals of civil society.

The end of history? Civil society and social capital

The story of civil society begins in the decades leading up to the fall of the Berlin Wall in 1989. For the democratic left, the fall of the Wall was the accomplishment of a new civil society movement, which served as a

---

[17] There is a curious definitional narrowing in Putnam's use of social capital. In the transition from Becker's promiscuous vision in which social capital applies to virtually everything, to Putnam's more contained application to civil society, social capital theory loses its ability to cure all the personal behaviors that so preoccupy Becker.

launching ground for self-organized bodies of political activists committed to democratic participation and autonomy from state coercion (Arato 1981, 1993, 2000; Cohen 1985, 1999; Cohen and Arato 1992; Habermas 1990; Isaac 1996; Keane 1994; Kennedy 1991, 1994, 2002). For neoliberals and conservatives, however, it signaled what Fukuyama (1992) famously labeled "the end of history" in his best-selling book of the same title. *The End of History* was a story and a prediction about the outcome to the decades-long duel to the death between capitalism and communism that had dominated the globe for the previous half-century. In Fukuyama's story the fall of the Wall represented the triumph of free-market capitalism, a victory over and against the totalitarianism loathed by neoliberals, conservatives, and progressive democrats alike. In retrospect, while there was unambiguous mobilization for civil and political rights, it is not at all clear what alternative economic system the European anticommunist movements envisioned. For Fukuyama and his end of history protégés, however, there was absolute clarity. Theirs was a conceptual and political landscape limited to a single manichaean dichotomy: the free versus the unfree, good versus evil, the market versus the state. The fall of one meant the absolute triumph of the other. This was the meaning of the end of history: With the end of communism there was only one possible future for the ex-communist world. Never again would history allow industrial nations to shift their centers of gravity from market to state, from freedom to tyranny, from notions of "personal responsibility" to those of social insurance History had in effect stopped with the end of Eastern European and Soviet communism. Any advocacy for political rules and regulations of markets would now be outside the realm of thinkable rational discourse. The end of history created a new political culture now ruled by Soros's (1998, 2000) market fundamentalism and Stiglitz's (1994, 1998, 2002) "Washington consensus," more commonly known as neoliberalism and/ or neoconservatism.

The pronouncement that history had ended, however, was more normative and ideological than empirically sound. For while history had in fact witnessed the defeat of state tyranny with the end of communism, Fukuyama's concurrent prediction of the future had no empirical model to build on. Never in history had any societies undergone the transition from communism to capitalism. There were no how-to models of democratization for societies that had had minimal, if any, institutional frameworks for administering the rule of law and mechanisms of democracy before becoming communist. The absence of such models thus made the end of history's view of the future a triumph of pure theory – an abstract model-driven commitment to remake the world in the image of the market, yet one not based on any existing successful transformation from a communist to a fully functioning market economy. To make matters worse, the "designer-capitalists" of the 1990s were so driven by antistatist ideology that they stubbornly refused even to draw lessons from what was the closest analogue to the contemporary situation, namely, the Marshall Plan's stunning success at nation building in Germany and Japan in the immediate aftermath of World War II (Glasman 1998). Instead, it was financiers and bankers at the IMF and the World Bank who made the global decisions about how market-driven "shock therapy" would be applied throughout Eastern Europe and Russia, and indeed in much of the developing world.

As Karl Polanyi ([1944] 2001) so brilliantly demonstrated over half a century ago, however, there is only one problem with the marketization of everything: it is impossible to achieve without threatening to destroy the fabric of society (Block and Somers 1984). Nurturing regulated markets as part of a healthy social order is something very different from the dream of *governance* by the self-regulating market mechanism, or what Polanyi called the "stark utopia" of a "market society." The rest of the story is thus as familiar as it would have been predictable to any student of economic sociology and history. Absent the complex, sometimes invisible rules in which successful markets are necessarily embedded, the neoliberal model of governance by self-regulating markets revealed its inherent weaknesses. It was not long before shock therapy gave way to social, political, and economic chaos. Profound international difficulties began in Thailand in July 1997, spread to Malaysia, Indonesia, and South Korea, and in 1998 to Russia and Brazil. As safety-net institutions that were once taken for granted began to disappear, the new ex-communist capitalist nations succumbed to currency crises and skyrocketing poverty. Without any constitutional institutional foundations, it was not democracy but the Mafia that took power in Russia. Soon there was a resurgence of pro-communist sentiment in parts of the ex-communist world (Holmes 1997; Kennedy 2002; Maier 1997; Soros 1998, 2000).

In the United States and the United Kingdom, neoliberals used the end of history thesis to facilitate dismantling the welfare state and to further degrade the public sphere. The corporate need for greater market flexibility in the interests of economic growth turns out to have been a code for the dissolution of the New Deal and Great Society regimes. With shock therapy capitalism, crises of public goods and much more inevitably ensued. Market failures and externalities, excess volatility and transaction costs proved to be the norm and not the exception for today's global economies (Stiglitz 1998, 2002). Clearly, the utopian dream that the self-regulating market could be the governing mechanism of the future had yet to become the end of history.

At this point, a crossroads had to be faced: how to solve these problems of externalities and diminishing public goods while continuing to privatize? Perhaps shock therapy was not working in quite the way the end of history had predicted. But in a zero-sum world of state versus market, there are no gray zones; any hint of return to the Keynesianism that had for so long saved capitalism from its own excesses would have betrayed marketizing ideals. Of course, there were, and are, plenty of societies – most of Western Europe, for example – that never succumbed to the either/or of market versus state but flourished successfully as social democracies. For the market fundamentalist project, however, even the most modest of welfare states meant no less than socialism and unfreedom – even under the moniker of a mixed economy. In this context, how to address the market's problems without turning back to the state became an urgent question.

Initially, the solution was to cling even more fervently to market models on the grounds that meddling politicians had prevented them from having had the opportunity to be fully implemented. So stubbornly did neoliberals cling to absolute belief in their model that even in those countries with successful economies the IMF started to withhold loans until there was a commitment to economic restructuring (e.g. McMichael 1998; Miller 1997). This in turn led to a rejection of any evidence that threatened to contradict the model. The practice was to save the model at all costs while blaming "reality" for the failings of the new world of marketization. This is precisely what happened when the giant hedge fund Long-Term Capital Management (LTCM) collapsed in 1998 under the weightlessness of its mathematically modeled reality. In a stunning inversion of the mantra of modern epistemology – theory proposes, data disposes – Martin Gruber, Nomura Professor of Finance at NYU's Stern School, remarked about LTCM: "A series of events occurred that were outside the norm. ... These catastrophes happen. The fault isn't with the models" (Morgenson and Neinstein 1998: 1). When challenged by the limits of its propositions, in other words, it is not the market model but *reality* that takes the blows for the failure of the world to conform to "the [model's] norms."

But for how long was reality going to lie down and take the blame for the failures of a "virtual" model of governance. In a repetition of much of the past two centuries, the either/or of market versus state was proving inadequate to the task of achieving its own goals. Then a *deus ex machina* appeared in the new vocabulary of social capital. Not only was it a concept that relied on methodological individualism, it was also one built on a foundational antistatism. But I get ahead of myself. To explain how these antistatists found their way to social capital we have to return to the struggle against communism and the rediscovery of civil society.

Enter civil society

Civil society is that sphere of social organization made famous by its political revival in Eastern Europe and South America's antiauthoritarian insurgencies of the 1980s (Arato 1981; Barber 1996; Calhoun 1993; Cohen 1999; Cohen and Rogers 1995; Ehrenberg 1999; Foley and Edwards 1996; Geremek 1992). Civil society, however, is an "essentially contested concept" (W. B. Gallie 1956, cited in Hollis and Lukes 1982). As I argue in chapter 7, the Tocquevillean-inspired view of civil society as a third sphere between market and state has always been rivaled by that of classical liberalism's. While both approaches pose civil society in sharp opposition to the state, for liberalism the manichaean dichotomy of public versus private overdetermines any gesture toward a genuine third sphere. In a bivalent conceptual landscape of only private and public, market and state, civil society can only be on the private side of the Rubicon that divides market from state.[18]

Following Locke, who first invented the idea of civil society in the seventeenth century as a self-sufficient social entity and countervailing source of political authority, late twentieth-century market fundamentalists unambiguously identify civil society as the cultural and social dimension of the market. Many conservatives were attracted especially to this cultural view of civil society as an antidote to what they characterized as the moral degeneration caused by years of dependence on the handouts of the public welfare state and the excesses of a rights-laden political culture (Huntington 1975; M. Crozier *et al.* 1975; Pharr and Putnam 2000). It is a vision of civil society that makes it at once a facilitator of the market and a cultural bulwark against the "nanny state" (and of the perverse dependences it encourages). As such, conservatives hoped that civil society would be a critical mechanism in the effort to shift responsibility for social problems away from the state *and* the market, and onto the shoulders of civil society's "little platoons" of family, church, and

---

[18] Hegel, of course, reversed Locke and reinstated a triadic conception of social organization. But, paradoxically, this did not create civil society as the sphere of citizenship but as the site of the market *tout court*. For the most important contemporary treatise on civil society in general and Hegel's understanding of it in particular, see Cohen and Arato (1992).

community (Berger and Neuhaus 1996; Fukuyama 1992, 1995a, 1995b). It thus became important as both an empirical and a normative site of private personal responsibility and moral autonomy.[19]

At first, civil society served these needs well. But shortly it became clear that the concept, like all essentially contested concepts, could not be owned by any single interpretation. For one thing, there was the testy little problem of origins. The Polish Solidarity movement that had contributed so much to the rebirth of the civil society idea was, after all, not one of Edmund Burke's traditional little platoons; it was, of all things, a *trade union* – one of neoliberalism's great anathemas. And even if some of Solidarity's leaders became avid free marketers and antistatist politicians, conservatives could not sit comfortably with civil society's trade union roots.

At the same time, with the success of the Eastern European revolutions against communism, civil society had increasingly become a rallying cry for the new social movements of the Western democratic and communitarian left. These civil society social movements, while they invoked their independence from the state, were no allies of neoliberalism (Dean 2004). History gave good reasons to renounce statism, but creating a market-governed society was not the default alternative. For the political democratic left, civil society was not captive to the limits of a public/private dichotomy but instead challenged the hegemony of *both* the coercion of administrative states *and* the predatory drives of the global marketplace (e.g. Arato 2000; Cohen and Arato 1992; Keane 1994; Kennedy 1991; Somers 2001). Gdansk, Solidarity, and the rediscovery of civil society thus became clarion calls not merely for freedom from state coercion but also for the *nonmarket* values of solidarity, reciprocity, horizontal ties, participatory civic values, and social justice, hardly the banner under which market fundamentalists or cultural conservatives could readily march. And for neoconservatism, there was yet another problem with the civil society moniker. In its sociological link to the political project of the democratic left, it was also implicated in the normative ideals of democratic participation, popular political empowerment, and the empowerment of rights-oriented social movements, all of which presupposed a deep engagement with the political public sphere (Rosenberg and Post 2002). Despite their full convergence with the norms of liberal democratic societies, these principles and projects evoked almost everything the neoconservatives had come to abhor, namely a rejection of not only the state but also market-centric foundations of social organization in favor of the

---

[19] For discussions of the relevant neoconservative literature, see also Demuth and Kristol (1995); Gershon (1996a, 1996b); Nicholson (1989); Kristol (1995).

primacy of democratic associations of rights-claiming citizens (Arato 1981, 2000; Cohen and Arato 1992).

From civil society to social capital

In 1993 social capital became something little remarked on in social theory: an epistemological public good.[20] Like all public goods, its resources became part of the "commons" – available to all, exploitable by many. When social capital entered the public sphere and became available as a public good, its epistemological powers were put into circulation. Those who perceived and appropriated this knowledge found themselves in possession of a remarkable kind of social, political, and economic power. Most public goods are characterized by their limited resources. But unlike these usual ones, epistemological public goods have unique powers by virtue of their abstract virtuality. They are infinitely elastic, and there are no limits to their capacity to provide goods. As an epistemological public good, social capital would prove to be the gift that keeps on giving.

It is hard to know what direction the juncture of neoconservativism and civil society would have taken if social capital had not suddenly become a public good. But it did, in large part thanks to the collision of neoconservative, neoliberal, and intellectual social capital streams. Timing was everything. Just as these multiple social capital trajectories collided, Robert Putnam's success catapulted the concept of social capital into the political public sphere. Across the ideological spectrum intellectuals moved quickly. Conservatives who saw in it all of the appeal and none of the deficits of the civil society concept, appropriated it, then tamed it, reframed it, and renamed it. In a truly Pygmalion-like achievement, civil society – the once unruly and unpredictable nurturing ground for the goals, practices, and normative ideals of democratic citizenship – reappeared in the 1990s in public and academic discourse as social capital. As a public good the capacity of social capital to solve political problems was perceived to be vast, and neoliberals and neoconservatives alike were able to fully exploit its epistemological powers. Above all, it provided an antistatist political language to explain, justify, and obfuscate the political project of shifting the burdens of social risk and market externalities from market and state, to the personal responsibility of individual families and communities. From

---

[20] My insistence on social capital as an epistemological public good distinguishes it from Coleman, for whom it is the functional effects of social capital's actual social relations (of family, community, etc.) that makes it what he calls a collective good (Coleman [1988] 2000: 317).

the social rights of the New Deal and the Great Society, to the commodified free agents of the 1980s and 1990s, the work of saving capitalism from its own excesses was about to shift once again – this time to the newly discovered gold mine of social capital.

The contributions of social capital to the political project of marketizing the social can be parsed into four dimensions:

1. Social capital provides a nonstate solution to those externalities the market is either unable or unwilling to solve. Call this the function of saving capitalism from its own excesses.
2. Social capital shifts the expectations of citizenship from rights claims to obligations and duties.
3. Social capital provides a nonstate alternative to what conservatives define as the entitlement-driven welfare state and the excesses of democratic rights claims. Call this the reconstitution of citizenship through the cultural sphere of moral regulation, self-help, and personal responsibility.
4. Finally, social capital provides a spatial substitute to civil society in the concept of "community" – the nonstate site in which the relationships of social capital are confined.

The site of community

Let us start with the last of the four and work backwards through the list. The great value of the term "civil society" is that it refers to a real *place* in the topography of social life. Social capital, by contrast, does not signify any particular domain; it is inherently placeless. To overcome this deficiency, conservatives coupled social capital with *community*, a concept with a long and noble place in the sociological landscape.[21]

The well-known phrase "It takes a village to raise a child" expresses nicely the relationship between social capital and community. This idealized approach to childcare is not free-floating and mobile but contained in a *particular* and *local* community. It thus carries the whiff of traditional values and of parenting practices dependent exclusively on family, kinship, and (face-to-face) community relationships. Traditional communities are seen to encourage respect for hard work, self-sufficiency, the values of the market, and disdain for dependence on the state. Yet the emphasis on the local village as the appropriate site of conscientious parenting is just as

---

[21] "Concerns about social capital thus represent a return to classical sociological preoccupations with community as the foundation of social solidarity and social cohesion" (Gamarnikow and Green 1999: 111). See also Bowles (1999) and Rose (1999, 2000).

strongly a negative injunction *against* expecting child support from the government. In lieu of looking to the state to deal with inadequately funded public schools, for example, "[i]t takes a village to raise a child" implicitly blames parents and the community – for their lack of personal responsibility in participating in the PTA, for their inadequate attention to the child's homework, perhaps even for not taking on the responsibility of home schooling – in short, for their insufficient exercise of social capital. The aphorism could easily be social capital's own clarion call as it at once celebrates the (private) family and community's burden of accountability for child-rearing even while, *sotto voce*, it intones "as opposed to the state and the public."

The first asset for social capital that the site of community provides is thus a negative one: it is the site that is *not* the state. The valorization of community by virtue of its absent statism and presence of personal responsibility cannot be overstated in the neoconservative project of redistributing the risks of market society from the market and state, to families and communities. In the words of one of its most influential craftsmen, Francis Fukuyama: "If society is not to become anarchic or otherwise ungovernable, then it must be capable of *self-government at levels of organization below the State*. Such a system depends ultimately not just on law but also on the *self-restraint of individuals*" (1995a: 357–8 emphasis added).

Fukuyama is one of the best-known US conservatives. But here is the British Labour Party's Home Secretary, Jack Straw, in his keynote speech to the 1998 Nexus Conference on "Mapping Out the Third Way": "*Community and personal responsibility* which have so long been buried in the futile arguments between Left and Right, are at the centre of everything we do ... [Therefore] we are literally handing over a *huge amount of power* to individual citizens and local communities *away from the central State*" (1998: 18; cited in Rose 2000, emphasis added). Note his almost evangelical celebration of community for being *not* the state. Community as the site of social capital is morally obligated to compensate for the loss of public services and social rights by providing shelter for the unemployed, the unemployable, and the socially excluded. When the Labour Party takes up the banner of social capital as the alternative to the state, it is clear that this shift of risk and responsibility from the public to the people does not require a wholesale commitment to market fundamentalism, but simply a rejection of the role of the public sphere in supporting social life. The *deus ex machina* of social capital, clearly, is an equal opportunity solution for all those committed to the superiority of market technologies in morally restoring society.

From the culture of entitlement to the ethos of self-help
and personal responsibility

Once social capital becomes identified with the traditionalist conceptual
terrain of community, the question of social action arises. This is the
third dimension in the work of social capital. For conservatives, the great
deficiency of civil society was its politically oriented content; the practices
of civil society could not easily be dissociated from a radical democratic
ethos, a strong emphasis on participatory citizenship rights, and activist
commitments to influence political and state policy (Habermas 1990;
Laarman 1995; Merkl and Weinberg 1993). As we know, the generative
value of social capital is not only that it rejects the state as the source of
support, rights, and entitlements; it also rejects the state as the locus of
social action. The community is responsible for its own moral and
economic viability. Social capital requires that people in their churches,
their communities, their city councils, their voluntary associations, their
Rotary clubs, their women's societies, and their bowling leagues assume
local civic duties and personal responsibilities. Its values are those of
self-help, moral autonomy, personal responsibility, and collective self-
restraint. These evoke Burke's conservative dream of "little platoons" as
the foundation of social order, as well as Durkheim's revelation that
society survives through moral constraint and normative regulation.
Thus, in contrast to the "dutiless rights" of "excessive" citizenship, social
capital works through networks of moral control, moral behavioral
norms for conduct and interaction, ethical imperatives of self-help and
personal responsibility. Here is Amitai Etzioni, the founder of communitarianism and a passionate advocate for social justice: "For a society to
be communitarian, much of the social conduct must be 'regulated' by
reliance on the moral voice rather than the law, and the scope of the law
itself must be limited largely to that which is supported by the moral
voice" (1997: 139).

From rights to duties: reinventing citizenship

The second dimension in the work of social capital may represent the
greatest distinction between civil society and social capital. The duties
associated with community activity are not complemented by an equally
robust set of rights. Recall the conservative outcry against the putative
excess of rights and unrestrained freedoms (i.e. in the 1960s) without the
corresponding sense of duties, merit, and personal responsibility, which
served as a major catalyst in the search for a site of social life untouched

by the state's entitlements (Berger and Neuhaus 1996). Here, echoing that sentiment, is the "Third Way" British Labour Party's Jack Straw again:

The old Left . . . failed to argue against . . . an extension of individual freedom [as] a license to do almost anything, and that the State existed as some sort of universal great provider, which made no moral judgments regardless of the merits of those who were dependent upon it . . . it has made rights appear like ready-made consumer items which the state can dispense at will and often for which the "consumer" never need pay. As the philosopher David Selbourne has written: "In its thrall, the citizen comes to be perceived and treated by the civic order (and its instruments, the state and government) not as a citizen but as a consumer, customer, and bundle of wants; and the citizen, perceiving himself in like fashion, loses sense of his duties, as a citizen, to himself, his fellows, and the civic order, at worst without sense of honour or shame" [Selbourne 1994: 70] . . . This led on to a culture of dutiless rights – where rights are exercised without due recognition being given to our mutual responsibilities towards each other. (1998: 6; cited in Rose 1999)

Third Way enthusiasm for social capital and the traditional community is driven mightily by a shift from rights to duties, from public service to private responsibility, from noncontractualism to a system of market-driven incentives. In depleting civil society of rights and loading it up with duties, the work of social capital in local communities becomes a peculiarly inverted antistatist version of *Leviathan*. Like the absolute political control exercised by the Hobbesian state, the source of social order and community sustenance shifts from the state to social capital and the community. But, just as in *Leviathan*, the Faustian bargain requires that in return for the secure moral values of honor and shame inherent in community regulation, individual rights must be abandoned at the entry. Social capital insulates the community from what the Trilateral Commission of the 1970s (Crozier *et al.* 1975) famously labeled the excesses of democracy.

It is one thing, however, to be seduced by the safety of community to give up some excessive expectations of the polity. It is something else altogether to define this shift from rights to duties, from the public sphere to the privatized community, as "the essential act of citizenship." Yet, this is exactly what Jack Straw says: "In many ways the most important example of our approach is our commitment greatly to extend the idea and practice of volunteering – of people doing something for each other rather than having the State doing it for them and so diminishing them. We have described this voluntary activity as *'the essential act of citizenship'*" (1998: 16: cited in Rose 2000: 1404; emphasis added).

Even for the moderate Third Wayers, then, social capital detaches the essential act of citizenship from the institutions of state and political community. Instead, in this reconstituted site of community, the essential acts of citizenship are those in which it is a duty to *donate* one's labor to the stock of social capital because it is social capital that in turn provides value to the nation's markets. This is the stuff of citizenship qua social capital – a radically antipolitical, anti-institutional, presocial, stateless and *rightless* kind of citizenship. Dutiful citizenship demands that we freely contribute our own labor to the project of transforming the previously noncontractual practices of citizenship into market-saving practices. Social capital's redesigned citizenship is driven by the duties of individuals to the market, not by the rights and obligations of public membership and the common good; by conditional desert based on merit, rather than by human rights and the equality of status; by moral restraints and self-sacrifice, rather than the irresponsible license of equitable redistribution (Berger and Neuhaus 1996; Fukuyama 1995a, 1995b; Selbourne 1994; Saegert and Thompson 2001).

If, after foregoing the state in favor of market solutions, markets now fail to solve the problems of poverty, the environment, persistent unemployment, and the risks of private insurance, instead of turning to the state, we are to seek succor in family, friends, relationships, and faith-based organizations. In place of welfare, let family and kin "wealth transfers" do the job; economists qua social capital advocates insist they are "more efficient" anyway (Durlauf 2002). This was the driving force behind the successful bipartisan American legislation that abolished Aid to Families with Dependent Children on the grounds that the welfare state created perverse incentives to moral compromise, irresponsible sexual behavior, and a disdain for the work ethic (Somers and Block 2005). As the alternative to the social state, social capital displaces the "culture of dependency" and the moral hazards associated with welfare. In place of federally funded policing, let neighborhood police paid by local taxes do the job. Better yet, let the neighborhood use its own rich reservoir of information capital (neighbors) as the eyes and ears of social control. In place of environmental regulations, let the community's voluntary civic associations exercise their own normative sanctions against free-riding corporate neighbors. And in place of public school funding, let the PTAs and home schoolers provide the moral and educational guidance so desperately needed by the children (Bowles and Gintis 2002; Orr 1999; Lin 2001; Saegert and Thompson 2001; Munch 2002).

Liberated from the "diminishment" of excessive rights and readmitted into the constraints and expectations of community, people are now made accountable through the moral approbation and sanctions – the naming, blaming, and shaming – that only friends, neighbors, and traditional communities can inflict to effectively govern behavior.

Saving the market from its externalities and excesses

Self-sacrifice, volunteerism, social control, reciprocal information sharing, the camaraderie of bowling leagues – this is the stuff of social capital (Åberg and Sandberg 2003; Putnam 2000, 2002; Putnam *et al.* 1993; Coleman [1988] 2000): it is a bundle of voluntary, self-help practices and values that promise to create a fountain of previously untapped economic value. But it is a peculiar kind of economic value. Recall that the turn to social capital on the part of the neoutilitarians was not motivated by assumptions of perfect market equilibrium. Rather, it was their recognition of the market's inevitable limits, externalities, and imperfections that drove them to transgress into social fields beyond the bounds of market analysis. The first item on my list of the work of social capital is therefore that of a collective citizen contributing economic value by performing the duties of modern citizenship – mopping up the nasty messes generated by neoliberalism's own privatizing reforms. Call this the function of saving capitalism from its own excesses. By absorbing the market's costs, social capital paradoxically adds value to the market's stream of utility functions. This is what makes it social *capital*.

In its job of saving the market from its own excesses and limits, it is social capital (that is us, by the way) that is now responsible for coping with unemployment, underemployment, loss of benefits, and low-wage jobs – and all without asking the market to pay. Citizenship morphs into a form of capital that adds value to the wealth of the nation while preserving property rights and competitive markets. By protecting markets from government interference, social capital turns citizenship into a prostitute for capitalism. It does not, however, put food on the table.

In the political epistemology of social capital, true citizens must take personal responsibility for their own welfare, treating relationships as investments and exploiting their friends, neighbors, relatives, fellow church-goers, and bowling teams. In the paradoxical new message of privatized citizenship, the social has been evacuated by an aggregate of purely instrumental connections "owned" by each individual, and funneled into the market. In this Orwellian world, exercising citizenship requires activating one's own personal stock of social capital by exploiting utility from friends. Here is Jack Straw again: "It [community] asserts our mutual responsibility, our belief in a common purpose. And it also asserts that there is no such 'thing' as society; not in the way in which

Mrs. Thatcher claimed, but because society is not a 'thing' external to our experiences and responsibilities. It is us, all of us" (1998: 17, cited in Rose 2000: 1395). Let "us," then, eat social capital.

Alternative knowledge: Solidarity and civil society

Whether in the hands of social scientists or self-styled imperialist econ-omists, the concept of social capital is grounded on the imperatives of duty, responsibility, coerced cooperation, moral and religious values, voluntary labor, and absolute trust in the market – but is devoid of rights. Hence one of the most consistent absences from the social capital liter-ature is trade unions. Yet (in their ideal-typical form), one could hardly think of a better normative and empirical exemplar for the kind of associational networks that the social capital concept claims to invoke. To garner the benefits of, say, a successful labor contract, a working person submits to the rules of membership regardless of whether these rules appeal or are convenient. The rules demand accountability; from which follow the obligations not of access and ownership but of belong-ing and membership. And from these foundational membership practices flows the capacity to bargain for and act on their hard-won rights to collective power and influence. These in turn require involvement of the state: not its degradation and privatization but its legal backing to the bargaining contract. Apparently, the social capital advocates managed to overlook the irreducibly public and rule-driven infrastructures at the heart of effective trade unions.

Poland's Solidarity, the union of Gdansk ship workers that first came to the world's notice in the early 1980s, exemplifies the empowerment generated by membership's rule-driven practices. Solidarity membership was based on sanctions and obligations, risks, and sacrifices. Yet the union both catalyzed and provided leadership in the struggle against communism. Such extraordinary power was only possible because the workers displayed commitment to act first and foremost as members of a collective entity. Solidarity's demonstration of how to win democratic rights is an example of the kind of agency characteristic of a membership-driven relational network. The union's membership practices were built on repositories of knowledge, skills, and rules that resided in the capacity of the social network to exercise associational power over the preferences and choices, even the "human capital," of individual agents. To be sure, individuals have choices within this relational entity, but they are framed within the rights and the obligations to participate in the union's rule-driven attachments. These are the choices of "voice" in an entity over which no one has ownership rights, and they are the rights of "exit" – knowing that to exit is to lose the inclusionary powers of membership.[22] These make relational networks and the attachments they embody not forms of capital but mechanisms of social belonging, mechanisms necessary to sustain the robust associational bodies that are required for social movements to be effective in their struggles for democratic freedoms: the kind of relationships, in other words, that enabled Solidarity to bring down a tyrannical state, the kinds of relationships characteristic *not* of social capital but of civil society.

More generally, the history of market societies suggests that meaningful citizenship practices and durable relationships that are robust, relationally sturdy, reciprocally empowered, and characterized by high degrees of trust depend on deep links to public spheres, the national state, and the rule of law. Democratic practices and social cooperation both require a legal apparatus embedded enough into the fabric of everyday life that the law is constitutive to the infrastructure of membership rules, practices, expectations, and sanctioned obligations. This in turn provides the foundations for a relational body peopled by rights-bearers, not social capitalists. The numerous voluntary associations that Skocpol (2003) and others have shown to be thickly distributed throughout much of US history as well as the modern university faculty are examples of relational bodies driven by membership practices (see also Collins 1979). The paradox is that although these are the very conditions that are essential to the survival of the kinds of social relationships that the idea of social capital claims to represent, they are precisely those that its advocates systematically exclude. The relational networks that the social capital concept wants to evoke cannot be isolated from their social and political environments, from the rules of law and state institutions that enforce the very strength and durability of those networks. Even the World Bank now recognizes "that the capacity of various social groups to act in their interest depends crucially on the support (or lack thereof) that they receive from the state as well as the private sector. Similarly, the state depends on social stability and widespread popular support. In short, economic and social development thrives when representatives of the state, the corporate sector, and civil society create forums in and through which they can identify and pursue common goals" (World Bank 2004).

Political and legal institutions are the mechanisms that actually allow democratic claims to be practiced by rights-bearing people. Without

[22] On exit and voice, see Hirschman (1970).

these institutional expressions of legal embeddedness, middle- and working-class communities would quickly dissolve into competition, unemployment, and despair – precisely the social conditions that, in the context of modern market dynamics, would lead to the dissolution of strong social relations and social supports. In theory, it would destroy "social capital." In reality, it *is* eroding civil society.

A militant antipositivism in positivist guise

Notwithstanding Becker's (1990: 30) and others' goal of colonizing the rest of the social sciences with economic imperialism, coupling the social with capital is often well intentioned; Robert Putnam, for example, can hardly be written off as either a neoconservative or a market fundamentalist. Because social capital ascribes value to nonmarket relationships, many see it as a way to civilize and humanize the otherwise brittle meanness of market forces. But even the most prestigious economists express serious qualms. Kenneth Arrow (2000) argues that the term social capital should be abandoned as the social relations to which it refers are not actually a type of capital. Instead, he suggests we focus on studying alternative forms of social interactions. Robert Solow (1990, 2000) concurs, suggesting that the theory suffers from confusion about what constitutes capital, thus canceling out the well-meaning intentions to valorize social relations (see also Akerlof 1984). It is time for the rest of us to follow suit.

One way to do so is to conclude by pointing to the politics of knowledge exhibited by the social capital stories – stories that demonstrate just how intimate is that link between what Foucault (1977b, 1995) calls the power/knowledge connection. It is a link that in the case of social capital demands more than merely assertion; it also demands demonstration. After all, at the end of the day social capital is just an *idea*, and it is fair to ask whether an idea can actually bear the influence I have ascribed to it throughout this chapter. My answer is twofold. First, to paraphrase the great Reinhard Bendix (1976), there are some ideas originally invented to conceptualize the empirical world that have such ideational powers that they end up becoming part of that world. Social capital is one such idea that has become more than an idea; it is now an essential empirical component to that world and, as such, should be subject to all the usual tools of empirical investigation. Second, as hard as it is for sociologists to come to grips with the independent causal powers of ideas, social capital is an exemplary case of ideational power. My argument is that social capital is not a term that emerged to reflect changes *actually* taking place in the social world. Rather, it is the idea of social capital that has pushed, prodded, and reconfigured our knowledge and understanding of that world, especially that of the appropriate distribution of power among the spheres of market, state, and civil society. As an ideational causal mechanism social capital has played (and continues to play) a mighty part in delegitimating and dismantling the once prevailing institutionalist/ Keynesian regime and converting it to the now dominant belief in market solutions. Social capital – not simply the words, of course, but the wider project of shifting the risks of market society from wealth to labor, from the public sector to individuals and families – has exercised its epistemic powers to successfully embed our contemporary market culture well within the larger ideational regime of marketization.[23]

This points us to "positivism and its epistemological others" (Steinmetz 2005b) in the construction of knowledge, where knowledge and power are so deeply entwined (Foucault 1977a). The social capital phenomenon entails three kinds of knowledge postulates, each of which has worked to reinforce its ideational role in shifting the study of the social from sociology to economics, and in shifting economic responsibility from the social state onto the shoulders of individuals and their communities. The first knowledge postulate is ontological. The social sciences were born in a stream of history driven forward by two centuries of struggle for the triumph of political liberalism – a struggle for natural individual rights not only against the perceived chronic threat of coercion from the state, but also from the perceived tyranny of feudal social relationships. Political liberalism, however, came attached to its inseparable twin of economic liberalism, which teaches that it is the natural freedoms of prepolitical market society and property exchange that provides for political freedom. As part of the liberal imagination, the social sciences came to life with an intractable ontological conflict: would society be a social entity, a site independent not only of the state but also of the market? Or would it be reduced to the antistatist site of natural liberties and the privatized freedoms of market exchange? Today's triumph of social capital over civil society and the state suggests that the conflict is currently being resolved in the direction of freedom as privatization, as pairing social with capital destroys the very social it aims to valorize. It is a theory of social values built on market theory and utilitarianism.

The second knowledge postulate is social naturalism. That which is natural is that which has its own laws and regularities. Social naturalism

---

[23] This concept of ideational embeddedness is developed at length in Somers and Block (2005).

extends the axiomatic laws of nature to society. The naturalist roots of utilitarianism's view of society as a prepolitical and presocial site endow it with lawlike regularities modeled on the self-regulating natural laws of the market. This in turn gives it the patina of a positivist science, one that lends itself to testable hypotheses. But ascribing the laws of nature to society does not really make it amenable to scientific analysis – it simply makes it appealing to the social sciences.

Finally, there is an epistemological postulate at work in the social capital phenomenon. Neoclassical economics, neoliberalism, and rational-choice theory all define capital as utility-generating investment decisions, which in turn require intentional and rational mental states. Yet intentions and rational thinking are unobservable processes without the evidential status demanded by positivist methodology. And absent epistemological access, unobservables become mere theoretical constructs derived from the logic of realist thought experiments. But if the capital in social capital is not an empirical but a theoretical entity, its causal properties can never be fully confirmed or disconfirmed. They cannot even be candidates for truth or falsehood. Its validity instead is entirely dependent on the logic of theoretical realism – a militantly antipositivist epistemology that mocks positivism for its naïve empiricist belief in the "illusion" of the empirical. "Real" causal mechanisms putatively operate at a deeper level of reality than the superficiality of appearance (see Somers 1998).

But here is the problem: if the capital in social capital is defined only by imputed causal mechanisms, when it rejoins the social half of the couplet, social capital's claim to science and positivism is radically undercut. The primacy of epistemologically inaccessible intentional states of mind leaves *power* as the sole arbiter of what counts as knowledge. Social capital claims the approval of scientific positivism, while it is actually dependent on a militant antipositivism. Combine this with an ontological individualism mapped onto the social and the result is an incoherent and unstable conceptual entity.

Conclusion

Where Solidarity once shined brightly in our political imaginations the Trojan horse of social capital now prevails. With its polysemic and protean language of social ties and community, social capital theorists have tried to appropriate the spirit of civil society. Social capital now inhabits some of the greatest symbols of participatory democratic ideals. By appropriating the language of civil society, but domesticating and evacuating its social, political, and egalitarian dimensions, social capital has turned the social against its natural constituents.

Clearly, the appeal of the social capital concept for the neoliberals and conservatives is in its indictment of public sector investment. It vindicates antistatism by blaming civic decline on the usual sociological suspects of the welfare state and its public services. Most conveniently, it explains the intractability of market failures and externalities not by neoliberalism's starvation of the public sector or its policies of privatization and structural readjustment, but by inadequate quantities of social capital. The message is clear: it is our fault, and our responsibility – yours and mine – for our excessive commitment to greater democratization of the polity, for our lapsed bowling league memberships, for our neglect of neighborhood barbeques, for our insufficient volunteer labor. Along with the privatization of citizenship has come the privatization of responsibility – and we are shamed by our loss of moral fortitude. Let *us* eat social capital.

In its glorious heyday of the Gdansk-based Solidarity movement, civil society was the nurturing ground for democratic associations of rights-claiming citizens. More than a decade after the fact, it has been hijacked and misshaped into social capital, an antistatist appendage for the compassionate side of market society. Militant antistatism, completely understandable in the case of Eastern Europe's repressed trade unions and social movements fighting heroically against communist state power, cannot be justified in the case of social capital. The exclusion of power, rights, and market inequities from the social capital agenda is not a heroic act; but it is a clever one. Responding to the seductive siren of community, an array of intellectuals, social justice advocates, and well-meaning communitarian proponents of the Third Way are caught in the web of the privatization of citizenship through the allure of social capital and the ever-receding utopia of community. Dazed by the golden glitter of the Trojan horse, we have been dazzled by the social in social capital to collude with a tragicomedy of social science – one in which social capital is bereft of the social, and Solidarity's vision of civil society has been turned into a neighborhood bowling league. Social capital is bad for reducing poverty or elevating civic cultures; and it is bad for sociology – as a discipline and as a social project. Above all, it is very bad for democratic citizenship.

7

Fear and loathing of the public sphere: how to unthink a knowledge culture by narrating and denaturalizing Anglo-American citizenship theory

This chapter further develops the basic elements of a *historical sociology of concept formation* – a new research program in the sociology of knowledge. The method is designed to analyze the complex and skewed relationship between the practical world of social organization and the cognitive maps with which we engage that world. Most simply, a historical sociology of concept formation is a cultural and historical approach to making sense of "how we think and why we seem obliged to think in certain ways" (Hacking 1990b: 362). In this chapter I use this research program to make sense of an intriguing but worrisome puzzle about contemporary politics and political argument: namely, the increasing privatization of citizenship and civil society, and the *fear and loathing of the public sphere* – the demonstrable antistatism of our times. After first elaborating on this puzzle, I propose that the concept of civil society is implicated in a knowledge culture that takes the form of a metanarrative – one I call Anglo-American citizenship theory. By exploring the genealogies of its invention, I suggest that at the causal heart of this metanarrative is the successful demonization of the institutional domain of the state and all that is associated with the public. It is this narrative of the fear and loathing of the public sphere that has been the driving force in defining modern liberal political argument and its equation of freedom with the privatization of citizenship.

A puzzling failure of conceptual space

After almost thirty years of scholarly neglect, citizenship has been redis-covered and reinvented. In this dual process intellectuals and politicians alike have recuperated the concept of civil society. This newly rejuvenated concept is one of the most significant in a conceptual cluster I call the citizenship concepts.[1] A recuperation inspired by the antistatist democratic revolutions of the 1980s and 1990s in Eastern Europe and the former Soviet Union, the notion of civil society holds immense conceptual promise. For one, it provides a unique political vocabulary liberated from the stifling constraints of Cold War manichaean dichotomies between state and market, public and private. At the same time, because of its association with the spread of democratic values and civic practices in Europe, the concept resonates with the increasingly expanding interest in theorizing the conditions for institutionalizing democratic and participatory political cultures in a completely reconfigured geopolitical global landscape.[2]

In proportion to its theoretical promise, however, the concept of civil society also bears an enormous burden. It has been asked to carry not only the theoretical but also the sociological and normative weight of explaining and conceptualizing what is considered to have been the foundational conditions for the Eastern European revolutions of the 1980s. Civil society has thus come to represent the flourishing of a seemingly novel political and social terrain, a space of popular social movements and collective mobilization, of informal networks, civic associations, and community solidarities all oriented toward sustaining a participatory democratic life. In addition to these extraordinary internal organizational traits, what makes the burden of this conception of civic life so enormous is the "place" the concept has been asked to occupy and defend in the post-Cold War social, political, and conceptual landscape. For over three hundred years, the terrain of liberal political thought has been fixed in the foundational premise that there were only two essential actors in forging the modern world – the modern administrative state and the property-based market.[3] This reading of the past was mapped onto a binary conceptual landscape with firm boundaries and epistemological closures that demarcated two mutually exclusive zones of public and private – what Bobbio has called the "great dichotomy" of modern political thought (Bobbio 1992: 2). It is a zero-sum dichotomy that continues to force social organization and political ideas into only one of the two binary possibilities.

---

[1] Elsewhere I have explored in detail the past and current uses of two other citizenship concepts – the public sphere and political culture (see chapter 5).
[2] For examples of theoretical efforts in the recent past, see Habermas's ([1962] 1989) work on the public sphere and Almond and Verba's (1963) work on civic cultures. On the conceptual rediscovery of civil society, see Cohen and Arato (1992) and Seligman (1992).
[3] I leave out the more complex model offered by Hegel's triadic inclusion of the family, because it does not change the basic claim regarding the relationship of state and market.

In the spirit of the discourse of the Eastern European revolutions of the 1980s, the concept of civil society was called on to break apart this dichotomous closure and to liberate a new social and political space – one in between and independent of both private markets and administrative state authority – where people can participate in the collective decision-making processes that shape their lives: in short, a place where citizens can participate in the practices of citizenship free of both coercion and competition. Because of its "in-betweenness," this conceptual space has come to be called a "third sphere" – referring now to an intermediate and autonomous zone in-between the two dominant spheres of state and market. Clearly, the revival of civil society reflects social and political theory's attempt to keep pace with history's exigencies as well as to embrace the normative ideal and the spirit of democratic practices. The appeal of the concept lies in its resonance with the strenuous efforts to theorize a third sphere, a space of social organization and free civic association believed to be uniquely capable of nurturing the same kinds of popular democratic practices and collective solidarities that launched the dramatic revolutionary successes of the late 1980s and early 1990s.

The premise of this chapter is that at the beginning of the twenty-first century, the civil society concept has not been able to bear the burden of sustaining its normative or sociological place in this third sphere. Instead, the conceptual space in which it is most commonly placed – subsumed, more accurately – is on the private, antipolitical, presocial, market side of the stubbornly entrenched dichotomy between public and private, state and society.[4] The evidence for this is multiple. Liberal democratic societies have been giddily romancing global markets armed with a muscular, bullying antistatism not seen since the 1920s – even while they vaunt the new-found virtues of civil society.[5] In the East, once-inspiring ideas about the freedoms of civil society have dissolved into a cultural commitment to freedom of exchange and freedom of market choice. And in East and West alike we have seen the precipitous withdrawal of social rights being justified by the needs of a healthy capitalist economy coupled with a stunning level of global poverty that is explained by the punitive

---

[4] This placing of the public sphere concept on the private side of the divide is especially evident in the work of those who draw directly either from Habermas's early work on the public sphere or in the work of those who draw on the political culture concept in the Parsonian tradition (see chapter 5).

[5] Holmes (1997) suggests we take a sobering look at the tragedy of 1997 Russia to be reminded that only a muscular legal apparatus backed by a state has the power to support a civic culture's normative principles.

nineteenth-century language of moral failure, individual blame, the shame of "dependency," and the celebration of "personal responsibility" (Somers and Block 2005).

How is it possible that a concept originally recuperated to do the theoretical work of liberating a third sphere now exhibits such a failure of conceptual space? This is a conundrum that needs to be explained. Given the extraordinary importance of civil society in contemporary social and political thought as well as practice, it also needs to be challenged. For this failure signals nothing less than the privatization of citizenship and the degradation of public life.

A knowledge culture: archeological and genealogical explorations

To address this conundrum I take a "cultural turn" in the history and sociology of knowledge. Whereas a traditional investigation in the sociology of knowledge might track down the social and economic interests expressed in ideas, and an intellectual history might trace their intellectual lineage, I suggest that the privatization of citizenship can only be explained by exploring the cultural, historical, and epistemological constraints embedded in the knowledge culture of Anglo-American citizenship theory. My approach builds on Ian Hacking's premise that concepts are "words in their sites," as I argue that all concepts are located and embedded in conceptual networks.[6] Because they are networks and sites of knowledge, I call them *knowledge cultures* (Somers 1996a). Knowledge, the first component of the term, is that which philosophy has deemed to be truth. Falsehoods, ignorance, mysticism, magic, even religion are not forms of knowledge, either because we know them to be untrue or because we cannot know for sure if they are true. We call statements, concepts, classificatory schemes, categories, formulas, and other signifiers knowledge when we believe they state accurately what is true about some thing or entity (the signified) – they know it. Categorizing a rock as mineral is an example of knowledge because "mineral" accurately states the truth about rocks. The attribution of knowledge is thus a great privilege that entails passing the rigorous test of epistemology – the body of rules and criteria (the lie detectors of intellectual claims) used to evaluate whether claims should count as truth, knowledge, and fact. My use of the term is thus capacious. Knowledge includes not only the "facts of the matter" but also the

---

[6] In taking inspiration from Hacking, I am also incorporating the early epistemological work of Foucault (1973, 1978).

presumption that those facts have gained the epistemic privilege of truth by passing the test of epistemological accountability and credibility.

The second element of a knowledge culture is the term culture. But instead of referring to a coherent set of subjectively held beliefs and values (Almond and Verba 1963), I use culture to refer to intersubjective public symbolic systems and networks of meaning-driven schemas organized by their own internal rules and structures that are (more or less, depending on the situation) loosely tied together in patterns of relationships.[7] Whereas the first definition makes culture inseparable from the psychology of those people who internalize beliefs and values, mine separates the realm of culture from other social forces by abstracting it out for heuristic purposes as a distinct analytic dimension of meaning. This makes it possible to explore the internal dynamics of a cultural schema on its own terms. Cultural schemas can take numerous forms such as narrative structures, binary codings, patterned metaphors or sets of metaphors, symbolic dualities, or practices of distinction (see Bourdieu 1984). Examples include gender codings in sexual conduct, grammatical syntaxes, the iconic schemas of a political party, rituals of public hanging in eighteenth-century London, the use of *Robert's Rules of Order* in civil associations, and the sacred and profane sumptuary laws of religious doctrine.

Because knowledge requires certainty and accountability, a knowledge culture must be buttressed by an epistemological infrastructure that verifies its truth claims. Thus in coupling knowledge with culture, I am insisting that no less than other kinds of meaning, claims to knowledge and truth are always transmitted to us via some kind of cultural schema. They are culturally embedded – that is, mediated through symbolic systems and practices, such as metaphors, ritualized codes, stories, analogies, or homologies. Fred Block, for example, shows how our most accepted truths about the state and economy derive from enduring cultural images and metaphors (e.g. the image of a "vampire state" that sucks the blood out of the economy), rather than from propositions that have been verified empirically (Block 1997: 6). To be sure, it is counterintuitive to accept that epistemology is founded not on the certainty of the unchanging laws of nature (as per standard philosophy) but on cultural schemas, conventional practices, and symbolic systems. Nonetheless, combining knowledge with

---

[7] My usage is loosely associated with the Bourdieuian/Foucauldian "new cultural history" as reflected in the work of Hunt (1989a); Durkheimian/Saussurian cultural sociology, e.g. Alexander (1992b, 2006); and especially the work of Hacking (1990b). The first reference is that of the Parsonian tradition of culture, e.g. Almond and Verba (1963). On the distinction between the two, see chapter 5.

culture simply makes explicit what is now increasingly being recognized: that truth claims have always gained legitimacy at least to some extent because of the cultural expressions by which they are articulated. In the case of Anglo-American citizenship theory, as I will show, this works in part through spatial and temporal regularities of the narrative form that substitute for nature's regularities, and in part through the binary code of social naturalism.

Embedded in my notion of a knowledge culture is also the assumption that concepts (the elements of knowledge) are cultural artifacts – rather than what Durkheim called "natural objects," or names of things that are believed to exist in nature in a precultural state, independently of symbolic classification systems. In a move that has been built on by the most influential social philosophers of our time, Mauss and Durkheim in their later work, insisted that our most primordial logical and factual knowledge categories, such as time, space, and causality, are themselves cultural creations: "The first logical categories were social categories; the first classes of things were classes of men, into which these things were integrated" (Durkheim and Mauss [1903] 1963: 82). To be clear: Durkheim is not suggesting that there is no reality outside of our conceptual representations. But since what counts as a fact is determined by a cultural metric that tells us to recognize it as a true fact in the first place (rather than, say, a wild speculation), it is the representational images of these metrics that we map onto natural phenomena that make the world accessible to us, and thus known, in the first place.

To look at the cultural infrastructure of knowledge is not a claim for the exclusively discursive constitution of the social world. It is, rather, a strategy with a twofold argument: first, there is no way to experience the world independently of the representational categories through which we engage it; and second, those representational categories have no empirical life of their own independent of their engagement with the social world. From the sociology of culture, this strategy derives and incorporates the crucial distinction between culture's analytic (or heuristic) autonomy on the one side, and its concrete (or empirical) autonomy on the other (Alexander and Smith 1993; Kane 1991). The distinction rests on the premise that the cultural dimension of life can never be "concretely" autonomous – that is, divorced empirically from social life and practices. At the same time, culture always exhibits a degree of analytic autonomy from empirical or scientific validation (Alexander 1995). To claim analytic autonomy for cultural structures and knowledge schemas, then, is a heuristic strategy of investigation, not an empirical claim that symbolic systems are the only sources of social determination. By examining the analytically autonomous cultural logic of a knowledge culture, we can identify and understand the degree to which cultural codes shape its rules for including and excluding evidence, its epistemological divides and demarcations, and its modes of structuring temporal and spatial patterns. The strategy thus allows us to understand how mechanisms of causal attribution can work very subtly through symbolic and cultural forms, as well as to examine in turn how these forms are also modalities of authority through which social life is given specific meanings.[8] So powerfully influential are the surrounding forces with which cultural structures are always empirically interacting – political, social, economic, and the like – that unless culture is *first* treated as an autonomous analytic abstraction it will be too easily overdetermined by the easier and more recognizable work of explaining culture as a reflection of the material world.

Treating cultural forms as analytically independent but concretely and empirically intertwined with the social world has important payoffs. First, it facilitates examining variations in how cultural schemas buttress knowledge claims. It does this by deciphering classificatory typologies and rules of procedure without immediately reducing or evaluating such schemas and rules by their degree of consistency or actual fit with the objects they represent. Acknowledging the analytic autonomy of a cultural structure prevents it from "belonging" *de facto* to any particular social class or organizational interest; we can instead examine empirically the historically contingent ways in which different groups may contest and appropriate its meaning.

Second, the strategy makes it possible to see variation in the degree to which a cultural structure can imprint itself on the course of institutional and discursive history, and thereby to test empirically how "the social theories that were advanced to interpret these [structural] transformations [of Western societies] have necessarily been a part of the societies they sought to comprehend" (Bendix 1976: 28). Looking in this way at the construction of social science thought allows us to see how concepts, and ultimately institutions, are built by men and women observing the empirical world through culturally constructed epistemological schemas and cognitive maps. It is the particular shape and logic of these cultural

---

[8] This, for example, is the meaning of economic sociology – the study of how the experience of economic relations and markets is, willy-nilly, mediated and given meaning by the cultural structures and schemas in which they are embedded. Thus Sewell (1999: 48) reminds us how a worker accepting the work of a wage laborer is not merely becoming an employee but entering into a culturally defined relation. See also Block (1990); Robertson and Friedland (1990); Joyce (1987); Somers (1995c); Zelizer (1997, 2005).

maps that makes it possible to see some things but not others, and to assign differential evaluative status to what is seen.

Another implication of joining the terms knowledge and culture together derives from the sense of culture as being those symbolic practices associated with a historically specific era or phenomenon – such as the "culture of modernity" or the "technological culture." In this use of the term, a knowledge culture can establish the boundaries of epistemic possibilities in thinking, reasoning, classifying, and conceptualizing within a given historical moment. Functioning similarly to other such ideas in the history and philosophy of science (e.g. Kuhn's "paradigm," Bourdieu's "doxa," Foucault's "episteme," or Hacking's "style of reasoning"), when a knowledge culture achieves this degree of epistemic closure it can exclude competing claims and so define the limits of the historically possible. Hence by setting parameters on contemporary rationality and reason it becomes an *epistemological gatekeeper*. Rather than advocating any single theory or truth, the mark of an epistemological gatekeeper is the capacity to define what counts as reasonable evidence and as rational investigation into truth or falsehood in the first place.[9]

Varieties of knowledge cultures

Narrative structures

A narrative structure is one in which meaning, structure, causality, and explanation are constituted through temporal and spatial relationality (Somers 1994b; Somers and Gibson 1994). A narrative structure arranges its relational elements in patterns of time and place. It contains a characteristic sequence (beginning = crisis; middle = struggle; end = resolution), and it contains a causal plot that assigns a narrative account of the cause and the resolution of the crisis at hand. Narratives are networks of patterned relationships connected and configured over time and space, and in which meaning, causality, and truth are ascribed based on these temporal and spatial arrangements. In a relational conceptual structure, agents and events do not have intrinsic meaning, causal powers, or epistemological validity but have meaning only in the context of their distribution across the temporal and spatial landscape of the overall structure. This is the narrative method of establishing causal emplotment – something causes something else, for example, because the first thing

---

[9] For further discussion of a knowledge culture, and a comparison with the more familiar notion of a paradigm, see Somers (1996a).

262 Genealogies of Citizenship

comes before the second in time. Cause, in this manner, is established through placement and sequence; joining later outcomes to earlier events provides explanation through chains of causality. (We will see, for example, how Locke uses his story of civil society's temporal anteriority to the government to justify its normative political priority.) This gives a narrative structure a theoretical and normative status: explanations and accounts are embedded in symbolic schemas that explain the present in terms of the past, and prescribe and justify actions that will dictate the future in terms of the demands of the present.

Within a knowledge culture, narratives thus not only convey information but serve epistemological purposes. They do so by establishing veracity through the integrity of their storied form. This suggests that in the first instance the success or failure of truth claims embedded in narratives depends less on empirical verification and more on the logic and rhetorical persuasiveness of the narrative. In this way the narrative – paradoxically, given its status as a cultural rather than a scientific account – takes on the mantle of epistemological truth and endows the information it conveys with the stature of knowledge, fact, and truth. In the long run, the success or failure of a narrative knowledge culture depends on its relationship to surrounding historical and political relations. But this interaction of cognitive and social forces is the usual starting point of all social science, and hence deserves less attention here. It is the first instance – the heuristic analysis of cultural phenomena – that has been relatively ignored and is thus deserving of extended discussion.

Binary codes and social naturalism

Another possible cultural schema of a knowledge culture can be a binary code or pattern of distinctions. Building from Durkheim's classifications between the sacred and the profane, Lévi-Strauss, Saussure, and others theorized that meanings are structured by systems of oppositions and distinction. To illustrate how they can shape a knowledge culture I focus here on the example of *social naturalism*.

In the work of judging truth value, the *laws of nature* set the template for reliable knowledge in mainstream philosophy. Naturalism is thus epistemology's ultimate reference point. Because it is not subject to the vicissitudes of culture, place, and time, only nature is credited by philosophers with having absolute regularities and escaping the fickleness and fortuitousness of culture and history. Only nature is what philosophers have increasingly come to call foundational – suggesting by this term that nature should be considered as the ultimate grounds of knowledge (Douglas [1970] 1982: 52; Rorty 1979). In naturalism, that represented as natural is more certain, more firm, and most appropriate to use as the highest standard against which all knowledge should be measured. By contrast, the not-natural is arbitrary/artificial/ideological. It lacks the quality of certainty because it is only a product of the thinker's conceptual schemas, while natural phenomena exist firmly and independently of the mind. Naturalism thus sets up a binary opposition between on the one side truth/certainty/nature and on the other, culture/uncertainty/contingency.

Social naturalism extends the epistemological criteria of the laws of nature from natural to social phenomena. It then evaluates the quality of social knowledge by apportioning conceptual arguments across the binary categories of nature versus culture. Higher epistemological status is attributed to all that falls on nature's side of the epistemological divide. Certain social phenomena – the market, for example – belong on nature's side, and are thus ascribed more foundational epistemological status. Others – the state, for example – are placed under the rubric of the not-natural, artificial, arbitrary, contingent, and thus are in an epistemologically inferior position. In these binary distinctions and in the privilege ascribed to the natural world are to be found the roots of social naturalism's powers and its complex epistemological metric.

Knowledge cultures as metanarratives

When a narrative structure is grafted onto the binary code of social naturalism the narrative is transformed into a *metanarrative*. A metanarrative is a cultural form that has been epistemologically naturalized by conjoining narrative with social naturalism. Metanarratives are among the most potent – and troubling – types of knowledge culture. This is because certain kinds of knowledge – we call them postulates or assumptions – are not accountable to the same standards of truth that apply to empirical claims; they are legitimated not by empirical evidence but by the self-evidential status of their seemingly naturalistic – hence preconstructed or presuppositional – qualities. Naturalized presuppositions are like economists' "as if" assumptions: they are not empirically accurate, but they are used to make empirical claims and predictions. When a naturalized knowledge claim is used, as is so often the case, *as if* it were the basis for an empirically justified argument, when charged with the inaccuracy of the original claim, economists justify this inconsistency with disclaimers about how it was never meant to be empirically true in the first place. Thus insulated from criticism by this Catch-22 situation, these foundational postulates and naturalized assumptions become serious troublemakers. When these troublemakers are arranged in storied form into public narratives, they reasonably can be called metanarratives.

Metanarratives have another kind of power. Recall that social naturalism establishes its legitimacy through an epistemology that looks to the laws of nature as the baseline for the foundations of knowledge, thereby making the reliable regularities of nature the absolute standards by which the validity of different kinds of knowledge are adjudicated. What gives this naturalistic epistemology so much conceptual authority is that what is viewed as natural and foundational, and what is viewed as cultural and contingent, form a series of hierarchical relationships. Concepts placed under the rubric of nature occupy a privileged position in an epistemological hierarchy, while those things deemed cultural are contingent, historical, and arbitrary – hence inferior to the natural. When mapped onto the epistemological grid of social naturalism, a narrative's temporal and spatial elements become subordinated to the hierarchical dichotomy between the natural and the cultural. Those categories of the narrative that fall under the natural side of the epistemological divide – for example, the anterior private sphere – immediately gain epistemological privilege as foundational objects over those that have been relegated to the not-natural/artificial side of the divide – for example, the public sphere and the state. Thus, in Locke's narrative, civil society and the market in property are grafted together to be narrated as temporally anterior to the government. When this temporal anteriority is mapped onto social naturalism, civil society and the market are transmuted from a temporal to an ontological condition of *being* natural, and thus unquestionably given in the nature of things. In an instant, then, in being naturalized the market now assumes a place at the summit of epistemological privilege.

It is therefore social naturalism that transforms knowledge cultures into metanarrative gatekeepers of conceptual authority. Its internal epistemological infrastructure imposes a field of relationships, demarcations, and boundaries that establish power, privilege, and hierarchy among the internal elements of its narrative representations. What is most paradoxical, and easiest to forget, is that social naturalism is itself a system of representations, a cultural schema. What is and is not defined as representational of nature is, after all, a social category rather than a social "fact," to use Durkheim's words against himself. Yet by its own naturalistic criteria this cultural aspect of its identity is obscured and reconstructed as natural. The "unnatural" fact, of course, is that all epistemologies are social and cultural conventions, and only through naturalizing analogies is some knowledge considered to be more natural – hence more foundational – than other knowledge.

While the notion of conceptual authority tied to boundary drawing and hierarchy invokes an image of vertical power and privilege, a meta-narrative's naturalizing power also gives it the gatekeeping authority to control the epistemological agenda. In this sense, a metanarrative is similar to a paradigm; it not only provides the range of acceptable answers but has the gatekeeping power to define both the questions to be asked and the rules of procedure by which they can rationally be answered. Even more than other kinds of knowledge cultures, a meta-narrative establishes the parameters of epistemic conceptual possibility through its power to adjudicate what counts as rational and reasonable investigation into competing knowledge claims.

A historical sociology of concept formation and historical epistemology

A metanarrative's power to reproduce epistemological hierarchies and boundaries even in the face of competing evidence could induce a deep pessimism about the possibility of "unthinking" the orthodoxy. There is, however, an approach that I believe to be well suited for the challenge. A historical sociology of concept formation is a research program in historical epistemology designed to analyze how we think, why we seem obliged to think in certain ways, and how to begin the process of unthinking (Hacking 1990b: 362).

Reflexivity

Social scientists in recent years have increasingly come to recognize that the categories and concepts we use to explain the social world should no longer be simply taken for granted; rather, they themselves should be made the objects of analysis. The work of examining the taken-for-granted categories of social science (individual, society, agent, structure, etc.) falls under the mandate of a reflexivity – meaning, literally, a turning back on itself (Bourdieu and Wacquant 1992). To turn social science back on itself entails treating terms like civil society and the public sphere not as instruments of analysis but as the objects to be explained, thus radically shifting the context of discovery (at least initially) from the external world to the cognitive tools by which we analyze this world. With this shift we suddenly have a whole new set of questions: why and how and to what effect did social scientists invent the idea that there exists something significant in the social world called civil society? And how have these terms been used to make sense of the world? Wallerstein calls this "unthinking social science," while Bourdieu felicitously calls it the practice of casting "radical doubt" (Wallerstein 1991; Bourdieu and Wacquant 1992: 235). Whatever we call it, looking reflexively at our presuppositional categories of social thought involves a vigorous retrieval and embrace of a new kind of sociology of knowledge – a historical sociology of concept formation. It is the first step in the work of destabilizing and unthinking a deeply entrenched knowledge culture.

Relationality

A historical sociology of concept formation requires a relational approach, for what appear to be autonomous concepts defined by isolated attributes are better conceived as relational signifiers, which are contingently stabilized in cultural structures usually made up of binary oppositions. In contrast to what Karl Popper calls "essentialism" – a philosophy that looks to the "essence" of a thing to discover its true nature – a historical sociology of concept formation looks at concepts as relational objects embedded in a relational configuration of concepts, cultural structures, or conceptual networks (Popper 1959). A conceptual network is a relational matrix or the "site" in which concepts are nested – a structured configuration of relationships among concepts that share the same conceptual net. Inspired by Hacking's notion that concepts are "words in their sites," the site-as-network metaphor can help take us "well on the way to a complex methodology" for generating "more specific conjectures about the ways in which the condition for the emergence and change of use of a word [or concept] also determined the space in which it could be used" (Hacking 1990b: 362). Indeed, conceptual networks are especially well suited to a methodology based on the spatial metaphor, as the network concept invokes images of concepts linked together across cultural and cognitive space. It is the full geometric shape and patterned logic of these ties that need to be reconstructed before we can make sense of the meaning of a single concept within that network.

A knowledge culture is a conceptual network that is dedicated specifically to epistemological concepts and categories of validity that are coordinated through specifically cultural idioms. A conceptual network qua knowledge culture implies that concepts in a knowledge culture are not only related to each other in the weak sense of being contiguous; they are also ontologically related. Like a point and a line in basic geometry, we only accept the definitional truth of one by its relational opposition to the other. In a knowledge culture, then, epistemological justifications for definitional truth convince by virtue of a concept's fit – its place – in the cultural schema of the knowledge culture as a whole.[10] Hence a relational approach to knowledge cultures foregrounds the importance of relational space in the work of epistemic reflexivity. Exploring the places and spaces of our conceptual vocabularies is a crucial step in understanding and, when necessary, being able to unthink the cognitive worlds we inhabit and impose on the social landscape.

A historical epistemology: the historicity of knowledge cultures

The stipulation that concepts are historical as well as relational objects is founded on a historical conception of knowledge, or a historical epistemology (Somers 1996a). A historical epistemology combines history and epistemology to emphasize what we now find to be relatively uncontroversial – namely, that successful truth claims are historically contingent rather than confirmations of absolute and unchanging reality. Based on the principle that all of our knowledge, our logics, our theories, indeed our very reasoning practices are indelibly (although often obscurely) marked with the signature of time, a historical epistemology underlies the method of a historical sociology of concept formation. Knowledge cultures are sited and sites have histories. Hence another of Hacking's imperatives: "If one took seriously the project of analysis, one would require *a history of the words [concepts] in their sites.*" The mandate to historicize in conceptual analysis is not simply a wave at some notion of looking back at the past; rather it is an injunction "to investigate the principles that cause [a concept] to be useful – or problematic" (Hacking 1990b: 362). Knowing how we got to where we are helps to clarify where we are. If we can understand what puts ideas and knowledge in place and what brings them into being – not a teleology but an account of contingencies and "might have beens" – we can hope to better grasp the meanings and the effects of those ideas, and their roles in problem-formation.

When knowledge is recognized as a historical and cultural object, we can worry less about whether it is true or false, and concentrate instead on how and to what effect certain concepts are even considered reasonable

---

[10] The term "place" as I use it here comes from Polanyi (1957b). For empirical application, see Somers (1993). A similar idea of "positions" in a "field" is suggested by Bourdieu and Wacquant (1992).

candidates for truth claims in the first place. Understanding how concepts gain and lose their currency and legitimacy is the task of historical epistemology, which entails reconstructing their making, resonance, and contestedness over time. When we explore the historical life of concepts, and the historicity of our conceptual semantics, we are likely to find that they themselves have histories of contestation, and transformation – histories not unlike the more straightforwardly social phenomena that we study regularly. A historical epistemology demonstrates that concepts are "history-laden" – a phrase meant to evoke, and invert, the now well-established Kuhnian understanding that all empirical claims are "theory-laden."

Taking stock

A historical sociology of concept formation argues that just as political ideas and social concepts are not mirrored reflections of external social facts, so also must our own social science concepts be understood not as labels for natural facts but as cultural and historical artifacts embedded within and assigned meaning by their location in symbolic and historically constructed conceptual networks. The method of a historical sociology of concept formation differs from the classical approach of Mannheim's or Marx's sociology of knowledge in that it does not look for class power and social interests behind the accepted ideas. Rather, it looks for the conditions of possibility within which concepts develop and are evaluated, and by which epistemological boundaries and hierarchies are created and sustained. It aims to account for how concepts do the work they do by reconstructing their construction, resonance, and contestedness over time. From the perspective of a historical sociology of concept formation, concepts do not have natures or essences; they have histories, networks, and narratives that can be subjected to historical and empirical investigation. In what follows, I use this method to do just that: to subject the histories, networks, and narratives of Anglo-American citizenship theory to a historical epistemology and to empirical investigation.

Narrating and naturalizing Anglo-American citizenship theory

Applying a historical sociology of concept formation to the concept of civil society generates three propositions:

Proposition 1. The civil society concept is not an isolated object but has a relational identity; its meaning is assigned by its place in its conceptual network/knowledge culture. Thus the subject of research should be the entire conceptual network, or the relational site, in which it is embedded.

Proposition 2. The knowledge culture of Anglo-American citizenship theory assumes the form of a metanarrative – a cultural structure that joins together a narrative form with the binary coding of social naturalism. This directs us to the task of analyzing the metanarrative's symbolic logic – especially its relationships of time, space, and emplotment – as well as its epistemological infrastructure of social naturalism.

Proposition 3. Metanarratives are structures of conceptual authority; they have the power to establish hierarchies, boundaries of inclusion and exclusion, tropes of good and bad, rules of what counts as rationality and evidence – all the characteristics of an *epistemological gatekeeper*. Hence the mandate of a historical epistemology: to challenge the power of a metanarrative by revealing its social naturalism to be nothing more and nothing less than a cultural schema constructed by historical contingency.

Anglo-American citizenship theory

The conceptual network of the civil society concept is the story of Anglo-American citizenship – a "conjectural history" of how popular sovereignty triumphed over coercive absolutist states to ensure individual liberties.[11] First adumbrated in the seventeenth century by John Locke, explicitly articulated by the eighteenth-century Scottish moralists (e.g. Adam Ferguson, Adam Smith), appropriated into the foundations of nineteenth-century classical sociological theory, and still the basic core of liberal political thought today, this story by my reading is a narrative political fiction less about citizenship per se than about the rise of markets and modernity and their heroic roles in establishing the social foundations for individual freedom and autonomy against the tyranny of the state. How Anglo-American citizenship theory developed can be reconstructed by exploring its narrative construction, its transformation, and its sedimentation over the course of the seventeenth through the twentieth century.[12] Here I begin that project by imagining the making

---

[11] By "citizenship theory," I refer not to one particular theory but to the deeper common features shared by those who have attempted to provide social science accounts of the conditions for individual protection *by* the state, as well as individual freedom *from* the state. The concept of conjectural history I take from Dugald Stewart's characterization of Adam Smith's historical sociology. See Collini *et al.* (1983); Meek (1976); Winch (1978).

[12] Although in this chapter I only explore seventeenth-century discourse, and then make the leap to the present, there is a very clear trajectory of both continuity and transformation from Locke through early eighteenth-century English social policy to the late eighteenth-century Scottish Enlightenment (Adam Smith, Dugald Stewart, Adam Ferguson), and to the

of a series of key narrative elements in their original seventeenth-century context.[13]

Anglo-American citizenship theory theorizes, explains, and makes political claims through narrative and naturalization. Because it is a story, its explanatory plausibility depends on the integrity of its temporal and spatial relationships, and the success or failure of the causal plot depends on the logic and rhetorical persuasiveness of the narrative – and not on empirical verification. Thus its power and durability rely on how well the elements of the story have been organized into a cohesive narrative logic that convinces us that it records and explains, rather than constructs, the empirical world it narrates.

Theorizing through crisis – what is to be explained?

At the heart of every narrative is a crisis or flash point that cries out for a solution. To gain access to the internal logic of a narrative thus requires first identifying the narrative's initial problematic – what is the crisis which this narrative account addresses? The crisis driving Anglo-American citizenship theory is the fear of the tyrannical coercion of the absolutist state: how to escape its ever-present threat to individual liberty? The crisis is formulated in manichaean terms: the threatening antagonist is the public realm of the administrative state – a domain characterized by unfreedom, constituted by coercion, domination, and constraint, which is backed up with physical compulsion and arbitrary personal dependencies. The job of the narrative is to solve the crisis and remove the danger by theorizing an epic struggle led by a heroic protagonist worthy and capable of defeating the tyrannical state.

The unprecedented suppression of personal liberties in seventeenth-century absolutist England thus catalyzed the first formulation of the crisis. Locke's revolutionary narration was a direct response to what he considered to be the limits to Hobbes's earlier solution to absolutist

---

nineteenth-century development of modern social and political theory as represented by, for example, Marx, Mill, Weber, Durkheim, Maine, Spencer, and Tonnies.

[13] I refer here to both texts and events that have since been dubbed as political or social theory (e.g. Hobbes, Smith, Marx), as well as lesser or hardly known arguments that were less texts in any lasting sense than institutionalized political interventions in the political dynamics of the time – how beheading a king, for example, was justified "by law," or how "the sovereignty of the people" was somehow made synonymous with free markets (see Morgan 1988 for treatment of this kind of informal intervention). As I indicated above, there is a significant alternative non-English story, which would include Montesquieu, Rousseau, Durkheim, Tocqueville, and the 1789, 1830, and 1848 French revolutions most prominently. See Taylor (1990) for an account of the two versions of the civil society concept and story.

authority.[14] Hobbes had been the first to conceptualize the "problem of order" – so named because in the context of the English civil war it asked how and from where, given the end of traditional monarchy, would authority and order come? Locke took as his starting point the problem he believed flowed from Hobbes's famous solution in a new Leviathan: how could personal liberty be maintained if the end of the story was again an all-powerful Leviathan to whom the people surrendered their rights? How could that Leviathan be truly contained? Over the course of the seventeenth, eighteenth, and nineteenth centuries, different iterations of the Lockean narrative were driven by an amalgam of successive formulations of this same problem, each new incarnation of the story resulting from the deficiencies of the previous narrative in solving the problem of a coercive state. But it is Locke's original narration that cemented the association of the public sphere with the tyrannical administrative state, thus setting the stage for the privatization of citizenship.

Narrating place: theorizing through political geography

A narrative requires a sense of space and place – a social and political geography. The prevailing conceptual landscape in Locke's time was represented in the famous frontispiece to Hobbes's *Leviathan* (see figure 7.1). In this allegorical engraving of political authority, Hobbes depicts a giant body of a wise, benevolent, and patriarchal-looking king standing godlike above a miniature landscape of country farms and churches. Yet what at first glance appears to be the king's suit of metal armor is on closer examination actually hundreds of miniature people, all facing reverently toward the giant head of the king. What Hobbes has done here is insert into the king's body "the people" – more aptly, the "subjects" – of his kingdom. Embedded as they are within the king's spatial corporeality, the message is that there is no separate terrain available for people to inhabit other than that internal to the king. The disappointment of Hobbes's narrative is that he allows only one social site and then places it under the dominion of political power. In so doing, he has robbed the people of any autonomous place of their own.

[14] In focusing on Locke, I demonstrate how a historical sociology of concept formation requires a difficult balance between ascribing anonymity to the cultural form and overly identifying it with any single thinker. Thus although Locke provides a subject for my reconstruction, this is not intellectual history and I use him primarily as a representative figure in the making of the narrative. In isolating Locke as the seventeenth-century representative of Anglo-American citizenship theory, I am of course not fully doing justice to his contemporary context, especially the wide range of other political treatises. This is a shortcoming, but one that is unavoidable given the limitations of space.

7.1 Frontispiece to *Leviathan or the Matter, Forme and Power of a Common Wealth Ecclesiasticall and Civil*, 1651, by Thomas Hobbes (1588–1679) of Malmesbury (engraving) (b&w photo), English School, (17th century) © Private Collection / The Bridgeman Art Library

Driven by the authoritarian experience of English absolutism, Locke fiercely rejected conflating the people into the political space of the king's body/state. He had an alternative vision that would permanently relocate a place for the people and reverse the direction and the source of political power – away from the state to that of the people. Even though Hobbes begins his story of *Leviathan* in the state of nature's domain of natural rights, his conclusion ultimately dissolves this original site of the people and in the end settles all of social life back in the domain of the state. Locke believed that Hobbes's solution of total state power calls for its own negation. To liberate the people from the state's domination, Locke envisioned an enduring social sphere distinct and independent from that of the state. He envisioned a civil (nonstate) society.

Locke invents civil society through a revolutionary remapping of the prevailing conceptual topography. He imagines, and narrates, a new locus of social organization – a prepolitical and private entity spatially separate and autonomous from the public sphere – a new place for the people alone. It was to be a permanent place of individual freedom and private property that would establish the grounds for an enduring collective entity. It would also serve as a normative reference for how to achieve freedom from the state. In endowing permanence to a private sphere, Locke's political vision broke decisively from Hobbes's and introduced the most enduring formulation of the conditions for popular freedom. In making a separate and prepolitical social space the sole realm of true freedom, he forever imprinted on our political imaginations a binary spatial divide between public and private. In this revolutionary narration, he recast forever our vision of the "social imaginary" (Taylor 2004).

Locke carried out his task through a manichaean dualism. The freeborn English people faced a crisis of evil in the Goliath-like character of the state. Like a *deus ex machina*, a social hero appears in the form of the autonomous site of a noncoercive prepolitical (hence private) realm of (civil) society – only within its private boundaries are the people's liberties safe from state power. Indeed, as is typical in narrative form there is even an element of surprise: it is actually the people themselves who create this new realm of social organization through their own heroic act of consenting to an enduring social contract. And also consistent with most narrations, the evil is never absolutely eliminated but remains in the shadowy background where it motivates a constant vigilance. Even after the sovereign people decide by contract to create a tamed representative government strictly under their control, Leviathan hovers as a permanent threat always ready to rear its coercive head against popular sovereignty.

Fear and loathing of the state is the wellspring of action in this story of popular freedom. It gives civil society its reason for existence.

We think of the nineteenth century as the age of the discovery of modern social theory. But as this narrative demonstrates, it is clearly Locke who first imagines the spatial possibility of a nonpolitical social domain of life that exists *sui generis*, free from political authority and control. It is the realm of popular freedom because it is a collective society with the robustness to exist independently of the state. It is this notion of an autonomous self-regulating prepolitical society that by the eighteenth century explicitly is termed civil society.[15] Since Locke, the story of ever-fragile popular liberties has been narrated as the fierce struggle of civil society to remain free from the regulative coercive reach of the administrative state.

Narrating time: establishing causality through sequence

Locke's invention of the new topographical site of prepolitical society, as revolutionary as it was, was not in itself sufficient to ensure permanently the people's freedom from state control. After all, what would prevent the state from subordinating anew even this separate society? To solve that problem, Locke invented a new narrative sequence through temporality. Rather than civil society emerging *after* the state, he reverses the story so that it *begins* with the people in the state of nature, who first contract into civil society, and who then finally consent to a representative popular government. By narrating the temporal sequence of the plot in this way, Locke is able to depict a government that exists only as a condition of the prior consent of the prepolitical community – specifically, their voluntary social contract to form a government. Because it was created as a conditional contract by a temporally anterior act of civil society, this consent to government could be revoked at any time. Sovereignty resides exclusively in the hands of the people in civil society.

Locke's imaginative use of time was political and moral; he uses civil society's temporal anteriority to explain and thereby justify its political authority over the government it had, after all, created. The temporality of the narrative is also doing the work of establishing moral justification for the subservience of the state to the people. Thus the syntax of narrative is used to establish normative authority: a legitimate government is one

---

[15] Locke still used the traditional language of political theory in which the terms "civil society" and "political society" were used interchangeably to refer to the state-centered domain of social organization.

morally reduced to being a contingent outcome of the people's consent voluntarily given as a fiduciary trust by an autonomous and self-regulating robust civil society. Through the use of narrative temporal sequence, Locke permanently reversed the source of political authority from the state to the people in civil society.

Narrative structure and causal explanation

A clear causal plot has emerged from Locke's mapping of the narrative structure of Anglo-American citizenship. He has taken as his point of departure in time (in the "beginning") the epic problem of free people with natural rights (the protagonists of a "natural community") confronting the chronic tyranny of the absolutist state – the temporal and spatial Other of the public sphere. The danger to individual liberties and rights lies explicitly with this visible institutional and administrative state power (its personnel and bureaucracy): "A right of making laws with penalties of death" is how Locke defines political power (a definition echoed two centuries later by Weber's characterization of the state bureaucracy as an "iron cage" of coercion). The crisis can only be resolved through a complete realignment of power and legitimacy, something that Locke accomplishes by renarrativizing the story on which the original problem was based. He plots the resolution not only by inventing a geographical domain of prepolitical civil society but also by having the people establish a representative government that is a mere provisional product of the private social contract. Through narrative Locke has established political causality: civil society is not only separate and autonomous from the state, but precedes it and thus, quite literally, *caused* government's very existence by its voluntary consent. Something that comes before something else, in this schema, causes it.[16] This is not chronological time but epistemological time – a narrative that endows cause and effect.

Locke's dramatic resolution is causally plotted by his inventing both a prepolitical civil society and a representative government that is in a fiduciary relationship to the people. The rule of law, the common law, parliament, and so on – all are narrated to be the outcome of the temporally and spatially prior and independent (of political rule) sphere of civil society. We now have a more balanced epic struggle between state

---

[16] Locke here capitalizes on a generic quirk built into English language narratives themselves: as Linde (1986: 194) explains, the "natural logic of English is *post hoc ergo propter hoc*," or that which comes before causes that which comes after.

and society, made possible by the new boundary between the shadowy threat of a Leviathan on the one side, and the tamed deinstitutionalized representative government under the control of the people on the other.

The place of political culture: the people's sociological glue

With Locke's invention of a private sphere of civil society, he faced a new sociological challenge: what would hold this society together? If the people were to have any sustained power against a tyrannical state – and this is of course the driving aspiration of the narrative – they had to constitute themselves not as an atomistic aggregation of random individuals but into a coherent and self-regulating entity. Authority of civil society over the state could only be achieved with a robust self-organized autonomous civil society that basically ruled itself. The presumption of a society self-organized enough to be able to make and break government rule, orderly enough to snub all government intervention except that of security and protection of property, pushed Locke into developing a theory of social organization to account for a robust normative social cohesion. Only with such cohesion could true autonomy be achieved (Calhoun 1993).

Locke found this in his notion of a civil community held together first through property and commercial exchange, and second through a political culture of public opinion and social trust. The integrative work of the market was the foundation of civil society. But Locke also believed that common moral concerns based on public opinion would ensure order, freedom, and moral cohesion enough to make state power unnecessary. Unlike political authority, for Locke both the authority of civil public opinion and the self-regulating civility of the market were free of "the legislative authority of man" because they are both voluntary, spontaneous, and noncoercive. For Locke, the idea of a civil society based on free market exchange and a normative political culture provided the glue of popular sovereignty and representational consent. He exalted civil society's economic and cultural harmoniousness free from public external political authority.

This is how Locke theorized through narrative a robust and durable self-activating civil society in parallel with the normative claim that authority, right of resistance, and consent must be located within the private sphere. His radical challenge was to reject the notion of ordered social relationships sustained by the power of a political center, in favor of a conception of society as a unit capable of generating a common moral order – spontaneous in its workings, self-activating, and functionally independent of the state. To give the people the capacity to make and unmake political power and sovereignty, Locke endowed their commercial life with the glue of cultural solidarity. Civil society cohered in this story through what we today call "informal social control" – rather than in any recognizably institutional form. Thus the social foundations of liberalism and freedom were found in Locke's story of the private world of civil society, held together through commercial property exchange and a normative political culture.[17]

An epistemological infrastructure of social naturalism

The privatization of freedom, moral order, and normative justice in tandem with fear and loathing of the public sphere have shown remarkable resiliency over the years, despite multiple challenges from both history and theory. Why has this Lockean Anglo-American citizenship theory been so invincible to direct empirical criticism – even in the face of evidence to the contrary? The answer lies in the epistemology of social naturalism.

In social naturalism, as I discussed above and as figure 7.2 demonstrates, the world of knowledge is divided into a set of binary relationships along the classic axis of nature/culture. Power is established through a matrix of internally constituted epistemological divides that ranks things located on the "natural" (and antipolitical) side of the divide as privileged over (i.e. as more valid than) those located on the cultural (and political) side. In this dichotomy culture and politics are nonnatural dimensions of knowledge. In Anglo-American citizenship theory, the division is articulated through a hierarchical delineation between that which is designated as "given" in the nature of things – unchanging, spontaneous, voluntary, natural, God-given, lawlike; and that designated as "contingent" – politically constructed, temporally contingent, coercive, arbitrary, vulnerable to change or manipulation. Most importantly, that which falls on the natural side of the epistemological divide exists ontologically independently of political or human intervention. It is thus deemed epistemologically more valid – more foundational – for knowledge and science, and hence becomes the criterion for epistemological adjudication. Knowledge is scientific, admissible, and true to the extent that it corresponds with these natural foundations – whether natural law (in the seventeenth century), natural liberty (in the eighteenth and nineteenth centuries), or the natural science of political economy

---

[17] For a similar vision of liberalism's constructed "social imaginary," see Taylor (2004).

Natural	Cultural/Historical
Natural law-regulated	Arbitrary
God-given	Man-made
Constant	Changeable
Universal	Particular
Foundational	Apparent
Rational	Irrational
Representational	Artificial
Certain	Uncertain
Determined	Fortuitous
Scientific	Anecdotal
Actual	Socially constructed
Necessary	Contingent
Self-regulating	Politically regulated

7.2 Table of social naturalism's binary oppositions

(in the nineteenth century). And although social naturalism is usually thought to begin with the late eighteenth and early nineteenth century's discovery of political economy, it is the social naturalism of Locke's inscription of prepolitical society that is the defining moment in modern political thought. Social naturalism became the basis for imputing a natural, rather than a contingent, logic to the workings of the market and the private sphere of civil society.

The metanarrative of Anglo-American citizenship theory

When a narrative structure is grafted onto the binary code of social natural-ism, the narrative is transformed into the much more potent cultural schema of a metanarrative, which then becomes a narrative structure "naturalized" – made true, that is – by social naturalism. Thus the metanarrative of liberal-ism's Anglo-American citizenship theory was produced by grafting Locke's sociopolitical narrative of civil society to the binary epistemological coding of social naturalism, as figure 7.3 illustrates. As I suggested above, meta-narratives exhibit an aura of inevitability and unchangingness and they cannot be destabilized or unthought through competing evidence or routine empirical investigation. Instead they wield extraordinary epistemological authority through social naturalism's ability to create boundaries of exclu-sion and inclusion. In this ability to exercise the power of inclusion and exclusion, privilege and illegitimacy, a metanarrative – like a paradigm – assumes the role of an epistemological gatekeeper. It defines not only the

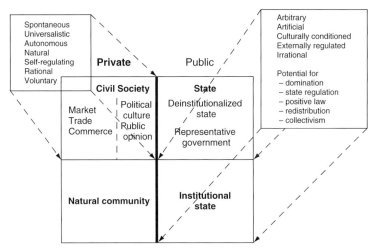

7.3 The making of a metanarrative: epistemological grid of social naturalism mapped onto the narrative structure of Anglo-American citizenship theory

range of rational argument and worthwhile questions but also the rules of procedure by which those questions can rationally be answered.

Anglo-American citizenship theory exercises its adjudicative authority through firm epistemological divides between civil society and the state, representative government and regulative law, spontaneity and domination, private and public, and so on. These boundaries assign evidence, argumentation, and hypothesis-formation into prestructured categories. Arguments that fall on the "wrong" side of an epistemological divide do not enjoy the privilege of being considered reasonable candidates in the competition to count as knowledge. In fact when a metanarrative is challenged by what should be disconfirming evidence it is able to subvert the challenge by ruling the evidence inadmissible by the metanarrative's standards of rationality. Social naturalism – an epistemological modality that adjudicates the truth or falsehoods of knowledge claims according to the regularities of nature – thus becomes embedded in the substantive ontological content of the story: Locke's antipolitical private sphere of civil commercial society actually becomes a natural, foundational, and privileged entity that has been constituted by, and functions according to, the laws of nature.

Figure 7.4 shows the outcome of this naturalizing process in its skeletal binary form. The temporal sequences and spatial mappings of the narrative

Natural – self-regulating and autonomous (functions independently of political interventions)	**Cultural/historical – artificial and constructed** (functions through arbitrary political power)
Private	**Public**
Public sphere	Legislature/parliament
Civil society	State
Free market	Managed economy
Public opinion	Artificial passions
Political culture	Political power
Natural law	Positive law
Natural rights	Political privilege
Right of resistance	Dominated subjecthood
Equality	Hierarchy
Bourgeois man	Master/slave
Impersonal order	Personal power
Independent	Dependent
Rational logic	Irrational force
Voluntary	Coercive
Spontaneous	Orchestrated

7.4 The Great Dichotomies of Anglo-American citizenship theory

of civil society have been redistributed across the binary nature/culture divide to become mutually exclusive naturalized oppositions (private versus public, civil society versus state, modernity versus tradition, the free/autonomous versus unfree/dominated agent). The meaning of any one entity does not reflect an external object but presupposes its oppositional other. Bobbio's great dichotomies of modern social and political thought emerge from this process – zero-sum dichotomies in which each term is the negation of the other: "From the moment that the space defined by the two terms (public and private) is completely covered they arrive at the point of mutually defining themselves in the sense that the public domain extends only as far as the start of the private sphere (and the reverse is also true)" (Bobbio 1992: 2). The naturalism of the private sphere, of modernity, of civil society, and of markets is fixed in opposition to the arbitrariness of the public sphere, of tradition, of the state, and of legal regulation. Markets, political cultures, and civil society all become natural entities. Locke's ascription of civil society as natural thus became the defining moment in modern political thought.

Figure 7.5 shows how Anglo-American citizenship theory arranges its political and sociological categories and organizes its temporal and spatial relationships across its epistemological divides. On the vertical axis the either/or of freedom and unfreedom is represented. On the horizontal axis, space is divided between the private naturalism of society and the arbitrary power of the public state. Locke's narrative begins with the

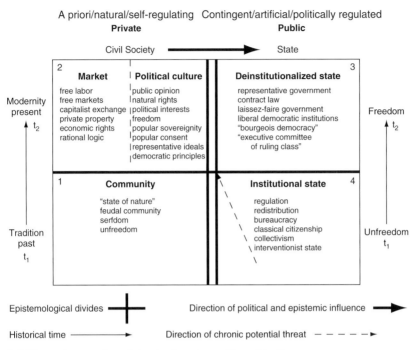

A priori/natural/self-regulating   Contingent/artificial/politically regulated
Private   **Public**

Civil Society ⟶ State

2 **Market**	**Political culture**	**Deinstitutionalized state** 3
free labor	public opinion	representative government
free markets	natural rights	contract law
capitalist exchange	political interests	laissez-faire government
private property	freedom	liberal democratic institutions
economic rights	popular sovereignty	"bourgeois democracy"
rational logic	popular consent	"executive committee
	representative ideals	of ruling class"
	democratic principles	

Modernity present ↑ t_2 Freedom ↑ t_2

1 **Community**	**Institutional state** 4
"state of nature"	regulation
feudal community	redistribution
serfdom	bureaucracy
unfreedom	classical citizenship
	collectivism
	interventionist state

Tradition past t_1 Unfreedom t_1

Epistemological divides ─┼─   Direction of political and epistemic influence ⟶

Historical time ⟶   Direction of chronic potential threat – – – – –►

7.5 The metanarrative of Anglo-American citizenship theory

"golden age" version of the state of nature in cell 1. Because it is natural and God-given, for Locke its time is the "abstract past" rather than the "concrete past," for the Scottish civil society thinkers it is the early "primitive" stage of eighteenth-century social theory, and for classical sociology it is the "traditional/feudal past" of modernization theory. The naturalism and God-given qualities of cell 1 give it narrative, moral and epistemological primacy as the original takeoff site for Locke's rights-bearing individuals to sign the first social contract to enter civil society. It is in cell 2 that the state of nature transforms into a naturalized civil society. Civil society is here an autonomous self-activated natural sphere based on noncoercive political culture and prepolitical market interchange. It was the naturalized commercial exchange of civil society that served as the seventeenth century's first social embodiment of a natural moral order based on freedom and natural rights. The private sphere of civil society thus assumed a privileged normative and epistemological status. Cell 3 represents the socially contracted political domain of representative government. As the locus of liberal democratic political institutions and the rule of law, this tamed government could be recalled and resisted when necessary by the social contractarians who created it. Although situated in the public zone, it is firmly tethered to the private sphere of the people in the epistemologically, historically, spatially, and morally anterior realm of civil society. Its publicness, however, means it is always on the brink of becoming coercive. This danger is kept in check by civil society's right to revoke its consent. Cell 4, by contrast, is the site of the permanently threatening administrative state – public, institutional, arbitrary, dangerous, nonnatural – but no less crucial to the metanarrative for all of that: its ever-threatening presence justifies a vigilant and fierce protecting of the private sphere of civil society.

By the eighteenth century, cell 1 bursts out of the abstract state of nature and becomes the real-time historical other of "primitive society." It is portrayed alternatively as either a full-blown "savage society" without private property (as in the Scottish "four-stages theory"), or as a generalized archaic feudal past from which the modern world of natural liberties (cell 2) evolves through the natural civilizing process. It is then an easy transition from this eighteenth-century version to the more starkly posed nineteenth-century binary oppositions between tradition and modernity, *Gemeinschaft* and *Gesellschaft*, feudalism and capitalism, preindustrial and industrial life, status and contract – each represented by cells 1 and 2 respectively. Note that when the past is specified as a traditional community organized through kinship, it is viewed as a natural, hence a necessary stage, of progression to modern freedom. This contrasts with cell 4's nonnatural arbitrary domain of public rule in the absolutist state whose threatening presence lurks in the background of Anglo-American citizenship theory. Finally there is cell 3 – the tamed and deinstitutionalized public arena of representative government where the rules that govern are those necessary to ensure the protection of civil society's essential natural freedom (e.g. criminal, contract, and civil law).

The privatization of citizenship

The privatization of civil society can be traced back to the metanarrative of Anglo-American citizenship theory. Driven by a fear of the tyranny of the state, Locke invented a private antipolitical sphere of social organization and market exchange separate from the state and strictly limited to the site of the private. His moral vision of a political culture within an autonomous civil society supplied liberal theory with a mechanism of social cohesion that could not be found in market exchange-based notions of community alone. It is within this self-regulating and prepolitical site of civil society that Locke locates the origins and practices of citizenship. In this paradoxical sense, what is "political," "public," even "civil" about citizenship in Anglo-American citizenship theory is that public opinion and individual rights are firmly rooted in the private sphere of civil society, despite their being contingently entrusted to a representative government accountable to the private interests from whence it came and from which its authority exclusively derives. The invention of a civil society inhabiting a space outside of and anterior to the public sphere of political institutions privatizes citizens and renders citizenship disembodied. It is devoid of the power and practices characteristic of public decision-making activities (Taylor 1990). The kind of citizenship born of liberal civil society may culminate in a government, but it is nonetheless decidedly antipolitical in the sense commonly associated with citizenship.

Constrained within this metanarrative network, the concept of civil society is frozen in its place – firmly on the nonpolitical, naturalistic, and antistatist side of the epistemological divide between public and private, nature/rationality and the arbitrary power attributed to the public sphere, as illustrated in figure 7.4. The demonization, the fear and loathing, of the public sphere and the state is what makes a nonpolitical private sphere a necessity. The concept of civil society endows the private sphere with the capacity to thrive independently of the state. The privatization of citizenship through civil society solidifies the bulwark against the constant threat of the public sphere. For Anglo-American citizenship theory, this inherently anti-institutional, antipublic form of authority becomes the normative guide for political organization, as democratic political structures are seen to emanate from the private anti-institutional political culture of civil society. From the needs and opinions of this marketized political culture – the social glue of civil society – putatively derive the ideas about politics that were the first expressions of liberal democratization. *Where do democratic ideals come from?* asked Locke. *From the private norms of society*, he answered. The "public-spirited man," Adam Smith echoed a century later, was he who respected the powers and opinions that operate in everyday life, not he who wanted to legislate and rearrange through institutional interventions (Wolin 1960: 299). It is much the same answer, and the same metanarrative structure, given some three hundred years later.

The metanarrative as gatekeeper

By grafting social naturalism to his story of civil society and the state, Locke hardened his story's temporal and spatial divides into a set of

impenetrable epistemological criteria for legitimate theories of democratization and freedom. The effect was paradigmatic, as the metanarrative
took on the role of an epistemological gatekeeper adjudicating how
evidence would rationally be distributed across the epistemological spectrum. If a historian's research into the premodern world, for example,
points to evidence of the existence of political rights in the wrong
temporal or spatial frame – the rights of citizens in the medieval country-
side, say – she learns very quickly that historiographical legitimacy is
only accorded when these same rights have been renamed and redefined
as "traditional," "premodern" rights, "prepolitical," "paternalistic"
forms of a "moral economy," or the "lagging" remnants of a feudal
order – thus stripped of any potentially destabilizing impact on the
metanarrative's story of political rights. The hallmark of an epistemological gatekeeper, like that of a paradigm, is the capacity to arbitrate the
boundaries of what counts as rational (hence admissible) investigation
into truth or falsehood. Not just the answers, but more important, the
criteria for what counts as reason and rationality are defined by the
gatekeeping parameters of the metanarrative – hence Anglo-American
citizenship theory's gatekeeping power over the distribution of evidence
and the adjudication of what counts as knowledge and truth. Once this
kind of closure has been established, evidential competition always runs
the risk of being neutralized by allegations of irrelevance or illogic. No
alternative empirical challenge to the privatization of citizenship or the
antistatism of Anglo-American citizenship theory has a chance of success
until the gatekeeping power of the dominant metanarrative is challenged
and transgressed.

The contemporary legacy

The epistemological divides and the gatekeeping demarcations depicted
in figure 7.5 represent the original seventeenth-century metanarrative of
Anglo-American citizenship theory. The institutionalized public sphere
is depicted as the site of external coercion, domination, and constraint,
backed up with physical compulsion and arbitrary personal dependencies. It is thus the domain of unfreedom. Private prepolitical/civil society
is the realm of freedom because it is autonomous from the state, impersonal, self-activating through commercial exchange (e.g. property contracts,
division of labor, markets), and natural. It is a robust entity whose
normative roots and coherence are in the idealized state of nature, the
harmony of its political culture, and the civility of the market. In lieu of
government authority in the work of maintaining social cohesion, the norms

and pressures of public opinion provide the means for both order and freedom in civil society. Combined, these characteristics constitute the essential infrastructure of Anglo-American citizenship theory with its binary opposition between the spontaneous free forces of prepolitical/civil society and the normative order of civil society on the one side and the tamed representative state on the other – and, in the background, always the potentially coercive, dominating, and enforced dependencies of public administrative power. It is a metanarrative born out of the ongoing "itch" to find the solution to the fear and loathing of the public sphere in a spatial domain of civil society where liberties and rights of representation could be organizationally grounded outside the powers of the coercive state (Baker 1990: 6). To ensure that these rights were themselves foundational and not granted at the behest of the crown or positive statutory laws, Locke made them natural rights, hence God-given and part of the prepolitical natural community. By this means he naturalized the organizational autonomy of society.

From this legacy, we have inherited the ineluctable connection between freedom, market exchange, and individual rights on the one side, in opposition to potential tyranny in the institutional domain of the state on the other. Since the seventeenth century, Anglo-American citizenship theory has proclaimed the normative guide for political organization to be the anti-institutional privatized market-based norms of civil society. Only by the criteria of the commercial culture of civil society can democratic political structures be judged as legitimate. Locke theorized and empowered a domesticated privately generated version of the law – rather than the command of the state – as the "constant and lasting force": "And so, whoever has the legislative or supreme power of any commonwealth, is bound to govern by established standing laws, promulgated and known to the people, and not by extemporary decrees" (Locke 1967: 191, 182). Habermas thus argues that ever since Locke the normative discourse of public opinion and political culture (Habermas's public sphere) has been articulated through the noninstitutionalized conception of the law as a cohesive force deriving from social norms. Law becomes a symbol not of the state but of society, and celebrated as the legitimate institutionalization of public opinion. But this was less an understanding of the law in the institutional form in which it had developed from medieval rule of law (e.g. administrative courts, and doctrinal principles of justice such as the "just wage") and more a vision of the law as embodying general and abstract norms (Habermas 1989: 53). Habermas brilliantly captures the processes of the law's conceptual deinstitutionalization as it proceeds from Hobbes through Locke and

Montesquieu: "In the 'law' the quintessence of general, abstract, and permanent norms, inheres a rationality in which what is right converges with what is just; *the exercise of power is to be demoted to a mere executor of such norms*" (Habermas 1989: 53).

To a striking degree ensuing social science and liberal political theory fit the parameters of the original seventeenth-century metanarrative. In the eighteenth century, for example, although Adam Smith maintained that political economy was a branch of statesmanship to be nurtured for the public good, he nonetheless insisted on the market as a "natural system of liberty" with a lawlike essence, and hence the inherent danger in any institutional "meddlings" from the public sphere (Winch 1978). From the physiocrats' notion that public opinion reflected the "*ordre naturel*" emanating from civil society (Calhoun 1992), to Marx's utopian postulate of freedom as emancipation from both the exploitation of capitalist labor and the dominion of institutional politics, we can observe a continuity in the idea that the rationality, naturalism, and civility of private exchange in civil society give rise to democratic beliefs, values, and even practices of public discourse. For Locke, Smith, and Marx, the freedoms of the liberal state embodied private interests alone. And although Marx saw these as bourgeois freedoms supporting the exploitation of labor, this contrary judgment did not in any way affect his deinstitutionalized view of the state. In perfect harmony with Anglo-American citizenship's metanarrative, Marx's source of freedom was also found in civil society – only in his case there is a normative reversal. Civil society is the site of capitalist exploitation and its "freedoms" are illusions of the bourgeois democratic state.

I cannot trace in this chapter the entire historical trajectory of Anglo-American citizenship theory and its associated arguments in liberal theory. Suffice it here to show that the Lockean invention set a template and that recognizing this template makes it possible to find iterations in later arguments. In so doing, I have tried to show how a historical sociology of concept formation differs from the usual approach to intellectual history. Intellectual historians tend to operate on the assumption that ideas are passed along in chains from one individual thinker to another, so the proof of continuity is to demonstrate these explicit links of influence between individuals or schools of thought. But influence does not necessarily work in quite that way. While finding direct connections does not hurt, they generally are not one-to-one but rather mediated by larger currents of thought. To demonstrate influence, a historical sociology of concept formation must find a basic similarity between the organizing assumptions and conceptual imagery of the modern approaches and those of earlier ones. It must show, for example, how the Anglo-American citizenship metanarrative's epistemological divides and narrative presuppositions remain the adjudicators of valid empirical argument in modern social science. Recursive use of the metanarrative, from this perspective, occurs not necessarily through chains of influence but through a constrained process of appropriation and evaluation from a limited number of available choices to the "exclusion of competing aspects that might turn choice in another direction" (DiMaggio and Powell 1991: 19). Metanarratives overdetermine data by working through the quasi-automatic self-activation of naturalized boundaries, classifications, distinctions, and assumptions. For the task at hand, then, reconstructing the inner logic of the arguments and demonstrating a similarity in that underlying logic is more important than pointing to the possible direct influence of one argument on another.

The paradoxical puzzle I set forth at the outset was how and why the newly rejuvenated civil society concept – recalled to normative and sociological service to represent a participatory third sphere between state and market – has again been privatized in political argument. The social revolutions it was called to explain now seem reduced to a cluster of prepolitical, antipublic, and naturalized attributes of the market, mechanisms of global commerce, and a political culture of antistatism. This now prevailing antistatist use of civil society fails to provide an adequate theorization of a social sphere of citizenship – one characterized by reciprocity, solidarities, and a robust public discourse and political culture of rights. Instead, citizenship has been reduced to only those rights hailed as derived from the morally superior natural private sphere of the market. But not only is this privatization of citizenship deeply counterintuitive; it is also deeply paradoxical. The concept of civil society can no longer explain the very historical events that precipitated its revival.

One purpose of this chapter has been to demonstrate how a historical epistemology and a historical sociology of concept formation can help to explain this paradox. The method suggests that the privatization of citizenship concepts can best be understood by making the primary subject of analysis not the isolated concept of civil society but the historically constituted larger knowledge culture of Anglo-American citizenship theory in which it is embedded. For a historical sociology of concept formation, concepts are best understood as words in their historical sites, and the sites most useful for making sense of knowledge are knowledge cultures. By deconstructing its making, narration, and naturalizing strategies we can see how the knowledge culture qua metanarrative of Anglo-American citizenship theory mediates knowledge through a narrative

cultural structure with its own gatekeeping criteria and normative pre-
scriptions, which because they have been naturalized are not answerable
to disconfirming evidence. The metanarrative's epistemological authority is established by grafting its temporal and spatial logics to the dichotomies of social naturalism.

For some three hundred years, what is natural and what is marketized
have been inexorably conjoined and epistemically privileged. Linking the
epistemology of social naturalism to the historicity of its production
enables us to question the "primordial" distinctions between nature and
culture. It also demonstrates the cultural roots of epistemic naturalism.
And if social naturalism's very standards of validity are culturally and
historically constructed, then so too are the hierarchies between natural
and constructed, civil society and the public sphere, private and public.
Perhaps, then, the greatest payoff of exploring the privatization of citizenship through a historical sociology of concept formation is the challenge it poses to the idea that epistemological boundaries and political
hierarchies are given in the nature of things. No political, social, conceptual, or epistemological boundary comes without a history.

References

Åberg, M. and Mikael Sandberg. 2003. *Social Capital and Democratisation: Roots of Trust in Post-Communist Poland and Ukraine.* Burlington, VT: Ashgate.

Adler, P. and S. Kwon. 1999. *Social Capital: The Good, the Bad and the Ugly.* World Bank Social Capital Library, Papers in Progress.

Agamben, Giorgio. 1998. *Homo Sacer: Sovereign Power and Bare Life.* Stanford, CA: Stanford University Press.

Aguilhon, Maurice. 1981. *Marianne into Battle: Republican Imagery and Symbolism in France. 1789–1880*, trans. Janet Lloyd. Cambridge: Cambridge University Press.

Akerlof, G. 1984. *An Economic Theorist's Book of Tales.* Cambridge: Cambridge University Press.

— 1990. "George A. Akerlof." In *Sociology and Economics: Redefining Their Boundaries: Conversations with Economists and Sociologists*, ed. Richard Swedberg: 61–77. Princeton, NJ: Princeton University Press.

Alexander, Jeffrey C. 1982a. *Positivism, Presuppositions, and Current Controversies.* Vol. I of *Theoretical Logic in Sociology.* Berkeley: University of California Press.

— 1982b. *The Antinomies of Classical Thought: Marx and Durkheim.* Vol. II of *Theoretical Logic in Sociology.* Berkeley: University of California Press.

— 1983a. *The Classical Attempt at Theoretical Synthesis: Max Weber.* Vol. III of *Theoretical Logic in Sociology.* Berkeley and Los Angeles: University of California Press.

— 1983b. *The Modern Reconstruction of Classical Thought: Talcott Parsons.* Vol. IV of *Theoretical Logic in Sociology.* Berkeley and Los Angeles: University of California Press.

1988. *Durkheimian Sociology: Cultural Studies*. New York: Cambridge University Press.

1989a. "Durkheimian Sociology and Cultural Studies Today." In *Structure and Meaning: Relinking Classical Sociology*, ed. Jeffrey Alexander: 15–73. New York: Columbia University Press.

1989b. "Habermas and Critical Theory: Beyond the Marxian Dilemma?" In *Structure and Meaning: Relinking Classical Sociology*, ed. Jeffrey Alexander: 217–19. New York: Columbia University Press.

1990. "Analytic Debates: On Understanding the Relative Autonomy of Culture." In *Culture and Society: Contemporary Debates*, ed. Jeffrey C. Alexander and Steven Seidman: 1–27. New York: Cambridge University Press.

1991. "Bringing Democracy Back In: Universalistic Solidarity and the Civil Sphere." In *Intellectuals and Politics: Social Theory in a Changing World*, ed. C. Lemert: 157–76. Newbury Park, CA: Sage.

1992a. "Citizen and Enemy as Symbolic Classification: On the Polarizing Discourse of Civil Society." In *Cultivating Differences: Symbolic Boundaries and the Making of Inequality*, ed. Michele Lamont and Marcel Fournier: 289–308. Chicago: University of Chicago Press.

1992b. "The Promise of a Cultural Sociology: Technological Discourse and the Sacred and Profane Information Machine." In *Theory of Culture*, ed. Richard Munch and Neil J. Smelser: 293–323. Berkeley: University of California Press.

1992c. "Some Remarks on 'Agency' in Recent Sociological Theory." *Perspectives: The Theory Section Newsletter of the American Sociological Association* 15: 1.

1993. "The Return to Civil Society." *Contemporary Sociology* 22 (6): 797–803.

1994. "Modern, Anti, Post, and Neo: How Intellectuals Have Coded, Narrated, and Explained the New World of our Time." *New Left Review* 210: 63–104.

2006. *The Civil Sphere*. Oxford: Oxford University Press.

Alexander, Jeffrey C. and Steven Seidman, eds. 1990. *Culture and Society: Contemporary Debates*. New York: Cambridge University Press.

Alexander, Jeffrey C. and Philip Smith. 1993. "The Discourse of American Civil Society: A New Proposal for Cultural Studies." *Theory and Society* 22: 151–207.

Alford, Robert R. and Roger Friedland. 1985. *Powers of Theory: Capitalism, the State, and Democracy*. Cambridge: Cambridge University Press.

Almond, Gabriel. 1980. "The Intellectual History of the Civic Culture Concept." In *The Civic Culture Revisited*, ed. Gabriel Almond: 1–37. Boston, MA: Little, Brown.

Almond, Gabriel and G. Bingham Powell. 1966. *Comparative Politics: A Developmental Approach*. Boston, MA: Little, Brown.

Almond, Gabriel and Sidney Verba. 1963. *The Civic Culture: Political Attitudes and Democracy in Five Nations*. Princeton, NJ: Princeton University Press.

American Prospect. 2007. "Special Report: Ending Poverty in America," *American Prospect* 18 (5).

Anderson, Carol. 2003. *Eyes Off the Prize: The United Nations and the African American Struggle for Human Rights, 1944–1955*. Cambridge: Cambridge University Press.

Anderson, Perry. 1964. "Origins of the Present Crisis." *New Left Review* 23: 26–54.

1974. *Lineages of the Absolute State*. London: New Left Books.

Arato, Andrew. 1981. "Civil Society Against the State: Poland 1980–81." *Telos* 47: 24.

1993. "Interpreting 1989." *Social Research* 60: 609–46.

2000. *Civil Society, Constitution, and Legitimacy*. Lanham, MD: Rowman and Littlefield.

Archer, Margaret S. 1988. *Culture and Agency: The Place of Culture in Social Theory*. Cambridge: Cambridge University Press.

Archibugi, D. and D. Held. 1995. *Cosmopolitan Democracy: An Agenda for a New World Order*. Cambridge, MA: Polity Press.

1998. *Re-imagining Political Community: Studies in Cosmopolitan Democracy*. Cambridge: Polity Press.

Arendt, Hannah. 1976. *Eichmann in Jerusalem: A Report on the Banality of Evil*. New York: Penguin.

[1951] 1979. *The Origins of Totalitarianism*. New York: Harcourt Brace.

[1958] 1998. *The Human Condition*. Chicago: University of Chicago Press.

Aronowitz, Stanley. 1992. *The Politics of Identity: Class, Culture, Social Movements*. New York: Routledge.

Arrow, K. 2000. "Observations on Social Capital". In *Social Capital: A Multifaceted Perspective*, ed. P. Dasgupta and I. Serageldin. Washington, DC: The World Bank.

Atkinson, Tony. 2002. "How Basic Income Is Moving up the Policy Agenda: News from the Future." Unpublished paper, presented at Ninth Congress of the Basic Income European Network (BIEN), Geneva.

Bain, R. 1933. "Scientist as Citizen." *Social Forces* 11 (3): 412–15.

Baker, Keith. 1982. "On the Problem of the Ideological Origins of the French Revolution." In *Modern European Intellectual History: Reappraisals and New Perspectives*, ed. Dominick LaCapra and Steven L. Kaplan: 197–219. Ithaca, NY: Cornell University Press.

1990. *Inventing the French Revolution: Essays on French Political Culture in the Eighteenth Century*. Cambridge: Cambridge University Press.

1992. "Defining the Public Sphere in Eighteenth-Century France: Variations on a Theme by Habermas." In *Habermas and the Public Sphere*, ed. Craig Calhoun. Cambridge, MA: MIT Press.

Balibar, Étienne. 1994. *Masses, Classes, Ideas: Studies on Politics and Philosophy before and after Marx*. New York: Routledge.

2002. *Politics and the Other Scene*. London: Verso.

2004a. "Is a Philosophy of Human Civic Rights Possible? New Reflections on Equaliberty." *South Atlantic Quarterly* 103 (2/3): 311–22.

2004b. *We, the People of Europe?: Reflections on Transnational Citizenship*. Princeton, NJ: Princeton University Press.

Banfield, Edward. 1965. *The Moral Basis of a Backward Society*. Glencoe, IL: Free Press.

Banting, Keith and Will Kymlicka, eds. 2006. *Multiculturalism and the Welfare State: Recognition and Redistribution in Contemporary Democracies*. New York: Oxford University Press.

Barry, B. M. 1970. *Sociologists, Economists and Democracy*. London: Collier Macmillan.

Barbalet, J. M. 1988. *Citizenship – Rights, Struggle, and Class Inequality*. Minneapolis: University of Minnesota Press.

Barber, Benjamin. 1996. "An American Civic Forum: Civil Society between Market Individuals and the Political Community." *Social Philosophy and Policy* 13: 269–83.

Baron, S., J. Field, and T. Schuller. 2000. *Social Capital: Critical Perspectives*. New York: Oxford University Press.

Barthes, Roland. 1974. "Introduction to the Structural Analysis of Narratives," trans. by Richard Miller. Occasional Paper, Centre for Contemporary Cultural Studies, University of Birmingham. New York: Hill and Wang.

Bauböck, R. 1991. *Immigration and the Boundaries of Citizenship*. Vienna: Institut für Höhere Studien.

1994. *From Aliens to Citizens: Redefining the Status of Immigrants in Europe*. Brookfield, VT: Avebury.

Bauböck, R. and J. F. Rundell, eds. 1998. *Blurred Boundaries: Migration, Ethnicity, Citizenship*. Aldershot: Ashgate.

Becker, G. S. 1975. "Human Capital: A Theoretical and Empirical Analysis, With Special Reference to Education." New York: National Bureau of Economic Research, Columbia University Press.

1976. *The Economic Approach to Human Behavior*. Chicago: University of Chicago Press.

1986. *An Economic Analysis of the Family*. Dublin: Argus.

1990. "Gary S. Becker," In *Sociology and Economics: Redefining their Boundaries: Conversations with Economists and Sociologists*, ed. Richard Swedberg: 27–46. Princeton: Princeton University Press.

1993. *Human Capital: A Theoretical and Empirical Analysis, with Special Reference to Education*, 3rd edn. Chicago: University of Chicago Press.

1996. *Accounting for Tastes*. Cambridge, MA: Harvard University Press.

Becker, G. S. and K. M. Murphy. 2000. *Social Economics: Market Behavior in a Social Environment*. Cambridge: Belknap Press.

Becker, G. S. and G. Nashat. 1997. *The Economics of Life: From Baseball to Affirmative Action to Immigration, How Real-World Issues Affect our Everyday Life*. New York: McGraw-Hill.

Beer, Samuel. 1962. *Patterns of Government: The Major Political Systems of Europe*, 2nd edn. New York: Random House.

Beiner, R. 1995. *Theorizing Citizenship*. Albany: State University of New York Press.

Bell, Daniel. 1981. "Models and Reality in Economic Discourse." In *The Crisis in Economic Theory*, ed. D. Bell and I. Kristol: 4–60. New York: Basic Books.

1989. "American Exceptionalism Revisited: The Role of Civil Society." *The Public Interest* 95: 38–56.

Bellah, Robert N., Richard Madsen, William M. Sullivan, Ann Swidler, and Steven M. Tipton. 1985. *Habits of the Heart: Individualism and Commitment in American Life*. New York: Harper and Row.

Bellamy, R. and A. Warleigh. 2001. *Citizenship and Governance in the European Union*. New York: Continuum.

Bendix, Reinhard. [1964] 1976. *Nation-Building and Citizenship*. Berkeley: University of California Press.

Bendix, Reinhard and Seymour Martin Lipset. 1957. "Political Sociology." *Current Sociology* 6: 79–99.

Benhabib, Seyla. 1995. *Feminist Contentions: A Philosophical Exchange*. New York: Routledge.

1996. *Democracy and Difference: Contesting the Boundaries of the Political*. Princeton, NJ: Princeton University Press.

2001. *Transformations of Citizenship: Dilemmas of the Nation State in the Era of Globalization: Two Lectures*. Assen: Koninklijke Van Gorcum.

2002. *The Claims of Culture: Equality and Diversity in the Global Era.* Princeton, NJ: Princeton University Press.

2004. *The Rights of Others: Aliens, Residents, and Citizens.* Cambridge: Cambridge University Press.

2007a. "Twilight of Sovereignty or the Emergence of Cosmopolitan Norms? Rethinking Citizenship in Volatile Times." *Citizenship Studies* 11(1): 19–36.

2007b. *Another Cosmopolitanism*, Tanner Lecture Series, with Jeremy Waldron, Bonnie Honig, and Will Kymlicka, ed. Robert Post. New York: Oxford University Press.

Benhabib, Seyla, Ian Shapiro and Danilo Petranovic. 2007. *Identities, Affiliations, and Allegiances.* Cambridge: Cambridge University Press.

Berezin, Mabel. 2005. "Emotions and the Economy." In N. J. Smelser and R. Swedberg, eds., *Handbook of Economic Sociology*: 109–27. New York: Russell Sage Foundation and Princeton University Press.

Berger, Peter L. and Richard John Neuhaus. 1996. *To Empower People: From State to Civil Society*, 2nd edn, ed. Michael Novak. Washington, DC: AEI Press.

Bernstein, Jared. 2007. "Is Education the Cure for Poverty?" *American Prospect*, April 22.

Black, C. E. 1966. *The Dynamics of Modernization.* New York: Harper and Row.

Blair, T. 1996. *New Britain: My Vision of a Young Country.* London: Fourth Estate.

1998. *The Third Way: New Politics for a New Century.* London: Fabian Society.

Block, Fred. 1990. *Post-Industrial Possibilities: A Critique of Economic Discourse.* Berkeley: University of California Press.

1997. *The Vampire State: And Other Myths and Fallacies about the US Economy.* New York: New Press.

2003. "Karl Polanyi and the Writing of *The Great Transformation.*" *Theory and Society* 32: 275–306.

2006. "A Moral Economy." *The Nation*, available at: www.thenation. com/doc/20060320/block (accessed March 11, 2007).

Block, Fred and Margaret R. Somers. 1984. "Beyond the Economistic Fallacy: The Holistic Social Science of Karl Polanyi." In *Vision and Method in Historical Sociology*, ed. Theda Skocpol: 47–84. Cambridge: Cambridge University Press.

Block, Fred and Margaret Somers. 2003. "In the Shadow of Speenhamland: Social Policy and the Old Poor Law." *Politics and Society* 31(2): 283–23.

Block, Fred, Anna C. Koreweg, Kerry Woodward, Zach Schiller and Imrul Mazid. 2006. "The Compassion Gap in American Poverty Policy." *Contexts* 5 (2): 14–20.

Bobbio, Norbert. 1992. *Democracy and Dictatorship: The Nature and Limits of State Power*, trans. Peter Kennealy. Minneapolis: University of Minnesota Press.

1996. *The Age of Rights*. Cambridge: Polity Press.

Body-Gendrot, S. and M. Gittell. 2003. *Social Capital and Social Citizenship*. Lanham, MD: Lexington Books.

Bollen, Kenneth and Robert Jackman. 1985. "Economic and Non-economic Determinants of Political Democracy in the 1960s." In *Research in Political Sociology*, vol. I: 27–48. Greenwich, CT: JAI Press.

Bonnell, Victoria and Lynn Hunt, eds. 1999. *Beyond the Cultural Turn*. Berkeley, CA: University of California Press.

Bosniak, Linda. 2006. *The Citizen and the Alien: Dilemmas of Contemporary Membership*. Princeton, NJ: Princeton University Press.

Bourdieu, Pierre. 1977. *Outline of a Theory of Practice*, trans. Richard Nice. Cambridge: Cambridge University Press.

[1979] 1984. *Distinction*, trans. Richard Nice. Cambridge, MA: Harvard University Press.

1986. "The Forms of Capital." In *Handbook of Theory and Research for the Sociology of Education*, ed. J. G. Richardson: 241–60. New York: Greenwood Press.

1998. *Acts of Resistance: Against the New Myths of our Time*. Cambridge: Polity Press.

Bourdieu, Pierre and Loïc J. D. Wacquant. 1992. *An Invitation to Reflexive Sociology*. Chicago: University of Chicago Press.

Bowles, Samuel. 1999. "'Social Capital' and Community Governance." *Focus* 20 (3): 6–10.

Bowles, Samuel and Herb Gintis. 2002. "Social Capital and Community Governance." *Economic Journal* 112 (November): F418.

Branford, V. V. 1906. "Science and Citizenship." *American Journal of Sociology* 11 (6): 721–62.

Brasch, Walter M. 2006. *'Unacceptable' The Federal Response to Hurricane Katrina*. Charleston, SC: BookSurge.

Brezina, Timothy. 2008. "What Went Wrong in New Orleans? An Examination of the Welfare Dependency Explanation." *Social Problems* 55 (1): 23–42.

Brinkley, Douglas. 2006. *The Great Deluge: Hurricane Katrina, New Orleans, and the Mississippi Gulf Coast*. New York: Morrow.

Brinkley, Douglas and Ronald Reagan. 2005. *The Boys of Pointe du Hoc: Ronald Reagan, D-Day and the US Army 2nd Ranger Battalion*. New York: W. Morrow.

Brodie, Mollyann, Erin Weltzien, Drew Altman, Robert J. Blendon, and John Benson. 2006. "Experiences of Hurricane Katrina Evacuees in Houston Shelters: Implications for Future Planning." *American Journal of Public Health* 96 (8): 1402–8.

Brown, Michael K. 1999. *Race, Money, and the American Welfare State*. Ithaca, NY: Cornell University Press.

Brubaker, Rogers. 1985. "Rethinking Classical Theory: The Sociological Vision of Pierre Bourdieu." *Theory and Society* 14: 74–75.

1992. *Citizenship and Nationhood in France and Germany*. Cambridge, MA: Harvard University Press.

Brunsma, David L., David Overfelt and J. S. Picou, eds. 2007. *The Sociology of Katrina: Perspectives on a Modern Catastrophe*. New York: Rowman and Littlefield.

Brysk, Alison. 2004. *Human Rights and Private Wrongs: Constructing Global Civil Society*. Oxford: Routledge.

Brysk, Alison and Gershon Shafir. 2004. *People Out of Place: Globalization, Human Rights, and the Citizenship Gap*. New York: Routledge.

Bulmer, M. and A. M. Rees. 1996. *Citizenship Today: The Contemporary Relevance of T. H. Marshall*. London: UCL Press.

Buxton, William. 1985. *Talcott Parsons and the Capitalist Nation-State*. Toronto: University of Toronto Press.

Calhoun, Craig. 1980. "Community: Toward a Variable Conceptualization of Comparative Research." *Social History* 5 (1): 10–29.

1991a. "Morality, Identity, and Historical Explanation: Charles Taylor on the Sources of the Self." *Sociological Theory* 9 (2): 232–63.

1991b. "The Problem of Identity in Collective Action." In *Macro-Micro Linkages in Sociology*, ed. Joan Huber. Beverly Hills, CA: Sage.

ed. 1992. *Habermas and the Public Sphere*. Cambridge, MA: MIT Press.

1993. "Civil Society and the Public Sphere." *Public Culture* 5(2): 267–80.

1994. "Social Theory and the Politics of Identity." In *Social Theory and the Politics of Identity*, ed. Craig Calhoun: 9–36. London: Basil Blackwell.

Camic, Charles. 1986. "The Matter of Habit." *American Journal of Sociology* 91 (5): 1039–87.

Canguilhem, Georges. [1966] 1978. *On the Normal and the Pathological*, trans. Carolyn R. Fawcett. Dordrecht: Reidel.

1988. *Ideology and Rationality in the History of the Life Sciences*, trans. Arthur Goldhammer. Cambridge, MA: MIT Press.

Carr, Edward. [1961] 1965. *What Is History?* New York: Vintage Press.

Carrithers, Michael, Steven Collins, and Steven Lukes, eds. 1985. *The Category of the Person: Anthropology, Philosophy, History*. Cambridge: Cambridge University Press.

Cass, Ronald. 2003. *The Rule of Law in America*. Baltimore, MD: Johns Hopkins University Press.

Chambers, Simone and Will Kymlicka. 2002. *Alternative Conceptions of Civil Society*. Princeton, NJ: Princeton University Press.

Chartier, Roger. 1982. "Intellectual History or Sociocultural History? The French Trajectories." In *Modern European Intellectual History*, ed. Dominick LaCapra and Steven L. Kaplan: 13–46. Ithaca NY: Cornell University Press.

1988. *Cultural History: Between Practices and Representations*, trans. Lydia G. Cochrane. Ithaca NY: Cornell University Press.

1991. *The Cultural Origins of the French Revolution*, trans. Lydia G. Cochrane. Durham, NC: Duke University Press.

Chatterjee, Partha. 1990. "A Response to Taylor's Mode of Civil Society." *Public Culture* 3 (1): 95–132.

Ciepley, D. 2000. "Why the State Was Dropped in the First Place: A Prequel to Skocpol's 'Bringing the State Back In.'" *Critical Review* 14 (2–3): 157–214.

Citizen's Income Trust. 2005. *Citizen's Income Newsletter* 1: 1–12.

Cohen, Jean L. 1982. *Class and Civil Society: The Limits of Marxian Critical Theory*. Amherst: University of Massachusetts Press.

1985. "Strategy or Identity: New Theoretical Paradigms and Contemporary Social Movements." *Social Research* 52 (4): 663–716.

1996. "Rights, Citizenship, and the Modern Form of the Social: Dilemmas of Arendtian Republicanism." *Constellations* 3 (2): 164–89.

1999. "American Civil Society Talk." In *Society, Democracy, and Civic Renewal*, ed. Robert K. Fullinwider. Lanham, MD: Rowman and Littlefield.

Cohen, Jean and Andrew Arato. 1992. *Civil Society and Political Theory*. Cambridge, MA: MIT Press.

Cohen, Joshua and Joel Rogers. 1995. *Associations and Democracy*. London: Verso.

Coleman, J. S. 1966. *Report on Equality of Educational Opportunity*. Washington, DC: U.S. Government Printing Office.

[1988] 2000. "Social Capital in the Creation of Human Capital." In *Knowledge and Social Capital: Foundations and Applications*, ed. E. L. Lesser: 17–42. Woburn, MA: Butterworth-Heinemann.

Collini, Stefan, Donald Winch, and John Burrow. 1983. *That Noble Science of Politics: A Study in Nineteenth-Century Intellectual History*. Cambridge: Cambridge University Press.

Collins, Randall. 1979. *The Credential Society: An Historical Sociology of Education and Stratification*. New York: Academic Press.

    1981. "Love and Property." In *Sociological Insight: An Introduction to Non-Obvious Sociology*, ed. Randall Collins: 119–54. New York: Oxford University Press.

    1985. *Three Sociological Traditions*. New York: Oxford University Press.

    1988. "The Durkheimian Tradition in Conflict Sociology." In *Durkheimian Sociology: Cultural Studies*, ed. Jeffrey C. Alexander: 107–28. New York: Cambridge University Press.

    1997. *Four Sociological Traditions*. New York: Oxford University Press.

Commission of the European Communities. 1997. *Citizenship of the Union: Second Report from the Commission*. Luxembourg: Office for Official Publications of the EC.

Converse, Philip E. 1964. "The Nature of Belief Systems in Mass Publics." In *Ideology and Discontent*, ed. David E. Apter: 206–61. New York: Free Press.

Coulter, Anne. 2003. *Treason: Liberal Treachery from the Cold War to the War of Terrorism*. New York: Crown Forum.

Cowen, Deborah. 2008. *Military Workfare: The Soldier and Social Citizenship in Canada*. Toronto: University of Toronto Press.

Crouch, C. 2001. "Citizenship and Markets in Recent British Education Policy." In *Citizenship, Markets and the State*, ed. K. Eder, C. Crouch, and D. Tambini: 111–33. London: Oxford University Press.

Crozier, Michel, Samuel P. Huntington, and Joji Watanuki. 1975. *The Crisis of Democracy: Report on the Governability of Democracies to the Trilateral Commission*. New York: New York University Press.

Dahl, Robert A. 1966. *Political Oppositions in Western Democracies*. New Haven, CT: Yale University Press.

    2000. *On Democracy*. New Haven, CT: Yale University Press.

Dahrendorf, Ralf. 1959. *Class and Class Conflict in Industrial Society*. London: Routledge and Kegan Paul.

    1996. "Citizenship and Social Class." In *Citizenship Today: The Contemporary Relevance of T. H. Marshall*, ed. M. Bulmer and A. M. Rees: 25–48. London: UCL Press.

Dasgupta, P. and I. Serageldin, eds. 1999. *Social Capital: A Multifaceted Perspective.* Washington, DC: World Bank.

Davis, Natalie Zemon. 1975. *Society and Culture in Early Modern France.* Stanford, CA: Stanford University Press.

Davidson, Arnold I. 2001. *The Emergence of Sexuality: Historical Epistemology and the Formation of Concepts.* Cambridge, MA: Harvard University Press.

Dean, H. 2004. "Popular Discourse and the Ethical Deficiency of 'Third Way' Conceptions of Citizenship." *Citizenship Studies* 8 (1): 65–82.

Dean, Mitchell. 1994. *Critical and Effective Histories: Foucault's Methods and Historical Sociology.* London: Routledge.

Demuth, Christopher and William Kristol, eds. 1995. *The Neoconservative Imagination: Essays in Honor of Irving Kristol.* Washington, DC: AEI Press.

Dershowitz, Alan M. 2004. *America on Trial: Inside the Legal Battles that Transformed our Nation.* New York: Warner Books.

Deutsch, Karl W. and William F. Foltz, eds. 1963. *Nation Building.* New York: Atherton Press.

DiMaggio, Paul. 1990. "Cultural Aspects of Economic Action." In *Beyond the Marketplace: Rethinking Economy and Society*, ed. Roger Friedland and A. F. Robertson: 113–31. Chicago: Aldine.

1992. "Cultural Boundaries and Structural Change: The Extension of the High Culture Model to Theater, Opera and the Dance, 1900–1940." In *Cultivating Differences: Symbolic Boundaries and the Making of Inequality*, ed. Michele Lamont and Marcel Fournier: 21–57. Chicago: University of Chicago Press.

DiMaggio, Paul J. and Walter W. Powell. 1991. "Introduction" in *The New Institutionalism in Organization Analysis*, ed. Walter W. Powell and Paul J. DiMaggio: 1–38. Chicago: University of Chicago Press.

Dobbin, Frank. 2004. *The New Economic Sociology.* Princeton, NJ: Princeton University Press.

Douglas, Mary. 1966. *Purity and Danger: An Analysis of the Concepts of Pollution and Taboo.* London: Penguin.

[1970] 1982. *Natural Symbols: Explorations in Cosmology.* New York: Pantheon.

Duncan, G. and S. Lukes. 1963. "The New Democracy." *Political Studies* 11: 156–77.

Durkheim, Émile. 1938. *The Rules of the Sociological Method.* Chicago: University of Chicago Press.

[1893] 1984. *Division of Labor in Society*. New York: Free Press.

[1912] 1995. *The Elementary Forms of Religious Life*, trans. Karen E. Fields. New York: Free Press

Durkheim, Emile and Marcel Mauss. [1903] 1963. *Primitive Classification*, trans. and ed. Rodney Needham. Chicago: Chicago University Press.

Durlauf, S. N. 2002. "On the Empirics of Social Capital." *Economic Journal* 112 (483): 459–79.

Dyson, Michael E. 2006. *Come Hell or High Water: Hurricane Katrina and the Color of Disaster*. New York: Basic Civitas.

Eckstein, Harry. 1964. *Internal War*. New York: Free Press.

1988. "A Cultural Theory of Political Change." *American Political Science Review* 82: 789–804.

1992. *Regarding Politics: Essays on Political Theory, Stability and Change*. Berkeley: University of California Press.

Economist. 1993. "Civic Lessons: Pro Bono Publico." February 6: 94.

2007. "A Widening Gap." Available at: www.economist.com/displays tory.cfm?story_id = 9358807 (accessed June 22, 2007).

Eder, K. and B. Giesen. 2001. *European Citizenship: Between National Legacies and Postnational Projects*. Oxford: Oxford University Press.

Eder, K., C. Crouch, and D. Tambini, eds. 2001. *Citizenship, Markets and the State*. Oxford: Oxford University Press.

Edwards, Bob, and Michael W. Foley. 1997. "Escape from Politics? Social Theory and the Social Capital Debate." *American Behavioral Scientist* 40: 550–61.

1998. "Civil Society and Social Capital Beyond Putnam." *American Behavioral Scientist* 42: 124–39.

Edwards, Bob, M.W. Foley, and M. Diani. eds. 2001. *Beyond Tocqueville: Civil Society and the Social Capital Debate in Comparative Perspective*. Hanover, NH: University Press of New England.

Ehrenberg, John. 1999. *Civil Society: The Critical History of an Idea*. New York: New York University Press.

Eldridge, Seba. 1928. "Community Organization and Citizenship." *Social Forces* 7 (1): 132–40.

Eley, Geoff. 1992. "Nations, Publics, and Political Cultures: Placing Habermas in the Nineteenth Century." In *Habermas and the Public Sphere*, ed. Craig Calhoun: 289–339. Cambridge, MA: MIT Press.

2002. *Forging Democracy: The History of the Left in Europe, 1850–2000*. Oxford: Oxford University Press.

Emirbayer, Mustafa and Jeff Goodwin. 1994. "Network Analysis. Culture, and the Problem of Agency." *American Journal of Sociology* 99 (6): 1411–54.

Epstein, Richard. 2005. *Takings: Private Property and the Power of Eminent Domain*. Cambridge, MA: Harvard University Press.

Esping-Anderson, Gosta. 1985. *Politics against Markets*. Princeton, NJ: Princeton University Press.

1990. *The Three Worlds of Welfare Capitalism*. Princeton, NJ: Princeton University Press.

Esping-Anderson, Gosta, Duncan Gallie, Anton Hemerijk and John Myles. 2002. *Why We Need a New Welfare State*. New York: Oxford University Press.

Estlund, Cynthia. 2003. *Working Together: How Workplace Bonds Strengthen a Diverse Democracy*. Oxford: Oxford University Press.

Etzioni, A. 1997. *The New Golden Rule: Community and Morality in a Democratic Society*. London: Profile.

Evans, Peter. 1996. "Government Action, Social Capital, and Development: Reviewing the Evidence on Synergy." *World Development* 24 (6): 1033–7.

Fagen, Richard. 1969. *The Transformation of Political Culture in Cuba*. Stanford, CA: Stanford University Press.

Fierlbeck, K. 1991. "Redefining Responsibility: The Politics of Citizenship in the United Kingdom." *Canadian Journal of Political Science / Revue Canadienne de Science Politique* 24 (3): 575–93.

Fine, Ben. 2001. *Social Capital versus Social Theory*. New York: Routledge.

Fitzpatrick, Peter. 1992. *The Mythology of Modern Law*. New York: Routledge.

Foley, Michael W. and Bob Edwards. 1996. "The Paradox of Civil Society." *Journal of Democracy* 7: 38–52.

Foner, Eric. 1998. *The Story of American Freedom*. New York: W. W. Norton.

2002. *Who Owns History?: Rethinking the Past in a Changing World*. New York: Hill and Wang.

Foucault, Michel. [1970] 1973. *The Order of Things: An Archaeology of the Human Sciences*. New York: Vintage.

1977a. "Nietzsche, Genealogy, History." In *Language, Counter-Memory, Practice: Selected Essays and Interviews*, trans. Donald F. Bouchard and Sherry Simon: 139–64. Ithaca, NY: Cornell University Press.

1977b. *Discipline and Punish: The Birth of the Prison*. New York: Pantheon Books.

[1966] 1978. "Introduction." In *On the Normal and the Pathological*, by Georges Canguilhem, trans. Carolyn R. Fawcett: ix–xx. Dordrecht: Reidel.

1983. "Interpretive Analytics." In *Beyond Structuralism and Hermeneutics*, ed. Hubert L. Dreyfus and Paul Rabinow: 104–25. Chicago: University of Chicago Press.

[1978] 1990. *The History of Sexuality: An Introduction*. New York: Random House.

Frank, Robert H. 2007a. *Falling Behind: How Rising Inequality Harms the Middle Class*. Berkeley, CA: University of California Press.

2007b. *The Economic Naturalist: In Search of Explanations for Everyday Enigmas*. New York: Basic Books.

Frank, Thomas. 2004. *What's the Matter with Kansas? How Conservatives Won the Heart of America*. New York: Metropolitan Books.

2005. "What's the Matter with Liberalism?" *New York Review of Books*, LII, 8, May 12, pp. 46–51.

2006. "What is K Street's Project?" *New York Times*, August 19.

Fraser, Nancy. 1989. *Unruly Practices: Power, Discourse and Gender in Contemporary Social Theory*. Minneapolis, MN: University of Minnesota Press.

1992. "Rethinking the Public Sphere: A Contribution to the Critique of Actually Existing Democracy." In *Habermas and the Public Sphere*, ed. Craig Calhoun: 109–42. Cambridge, MA: MIT Press.

1997. *Justice Interruptus: Critical Reflections on the "Postsocialist" Condition*. New York: Routlege.

1997. "From Redistribution to Recognition? Dilemmas of Justice in a 'Postsocialist' Age." In *Justice Interruptus: Critical Reflections on the "Postsocialist" Condition*, ed. Nancy Fraser: 11–40. New York: Routledge.

Fraser, Nancy and Linda Gordon. 1997. "A Genealogy of 'Dependency': Tracing a Keyword of the US Welfare State." In *Justice Interruptus: Critical Reflections on the "Postsocialist" Condition*, ed. Nancy Fraser: 121–50. New York: Routledge.

1998. "Contract Versus Charity: Why Is There No Social Citizenship in the United States." In *The Citizenship Debates*, ed. G. Shafir: 113–27. Minneapolis: University of Minnesota Press.

Fraser, Nancy and Axel Honneth. 2003. *Redistribution or Recognition?: A Political-Philosophical Exchange*. London: Verso.

Freedland, M. 2001. "The Marketization of Public Services." In *Citizenship, Markets and the State*, ed. D. Tambini: 91–110. London: Oxford University Press.

Friedland, Roger and Robert R. Alford. 1991. "Bringing Society Back In: Symbols, Practices, and Institutional Contradictions." In *The New Institutionalism in Organizational Analysis*, ed. Walter W. Powell and Paul J. DiMaggio: 232–63. Chicago: University of Chicago Press.

Friedman, Milton. 1953. "The Methodology of Positive Economics." In *Essays in Positive Economics*, ed. Milton Friedman: 3–43. Chicago: University of Chicago Press.

Fukuyama, Francis. 1992. *The End of History and the Last Man*. New York: Free Press.

1995a. *Trust: Social Virtues and the Creation of Prosperity*. New York: Free Press.

1995b. "The Primacy of Culture." *Journal of Democracy* 6: 6.

Furet, François. 1981. *Interpreting the French Revolution*, trans. Elborg Forster. Cambridge: Cambridge University Press.

Galbraith, James K. 2000. "How the Economists Got it Wrong." *American Prospect*, February 14.

Gallagher, Catherine. 1986. "The Body Versus the Social Body in the Works of Thomas Malthus and Henry Mayhew." *Representations* 14 (special issue on "The Making of the Modern Body: Sexuality and Society in the Nineteenth Century"): 83–106.

Gamarnikow, E. and A. Green. 1999. "Social Capital and the Educated Citizen," *The School Field* 10 (3/4): 103–26.

Gambetta, D. 1987. *Were They Pushed or Did they Jump?: Individual Decision Mechanisms in Education*. Cambridge: Cambridge University Press.

1988. *Trust: Making and Breaking Cooperative Relations*. New York: Blackwell.

Gault, Barbara, Heidi Hartmann, Avis Jones-DeWeever, Misha Werschkul, and Erica Williams. 2005. "The Women of New Orleans and the Gulf Coast: Multiple Disadvantages and Key Assets for Recovery." Part I. Poverty, Race, Gender, and Class. Washington DC: Institute for Women's Policy Research Briefing Paper.

Geertz, Clifford. 1973. *The Interpretation of Cultures*. New York: Basic Books.

1983. *Local Knowledge: Further Essays in Interpretative Anthropology*. New York: Basic Books.

1988. "A Methodological Framework for the Sociology of Culture." *Sociological Methodology* 17: 1–35.

Geremek, Bronislaw. 1992. "Civil Society Then and Now." *Journal of Democracy* 3: 4.

Gershon, Mark. 1996a. *The Neoconservatism Vision*. New York: Madison Books.

ed. 1996b. *The Essential Neoconservative Reader*. Reading, MA: Addison Wesley.

Giddens, Anthony. 1982. *Profiles and Critiques in Social Theory*. London: Macmillan.

1998. *The Third Way: The Renewal of Social Democracy*. Cambridge: Polity Press.

Gitlin, T. 1995. *The Twilight of Common Dreams: Why America is Wracked by Culture Wars*. New York: Metropolitan Books.

Glaeser, E., David Laibson, and Bruce Sacerdote. 2002. "The Economic Approach to Social Capital." *Economic Journal* 112 (483): F437–58.

Glasman, Maurice. 1998. *Unnecessary Suffering*. London: Verso.

Gordon, Linda, ed. 1990. *Women, the State, and Welfare*. Madison: University of Wisconsin Press.

Goulden, Joseph C. 1972. *The Superlawyers: The Small and Powerful World of the Great Washington Law Firms*. New York: Weybright and Talley.

Granovetter, Mark. 1985. "Economic Action and Social Structure: The Problem of Embeddedness." *American Journal of Sociology* 91: 481–510.

Granovetter, Mark and Richard Swedberg, eds. 2001. *The Sociology of Economic Life*. 2nd edn. Boulder, CO: Westview Press.

Grew, R. 1985. "The Comparative Weakness of American History." *Journal of Interdisciplinary History* 16 (1): 87–101.

Griswold, Wendy. 1987. "The Fabrication of Meaning: Literary Interpretation in the United States, Great Britain, and the West Indies." *American Journal of Sociology* 92 (5): 1077–1117.

1992. "The Sociology of Culture: Four Good Arguments (and One Bad One)." *Acta Sociologica* 35: 323–8.

Grootaert, C. 1997. "Social Capital: The Missing Link?" World Bank website on Social Capital: www.worldbank.org/poverty/scapital/whatsc.htm.

Grootaert, C. and T. Van Bastelaer. 2002. *The Role of Social Capital in Development: An Empirical Assessment*. Cambridge: Cambridge University Press.

Gross, Daniel. 2007. "Income Inequality, Writ Larger." *New York Times*, June 10.

Grossberg, Lawrence, Cary Nelson, and Paula A. Treichler. eds. 1992. *Cultural Studies*. New York: Routledge.

Gunsteren, Herman R.v. 1998. *A Theory of Citizenship: Organizing Plurality in Contemporary Democracies*. Boulder, CO: Westview Press.

Gutting, Gary. 1989. *Michel Foucault's Archaeology of Scientific Reason*. Cambridge: Cambridge University Press.

Habermas, Jürgen. 1974. "The Public Sphere: An Encyclopedia Article (1946)." *New German Critique* 3: 49–55.

[1962] 1989. *The Structural Transformation of the Public Sphere: An Inquiry into a Category of Bourgeois Society*, trans. Thomas Burger and Frederick Lawrence. Cambridge, MA: MIT Press.

1990. "What does Socialism Mean Today? The Revolutions of Recuperation and the Need for New Thinking." In *After the Fall: The Failure of Communism and the Future of Socialism*, ed. Robin Blackburn: 25. London: Verso.

1992. "Further Reflections on the Public Sphere." In *Habermas and the Public Sphere*, ed. Craig Calhoun: 421–61. Cambridge, MA: MIT Press.

1996. *Between Facts and Norms*. Cambridge, MA: MIT Press.

2001. *The Postnational Constellation: Political Essays*. Cambridge: Polity Press.

Hacker, Jacob S. 2006. *The Great Risk Shift: The Assault on American Jobs, Families, Health Care and Retirement and How You Can Fight Back*. New York: Oxford University Press.

Hacking, Ian. 1979. "Michel Foucault's Immature Science." *Nous* 13: 39–51.

1982. "Language, Truth and Reason." In *Rationality and Relativism*, ed. S. Lukes and M. Hollis: 48–66. Cambridge, MA: MIT Press.

1988. "The Sociology of Knowledge about Child Abuse." *Nous* 22: 53–63.

1990a. *The Taming of Chance*. Cambridge: Cambridge University Press.

1990b. "Two Kinds of 'New Historicism' for Philosophers." *New Literary History* 21: 343–76.

Haddow, George, Jane Bullock, and Damon P. Coppola. 2008. *Introduction to Emergency Management*, 3rd edn. London: Butterworth-Heinemann.

Hall, J. A., ed. 1995. *Civil Society: Theory, History, Comparison*. Cambridge: Polity Press.

Hall, John R. 1987. *Gone from the Promised Land: Jamestown in American Cultural History*. New Brunswick, NJ: Transaction.

1992. "The Capital[s] of Cultures: A Nonholistic Approach to Status Situations, Class, Gender, and Ethnicity." In *Cultivating Differences: Symbolic Boundaries and the Making of Inequality*, ed. Michele Lamont and Marcel Fournier: 257–85. Chicago: University of Chicago Press.

Hall, S. and D. Held. 1989. "Left and Rights." *Marxism Today* June: 16–23.

Halsey, A. H. 1982. "Provincials and Professionals: The British Post-War Sociologists." *Archives Européennes de Sociologie* 23 (1): 150–75.

1984. "T. H. Marshall: Past and Present 1893–1981: President of the British Sociological Association 1964–1969." *Sociology* 18: 1–18.

Hammar, Tomas. 1990. *Democracy and the Nation State: Aliens, Denizens, and Citizens in a World of International Migration.* Brookfield, VT: Gower.

Handler, Joel F. 2004. *Social Citizenship and Workfare in the United States and Western Europe: The Paradox of Inclusion.* Cambridge: Cambridge University Press.

2006. "On Welfare Reform's Hollow Victory." *Daedalus* 135: 114–17.

Hanifan, L. J. 1920. *The Community Center.* Boston, MA: Silver Burdett.

Harriss-White, Barbara. 1996. "Free Market Romanticism in an Era of Deregulation." *Oxford Development Studies* 24 (1): 27–46.

Hartman, Chester W. and Gregory D. Squires. 2006. *There Is no such Thing as a Natural Disaster: Race, Class, and Hurricane Katrina.* New York: Routledge.

Hayek, F. A. 2007. *The Road to Serfdom: Texts and Documents.* Chicago: University of Chicago Press.

Heater, D. B. 1996. *World Citizenship and Government: Cosmopolitan Ideas in the History of Western Political Thought.* Basingstoke: Macmillan.

Hegel, G. W. F. 1955. *The Philosophy of Right*, ed. T. M. Know and John Sibree. Chicago: Encyclopedia Britannica.

[1822] 1975. *Lectures on the Philosophy of World History*, trans. H. B. Nisbet. New York: Oxford University Press.

Heilbroner, R. and W. Milberg. 1995. *The Crisis of Vision in Modern Economic Thought.* Cambridge: Cambridge University Press.

Held, D. 1995. *Democracy and the Global Order: From the Modern State to Cosmopolitan Governance.* Stanford, CA: Stanford University Press.

1999. *Global Transformations: Politics, Economics and Culture.* Stanford, CA: Stanford University Press.

Held, D. and A. G. McGrew. 2002. *Governing Globalization: Power, Authority and Global Governance.* Cambridge: Polity.

Hertz, F. 1941. "The Nature of Nationalism." *Social Forces* 19 (3): 409–15.

Hertzberg, Hendrik. 2002. "Manifesto." *The New Yorker.* October 14 and 21: 63–6.

Hirschman, Albert. 1970. *Exit, Voice, and Loyalty: Responses to Decline in Firms, Organizations, and States.* Cambridge, MA: Harvard University Press.

1984. "Against Parsimony: Three Easy Ways of Complicating Some Categories of Economic Discourse." *American Economic Review*, 74 (2): 89–96.

1990. *The Rhetoric of Reaction: Perversity, Futility, Jeopardy*. Cambridge, MA: Harvard University Press.

HM Government. 1991a. *The Citizen's Charter: A Guide*. London: HMSO.

1991b. *The Citizen's Charter: Raising the Standard*. London: HMSO.

1991c. *Competing for Quality*. London: HMSO.

Hobbes, Thomas. [1651] 1973. *Leviathan*. London: Dent.

[1642] 1998. *On the Citizen*, ed. Richard Tuck and Michael Silverthorne. Cambridge: Cambridge University Press.

Hobhouse, L. T. [1911] 1964. *Liberalism*. New York: Oxford University Press.

Hodgson, Geoffrey M. 1988. *Economics and Institutions*. Cambridge: Polity Press.

Hollinger, David A. 1995. *Post-Ethnic America: Beyond Multiculturalism*. New York: Basic Books.

Hollis, Martin and Steven Lukes. 1982. *Rationality and Relativism*. Cambridge, MA: MIT Press.

Holmes, Stephen. 1997. "What Russia Teaches Us Now." *American Prospect* 33 (July–August): 30–40.

Horne, Jed. 2006. *Breach of Faith: Hurricane Katrina and the near Death of a Great American City*. New York: Random House.

Hover, E. J. 1932. "Citizenship of Women in the United States." *American Journal of International Law* 26 (4): 700–19.

Huber, E. and J. D. Stephens. 2001. *Development and Crisis of the Welfare State: Parties and Policies in Global Markets*. Chicago: University of Chicago Press.

Hunt, Lynn. 1984. *Politics, Culture, and Class in the French Revolution*. Berkeley: University of California Press.

1986. "French History in the Last Twenty Years: The Rise and Fall of the *Annales* Paradigm." *Journal of Contemporary History* 21 (2): 209–24.

1988. "The Sacred and the French Revolution." In *Durkheimian Sociology: Cultural Studies*, ed. Jeffrey C. Alexander: 25–43. New York: Cambridge University Press.

ed. 1989a. *The New Cultural History*. Berkeley: University of California Press.

1989b. "Political Culture and the French Revolution." *States and Social Structures*, Newsletter of the American Sociological Association 10 (11): 1–6.

ed. and trans. 1996. *The French Revolution and Human Rights: A Brief Documentary History*. Boston, MA: Bedford Books of St. Martin's Press.

Huntington, Samuel. 1975. "The Democratic Distemper." *The Public Interest* 41: 9–38.

Hurd, Michael J. 2005. "Rebuilding New Orleans." *Capitalism Magazine*, available at: www.capmag.com/article.asp?ID=4409 (accessed December 16, 2007).

Hutchings, K. and R. Dannreuther. 1999. *Cosmopolitan Citizenship*. Houndmills: Macmillan.

Ignatieff, Michael. 2005. "The Broken Contract." *New York Times Magazine*, September 25: 15–17.

Isaac, Jeffrey C. 1996. "The Meanings of 1989." *Social Research* 63: 291–344.

Isin, E. F. 1992. *Cities Without Citizens*. Montreal: Black Rose Books.
  2002. *Being Political: Genealogies of Citizenship*. Minneapolis: University of Minnesota Press.

Isin, E. F. and B. S. Turner. 2002. *Handbook of Citizenship Studies*. London: Sage.

Isin, E. F. and P. K. Wood 1999. *Citizenship and Identity*. London: Sage.

Jacobs, J. 1961. *The Death and Life of Great American Cities*. New York: Random House.

Jaeger, Gertrude and Philip Selznick. 1964. "A Normative Theory of Culture." *American Sociological Review* 29: 653–99.

Janoski, T. 1998. *Citizenship and Civil Society: A Framework of Rights and Obligations in Liberal, Traditional, and Social Democratic Regimes*. Cambridge: Cambridge University Press.

Janowitz, Morris. 1980. "Observations on the Sociology of Citizenship: Obligations and Rights." *Social Forces* 59: 1–24.

Jepperson, Ronald L. 1991. "Institutions, Institutional Effects, and Institutionalism." In *The New Institutionalism in Organizational Analysis*, ed. W. W. Powell and P. J. DiMaggio: 143–63. Chicago: University of Chicago Press.

Jessop, Bob. 1978. "Capitalism and Democracy: The Best Possible Political Shell?" In *Power and the State*, ed. Gary Littlejohn: 10–51. London: Croom Helm.

Jones-DeWeever, Avis and Heidi Hartmann. 2006. "Abandoned Before the Storms: The Glaring Disaster of Gender, Race, and Class Disparities in the Gulf." In Heidi Hartman and Gregory D. Squires, eds., *There's No Such Thing as a Natural Disaster: Race, Class, and Hurricane Katrina*: 85–102. New York: Routledge.

Joppke, C. 1998. *Challenge to the Nation-State: Immigration in Western Europe and the United States*. Oxford: Oxford University Press.

Joppke, Christian and Steven Lukes, eds. 1999. *Multicultural Questions.* Oxford: Oxford University Press.

Kahneman, Daniel, Paul Slovic and Amos Tversky. 1985. *Judgment under Uncertainty: Heuristics and Biases.* Cambridge: Cambridge University Press.

Kane, Anne. 1991. "Cultural Analysis in Historical Sociology: The Analytic and Concrete Forms of the Autonomy of Culture." *Sociological Theory* 9 (1): 53–69.

Karst, Kenneth. 1989. *Belonging to America: Equal Citizenship and the Constitution.* New Haven, CT: Yale University Press.

Katz, Michael. 2001. *The Price of Citizenship: Redefining the American Welfare State.* New York: Henry Holt.

Katznelson, Ira. 2005. *When Affirmative Action Was White.* New York: W. W. Norton.

Keane, John. 1988. *Democracy and Civil Society.* London: Verso.

1994. "Nations, Nationalism and Citizens in Europe." *International Social Science Journal* 46: 169–84.

Kennedy, Michael D. 1990. *The Intelligentsia in the Constitution of Civil Societies and Post Communist Regimes in Hungary and Poland.* Ann Arbor: University of Michigan Press.

1991. *Professionals, Power, and Solidarity in Poland: A Critical Sociology of Soviet-Type Society.* Cambridge: Cambridge University Press.

1992. "The Intelligentsia in the Constitution of Civil Societies and Postcommunist Regimes in Hungary and Poland." *Theory and Society* 12 (1): 29–76.

1994. *Envisioning Eastern Europe: Postcommunist Cultural Studies.* Ann Arbor: University of Michigan Press.

2002. *Cultural Formations of Postcommunism: Emancipation, Transition, Nation, and War.* Minneapolis: University of Minnesota Press.

Kessler-Harris, Alice. 2001. *In Pursuit of Equity: Women, Men, and the Quest for Economic Citizenship in 20th Century America.* New York: Oxford University Press.

Kimeldorf, Howard. 1990. "Bringing Unions Back In, or Why We Need a New Old Labor History." *Labor History* 32 (1): 91–103.

Kitschelt, Herbert. 1993. "Social Movements, Political Parties, and Democratic Theory." *Annals of the American Academy of Political and Social Sciences* 528 (July): 13–29.

Knorr-Cetina, Karin and Michael Mulkay, eds. 1983. *Science Observed: Perspectives on the Social Study of Science.* London: Sage.

Kohn, Jerome. 2002. "Arendt's Concept and Description of Totalitarianism." *Social Research,* 69 (2): 621–56.

Kotkin, Joel. 2006. "Ideological Hurricane." *American Enterprise* January/February: 24–9.

Krippner, Greta. 2001. "The Elusive Market: Embeddedness and the Paradigm of Economic Sociology." *Theory and Society* 30: 775–810.

Krishna, A. 2002. *Active Social Capital: Tracing the Roots of Development and Democracy*. New York: Columbia University Press.

Kristol, Irving. 1995. *Neoconservatism: The Autobiography of an Idea*. New York: Free Press.

Kroeber, A. L. and Talcott Parsons. 1958. "The Concepts of Culture and of Social System." *American Sociological Review* 23: 582–83.

Krugman, Paul R. 2003a. *The Great Unraveling: Losing our Way in the New Century*. New York: W. W. Norton.

2003b. "The Tax-Cut Con." *New York Times Magazine*, September 14.

Kuhn, Thomas. 1970. *The Structure of Scientific Revolutions*, 2nd edn. Chicago: University of Chicago Press.

Kuttner, Robert. 1997. *Everything for Sale*. New York: Alfred A. Knopf.

2007. *The Squandering of America*. New York: Alfred A. Knopf.

Kymlicka, W. 1995. *Multicultural Citizenship: A Liberal Theory of Minority Rights*. Oxford: Clarendon Press.

1997. *State, Nations and Cultures*. Assen: Van Gorcum.

2001. *Politics in the Vernacular: Nationalism, Multiculturalism, and Citizenship*. New York: Oxford University Press.

Kymlicka, W. and W. Norman. 1995. "Return of the Citizen: A Survey of Recent Work on Citizenship Theory." In *Theorizing Citizenship*, ed. R. Beiner: 283–322. Albany, NY: SUNY Press.

Laarman, Peter. 1995. "Religious Right Thrives in a Red-Hot Vacuum." *Dissent* 42: 389–92.

Laitin, David. 1988. "Political Culture and Political Preferences." *American Political Science Review* 88: 589–93.

Lamont, Michele. 1989. "The Power-Culture Link in a Comparative Perspective. In *Comparative Social Research*, vol. XI, ed. Craig Calhoun: 131–50. Greenwich, CT: JAI Press.

1992a. "Introduction." In *Cultivating Differences: Symbolic Boundaries and the Making of Inequality*, ed. Michele Lamont and Marcel Fournier: 1–17. Chicago: University of Chicago Press.

1992b. *Money, Morals. and Manners: The Culture of the French and American Upper-Middle Class*. Chicago: University of Chicago Press.

2000. *The Dignity of Working Men: Morality and the Boundaries of Race, Class, and Immigration*. Cambridge, MA: Harvard University Press.

Lamont, Michele and Marcel Fournier, eds. 1992. *Cultivating Differences: Symbolic Boundaries and the Making of Inequality*. Chicago: University of Chicago Press.

Lamont, Michele and Robert Wuthnow. 1990. "Betwixt and Between: Recent Cultural Sociology in Europe and the United States." In *Frontiers of Social Theory: The New Synthesis*, ed. George Ritzer: 287–315. New York: Columbia University Press.

Lancaster, L. W. 1930. "Possibilities in the Study of 'Neighborhood' Politics." *Social Forces* 8 (3): 429–32.

Landes, Joan. 1988. *Women and the Public Sphere in the Age of the French Revolution*. Ithaca, NY: Cornell University Press.

Latour, Bruno. 1988. "Response to Hacking." *Nous* 22: 64–73.

1993. *We Have Never Been Modern*, trans. Catherine Porter. Cambridge. MA: Harvard University Press.

Leibfried, S. and P. Pierson 1995. *European Social Policy: Between Fragmentation and Integration*. Washington, DC: Brookings Institution.

Leonhardt, David. 2007. "Larry Summer's Evolution." *New York Times Magazine*, June 10: 22.

Lesser, Eric L. 2000. *Knowledge and Social Capital: Foundations and Applications*. Boston, MA: Butterworth Heinemann.

Levi, Margaret. 1996. "Social and Unsocial Capital." *Politics and Society* 24, 1: 45–55.

Lévi-Strauss, Claude. [1964] 1969. *The Raw and the Cooked*. Chicago: University of Chicago Press.

Levitt, Steven D. and Stephen J. Dubner. 2005. *Freakonomics: A Rogue Economist Explores the Hidden Side of Everything*. New York: William Morrow.

Lewis, N. 1993. "The Citizen's Charter and Next Steps: A New Way of Governing?" *Political Quarterly* 64 (3): 316–26.

Leys, Colin. 2003. *Market-Driven Politics: Neoliberal Democracy and the Public Interest*. London: Verso.

Lieberman, Robert C. 1998. *Shifting the Color Line: Race and the American Welfare State*. Cambridge, MA: Harvard University Press.

Lin, N. 2001. *Social Capital: A Theory of Social Structure and Action*. Cambridge: Cambridge University Press.

Lindblom, Charles E. 2001. *The Market System: What it Is, How it Works, and What to Make of It*. New Haven, CT: Yale University Press.

Linde, Charlotte. 1986. "Private Stories in Public Discourse: Narrative Analysis in the Social Sciences." *Poetics* 15: 183–202.

Linklater, A. 1990. *Men and Citizens in the Theory of International Relations*. London: Macmillan.

2000. *International Relations: Critical Concepts in Political Science.* London: Routledge.

Liphart, Arend. 1980. "The Structure of Inference." In *The Civic Culture Revisited*, ed. Gabriel A. Almond and Sidney Verba: 37–56. Boston, MA: Little, Brown.

Lipset, Seymour Martin. 1964. "Introduction." In *Class, Citizenship, and Social Class*, ed. T. H. Marshall: v–xx. New York: Doubleday.

1967. *The First New Nation: The United States in Historical and Comparative Perspective.* New York: Doubleday.

[1960] 1981. *Political Man: The Social Bases of Politics.* New York: Anchor.

1983. "Radicalism or Reformism: The Sources of Working-Class Politics." *American Political Science Review* 77: 1–18.

1990. "The Centrality of Political Culture." *Journal of Democracy* 1 (4): 80–3.

Lipset, Seymour Martin and Stein Rokkan. 1967. "Cleavage Structures, Party Systems and Voter Alignments." In *Party Systems and Voter Alignments*, ed. Seymour Martin Lipset and Stein Rokkan: 1–64. New York: Free Press.

Liptak, Adam. 2007. "Full Constitutional Protection for Some, but no Privacy for the Poor." *New York Times*, July 16.

Lister, R. 1997. *Citizenship: Feminist Perspectives.* Washington Square, NY: New York University Press.

Locke, John. [1690] 1952. *The Second Treatise of Government*, ed. T.P. Peardon. New York: Bobbs-Merrill.

[1690] 1961. *An Essay Concerning the True Original Extent and End of Civil Government.* Chicago: Great Books Foundation.

[1690] 1967. *Two Treatises of Government*, 2nd edn, ed. Peter Laslett. Cambridge: Cambridge University Press.

Lockwood, David. 1974. "For T. H. Marshall." *Sociology* 8: 363–8.

Loury, G. 1977. "A Dynamic Theory of Racial Income Differences." In *Women, Minorities, and Employment Discrimination*, ed. P. Wallace and A. LaMond: 153–86. Lexington, KY: Lexington Books.

Lowenstein, Roger. 2007. "The Inequality Conundrum." *New York Times Magazine*, June 10: 11–14.

Lukes, Steven. 2004. "Invasions of the Market." In *Worlds of Capitalism: Institutions, Governance and Economic Change in the Era of Globalization*: 298–321. London: Routledge.

2007. "Pathologies of Markets and States." In *Crime, Social Control and Human Rights: From Moral Panics to States of Denial, Essays in*

Honour of Stanley Cohen, ed. David Downes, Paul Rock, Christine Chinkin, and Conor Gearty. Uffculme, Devon: Willan Publishing.

McAdam, Douglas, S. G. Tarrow, and Charles Tilly. 2001. *Dynamics of Contention*. New York: Cambridge University Press.

McCloskey, Deirdre N. 1994. *Knowledge and Persuasion in Economics*. Cambridge: Cambridge University Press.

MacIntyre, Alasdair. 1981. *After Virtue: A Study in Moral Theory*. Notre Dame, IN: University of Notre Dame Press.

    1989. *Whose Justice? Which Rationality?* Notre Dame, IN: University of Notre Dame Press.

McLean, S. L., D. A. Schultz, and Manfred B. Steger. 2002. *Social Capital: Critical Perspectives on Community and "Bowling Alone."* New York: New York University Press.

McMichael, Philip. 1998. "Development and Structural Adjustment." In *Virtualism: A New Political Economy*, ed. J. G. Carrier and D. Miller: 95–116. New York: Berg.

McNall, Scott, Ronda Levine, and Rick Fantasia, eds. 1991. *Bringing Class Back In: Contemporary and Historical Perspectives*. Boulder, CO: Westview Press.

Maier, Charles S. 1994. "Democracy and its Discontents." *Foreign Affairs* 73: 48–64.

    1997. *Dissolution: The Crisis of Communism and the End of East Germany*. Princeton, NJ: Princeton University Press.

Malthus, T. R. 1989. *Principles of Political Economy*, ed. J. Pullen. Cambridge: Cambridge University Press.

    [1803] 1992. *An Essay on the Principle of Population*, ed. Donald Winch. Cambridge: Cambridge University Press.

Mann. Michael. 1970. "The Social Cohesion of Liberal Democracy." *American Sociological Review* 35: 423.

    1986. *The Sources of Social Power*, vol. I: *A History of Power From the Beginning to A.D. 1760*. Cambridge: Cambridge University Press.

    1987. "Ruling Class Strategies and Citizenship." *Sociology* 21 (3): 339–54.

Marcella, R. and G. Baxter. 1999. "The Information Needs and the Information Seeking Behaviour of a National Sample of the Population in the United Kingdom, with Special Reference to Needs Related to Citizenship." *Journal of Documentation* 55 (2): 159–83.

March, James and Johan P. Olsen. 1984. "The New Institutionalism: Organizational Factors in Political Life." *American Political Science Review* 78: 734–49.

Marshall, T. H. 1963. *Sociology at the Crossroads, and Other Essays*. London: Heinemann.

[1950] 1964. "Citizenship and Social Class." In *Class, Citizenship, and Social Development*, intro. S. M. Lipset: 65–123. Garden City, NY: Doubleday.

1981. *The Right to Welfare and Other Essays*. New York: Free Press.

Marshall, T. H. and Tom Bottomore. 1992. *Citizenship and Social Class*. Concord, MA: Pluto.

Marx, Karl. [1843] 1975. "On the Jewish Question." In *Early Writings*, ed. T. B. Bottomore. London: Watts.

1977a. "The Working Day." In Karl Marx, *Capital*, vol. I. New York: Vintage Books.

1977b. "The German Ideology." In *Karl Marx: Selected Writings*, ed. David McLellan: 15–91. Oxford: Oxford University Press.

[1932] 1977c. "Economic and Philosophical Manuscripts." In *Karl Marx: Selected Writings*, ed. David McLellan: 75–112. Oxford: Oxford University Press.

[1867] 1978. *Capital*, vol. I. In *The Marx–Engel's Reader*, ed. Robert Tucker. New York: Norton.

Mauss, Marcel. [1927] 1985. "A Category of the Human Mind: The Notion of Person; the Notion of Self." In *The Category of the Person: Anthropology, Philosophy, History*, ed. Michael Carrithers, Steven Collins, and Steven Lukes: 1–25. Cambridge: Cambridge University Press.

Mead, L. M. 1997. "Citizenship and Social Policy: T.H. Marshall and Poverty." *Social Philosophy and Policy* 14 (2): 197–230.

Meek, Ronald L. 1976. *Social Science and the Ignoble Savage*. Cambridge: Cambridge University Press.

Mekeel, S. 1944. "Citizenship, Education, and Culture." *American Journal of Sociology* 50 (3): 208–13.

Mendelsohn, Daniel. 2006. *The Lost: A Search for Six of Six Million*. New York: Harper Perennial.

Merkl, Peter and Lenard Weinberg, eds. 1993. *Encounters with the Contemporary Radical Right*. Boulder, CO: Westview Press.

Miller, Daniel. 1997. *Capitalism: An Ethnographic Approach*. New York: Berg.

Mills, C. Wright. 1959. *The Sociological Imagination*. New York: Oxford University Press.

Minow, Martha. 1985. "'Forming Underneath Everything that Grows': Toward a History of Family Law." *Wisconsin Law Review* 4: 819–98.

1987. "Interpreting Rights: An Essay for Robert Cover." *Yale Law Review* 96: 1860–1915.

Mirowski, Philip. 2005. "How Positivism Made a Pact with the Postwar Social Sciences in the United States." In *The Politics of Method in The Human Sciences*, ed. G. Steinmetz: 142–72. Durham, NC: Duke University Press.

Mishel, Lawrence, Jared Bernstein and Sylvia Allegretto. 2006. *The State of Working America, 2006/2007*. An Economic Policy Institute Book. Ithaca, NY: ILR Press, imprint of Cornell University Press.

Mitchell, Timothy. 2002. *Rule of Experts*. Berkeley: University of California Press.

  2005. "Economists and the Economy in the Twentieth Century." In *The Politics of Method in The Human Sciences*, ed. G. Steinmetz: 126–41. Durham, NC: Duke University Press.

Mizrachi, Nissim, Israel Drori and Renee R. Anspach. 2007. "Repertoires of Trust: The Practice of Trust in a Multinational Organization amid Political Conflict." *American Sociological Review* 72: 143–65.

Moore, Barrington, Jr. 1965. *Soviet Politics – The Dilemma of Power: The Role of Ideas in Social Change*. New York: Harper and Row.

Morgan, Edmund S. 1988. *Inventing the People: The Rise of Popular Sovereignty in England and America*. New York: W. W. Norton.

Morgenson, Gretchen and Michael M. Weinstein. 1998. *New York Times*, November 14: 1–3.

Morley, D. and K. Robins. 1995. *Spaces of Identity: Global Media, Electronic Landscapes and Cultural Boundaries*. London: Routledge.

Mouffe, C. 1995. "Democratic Politics and the Question of Identity." In *The Identity in Question*, ed. J. Rajchman. New York: Routledge.

Mukerji, Chandra and Michael Schudson. 1991. *Rethinking Popular Culture: Contemporary Perspectives in Cultural Studies*. Berkeley: University of California Press.

Munch, R. 2002. "The Limits of the Self-organization of Civil Society: The American Debate on Multiculturalism, Public Spirit, and Social Capital from the Point of View of Modernization Theory." *Berliner Journal fur Soziologie* 12 (4): 445ff.

Murray, C. A. 1984. *Losing Ground – American Social Policy, 1950–1980*. New York: Basic Books.

New York Times Magazine. 2007. "Special issue: Inside the Income Gap," June 10.

Nicholson, Shierry Weber, ed. 1989. *The New Conservatism*. Cambridge, MA: MIT Press.

Nolan, Bruce. 2005. "In Storm, N.O. Wants No One Left Behind; Number of People without Cars Makes Evacuation Difficult." *The Times-Picayune*, July 24, Metro.

2006. "Real Katrina Lesson: Blacks in New Orleans Were Duped Into Social Dependency.", available at: www.azcentral.com/arizonarepublic/ eastvalleyopinionseastvalleyopinions/articles/1005gr-pinkney05.html (accessed March 1, 2006 by Tim Brezina).

Norquist, Grover. 2004. "The Democratic Party is Toast." *Washington Monthly.* September, and online at www.washingtonmonthly.com/ features/2004/0409.norquist.html.

2005. "Ownership can be Revolutionary." *American Enterprise.* March, and online at www.taemag.com/issues/issue ID.169/toc.asp.

Nozick, Robert. 1974. *Anarchy, State, and Utopia.* New York: Basic Books.

Nussbaum, M. C. 2000. *Women and Human Development: The Capabilities Approach.* Cambridge: Cambridge University Press.

Nussbaum, M. C. and J. Cohen. 1996. *For Love of Country: Debating the Limits of Patriotism.* Boston, MA: Beacon Press.

O'Connor, Alice. 2002. *Poverty Knowledge: Social Science, Social Policy, and the Poor in Twentieth-Century US History.* Princeton, NJ: Princeton University Press.

O'Connor, Julia S., Ann Shola Orloff, and Sheila Shaver. 1999. *States, Markets, Families.* New York: Cambridge University Press.

Ogilvie, Sheila. 2004. "How Does Social Capital Affect Women? Guilds and Communities in Early Modern Germany." *American Historical Review* 109, 2 (April): 325–59.

Okin, S. M., J. Cohen, M. Howard and M. Nussbaum. 1999. *Is Multiculturalism Bad for Women?* Princeton, NJ: Princeton University Press.

Olasky, M. N. 1992. *The Tragedy of American Compassion.* Washington, DC: Regnery Gateway.

Oldfield, A. 1990. *Citizenship and Community: Civic Republicanism and the Modern World.* London: Routledge.

Ong, Aihwa. 2003. *Buddha Is Hiding: Refugees, Citizenship, the New America.* Berkeley: University of California Press.

2006. *Neoliberalism as Exception: Mutations in Citizenship and Sovereignty.* Durham, NC: Duke University Press.

Oommen, T. K. 1997a. *Citizenship and National Identity: From Colonialism to Globalism.* Thousand Oaks, CA: Sage.

1997b. *Citizenship, Nationality, and Ethnicity: Reconciling Competing Identities.* Cambridge: Polity Press.

Orloff, Ann. 1993. "Gender and the Social Rights of Citizenship: The Comparative Analysis of State Policies and Gender Relations." *American Sociological Review* 58 (3): 303–28.

2005. "Social Provision and Regulation: Theories of States, Social Policies, and Modernity." In *Remaking Modernity: Politics, History, and Sociology*, ed. Julia Adams, Elisabeth S. Clemens, and Ann Shola Orloff: 190–224. Durham, NC: Duke University Press.

Orr, M. 1999. *Black Social Capital: The Politics of School Reform in Baltimore, 1986–1998*. Lawrence: University Press of Kansas.

Ozouf, Mona. 1988. *Festivals and the French Revolution*, trans. Alan Sheridan. Cambridge. MA: Harvard University Press.

Parsons, Talcott. 1937. *The Structure of Social Action*. New York: McGraw-Hill.

1967. "Durkheim's Contribution to the Theory of the Integration of Social Systems." In *Sociological Theory and Modern Society*: 3–34. New York: Free Press.

1969. "On the Concept of Political Power." In *Political Power: A Reader in Theory and Research*, ed. R. Bell, D. V. Edwards and H. R. Wagner: 251–84. New York: Free Press.

1971. *The System of Modern Societies*. Englewood Cliffs, NJ: Prentice-Hall.

Parsons, Talcott and Edward A. Shils. 1951. "Values, Motives, and Systems of Action." In *Toward a General Theory of Action*, ed. Talcott Parsons and Edward A. Shils: 47–245. Cambridge, MA: Harvard University Press.

Pateman, Carole. 1980. "The Civic Culture: A Philosophic Critique." In *The Civic Culture Revisited*, ed. Gabriel Almond and Sidney Verba: 57–107. Boston, MA: Little, Brown.

1989. *The Disorder of Women: Democracy, Feminism and Political Theory*. Stanford, CA: Stanford University Press.

Pearson, Harry. 1977. "Editor's Introduction." In Karl Polanyi, *The Livelihood of Man*, ed. Harry Pearson. New York: Academic Press.

Peck, Jamie. Forthcoming 2008. "Remaking Laissez-Faire." *Progress in Human Geography*.

Peck, J. and A. Ticknell. 2002. "Neoliberalizing Space." *Antipode* 34 (3): 380–404.

Pharr, S. J. and R. D. Putnam. 2000. *Disaffected Democracies: What's Troubling the Trilateral Countries?* Princeton, NJ: Princeton University Press.

Pickering, Andrew. 1984. *Constructing Quarks: A Sociological History of Particle Physics*. Chicago: University of Chicago Press.

1992. "From Science as Knowledge to Science as Practice." In *Science as Practice and Culture*, ed. Andrew Pickering: 1–26. Chicago: University of Chicago Press.

1993. "The Mangle of Practice: Agency and Emergence in the Sociology of Science." *American Journal of Sociology* 99 (3): 559–89.

Pierson, P. 1994. *Dismantling the Welfare State?: Reagan, Thatcher, and the Politics of Retrenchment*. Cambridge: Cambridge University Press.

2001. *The New Politics of the Welfare State*. Oxford: Oxford University Press.

Pizzorno, Alessandro, ed. 1971. *Political Sociology: Selected Readings*. Harmondsworth: Penguin.

Pocock, J. G. A. 1998. "The Ideal of Citizenship since Classical Times." In *The Citizenship Debates*, ed. Gershon Shafir: 2–32. Minneapolis: University of Minnesota Press.

Polanyi, Karl. 1957a. "Aristotle Discovers the Economy." In *Trade and Market in the Early Empires: Economies in History and Theory*, ed. Karl Polanyi, Conrad M. Arensberg, and Harry W. Pearson: 64–96. New York: Free Press.

1957b. "The Economy as an Instituted Process." In *Trade and Market in the Early Empires*, ed. Karl Polanyi, Conrad M. Arensberg, and Harry W. Pearson: 243–69. New York: Free Press.

[1944] 1957c. *The Great Transformation: The Political and Economic Origins of our Time*. Boston, MA: Beacon Press.

1977. *The Livelihood of Man*, ed. Harry Pearson. New York: Academic Press.

[1944] 2001. *The Great Transformation*, ed. Fred Block, foreword by Joseph Stiglitz. Boston: Beacon Press.

Pollner, Melvin. 1987. *Mundane Reason: Reality in Everyday and Sociological Discourse*. New York: Cambridge University Press.

Popper, Karl. [1934] 1959. *The Logic of Scientific Discovery*. London: Hutchinson.

Poranski, Diana M. 2005. "Government Dependency Exposed." Opinion Editorials.com, available at: www.opinioneditorials.com/freedom writers/dporanski_20050907.html (accessed December 16, 2007).

Portes, A. 1998. "Social Capital: Its Origins and Applications in Modern Sociology." *Annual Review of Sociology* 24: 1–24.

Powell, John A., Hasan K. Jeffries, Daniel W. Newhart and Eric Stiens. 2006. "Towards a Transformative View of Race: The Crisis and Opportunity of Katrina." In *There is No Such Thing as a Natural Disaster*, ed. C. Hartman and G. D. Squires: 59–84. New York: Routledge.

Powell, Walter and Paul J. DiMaggio, eds. 1991. *The New Institutionalism in Organizational Analysis*. Chicago: University of Chicago Press.

Power, Samantha. 2004. "The Lesson of Hannah Arendt." *New York Review of Books* 51, April 29.

Preuss, U. 1995. "Citizenship and Identity: Aspects of a Theory of Citizenship." In *Democracy and Constitutional Culture in the Union of Europe*, ed. Richard Bellamy, V. Buffachi, and Dario Castiglione. London: Lothian Foundation Press.

Procacci, G. 2001. "Poor Citizens." In *Citizenship, Markets, and the State*, ed. K. Eder, C. Crouch and D. Tambini: 49–68. Oxford: Oxford University Press.

Procacci, G. and N. Salamone. 2000. *Mutamento sociale e identità: la sociologia di fronte alla contemporaneità*. Milan: Guerini Studio.

Putnam, Robert D. 1993. "The Prosperous Community: Social Capital and Public Life." *American Prospect* 4 (13): 35–42.

1995. "Bowling Alone: America's Declining Social Capital." *Journal of Democracy* 6 (1): 65–78.

1996. "The Strange Disappearance of Civic America." *American Prospect* 24: 34–48.

2000. *Bowling Alone: The Collapse and Revival of American Community*. New York: Simon and Schuster.

2002. *Democracies in Flux: The Evolution of Social Capital in Contemporary Society*. Oxford: Oxford University Press.

Putnam, Robert D., Robert Leonardi and Rafaella Y. Nanetti. 1993. *Making Democracy Work: Civic Traditions in Modern Italy*. Princeton, NJ: Princeton University Press.

Pye, Lucian W. 1962. *Politics, Personality, and Nation Building*. New Haven, CT: Yale University Press.

1965. "Introduction: Political Culture and Political Development." In *Political Culture and Political Development*, ed. Lucian W. Pye and Sidney Verba: 1–26. Princeton, NJ: Princeton University Press.

Pye, Lucian and Sidney Verba, eds. 1965. *Political Culture and Political Development*. Princeton, NJ: Princeton University Press.

Quadagno, Jill S. 1994. *The Color of Welfare: How Racism Undermined the War on Poverty*. New York: Oxford University Press.

Rajchman, J. 1995. *The Identity in Question*. New York: Routledge.

Rambo, Eric and Elaine Chan. 1990. 'Text, Structure and Action in Cultural Sociology." *Theory and Society* 19: 635–48.

Rawls, J. 1971. *A Theory of Justice*. Cambridge, MA: Belknap Press of Harvard University Press.

Reidy, David A., Jr. 1992. "Eastern Europe, Civil Society and the Real Revolution." *Praxis International* 12: 169.

Rex, J. 1996. *Ethnic Minorities in the Modern Nation State: Studies in the Theory of Multiculturalism and Political Integration*. Houndmills:

Macmillan, in association with Centre for Research in Ethnic Relations, University of Warwick.

Rex, J. and B. Drury. 1994. *Ethnic Mobilisation in a Multi-cultural Europe.* Aldershot: Avebury.

Ricardo, David. [1817] 1996. *Principles of Political Economy and Taxation.* Amherst, NY: Prometheus Books.

Robalino, D. A. 2000. *Social Capital, Technology Diffusion, and Sustainable Growth in the Developing World.* Santa Monica, CA: Rand.

Robertson, Sandy and Roger Friedland. 1990. *Beyond the Marketplace: Rethinking Economy and Society.* New York: Aldine Transaction.

Rogowski, Ronald. 1976. *A Rational Theory of Legitimacy.* Princeton, NJ: Princeton University Press.

Rorty, Richard. 1979. *Philosophy and the Mirror of Nature.* Princeton, NJ: Princeton University Press.

Rose, Nikolas. 1999. *Powers of Freedom: Reframing Political Thought.* Cambridge: Cambridge University Press.

Rose, R. and University of Strathclyde, Centre for the Study of Public Policy. 2000. *How Much Does Social Capital Add to Individual Health?: A Survey Study of Russians.* Glasgow: Centre for the Study of Public Policy, University of Strathclyde.

Rosen, Jeffrey. 2005. "The Unregulated Offensive." *New York Times Magazine.* April 17.

Rosenbaum, Walter A. 1975. *Political Culture.* New York: Praeger.

Rosenberg, N. L. and R. C. Post. 2002. *Civil Society and Government.* Princeton, NJ: Princeton University Press.

Rotberg, R. I. and G. A. Brucker. 2001. *Patterns of Social Capital: Stability and Change in Historical Perspective.* Cambridge: Cambridge University Press.

Rueschemeyer, Dietrich, Evelyne Huber Stephens, and John D. Stephens. 1992. *Capitalist Development and Democracy.* Chicago: University of Chicago Press.

Runciman, Walter G. 1969. *Social Science and Political Theory.* 2nd edn. London: Cambridge University Press.

Saegert, S., J. P. Thompson, and M. R. Warren, eds. 2001. *Social Capital and Poor Communities.* New York: Russell Sage Foundation.

Sahlins, Marshall. 1976. *Culture and Practical Reason.* Chicago: University of Chicago Press.

Sandel, M. J. 1982. *Liberalism and the Limits of Justice.* Cambridge: Cambridge University Press.

   ed. 1984. *Liberalism and its Critics.* Oxford: Blackwell.

1996. *Democracy's Discontent: America in Search of a Public Philosophy.* Cambridge, MA: Belknap Press of Harvard University Press.

Sartori, Giovanni. 1969. "From the Sociology of Politics to Political Sociology." In *Politics and the Social Sciences,* ed. Seymour Martin Lipset: 65–100. New York: Oxford University Press.

Sassen, S. 1996. *Losing Control?: Sovereignty in an Age of Globalization.* New York: Columbia University Press.

1998. *Globalization and its Discontents: Essays on the New Mobility of People and Money.* New York: New Press.

2001. *The Global City: New York, London, Tokyo.* Princeton, NJ: Princeton University Press.

2006a. *Territory, Authority, Rights.* Princeton: Princeton University Press.

2006b. "The Repositioning of Citizenship and Alienage: Emergent Subjects and Spaces for Politics." In *Migration, Citizenship, Ethnos,* ed. M. Y. Bodemann and G. Yurdakul: 13–34. New York: Palgrave Macmillan.

Saussure, Ferdinand de. [1916] 1959. *Course in General Linguistics.* New York: Philosophical Library.

Schlesinger, A. M. 1992. *The Disuniting of America: Reflections on a Multicultural Society.* New York: W. W. Norton.

Schmitt, Mark. 2007a. "How Did Tax Credits Become the Answer to Everything? Are There no Other Tools?" *American Prospect* 18 (4): 9.

2007b. "Whose Big Government?" *American Prospect,* May 20.

Schnapper, Dominique. 1998. *Community of Citizens: On the Modern Idea of Nationality.* New Brunswick, NJ: Transaction Publishers.

Schuech, Erwin K. 1969. "Social Context and Individual Behavior." In *Quantitative Ecological Analysis in the Social Sciences,* ed. Mattei Dogan and Stein Rokkan: 138–59. Cambridge. MA: MIT Press.

Schumpeter, Joseph. 1943. *Capitalism, Socialism, and Democracy.* London: Allen and Unwin.

Scott, Joan Wallach. 1988. *Gender and the Politics of History.* New York: Columbia University Press.

Scruggs, W. L. 1886. "Ambiguous Citizenship." *Political Science Quarterly* 1 (2): 199–205.

Selbourne, David. 1994. *The Principle of Duty: An Essay on the Foundations of the Civic Order.* London: Abacus.

Seligman, Adam. 1992. *The Idea of Civil Society.* New York: Free Press.

1993. "The Fragile Ethical Vision of Civil Society." In *Citizenship and Social Theory,* ed. Bryan S. Turner: 139–61. London: Sage.

Sen, Amartya. 1981. *Poverty and Famines: An Essay on Entitlement and Deprivation*. Oxford: Clarendon Press.

    1982. "The Right not to be Hungry." In *Contemporary Philosophy: A New Survey*, ed. F. Guttom: 343–60. The Hague: Martinus Nijhoff.

Sennett, Richard. 2006. *The Culture of the New Capitalism*. New Haven, CT: Yale University Press.

Sewell, William H. Jr. 1980. *Work and Revolution in France*. Cambridge: Cambridge University Press.

    1992. "A Theory of Structure: Duality, Agency, and Transformation." *American Journal of Sociology* 91: 1–29.

    1993. "Toward a Post-Materialist Rhetoric for Labor History." In *Rethinking Labor History, Essays on Discourse and Class Analysis*, ed. Lenard R. Berlanstein: 15–38. Urbana: University of Illinois Press.

    1999. "The Concept(s) of Culture." In *Beyond the Cultural Turn: New Directions in the Study of Society and Culture*, ed. Victoria E. Bonnell and Lynn Hunt: 35–61. Berkeley: University of California Press.

Shachar, Ayelet. 2001. *Multicultural Jurisdictions: Cultural Differences and Women's Rights*. Cambridge: Cambridge University Press.

Shafir, G., ed. 1998. *The Citizenship Debates: A Reader*. Minneapolis: University of Minnesota Press.

Shapin, Steven and Simon Schaffer. 1986. *Leviathan and the Air Pump: Hobbes, Boyle and the Experimental Life*. Princeton, NJ: Princeton University Press.

Shapiro, Ian. 1995. "Resources, Capacities, and Ownership: The Workmanship Ideal and Distributive Justice." In *Early Modern Conceptions of Property*, ed. John Brewer and Susan Staves: 21–42. London: Routledge.

Sherwood, H. N. 1923. "Problems of Citizenship." *Journal of Negro History* 8 (2): 162–6.

Sherwood, Steven Jay, Philip Smith, and Jeffrey C. Alexander. 1993. "The British Are Coming ... Again! The Hidden Agenda of 'Cultural Studies'." *Contemporary Sociology* 22 (3): 370–5.

Shklar, Judith N. 1991. *American Citizenship: The Quest for Inclusion*. Cambridge, MA: Harvard University Press.

Siim, Birte. 2000. *Gender and Citizenship: Politics and Agency in France, Britain, and Denmark*. Cambridge: Cambridge University Press.

Skocpol, Theda. ed. 1984. *Vision and Method in Historical Sociology*. New York: Cambridge University Press.

2003. *Diminished Democracy: From Membership to Management in American Civil Life*. Norman: University of Oklahoma Press.

Smelser, Neil. 1992. "Culture: Coherent or Incoherent?" In *Theory of Culture*, ed. Richard Munch and Neil J. Smelser: 3–28. Berkeley: University of California Press.

Smelser, Neil J. and Richard E. Swedberg. 2005. *Handbook of Economic Sociology*, 2nd edn. New York: Russell Sage Foundation and Princeton University Press.

Smircich, Linda. 1983. "Concepts of Culture and Organizational Analysis." *Administrative Science Quarterly* 28 (3): 339–58.

Smith, Adam. [1776] 1976. *An Inquiry into the Nature and Causes of the Wealth of Nations*, ed. R. H. Campbell, A. S. Skinner, and W. B. Todd. Oxford: Clarendon Press.

Smith, Michael. G. 1966. "A Structural Approach to Comparative Politics." In *Varieties of Political Theory*, ed. D. Easton: 113–28. Englewood Cliffs, NJ: Prentice-Hall.

Smith, Rogers M. 1993. "Beyond Tocqueville, Myrdal, and Hartz: The Multiple Traditions in America." *American Political Science Review* 87 (3): 549–66.

1999. *Civic Ideals: Conflicting Visions of Citizenship in US History*. New Haven, CT: Yale University Press.

2003. *Stories of Peoplehood: The Politics and Morals of Political Membership*. New York: Cambridge University Press.

Solow, Robert M. 1990. "Robert M. Solow." In *Sociology and Economics: Redefining their Boundaries: Conversations with Economists and Sociologists*, ed. Richard Swedberg: 268–84. Princeton, NJ: Princeton University Press.

2000. "Notes on Social Capital and Economic Performance." In *Social Capital: A Multifaceted Perspective*, ed. P. Dasgupta and I. Serageldin. Washington, DC: World Bank.

Somers, Margaret R. 1990. "Karl Polanyi's Intellectual Legacy." In *The Life and Work of Karl Polanyi*, ed. Kari Polanyi-Levitt. Montreal: Black Rose Books.

1992. "Narrativity, Narrative Identity, and Social Action: Rethinking English Working-Class Formation." *Social Science History* 16 (4): 591–630.

1993. "Citizenship and the Place of the Public Sphere: Law, Community, and Political Culture in the Transition to Democracy." *American Sociological Review* 58 (5): 587–620.

1994a. "Rights, Relationality, and Membership: Rethinking the Making and Meaning of Citizenship." *Law and Social Inquiry* 19 (1): 63–112.

1994b. "The Narrative Constitution of Identity: A Relational and Network Approach." *Theory and Society* 23 (5): 605–49.

1995a. "What's Political or Cultural about the Political Culture Concept? Toward an Historical Sociology of Concept Formation." *Sociological Theory* 13 (2): 113–44.

1995b. "Narrating and Naturalizing Civil Society and Citizenship Theory: The Place of Political Culture and the Public Sphere." *Sociological Theory* 13 (3): 229–74.

1995c. "The 'Misteries' of Property: Relationality, Rural Industrialization, and Community in Chartist Narratives of Political Rights." In *Early Modern Conceptions of Property*, ed. John Brewer and Susan Staves: 62–92. London: Routledge.

1996a. "Where is Sociology after the Historic Turn? Knowledge Cultures, Narrativity, and Historical Epistemologies." In *The Historic Turn in the Human Sciences*, ed. T. J. McDonald: 53–90. Ann Arbor: University of Michigan Press.

1996b. "Class Formation and Capitalism: A Second Look at a Classic." *Archives de Sociologie Européene* 37 (1): 180–202.

1997. "Deconstructing and Reconstructing Class Formation Theory: Narrativity, Relational Analysis, and Social Theory." In *Reworking Class*, ed. John Hall: 73–106. Ithaca, NY: Cornell University Press.

1998. "We're No Angels: Realism, Rational Choice, and Relationality in Social Science." *American Journal of Sociology* 104: 722–84.

1999. "The Privatization of Citizenship: How to Unthink a Knowledge Culture." In *Beyond the Cultural Turn: New Directions in the Study of Society and Culture*, ed. Victoria E. Bonnell and Lynn Hunt: 121–61. Berkeley: University of California Press.

2001. "Romancing the Market, Reviling the State: Historicizing Liberalism, Privatization, and the Competing Claims to Civil Society." In *Citizenship, Markets, and the State*, ed. K. Eder, Colin Crouch and D. Tambini: 23–48. New York: Oxford University Press.

2005a. "Citizenship Troubles: Genealogies of Struggle for the Soul of the Social." In *Remaking Modernity*, ed. Julia Adams, Lis Clemens, and Ann Orloff: 438–69. Durham, NC: Duke University Press.

2005b. "Beware Trojan Horses Bearing Social Capital: How Privatization turned *Solidarity* into a Bowling Team." In *The*

Politics of Method in the Human Sciences, ed George Steinmetz: 346–411. Duke University Press.

2006. "Citizenship, Statelessness and Market Fundamentalism: Arendtian Lessons on Losing the Right to Have Rights." In *Migration, Citizenship, Ethnos: Incorporation Regimes in Germany, Western Europe and North America*, ed Y. M. Bodemann and G. Yurdakul: 35–62. London: Palgrave Macmillan.

Somers, Margaret R. and Fred Block. 2005. "From Poverty to Perversity: Ideas, Markets, and Institutions over Two Centuries of Welfare Debate." *American Sociological Review* 70 (2): 260–87.

2006. "Poverty and Piety." *American Sociological Review* 71 (3): 511–13.

Somers, Margaret R. and Gloria D. Gibson. 1994. "Reclaiming the Epistemological 'Other': Narrative and the Social Constitution of Identity." In *Social Theory and the Politics of Identity*, ed. Craig Calhoun: 37–99. Oxford: Basil Blackwell.

Somers, Margaret R. and Christopher Roberts. Forthcoming 2009. "Toward a New Sociology of Rights," *Annual Review of Law and Social Science* 5.

Soros, George. 1998. *The Crisis of Global Capitalism*. New York: Public Affairs Press.

2000. *Open Society: Reforming Global Capitalism*. New York: Public Affairs Press.

South End Press Collective, ed. 2007. *What Lies Beneath: Katrina, Race, and the State of the Nation*. Cambridge, MA: South End Press.

Soysal, Yasemin. 1994. *Limits of Citizenship: Migrants and Postnational Membership in Europe*. Chicago: University of Chicago.

Standing, Guy. 1999. *Global Labour Flexibility: Seeking Distributive Justice*. New York: Macmillan.

2002. *Beyond the New Paternalism. Basic Security as Equality*. London: Verso.

ed. 2005. *Promoting Income Security as a Right*. London: Anthem Press.

Stark, David. 1992. "Path Dependence and Privatization Strategies in East Central Europe." *East European Politics and Societies* 6 (1): 17–54.

Starr, Paul. 2007. *Freedom's Power: The True Force of Liberalism*. New York: Basic Books.

Steinmetz, George. 1992. "Reflections on the Role of Social Narratives in Working Class Formation: Narratives and Social Sciences." *Social Science History* 16 (3): 489–516.

2005a. "The Epistemological Unconscious of U.S. Sociology and the Transition to Post-Fordism: The Case of Historical Sociology." In

Remaking Modernity: Politics, History, and Sociology, ed. Julia Adams, Elisabeth S. Clemens, and Ann Shola Orloff: 109–57. Durham, NC: Duke University Press.

2005b. *The Politics of Method in the Human Sciences: Positivism and its Epistemological Others*. Durham, NC: Duke University Press.

Steinmo, Sven, Kathleen Thelen and Frank Longstreth, eds. 1992. *Structuring Politics: Historical Institutionalism in Comparative Analysis*. Cambridge: Cambridge University Press.

Stewart-Weeks, M. and C. Richardson, eds. 1998. *Social Capital Stories: How 12 Australian Households Live Their Lives*. St. Leonards, NSW: Centre for Independent Studies.

Stiglitz, Joseph E. 1989. "Markets, Market Failures and Development." *American Economic Review* 79 (2): 197–202.

1994. *Whither Socialism?* Cambridge, MA: MIT Press.

1998. "More Instruments and Broader Goals: Moving Toward the Post-Washington Consensus." The 1998 WIDER Annual Lecture, January 7, Helsinki.

2000. *Economics of the Public Sector*, 3rd edn. New York: Norton.

2002. *Globalization and its Discontents*. New York: Norton.

Stinchcombe, Arthur L. 1975. "Social Structure and Politics." In *Macropolitical Theory*, ed. F. Greenstein and N. Polsby: 557–622. Reading, MA: Addison-Wesley.

[1978] 1982. "The Deep Structure of Moral Categories: Eighteenth-Century French Stratification and the Revolution." In *Structural Sociology*, ed. Eno Rossi: 67–95. New York: Columbia University Press.

1991. "The Conditions of Fruitfulness of Theorizing about Mechanisms in Social Science." In *Social Theory and Social Policy: Essays in Honor of James S. Coleman*, ed. A. B. Sorensen and S. Spilerman: 24–41. Westport, CT: Praeger.

Stoler, Ann L. 1995. *Race and the Education of Desire: Foucault's History of Sexuality and the Colonial Order of Things*. Durham, NC: Duke University Press.

2002. *Carnal Knowledge and Imperial Power: Race and the Intimate in Colonial Rule*. Berkeley: University of California Press.

Straw, J. 1998. "Building Social Cohesion, Order and Inclusion in a Market Economy." Paper presented to the Nexus Conference on Mapping out the Third Way, available at www.netnexus.org/events/july98/talks/strawspeech.htm.

Sunstein, Cass. 2003. "The Right-Wing Assault: What's at Stake, What's Already Happened and What Could Yet Occur."

American Prospect 14 (3), available at www.prospect.org/cs/ articles?article = the_rightwing_assault.

2004. *The Second Bill of Rights: FDR's Unfinished Revolution and Why We Need it More Than Ever.* New York: Basic Books.

Swedberg, Richard. 1987. "Economic Sociology: Past and Present." *Current Sociology* 35: 1–221.

Swidler, Ann. 1986. "Culture in Action: Symbols and Strategies." *American Sociological Review* 51 (2): 273–86.

1987. "The Uses of Culture in Historical Explanation." Paper presented at the American Sociological Association annual meeting, Chicago.

Tamanaha, Brian. 2004. *On the Rule of Law: History, Politics, Theory.* Cambridge: Cambridge University Press.

Tarrow, Sidney. 1992. "Mentalities, Political Cultures, and Collective Action Frames: Constructing Meanings through Action." In *Frontiers in Social Movement Theory*, ed. Aldon D. Morris and Carol McClurg Mueller: 174–203. New Haven, CT: Yale University Press.

1996. "Making Social Science Work Across Space and Time: A Critical Reflection on Robert Putnam's *Making Democracy Work*." *American Political Science Review* 90, 2: 389–97.

Taylor, Charles. 1989. *Sources of the Self: The Making of the Modern Identity.* Cambridge, MA: Harvard University Press.

1990. "Modes of Civil Society." *Public Culture* 3 (1): 95–118.

2002. "Modern Social Imaginaries." *Public Culture* 14 (1): 91–124.

2004. *Modern Social Imaginaries.* Durham, NC: Duke University Press.

Taylor, Charles and Amy Gutmann. 1992. *Multiculturalism and the Politics of Recognition: An Essay.* Princeton, NJ: Princeton University Press.

Taylor, M. and S. Leonard. 2002. *Embedded Enterprise and Social Capital: International Perspectives.* Aldershot: Ashgate.

Thelen, Kathleen. 1999. "Historical Institutionalism in Comparative Politics." *Annual Review of Political Science* 2: 369–404.

Therborn, Goran. 1977. "The Rule of Capital and the Rise of Democracy." *New Left Review* 103: 3–41.

Thompson, E. P. 1963. *The Making of the English Working Class.* New York: Vintage.

1975. *Whigs and Hunters: The Origin of the Black Act.* New York: Pantheon.

Thompson, Michael, Richard Ellis, and Aaron Wildavsky. 1990. *Cultural Theory.* Boulder, CO: Westview Press.

References

Tierney, Kathleen. 2006. "Foreshadowing Katrina: Recent Sociological
Contributions to Vulnerability Science." *Contemporary Sociology* 35
(3): 207–12.
Tilly, Charles. ed. 1975. *The Formation of National States in Western
Europe*. Princeton, NJ: Princeton University Press.
    1984. *Big Structures, Large Processes, Huge Comparisons*. New York:
    Russell Sage.
    ed. 1995. *International Review of Social History: Special Issue: Citizenship
    Identity and Social History*. Amsterdam: Cambridge Press.
    1998. "Where Do Rights Come From?" In *Democracy, Revolution, and
    History*, ed. T. Skocpol: 55–72. Ithaca, NY: Cornell University Press.
Toner, Robin. 2007. "A New Populism Spurs Democrats on the
Economy." *New York Times* July 16.
Touraine, Alain. 1985. "An Introduction to the Study of Social Movements."
Social Research 52 (4): 749–87.
Townsend, Joseph. [1786] 1979. *A Dissertation on the Poor Laws. By a
Well-Wisher to Mankind*. Berkeley: University of California Press.
Tracinski, Robert. 2005. *The Intellectual Activist*, available at: http://tiadaily.
com/php-bin/news/showArticle.php?id = 1026 (accessed December 16,
2007).
Trend, D. 1996. *Radical Democracy: Identity, Citizenship, and the State*.
New York: Routledge.
Tritter, J. 1994. "The Citizen's Charter: Opportunities for Users'
Perspectives?" *Political Quarterly* 65: 397–414.
Trout, David D. 2007. *After the Storm: Black Intellectuals Explore the
Meaning of Hurricane Katrina*. New York: New Press.
Tucker, Robert C. 1973. "Culture, Political Culture, and Communist
Society." *Political Science Quarterly* 20: 173–90.
    1978. *The Marx–Engels Reader*. New York: Norton.
Turner, Bryan S. 1986. *Citizenship and Capitalism: The Debate over
Reformism*. London: Allen and Unwin.
    1990. *Theories of Modernity and Postmodernity*. London: Sage.
    1993. "Outline of a Theory of Human Rights." *Sociology* 27: 489–512.
    2006. *Vulnerability and Human Rights*. University Park, PA: Penn State
    University.
Twine, Fred. 1994. *Citizenship and Social Rights: The Interdependence of
Self and Society*. London: Sage.
Uchitelle, Louis. 2006. *The Disposable American: Layoffs and their
Consequences*. New York: Knopf.
    2007. "Age of Riches: The Richest of the Rich, Proud of a New Gilded
    Age." *New York Times*, July 15.

United Kingdom Commission on Citizenship. 1990. *Encouraging Citizenship: Report of the Commission on Citizenship*. London: HMSO.

Valenze, Deborah M. 1995. *The First Industrial Woman*. New York: Oxford University Press.

Van Heerden, Ivor and Mike Bryan. 2006. *The Storm: What Went Wrong and Why During Hurricane Katrina*. New York: Viking.

Verba, Sidney and Norman Nie. 1973. *Political Participation*. New York: Harper and Row.

Voet, R. 1998. *Feminism and Citizenship*. London: Sage.

Wallerstein, Immanuel. 1974. *The Modern World System*, vol. I. New York: Academic Press.

1991. *Unthinking Social Science: The Limits of Nineteenth-Century Paradigms*. Oxford: Polity Press.

Walzer, Michael. 1983. *Spheres of Justice: A Defense of Pluralism and Equality*. New York: Basic Books.

1988. *The Company of Critics: Social Criticism and Political Commitment in the Twentieth Century*. New York: Basic Books.

1991. "The Idea of Civil Society: A Path to Social Reconstruction." *Dissent* 38: 293–304.

1995. "The Civil Society Argument." In *Theorizing Citizenship*, ed. R. Beiner: 153–75. Albany, NY: SUNY Press.

1997. *On Toleration*. New Haven, CT: Yale University Press.

2005. *Politics and Passion: Toward a More Egalitarian Liberalism*. New Haven, CT: Yale University Press.

Warren, Earl. 1958. "Clemente Martinez Perez v. Herbert Brownell, Jr., Attorney General." 536 U.S. 44, US Supreme Court.

Warren, M. 1999. *Democracy and Trust*. Cambridge: Cambridge University Press.

Weintraub, Jeff. 1992. "Democracy and the Market: A Marriage of Inconvenience." In *From Leninism to Freedom: The Challenges of Democratization*, ed. Margaret Latus Nugent: 47–66. Boulder, CO: Westview Press.

1995. "Varieties and Vicissitudes of Public Space." In *Metropolis: Center and Symbol of Our Times*, ed. Philip Kasinitz: 280–319. New York: New York University Press.

Wellman, Barry. 1983. "Network Analysis: Some Basic Principles." In *Sociological Theory*, ed. Randall Collins: 155–200. San Francisco: Jossey-Bass.

Wellman, Barry and S. D. Berkowitz. 1988. *Social Structures: A Network Approach*. Cambridge: Cambridge University Press.

White, Harrison. 1976. "Social Structure from Multiple Networks II." *American Journal of Sociology* 81: 1265.

1992. *Identity and Control: A Structural Theory of Social Action.* Princeton, NJ: Princeton University Press.

White, Harrison, Scott A. Boorman, and Ronald L. Breiger. 1976. "Social Structure from Multiple Networks: Part I. Blockmodels of Roles and Positions." *American Journal of Sociology* 81 (4): 730–80.

Wildavsky, Aaron. 1987. "Choosing Preferences by Constructing Institutions: A Cultural Theory of Preference Formation." *American Political Science Review* 81: 3–21.

Winch, Donald. 1978. *Adam Smith's Politics: An Essay in Historiographic Revision.* Cambridge: Cambridge University Press.

Wolfe, Alan. 1989. *Whose Keeper? Social Science and Moral Obligation.* Berkeley: University of California Press.

1992. "Democracy versus Sociology: Boundaries and their Political Consequences." In *Cultivating Differences: Symbolic Boundaries and the Making of Inequality*, ed. Michele Lamont and M. Fournier: 309–25. Chicago: University of Chicago Press.

Wolin, Sheldon. 1960. *Politics and Vision: Continuity and Innovation in Western Political Thought.* Boston, MA: Little Brown.

Woolcock, M. 1998. "Social Capital and Economic Development: Toward a Theoretical Synthesis and Policy Framework." *Theory and Society* 27 (2): 151–208.

Woolgar, Steve. 1988. *Knowledge as Reflexivity.* London: Sage.

1992. "Some Remarks about Positionism: A Reply to Collins and Yearley." In *Science as Practice and Culture*, ed. Andrew Pickering: 327–42. Chicago: University of Chicago Press.

World Bank. 2004. "What is Social Capital?" Website on social capital, available at www.worldbank.org/poverty/scapital/whatsc.htm.

Wuthnow, Robert. 1987. *Meaning and Moral Order: Explorations in Cultural Analysis.* Berkeley: University of California Press.

1990. *Communities of Discourse.* Cambridge, MA: Harvard University Press.

Young, I. M. 1990. *Justice and the Politics of Difference.* Princeton, NJ: Princeton University Press.

2000. *Inclusion and Democracy.* Oxford: Oxford University Press.

Zaret, David. 1992. "Religion, Science, and Printing in the Public Spheres in Seventeenth-Century England." In *Habermas and the Public Sphere*, ed. Craig Calhoun: 212–35. Cambridge. MA: MIT Press.

Zelizer, Viviana. 1988. "Beyond the Polemics of the Market: Establishing a Theoretical Agenda." *Social Forces* 3: 614.

1997. *The Social Meaning of Money. Pin Money, Paychecks, Poor Relief, and Other Currencies.* Princeton, NJ: Princeton University Press.

2005. *The Purchase of Intimacy.* Princeton, NJ: Princeton University Press.

Zimmerman. Don H. and Melvin Pollner. 1970. "The Everyday World as a Phenomenon." In *Understanding Everyday Life*, ed. Jack Douglas: 1–103. Chicago: Aldine.

Index